1ST COMPETITION — 1947
AMERICAN MUSEUM OF NATURAL HISTORY

A WHITETAIL RETROSPECTIVE:

Vintage Photos and Memorabilia from the Boone and Crockett Club Archives

A WHITETAIL RETROSPECTIVE:

Vintage Photos and Memorabilia from the Boone and Crockett Club Archives

First Edition 2006
Second Printing

Library of Congress Catalog Card Number: 2006933015
ISBN Number: 978-0-940864-56-6
Published November 2006

Published in the United States of America
by the
Boone and Crockett Club
250 Station Drive
Missoula, MT 59801
406/542-1888
406/542-0784 (fax)
www.booneandcrockettclub.com

Manufactured in Canada

A WHITETAIL RETROSPECTIVE:

Vintage Photos and Memorabilia from the Boone and Crockett Club Archives

Published by the Boone and Crockett Club

Missoula, Montana

2006

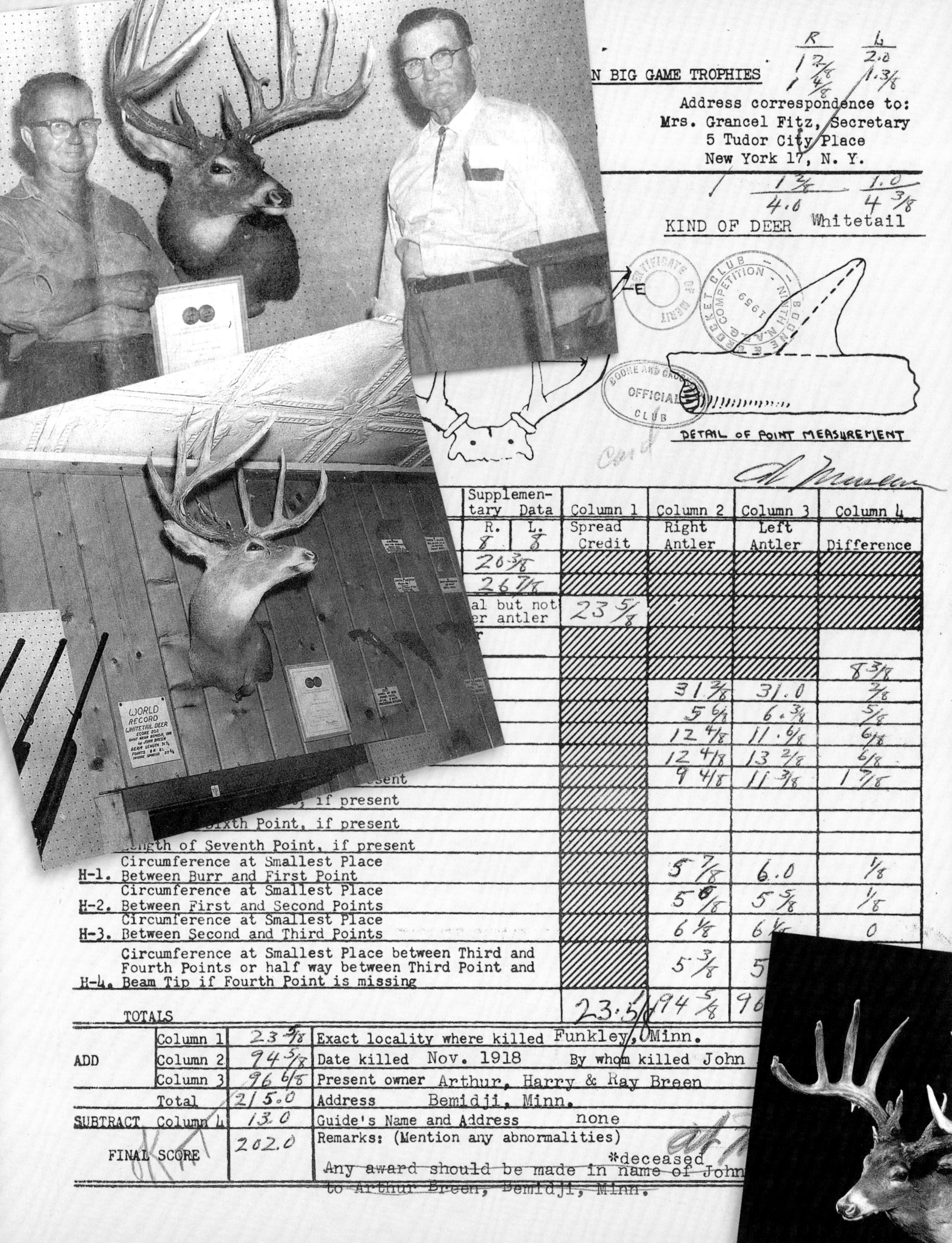

N BIG GAME TROPHIES

R	L
1 2/8	2.0
1 4/8	1.3/8

Address correspondence to:
Mrs. Grancel Fitz, Secretary
5 Tudor City Place
New York 17, N. Y.

1 3/8	1.0
4.0	4 3/8

KIND OF DEER Whitetail

CERTIFICATE OF MERIT

BOONE AND CROCKETT CLUB — NINTH NAT'L COMPETITION 1959

BOONE AND CROCKETT OFFICIAL CLUB

DETAIL OF POINT MEASUREMENT

	Supplementary Data R.	Supplementary Data L.	Column 1 Spread Credit	Column 2 Right Antler	Column 3 Left Antler	Column 4 Difference
	8	8				
	20 3/8					
	26 7/8					
al but not er antler			23 5/8			
r						
						8 3/8
				31 2/8	31.0	2/8
				5 6/8	6.3/8	5/8
				12 4/8	11.6/8	6/8
				12 4/8	13 2/8	6/8
esent				9 4/8	11 3/8	1 7/8
, if present						
Sixth Point, if present						
Length of Seventh Point, if present						
H-1. Circumference at Smallest Place Between Burr and First Point				5 7/8	6.0	1/8
H-2. Circumference at Smallest Place Between First and Second Points				5 6/8	5 5/8	1/8
H-3. Circumference at Smallest Place Between Second and Third Points				6 1/8	6 1/8	0
H-4. Circumference at Smallest Place between Third and Fourth Points or half way between Third Point and Beam Tip if Fourth Point is missing				5 3/8	5	
TOTALS			23.5/8	94 5/8	96	

ADD	Column 1	23 5/8	Exact locality where killed Funkley, Minn.
	Column 2	94 5/8	Date killed Nov. 1918 By whom killed John
	Column 3	96 6/8	Present owner Arthur, Harry & Ray Breen
	Total	215.0	Address Bemidji, Minn.
SUBTRACT	Column 4	13.0	Guide's Name and Address none
FINAL SCORE		202.0	Remarks: (Mention any abnormalities) *deceased ~~Any award should be made in name of John~~ ~~to Arthur Breen, Bemidji, Minn.~~

PREFACE

HALLOWED GROUND BY RYAN HATFIELD

Take a moment and imagine the following vision. You walk into a room, and there before you are all the hunters who have ever taken the most outstanding big-game trophies in our century-or-so-old recorded history of such things. All you have to do is approach any one of them, and they are more than happy to put their arm around you and paint the picture of the events surrounding one of hunting's most outstanding days. How would you like to visit with Mel Johnson, Del Austin, or John Breen about the day they bagged one of the most exceptional whitetails in history? The analogy of a kid in a candy store merely brushes the surface of what such an opportunity would offer.

Such was the case when I came to work for the Boone and Crockett Club and first visited "the archives." Being a person who takes great interest in hunting's heritage, history, and traditions, working for B&C represented the pinnacle of each of these.

Visiting the archives can be overwhelming. It is hunting's *Hallowed Ground*. All of the documented history surrounding North America's most outstanding big-game animals are there. Let your imagination run and you can nearly hear the whispers emanating from the files themselves. Priceless history, important events, and simple documentation all help to complete the story contained in every file.

I'll never forget the first time I went into the archives. I went in to perform a simple record update, and proceeded to lose myself in those files for hours. File after file, I flipped through them, admiring accompanying field photos, reading correspondence, seeing authentic signatures, all the while being thoroughly riveted. I wanted to turn to someone and say, "Wow! Would you look at that!" At the same time, however, it was just as exciting because I could enjoy it alone and at my own pace.

It didn't take a big leap to realize that the history that lay dormant in these files was far too valuable to simply leave stuffed in a file cabinet to do nothing more than collect dust and slowly deteriorate. These stories, photos, and memorabilia needed to be shared.

As hunting changes and time marches on, the chance to hop on a time machine and transport oneself back to simpler, grander days becomes all the more tantalizing. For whitetail fanatics, *A Whitetail Retrospective* is that chance. Most of what you will see in the following pages has never been seen before – some of it was never intended to be seen. Opening Boone and Crockett Club's private vaults for the world to see was not a simple process, but it was more than worth the effort.

I had the honor to select many of the following photos, using the "you know it when you see it" approach. Of course, all of the 33,000 files are worth seeing, but in the interests of time and space, we have selected some of the most intriguing for publication here.

Some of the photos will be questionable by today's standards, but to sanitize the true history would be a mistake. As such, we have chosen to leave it in its raw, unadulterated state. This serves not only to show were done in the past, but also as a reminder of our expectations of today. Just because our photo standards have changed doesn't mean we should shy away from embracing these great historic photos.

I hope you will be as enamored with the following items as we here at B&C are, and that they will leave you yearning for more. Enjoy!

TABLE OF CONTENTS

A WHITETAIL RETROSPECTIVE

PREFACE................ V
By Ryan Hatfield

INTRODUCTION IX
By Eldon L. "Buck" Buckner

CHAPTER ONE..........1

Score Charts
Boone and Crockett Club's long-time Director of Big Game Records discusses the development of records keeping and the metamorphosis of the whitetail score charts from the turn of the century through today.

By Jack Reneau

CHAPTER TWO.... 14

Distribution
Past efforts and resources of hunters, conservation organizations and government agencies were realized with the overall population of whitetail deer growing from 500,000 in the early 1900s to nearly 12 million by the 1970s. That expansion is evident with the number of entries in the Club's Big Game Records Program. You can see this with the inclusion of detailed maps, separated by decade, that highlight the top trophy-producing counties.

By Joel W. Helmer

CHAPTER THREE 24

The Early Years
Members of the Boone and Crockett Club have history in records-keeping dating back to 1891 when Theodore Roosevelt, George Bird Grinnell, and Archibald Rogers judged a trophy competition in New York City. In the late 1800s, it was believed that many species of big game were going the way of the bison. Therefore, B&C members helped establish the New York Zoological Society to preserve a collection of species for future generations to enjoy. This action ultimately led to the creation of the first scoring methods used by the Club, which were in place through the 1949 Competition.

By John P. Poston

Vintage Photos 28
Award-Winning Whitetails......... 32
Publicity 38
Correspondence.......................... 42
Score Charts.............................. 48
Special Trophies 50

WHITETAIL ENTRY DISTRIBUTION: 1830-1979

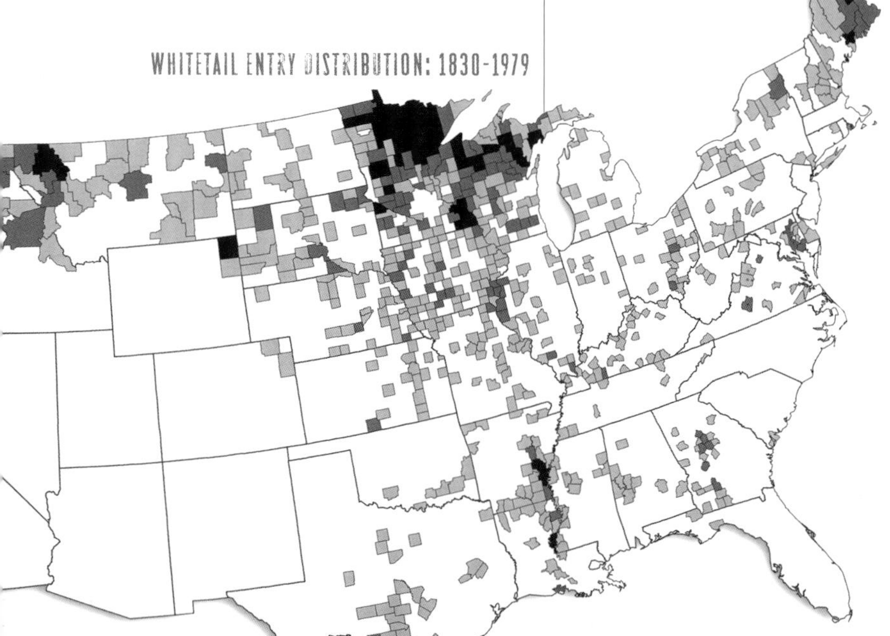

A New System

At the end of World War II there was renewed interest for the Boone and Crockett Club to direct attention to designing a new system for measuring North American big-game trophies. Samuel B. Webb chaired the committee, which included Grancel Fitz, James L. Clark, Harold E. Anthony, Milford Baker, and Frederick K. Barbour. The system was officially adopted in 1950 and quickly became the universally accepted standard for measuring native North American big game. The new system was in effect beginning with the 4th Competition held at the American Museum of Natural History in New York City in 1950.

By Frederick J. King

Carnegie Museum

After 16 years at the American Museum of Natural History in New York City, the Club's records-keeping activities and competitions moved to the Carnegie Museum in Pittsburgh, Pennsylvania. The success of six decades of big-game conservation became evident resulting in two major increases in minimum entry scores within five years. Several noteworthy whitetail deer were entered during this time period (1964-1971) including Melvin J. Johnson's Illinois buck that received the coveted Sagamore Hill Award – the only whitetail to ever do so.

By Gilbert T. Adams

NABGAP Begins

In June of 1973, the Boone and Crockett Club and the National Rifle Association signed an agreement to cosponsor what would then be called the North American Big Game Awards Program (NABGAP). This era in big-game records keeping lasted for seven years and included three Big Game Awards Programs. Other strides in improving the scoring system were also seen at this time. They included the creation of a uniform scoring manual for training measurers and a standard of entry requirements. Such changes provided the program a much greater ability to detect unscrupulous or erroneous entries, as well as enforce the accurate and consistent measurement of trophies.

By Tommy Caruthers

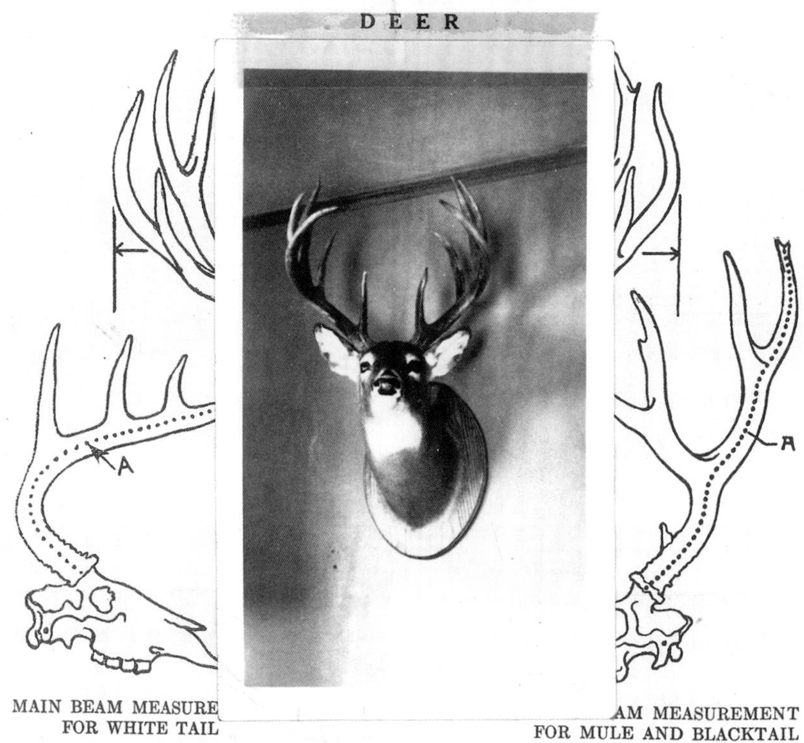

Method of Measuring

All measurements <u>**must**</u> be made with a flexible steel tape.

A Length of outside curve: Measured along the main beam from the base of the burr to the tip of the most distant point on the main beam.

B Greatest spread: Measured between parallels and at right angles to the center line of the skull.

C Circumference: Measured midway between the basal snag and the first fork.

Points: No point shall be counted unless it extends at least one inch.

D Circumference of burr.

Remarks: State whether the trophy has any characteristics which depart from the normal for this species.

INTRODUCTION

BY ELDON L. "BUCK" BUCKNER

Many of my most memorable hunts have been for North America's most numerous and widespread big game—the whitetail deer. A wily and adaptable animal, he has not only managed to hold his own, but has increased both his numbers and range despite man's invasion and destruction of much of his habitats. For example, the first dozen years of my life were spent on a central Missouri farm. Back then, during the 1940s, there were no deer in the area. A couple years ago, I saw many in the same area while driving the highway. Similarly, when we moved from Arizona to northeast Oregon in 1972, we found only mule deer on our ranch. Now, whitetails are common and have been for the past ten years.

It is not surprising that this most popular of all big-game animals, whether the Southwest's version known as Coues' deer or the more northern variety, has developed a near fanatical following in many cases. From personal experience, first with the Coues' deer of Arizona and Sonora, and later with their cousins in Oregon, Montana, Texas, Kansas, and Pennsylvania, I think the whitetail addiction stems from a challenging combination of admiration, frustration, and exasperation. After all, what hunter can resist the thrown gauntlet of a deer who brazenly devours his wife's roses on the front porch one day, then becomes an invisible ghost the next day when the season opens!

An example of a far-gone Coues' deer addict was the late John Doyle, a Tucson taxidermist and B&C Official Measurer. He was responsible for introducing me to the Club's records program when I was barely a teenager. When I finally bagged a record-book buck at age 20, he measured it for me. Shortly after, the increased minimum score negated my trophy's record-book status. I've been trying to repeat my initial success ever since, in vain!

LEFT: The back of the score chart shown here is from the 1947 Competition. Back then, there was only one chart for all types of deer (whitetail, mule deer, blacktail, and Arizona whitetail). The buck shown here was taken in 1938 in Oneida County, Wisconsin.

This book will evoke fond memories for many, like me, who can remember when hunting was a less crowded sport, permission to hunt private land was available for the asking, and major newspapers lauded the accomplishments of hunters without fear of reprisals from readers. Equipment was simpler, too; 4-wheel-drive vehicles and camouflage clothing were rarities, variable-power scopes didn't exist, and ATVs and trail cameras were not dreamed of.

Younger sportsmen with even the slightest interest in trophy whitetails and hunting history will find a real treasure in Joel Helmer's periodic whitetail distribution maps that show locations of record entries by county over the years. The maps show the spread of whitetails alluded to earlier.

The history and development of the Boone and Crockett scoring system, from a measure of

47

Records of North American Big Game

A PUBLICATION OF
THE BOONE AND CROCKETT CLUB
IN CARE OF
AMERICAN MUSEUM OF NATURAL HISTORY
COLUMBUS AVENUE AND 77TH STREET
NEW YORK, N. Y.

COMMITTEE
ALFRED ELY, CHAIRMAN
HAROLD E. ANTHONY
R. R. M. CARPENTER

UNDER THE AUSPICES
OF
THE NATIONAL MUSEUM
OF HEADS AND HORNS
OF THE
NEW YORK ZOOLOGICAL
SOCIETY

DEER

SPECIES Arizona Whitetail

MEASUREMENTS	RIGHT	LEFT
Length on outside curve **A**	18 1/4	18 3/8
Circumference of main beam **B**		
Circumference of burr **C**	4 3/8	4 1/4
Number of points on antler	4	4

Greatest spread: **D** 19

Exact locality where killed Las Mochis Rg., Sonora, Mex.

Date killed 1937

By whom killed Lion

Owner Jack O'Connor

Address Tucson, Ariz.

Remarks:

Photographs: Front view..........Profile..........
(Please place V mark to indicate photographs furnished.)

We hereby certify that we have measured the above described trophy on..........193 , and that these measurements are correct and made in accordance with the directions overleaf.

....

By ....

O'Connor 10.2.38

X

just one antler feature to the current system adopted in 1950, is thoroughly covered by Records Committee members John Poston and Fred King, and augmented by a special section on the evolution of score charts put together by Jack Reneau.

Concurrent with changes in scoring systems were changes in periodic trophy displays. Originally labeled "competitions," these were later named "Awards Programs," as described by Tommy Caruthers, former B&C Director of Hunting and Big Game Records.

During its century-plus history, Boone and Crockett Club has headquartered at several locations. The move to the Carnegie Museum in Pittsburgh for the 1964-1971 period came right after the minimum score for whitetails was increased in 1965 and is ably documented by Records Committee member Gilbert T. Adams. I have special memories of this period because I was appointed an Official Measurer in 1968 under sponsorship of John Doyle. Then–Records Chairman Elmer Rusten and I were frequent correspondents.

The unique feature of this book is the inclusion of so many informal trophy photos, news articles and fascinating correspondence related to special trophies. An example is the documentation concerning the bagging of a 29-year-old buck shot in Nova Scotia in 1917 that was reportedly one of three tagged deer released there in the 1880s. Other items that caught my interest included a lion-killed Coues' deer picked up in Sonora in 1937 by my friend, the late Jack O'Connor; the extended correspondence over a wrongly-classified Arizona mule deer that was once pictured as the World's Record Coues' deer, reported burned in a fire but resurrected in Montana 20 years later; the controversial correspondence between long-time records secretary Betty Fitz, former Measurer and Grand Slam Club founder Bob Householder, and Arizona Game Ranger Bob Hernbrode, over a possible mule deer/Coues' deer cross. I knew all three people well, now all departed, and found it interesting that B&C Club is now initiating research efforts through DNA studies to help prevent such problems in the future.

I'll have to admit that seeing so many photos of old friends and acquaintances no longer with us and reading the words of others who have passed on has caused me to shed a nostalgic tear or two. But that's not all bad; books like this help remind us of our rich hunting heritage and encourage us to carry on those traditions we so greatly cherish.

LEFT: In the early years, Coues' whitetail deer were identified as Arizona whitetails. The chart shown here describes a picked-up trophy submitted by Jack O'Connor. Unfortunately, no photograph was attached.

MEASUREMENT CHART

D

B

A

BEAM MEASUREMENT
R WHITE TAIL

DEER
Measurement Chart

Species - Whitetail Deer

EASUREMENTS:-

	Animals Right Ant
Length on outside curve - A	24
Circumference, main beam - B	$4\frac{1}{2}$
Number of points, each horn	5
Greatest Spread - D	
Exact locality where killed	U
Year killed	
By whom killed	
Make & bore rifle used	Savage,
Kind of ammunition used	Remingto
Owner	

Remarks: Measured by ROGER SEAMANS, Biologi
Montpelier, Vermont or

NORTH AMERICAN BIG GAME

OFFICIAL MEASUREMENT RECORDS

ENTISS N. GRAY

1: SCORE CHARTS

BY JACK RENEAU

Records-keeping of native North American big-game animals has deep roots in Boone and Crockett Club's history. While little is known of the earliest days (1800s) of the Club's records-keeping interest and activities, we do know that Theodore Roosevelt, the Club's founder and first president, was personally involved. On July 16, 1902, the Club's Executive Committee Chairman assigned Theodore Roosevelt, Caspar Whitney, and Archibald Rogers to a subcommittee with the sole purpose of devising an objective method for recording measurements of big-game animals.

Knowing Theodore Roosevelt's character, there is no doubt he enthusiastically embraced this assignment, and that his committee likely created the Club's first scoring system. I say likely, because unfortunately, no record or report of their deliberations has ever been found in the Club's archives. It wasn't until 1932, the year the first edition of the records book, *Records of North American Big Game*, was published that the hunting public was introduced to the Club's interest in records-keeping on native North American big game animals.

Contrary to the perception of many people today, the Club did not get into records keeping for recording abundant game populations or bragging rights. On the contrary, populations of many North American big-game species were at all-time lows in the early 1900s because of western expansion, market hunting, and the fact that there were absolutely no restrictions on the taking of animals.

Market hunting was a 24/7, 365 days a year occupation that many enthusiastically participated in to make a living or simply feed themselves and their families. There were no bag limits, restrictions on methods of take, etc. As hard as it may be to believe today, the Club became involved in records-keeping at the turn of the 20th century because many knowledgeable people at that time thought extinction was a possibility for many large mammals in North America. The National Collection of Heads and Horns, which was established in 1906 at the Bronx Zoo in New York City by B&C Club members William T. Hornaday and Madison Grant, was dedicated to the "Vanishing Big Game of the World."

Prentiss N. Gray, editor of the first edition, noted in his foreword that, "This record [book] seems timely as preserving an authentic history of the many splendid trophies taken before some of our big game animals have been brought practically to the point of extinction." In other words, the Club was devising a scoring system to record measurements of big-game animals so that future generations might know the dimensions these animals attained if they went extinct or if Club members' conservation efforts proved futile. Records-keeping and the National Collection of Heads and Horns were intended to draw attention to the plight of North American big-game animals.

The concept of extinction may sound far-fetched today when whitetail deer are so widespread and still expanding into new habitats, but don't forget that bison were brought to the edge of extinction before the turn of the 20th century from an estimated 60 million animals in the 16th century. It is further estimated that bison were reduced from 4 million in 1880 to less than 5,000

FIGURE A: Possibly the first chart — it appeared in the 1934 Remington Arms reprint.

DEER

MEASUREMENT CHART

Species________________________________

Measurements

	Animal's Right Antler	*Animal's Left Antler*
Length on outside curve *A*	__________	__________
Circumference of main beam *B*	__________	__________
Number of points on each horn	__________	__________

Greatest spread *D*____________________

Exact locality where killed____________________

Year killed____________________

By whom killed____________________

Make and bore rifle used____________________

Kind of ammunition used____________________

Owner____________________

Address____________________

Remarks:____________________

Return this chart when completed

to

Prentiss N. Gray
Records of North American Big Game
46 William Street
New York, N. Y.

(over)

MAIN BEAM MEASUREMENT FOR WHITETAIL

FIGURE B: The original main beam measurement for whitetail deer.

in 1887, the year the Club was founded, and the decline continued.

Unfortunately, B&C does not have a single example of the Club's first score charts, including those used for whitetail deer, that Prent, as he was known by his friends, used to gather data for the first edition of the records book released in 1932. Copies of the score charts were not reproduced in the first edition, so we cannot be positively sure what they looked like.

Prent was collecting more data for the second edition when he unexpectedly passed away in 1935 in a tragic boating accident in the Everglades. It is believed that the bank where Prent worked at the time of his untimely death put all of his papers and personal belongings, including the score charts collected for the first edition, in storage where they have been ever since. Hopefully, these score charts will be located and returned to the Boone and Crockett Club in the near future as Prent's son, Sherman Gray, recently renewed efforts to obtain Prent's belongings from his father's former employer.

In the meantime, we have a good idea of what the score charts used for the 1932 edition might have looked like. In 1934, Remington Arms published a booklet titled, *North American Big Game: Official Measurement Records Compiled by Prentiss N. Gray* (cover shown opposite of page 1). The cost was 25¢, including shipping and handling.

On page 39 of this rare and very collectible booklet is an example of what must have been the score chart (**Figure A**) used to collect data for whitetail deer for the 1932 edition, likely making it B&C's first official whitetail deer score chart. Included on this score chart is Prent's return address. Whether all or even part of the whitetail deer scoring system devised by Theodore Roosevelt's committee was used for this score chart and the 1932 book was not noted for posterity.

There were 28 categories of North American big game, including whitetail deer and Arizona whitetail deer, listed in the 1932 edition. The latter is obviously listed as Coues' whitetail deer in today's records books.

As you can see in **Figure A**, only seven measurements were recorded on the first whitetail score chart. Only five, namely length of outside curve (of main beam), circumference of main beam, greatest spread, and number of points on both antlers, were listed in the 1932 records book. Whitetails were listed and ranked only by the "length of the outside curve" or the longer main beam. According to the drawing (**Figure B**) on the back of the score chart, main beam length started at the top edge of the burr and was taken along the front and underside of the main beam to its tip, which is obviously different than how it is taken today. The highest-ranking whitetail specimen in this first edition, or "World's Record," so to speak, had a main beam length of 30-3/4 inches, while the length of the smallest (minimum score probably) was 23-1/4 inches.

There was no distinction between typical and non-typical whitetail deer in the 1932 records book. Specimens of both categories were listed under the whitetail deer heading. The number of points on the animals listed ranged from 4x4 for the fewest points to 18x19 for the most.

The problems with this whitetail deer scoring system were as obvious to Prent in 1932 as they are to us now. Prent noted in his foreword, "We recognize fully that no one dimension is the controlling factor, and we hope that eventually some fair method of scoring a head may be devised which will be acceptable."

In 1950, Boone and Crockett Club adopted its universally recognized scoring system that is still in use today with minimal modifications. Unlike earlier B&C systems, whitetail scores and ultimate ranking are determined through a series of somewhat complicated measurements that arrive at a final score for a trophy based on two characteristics—massiveness and symmetry. Massiveness is accounted for by measuring the inside spread, main beams, points, and four circumferences on each antler. Symmetry is accounted for by deducting for differences between main beams, points, and circumferences. The numbers of points on each antler, greatest spread, and tip-to-tip spread

RIGHT: The typical frame of the World's Record non-typical whitetail deer from Missouri is clearly visible.

OPPOSITE: The Hole-in-the-Horn buck, which was picked up in Portgage County, Ohio, in the 1940s, would score higher than the current World's Record shown on this page if it wasn't for the focus on symmetry in the Club's scoring system.

are recorded as supplementary data that do not add into the final score.

Contrary to common belief, there is no difference in scoring typical and non-typical whitetails. A normal point is a normal point, and an abnormal point is an abnormal point for specimens of both categories. The only difference is that the abnormal point total is deducted from typical scores but added into the scores of non-typicals. If a trophy meets the minimum score for both categories, the choice of which category it is listed in is left up to the owner because it cannot be listed in both categories. B&C recommends that it be listed in the category where it has the highest relative rank.

Symmetry is a unique aspect of the Club's scoring system, and the decision to account for symmetry was not taken lightly at the time the system was devised. Critics of B&C's system say, "give it credit for what it grows." However, if it wasn't for symmetry, the freakiest and most irregular trophies would score the highest. For example, the "Hole in the Horn Buck" picked up in Portage County, Ohio, in the 1940s would score 3-7/8ths points higher than the Missouri Monarch, the current World's Record, if there wasn't a penalty for lack of symmetry. The 19th Awards Program Judges Panel had a difficult time identifying the four normal points they selected on the left antler of the former to match with the easily-recognizable points on the right antler, while the typical frame of the latter is clearly visible in almost any photo of it.

Beginning in 1950, trophies were scored and ranked for B&C using the typical and non-typical whitetail deer score charts in **Figures C** and **D**, though it really isn't completely clear when the non-typical forms were finalized and released. While the non-typical form has a copyright date of 1950, none of these forms appear in our files until the 6th Competition held in 1953. Prior to that, all non-typical whitetails were scored on typical forms with necessary adjustments made for calculating the non-typical score and a handwritten notation on each score chart that the deer was non-typical. There are three sets of the 1950 score charts in B&C's archives, and none of them include a separate score chart for non-typical whitetail or non-typical mule deer.

Interestingly, the typical and non-typical forms did not have separate boxes for recording abnormal point lengths until 1981 and 1963, respectively. Prior to that, abnormal point lengths were noted and calculated in the margins of both score charts or on a separate piece of paper, which frequently became detached and lost.

It is obvious, even to the casual observer, that considerable effort and discussion went into the creation of the whitetail deer scoring system. The typical and non-typical whitetail score charts in **Figures C** and **D**, respectively, are the result of the Club's Committee on Revisions created in 1949. Members of this committee included Sam Webb, Chairman; Harold E. Anthony, Milford Baker, Frederick K. Barbour, James L. Clark, and Grancel Fitz, a well-known big-game hunter and free-lance outdoor writer in his day. According to

FIGURE C: 1950 typical whitetail deer

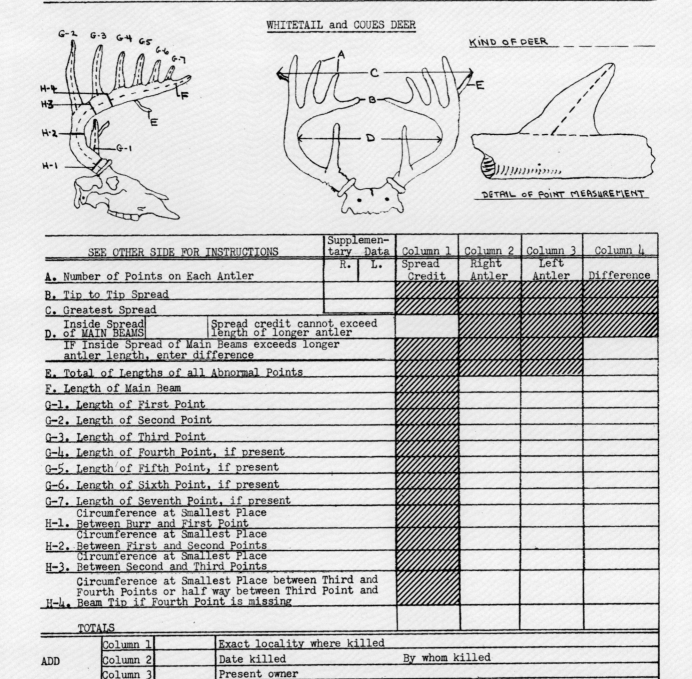

OFFICIAL SCORING SYSTEM FOR NORTH AMERICAN BIG GAME TROPHIES

Records of North American
Big Game and North American
Big Game Competition

BOONE AND CROCKETT CLUB

℅ Am. Museum of Natural History
Central Park West at 79th Street
New York 24, New York

WHITETAIL and COUES DEER

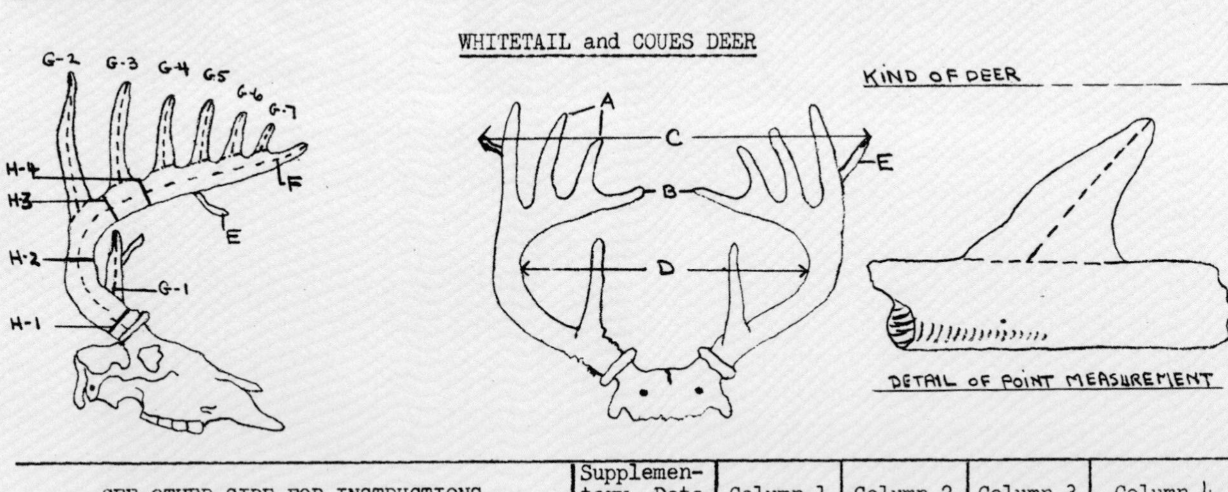

SEE OTHER SIDE FOR INSTRUCTIONS	Supplementary Data R.	Supplementary Data L.	Column 1 Spread Credit	Column 2 Right Antler	Column 3 Left Antler	Column 4 Difference
A. Number of Points on Each Antler						
B. Tip to Tip Spread						
C. Greatest Spread						
D. Inside Spread of MAIN BEAMS — Spread credit cannot exceed length of longer antler						
IF Inside Spread of Main Beams exceeds longer antler length, enter difference						
E. Total of Lengths of all Abnormal Points						
F. Length of Main Beam						
G-1. Length of First Point						
G-2. Length of Second Point						
G-3. Length of Third Point						
G-4. Length of Fourth Point, if present						
G-5. Length of Fifth Point, if present						
G-6. Length of Sixth Point, if present						
G-7. Length of Seventh Point, if present						
H-1. Circumference at Smallest Place Between Burr and First Point						
H-2. Circumference at Smallest Place Between First and Second Points						
H-3. Circumference at Smallest Place Between Second and Third Points						
H-4. Circumference at Smallest Place between Third and Fourth Points or half way between Third Point and Beam Tip if Fourth Point is missing						
TOTALS						

ADD	Column 1		Exact locality where killed
	Column 2		Date killed By whom killed
	Column 3		Present owner
	Total		Address
SUBTRACT	Column 4		Guide's Name and Address
FINAL SCORE			Remarks: (Mention any abnormalities)

FIGURE D: 1950 non-typical whitetail deer

OFFICIAL SCORING SYSTEM FOR NORTH AMERICAN BIG GAME TROPHIES

Records of North American Big Game Committee

BOONE AND CROCKETT CLUB

Address Correspondence to:
Mrs. Grancel Fitz, Secretary
5 Tudor City Place, NYC 17, NY.

NON-TYPICAL WHITETAIL DEER

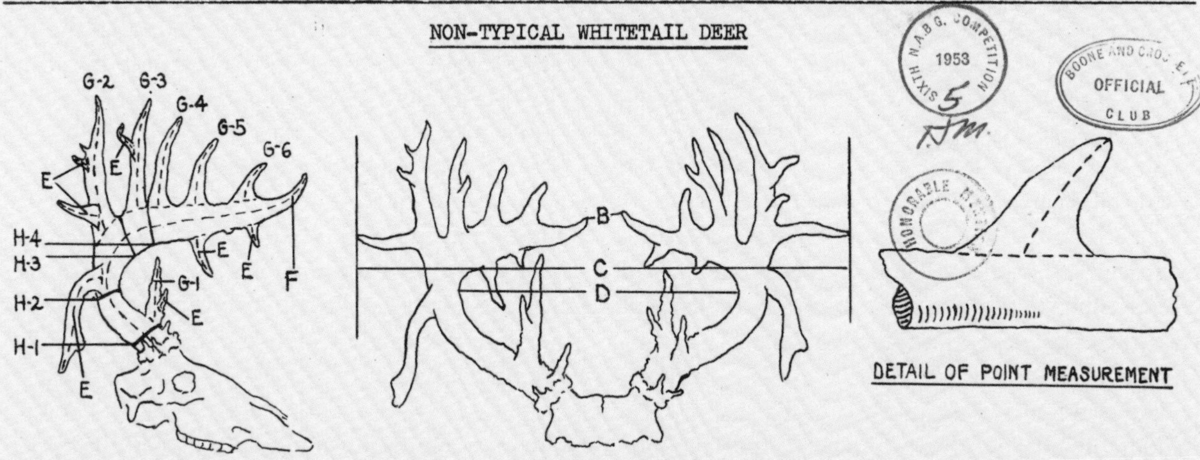

SEE OTHER SIDE FOR INSTRUCTIONS	Supplementary Data R.	Supplementary Data L.	Column 1 Spread Credit	Column 2 Right Antler	Column 3 Left Antler	Column 4 Difference
A. Number of Points on Each Antler	13	12				
B. Tip to Tip Spread	20 2/8					
C. Greatest Spread	29 3/8					
D. Inside Spread of MAIN BEAMS: 22 — Spread credit may equal but not exceed length of longer antler			22			
IF Inside Spread of Main Beams exceeds longer antler length, enter difference						
E. Total of Lengths of all Abnormal Points	36 2/8					
F. Length of Main Beam				25	25 1/8	1/8
G-1. Length of First Point, if present				3	6 1/8	3 1/8
G-2. Length of Second Point				10 3/8	8 5/8	1 6/8
G-3. Length of Third Point				9 2/8	8 4/8	6/8
G-4. Length of Fourth Point, if present				6 2/8	7	6/8
G-5. Length of Fifth Point, if present				7 6/8	3 1/8	4 5/8
G-6. Length of Sixth Point, if present				2 7/8	-	2 7/8
G-7. Length of Seventh Point, if present				-	-	
H-1. Circumference at Smallest Place Between Burr and First Point				4 6/8	4 5/8	1/8
H-2. Circumference at Smallest Place Between First and Second Points				4 2/8	4 2/8	-
H-3. Circumference at Smallest Place Between Second and Third Points				4 7/8	4 6/8	1/8
H-4. Circumference at Smallest Place Between Third and Fourth Points				4 6/8	4 4/8	2/8
TOTALS	36 2/8		22	83 1/8	76 5/8	14 4/8

ADD	Column 1	22	Exact locality where killed Live Oak Co, Texas
	Column 2	83 1/8	Date killed 1916 By whom killed Alec Coker
	Column 3	76 5/8	Present owner Henderson Coquat
	Total	181 6/8	Address San Antonio, Texas
SUBTRACT	Column 4	14 4/8	Guide's Name and Address none
	Result	167 2/8	Remarks: (Mention any abnormalities)
Add Line E Total		36 2/8	
FINAL SCORE		203 4/8	

a letter Sam Webb sent to Grancel Fitz on September 28, 1949, the committee's "... main objective is to formulate a scoring system for North American big game trophies that will work and be universally adopted."

The Club's 1950 score charts for scoring typical and non-typical whitetail deer were an amalgamation of two separate systems, tempered with the insight and guiding hand of Sam Webb. Clark was the head taxidermist at the American Museum of Natural History in New York City for many years and operated a taxidermy business of his own. He devised and copyrighted his scoring system in 1935, which he called, "The James L. Clark Standard Code for Scoring Big Game Trophies," for the purpose of judging and recognizing trophies mounted in his own taxidermy shop.

FIGURE E: James L. Clark's whitetail deer score chart.

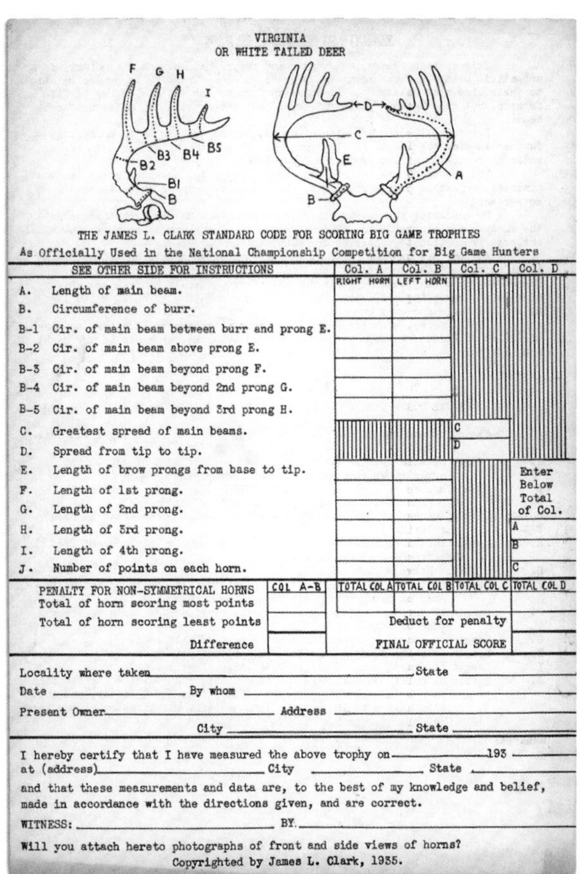

VIRGINIA
OR WHITE TAILED DEER

THE JAMES L. CLARK STANDARD CODE FOR SCORING BIG GAME TROPHIES
As Officially Used in the National Championship Competition for Big Game Hunters

SEE OTHER SIDE FOR INSTRUCTIONS		Col. A RIGHT HORN	Col. B LEFT HORN	Col. C	Col. D
A.	Length of main beam.				
B.	Circumference of burr.				
B-1	Cir. of main beam between burr and prong E.				
B-2	Cir. of main beam above prong E.				
B-3	Cir. of main beam beyond prong F.				
B-4	Cir. of main beam beyond 2nd prong G.				
B-5	Cir. of main beam beyond 3rd prong H.				
C.	Greatest spread of main beams.			C	
D.	Spread from tip to tip.			D	
E.	Length of brow prongs from base to tip.				Enter Below Total of Col.
F.	Length of 1st prong.				
G.	Length of 2nd prong.				
H.	Length of 3rd prong.				A
I.	Length of 4th prong.				B
J.	Number of points on each horn.				C

PENALTY FOR NON-SYMMETRICAL HORNS	COL A-B	TOTAL COL A	TOTAL COL B	TOTAL COL C	TOTAL COL D
Total of horn scoring most points					
Total of horn scoring least points		Deduct for penalty			
Difference		FINAL OFFICIAL SCORE			

Locality where taken ______ State ______
Date ______ By whom ______
Present Owner ______ Address ______
City ______ State ______

I hereby certify that I have measured the above trophy on ______ 193 ______
at (address) ______ City ______ State ______
and that these measurements and data are, to the best of my knowledge and belief, made in accordance with the directions given, and are correct.
WITNESS: ______ BY ______

Will you attach hereto photographs of front and side views of horns?
Copyrighted by James L. Clark, 1935.

Figure E is a copy of his score chart for whitetail deer. Clark did not have a separate form for non-typical specimens or "freaks" as non-typicals were known at that time. There just weren't that many non-typicals known to exist at that time because most deer didn't live long enough to attain non-typical status.

Clark's system for scoring whitetail deer was considerably different than that adopted by the Club in 1950. Clark did not include the inside spread measurement in his system or calculations. However, he did record the tip-to-tip and greatest spreads, which added into a trophy's final official score.

Clark measured the lengths of the main beams and all the normal points as with the current system. He also allowed room for as many as six circumferences, including a burr circumference. Finally, Clark provided boxes for including the total number of points on each antler that were added into the score. The number of points included the total number of normal and abnormal points, plus the beam tips. Abnormal points were not measured, but added into the final score as in some European systems, where each abnormal projection over one inch that was not one of the normal "pattern points" simply received a credit of one point. It is very evident that Clark put a lot of thought into his scoring system.

Fitz introduced his suggestions for a scoring system in the Club's second edition of the records book, *North American Big Game*, published by the Club in 1939 in a chapter he authored titled, "Rating of Trophies." **Figure F** is a copy of his proposed score chart. It is very evident that he also put a lot of thought into how trophies should be scored.

Figure G is a copy of the score chart used to collect whitetail data for the 1939 records book. There are several versions of this score chart in B&C's files, but all are similar to the score chart that appeared in the 1934 Remington reprint (**Figure A**), except the line of measurement for length of main beams on whitetails changed from 1932 to 1939, as mentioned earlier. The length of main beam for the 1939 records book

FIGURE F: Fitz's proposed score chart reproduced from page 81 of the 1939 records book

WHITETAIL DEER
ARIZONA WHITETAIL DEER

	SUPPLEMENTARY DATA R.	SUPPLEMENTARY DATA L.	COLUMN 1 INSIDE SPREAD	COLUMN 2 ANIMAL'S RIGHT ANTLER	COLUMN 3 ANIMAL'S LEFT ANTLER	COLUMN 4 NON-SYMMETRY PENALTIES
N-NUMBER OF POINTS ON EACH ANTLER						
E-EXTREME SPREAD						
T-TIP TO TIP SPREAD						
S-GREATEST SPREAD INSIDE MAIN BEAMS						
P-TOTAL OF LENGTHS OF ALL ABNORMAL POINTS						
L-1-LENGTH OF MAIN BEAM						
L-2- " " BROW POINT						
L-3- " " SECOND "						
L-4- " " THIRD "						
L-5- " " FOURTH " (IF PRESENT IN NORMAL PATTERN)						
L-6- " " FIFTH " " " " " "						
L-7- " " SIXTH " " " " " "						
L-8- " " SEVENTH " " " " " "						
C-1-CIRCUMFERENCE OF BURR						
C-2-CIR. AT SMALLEST PLACE BETWEEN BROW AND SECOND POINTS						
C-3- " " " " " SECOND AND THIRD POINTS						
C-4- " " " " " THIRD " FOURTH " (IF PRESENT)						
C-5- " " " " " FOURTH " FIFTH " " "						
C-6- " " " " " FIFTH " SIXTH " " "						
C-7- " " " " " SIXTH " SEVENTH " " "						
TOTALS						

ADD	COL. 1		Exact locality where killed
	" 2		Date By whom killed
	" 3		Owner
	TOTAL		Address
SUBTRACT	COL. 4		Remarks
FINAL SCORE			Scored and measured by Date

FIGURE G: 1939 B&C deer score chart

1 1947

Boone and Crockett Club

RECORDS OF NORTH AMERICAN BIG GAME
AND
NORTH AMERICAN BIG GAME COMPETITION
IN CARE OF
AMERICAN MUSEUM OF NATURAL HISTORY
CENTRAL PARK WEST AT 79TH STREET
NEW YORK 24, N. Y.

COMMITTEE
—
HAROLD E. ANTHONY, CHAIRMAN
R. R. M. CARPENTER
ALFRED ELY
KARL T. FREDERICK
A. C. GILBERT

UNDER THE AUSPICES
OF
THE NATIONAL MUSEUM
OF HEADS AND HORNS
OF THE
NEW YORK ZOOLOGICAL
SOCIETY

DEER

SPECIES: White Tail Deer.

MEASUREMENTS

	RIGHT	LEFT
Length of outside curve A	27½"	26½"
Greatest spread B 20"		
Circumference of main beam C	5"	4⅞"
Number of points on antler	7	5
Circumference of burr D	7¼"	7⅛"

Exact locality where killed Township Lynne, Oneida County, Wisconsin.

Date killed November 27, 1938.

By whom killed Jesse E Sherwood, Rhinelander, Wis.

Owner Jesse Sherwood,

Address

Present location of trophy Thayer St, Rhinelander Wis.

Remarks:

We hereby certify that we have measured the above described trophy on December 15 1947, and that these measurements are correct and made in accordance with the directions overleaf.

By Jesse Sherwood

MAIN BEAM MEASUREMENT
FOR WHITE TAIL

A

FIGURE H: 1939 length of main beam measurement (A) for deer score chart was taken along the midpoint of the outside edge of the main beam (**Figure H**) as it is still done today.

The 1932 and 1939 records book score charts (**Figures A** and **G**) were multi-species score charts. That is, both score charts were used to score all four categories of deer recognized by the Club at that time—whitetail deer, Arizona whitetail deer, mule deer, and Columbian blacktail deer. In fact, the mule deer and whitetail deer drawings on the back of the score chart show through in **Figure G**.

There are many unique features to both Clark's and Fitz's scoring systems, **Figures E** and **F**, respectively, worth highlighting. To start with, Fitz recorded the number of points on each antler, as well as an extreme spread (greatest spread), and tip-to-tip spread. Unlike Clark's system, these measurements were supplementary data on Fitz's score chart and did not add into the final score. On the other hand, Fitz included a line for the inside spread that added into the final score while Clark didn't. According to Fitz, the inside spread was a characteristic integral to a number of European systems he had examined.

Both Fitz and Clark were proponents for symmetry penalties. However, the techniques each used to account for symmetry were significantly different. Fitz deducted for differences between the lengths of the main beams, points, and circumferences, as is done today, while the only deduction that Clark took for non-symmetry was the difference between the column totals for the right and left antlers.

Fitz did not like Clark's method of accounting for symmetry because of compensating differences. Under a worst-case scenario, for example, there could be significant differences between the main beams, numbers and lengths of points, and circumferences, but there would be no deduction for lack of symmetry under Clark's system if the column totals added up identically the same because of compensating differences.

Fitz's system recorded the number of projections that qualified as points, but they were recorded as supplementary data and did not add into the Final Score. Clark's point totals, including what we now call abnormal points, added into the column totals in keeping with other scoring systems, especially European, in use at that time, though abnormal points were not measured. Fitz noted, "Adding a single 'score point' for each antler point would be a meaningless complication." The more normal points a trophy had, the more credit it already received in lengths measured.

The basic determination of what constituted a point between Fitz's and Clark's systems was how point lengths were measured. Both agreed points had to be an inch long, but their method of scoring them varied. Fitz proposed that the length of each point be measured to the *midpoint* of the main beam (**Figure F**), while Clark actually measured all "pattern points," as normal points were known at that time, to the bottom edge of the main beam (**Figure E**) except for brow tines, which he measured to their base off the top of the main beam.

Webb's influence on the committee's outcome is evident. He was the referee who tempered egos and kept things moving towards their ultimate goal—a relatively simple, universally accepted scoring system. When the Committee for Revisions finished its work, copies of the score charts were distributed in early 1950 to 250 individuals, including outdoor writers, scientists, taxidermists, big-game hunters, guides, outfitters, game officials, and other individuals with a strong interest in records-keeping for review and comments.

The success of Webb's committee in devising a scoring system for typical and non-typical whitetail deer stands as a testimonial to their efforts. The only significant difference between the 1950 and 2006 score charts (**Figures I** and **J**) for typical and non-typical whitetail deer is the fact that the penalty for excessive inside spread (**Figures C** and **D, Line E, Column 4**), which became known as "double penalty," was deleted in the 1980s. Otherwise, there have been no significant changes to the typical and non-typical score charts that require re-measuring of all the entries.

FIGURE I: 2006 typical whitetail deer score chart

Records of North American Big Game

250 Station Drive
Missoula, MT 59801
(406) 542-1888

BOONE AND CROCKETT CLUB®

OFFICIAL SCORING SYSTEM FOR NORTH AMERICAN BIG GAME TROPHIES

MINIMUM SCORES	AWARDS	ALL-TIME
whitetail	160	170
Coues'	100	110

TYPICAL WHITETAIL AND COUES' DEER

KIND OF DEER (check one)
☐ whitetail
☐ Coues'

G2 G3 G4 G5 G6 G7 H4 H3 H2 H1 G1 E F
Detail of Point Measurement
C B D E

	Abnormal Points	
	Right Antler	Left Antler
SUBTOTALS		
TOTAL TO E		

SEE OTHER SIDE FOR INSTRUCTIONS				COLUMN 1	COLUMN 2	COLUMN 3	COLUMN 4
A. No. Points on Right Antler		No. Points on Left Antler		Spread Credit	Right Antler	Left Antler	Difference
B. Tip to Tip Spread		C. Greatest Spread					
D. Inside Spread of Main Beams		SPREAD CREDIT MAY EQUAL BUT NOT EXCEED LONGER MAIN BEAM					
E. Total of Lengths of Abnormal Points							
F. Length of Main Beam							
G-1. Length of First Point							
G-2. Length of Second Point							
G-3. Length of Third Point							
G-4. Length of Fourth Point, If Present							
G-5. Length of Fifth Point, If Present							
G-6. Length of Sixth Point, If Present							
G-7. Length of Seventh Point, If Present							
H-1. Circumference at Smallest Place Between Burr and First Point							
H-2. Circumference at Smallest Place Between First and Second Points							
H-3. Circumference at Smallest Place Between Second and Third Points							
H-4. Circumference at Smallest Place Between Third and Fourth Points							
			TOTALS				

ADD	Column 1		Exact Locality Where Killed:
	Column 2		Date Killed: Hunter:
	Column 3		Trophy Owner: Telephone #:
	Subtotal		Trophy Owner's Address:
	SUBTRACT Column 4		Trophy Owner's E-mail: Guide's Name:
	FINAL SCORE		Remarks: (Mention Any Abnormalities or Unique Qualities) OM I.D. Number

FIGURE J: 2006 non-typical whitetail deer score chart

Records of North American Big Game

250 Station Drive
Missoula, MT 59801
(406) 542-1888

BOONE AND CROCKETT CLUB®

OFFICIAL SCORING SYSTEM FOR NORTH AMERICAN BIG GAME TROPHIES

NON-TYPICAL WHITETAIL AND COUES' DEER

MINIMUM SCORES	AWARDS	ALL-TIME
whitetail	185	195
Coues'	105	120

KIND OF DEER (check one)
☐ whitetail
☐ Coues'

G2 G3 G4 G5 G6 E E E F H4 H3 G1 H2 H1

Detail of Point Measurement

B C D

Abnormal Points	
Right Antler	Left Antler
SUBTOTALS	
E. TOTAL	

SEE OTHER SIDE FOR INSTRUCTIONS				COLUMN 1	COLUMN 2	COLUMN 3	COLUMN 4
A. No. Points on Right Antler		No. Points on Left Antler		Spread Credit	Right Antler	Left Antler	Difference
B. Tip to Tip Spread		C. Greatest Spread					
D. Inside Spread of Main Beams		SPREAD CREDIT MAY EQUAL BUT NOT EXCEED LONGER MAIN BEAM					
F. Length of Main Beam							
G-1. Length of First Point							
G-2. Length of Second Point							
G-3. Length of Third Point							
G-4. Length of Fourth Point, If Present							
G-5. Length of Fifth Point, If Present							
G-6. Length of Sixth Point, If Present							
G-7. Length of Seventh Point, If Present							
H-1. Circumference at Smallest Place Between Burr and First Point							
H-2. Circumference at Smallest Place Between First and Second Points							
H-3. Circumference at Smallest Place Between Second and Third Points							
H-4. Circumference at Smallest Place Between Third and Fourth Points							
			TOTALS				

ADD	Column 1		Exact Locality Where Killed:
	Column 2		Date Killed: Hunter:
	Column 3		Trophy Owner: Telephone #:
Subtotal			Trophy Owner's Address:
SUBTRACT Column 4			Trophy Owner's E-mail: Guide's Name:
Subtotal			Remarks: (Mention Any Abnormalities or Unique Qualities)
ADD Line E Total			
FINAL SCORE			OM I.D. Number

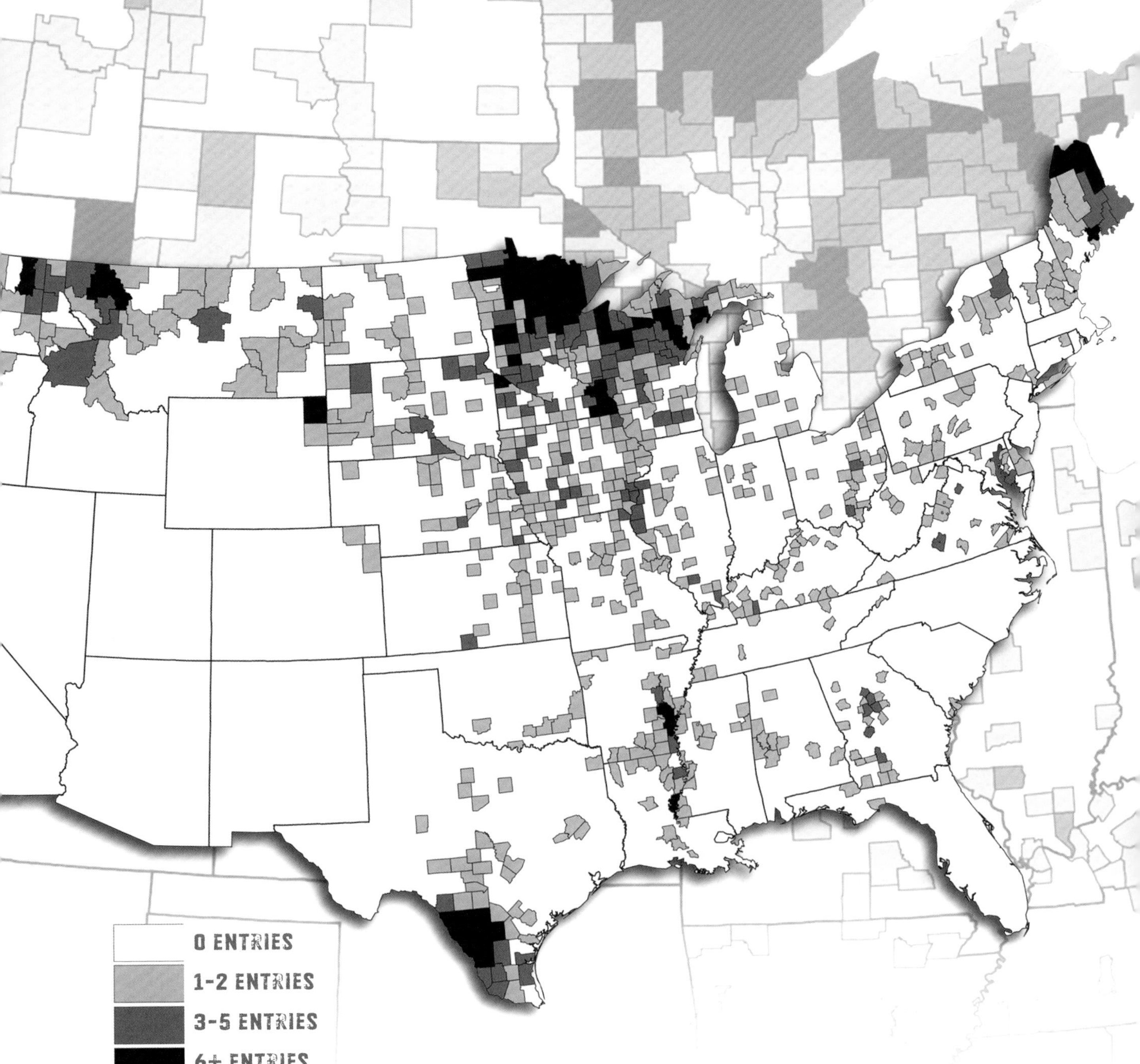

DISTRIBUTION MAP FOR WHITETAIL DEER ENTRIES

1830 UP THROUGH 1979

The map shown above includes trophy entries from 1830 through 1979. Several key areas for outstanding trophy entries are evident — south Texas, Minnesota, Wisconsin, and Idaho/Montana. You will see on the maps that follow how these different areas performed throughout the years.

2: DISTRIBUTION

BY JOEL W. HELMER PH.D.

"American sportsmen, those who hunted and fished for pleasure rather than commerce or necessity, were the real vanguard of conservation."
—John F. Reiger

Many today probably do not perceive the Boone and Crockett Club's records program as a historical archive of American conservation. For most it is a celebration of hunting, recognition of individual hunting success, a system of keeping score, or a way of honoring mature big-game specimens. Although all valid views, it is also a unique and important historical archive. Indeed, it was the desire to pay tribute to our natural history that motivated Prentiss N. Gray and other Club members to begin the process of compiling records of North American big game in the late 1920s.

What makes the Club's records program archive particularly notable is its consistency, supporting documentation, and location information. Each entry is measured using the same patented scoring system that is relatively unchanged since its most recent refinement in 1950. All entries are therefore comparable over time. The official score sheet verifies authenticity and includes hunter information. An entry affidavit certifies that the trophy was taken in an ethical and sporting manner. Pictures, letters, hunting tags and licenses, and other materials complete the file of each entry.

Finally, each entry has a geographic location (most commonly a county) and a date, allowing for its placement in time and space. By mapping the whitetail records book over time, we can "see" the interconnected natural history of deer, American conservation, and the Boone and Crockett Club's records book.

1830-1939

The earliest entry in the records book is particularly fascinating. Although shot in "about" 1830, the buck would not be officially scored for another 135 years! C.R. Studholme finally had the buck scored in 1965, providing a letter detailing the story. The 175-4/8 inch buck was shot by his great grandfather, Arthur Young, in McKean County, Pennsylvania, near the town of Norwich. He eventually died in 1878, nine years prior to the formation of the Boone and Crockett Club. Mr. Studholme continues by assuring the Club that the animal was taken in fair chase since "there were no motor powered vehicles at that time." Amazingly, the rack and rifle used to shoot the buck stayed in the family. Perhaps most revealing, Arthur Young was a market hunter, credited with taking "over 1,500 deer" during his lifetime.

The presence of a market hunter in the records book is historically appropriate. When Europeans arrived in North America, there were probably anywhere from 15 million to perhaps 30 million whitetails. From the 1500s to the end of the 1800s this number declined precipitously. The mid-1800s was the apex of the exploitation of whitetail deer and other big-game animals. There were few game laws, and those that did exist were rarely enforced. Wild game of all varieties was commonly sold and traded. Market hunting was commonplace, legal, and provided income to some and food to settlers, military personnel, and urbanites wanting fresh meat. Many areas, especially the Midwest, were cleared and converted to agricultural uses.

The events during the Iowa winter of 1856-57 are illustrative. A particularly nasty snowstorm during early December forced deer down into the valleys, nearer settlements, and into deep snows. Settlers, who were probably half-starved themselves, set upon the struggling deer with guns and clubs. One young boy of 15 reportedly crawled atop a struggling deer and killed it with a knife. During that same winter, Dick Chamberlain alone killed 78 deer in Montgomery County. By the 1880s deer were rare in Iowa and considered extinct by 1900, although a remnant herd may have survived in the extreme northeastern part of the state.

The nadir for whitetail deer in America occurred sometime during the first decade of the 20th century, when the population was estimated at 500,000. Whitetails were officially extinct in many states, including Ohio, Kansas, Indiana, and Illinois. In most other areas they were extremely rare. There were an estimated 500 deer in both Oklahoma and Arkansas, while Missouri had a mere 395. Just seeing a deer was a newsworthy event. For perspective, Wisconsin hunters currently shoot over 300,000 deer during a nine-day gun season. The destruction of whitetails and other big game was so complete that Club member William T. Hornaday worked diligently to establish the National Collection of Heads and Horns at the Bronx Zoo to, in part, preserve "vanishing" species.

It would be hunter-conservationists who would clamor for an end to the destruction. Continuing a process that actually began in the early 1800s, sportsmen increased their efforts to establish game laws, lobbied for more enforcement, and worked to instill in hunters the concept of fair chase. In 1887 the Boone and Crockett Club was formed with the stated goal of preserving and protecting big-game animals and their habitat. Soon thereafter, Club member John F. Lacey worked successfully to pass the Lacey Act. This watershed legislation regulated interstate commerce in wild game, ending market hunting and ushering in the era of state and federal collaboration in wildlife management.

Although encouraging first steps, deer populations would remain relatively low for the next 50 years. In many states, the deer season was either closed or exceedingly limited. Despite the decline in deer and limited opportunity, hunters still continued to pursue deer throughout the 109-year period from 1830 to 1939. The majority of records-book whitetails during this period came from the rugged fringes of the country. In the northern woodlands of Minnesota, Wisconsin, and Maine, the brush country of southern Texas, and the mountains of Idaho and Montana, deer were never extirpated. For example, in 1917-18 Wisconsin hunters shot approximately 18,000 deer. Later it would be whitetails from these regions that would be trapped and transplanted to repopulate other regions of the country.

1940-49

With increasing protection during the early 1900s, whitetail deer slowly began to repopulate their former range. The Pittman-Robertson Federal Aid in Wildlife Restoration Act of 1937 played a key role by placing a federal excise tax on sporting arms and ammunition. Each year millions of dollars were distributed back to state wildlife agencies to purchase and protect habitat and restore game populations. Much of this money was spent reestablishing whitetail deer. Pittman-Robertson continues today, and since its inception has generated over $4 billion for wildlife conservation.

With increasing funding, state biologists began actively transplanting deer. Georgia provides a good example. After the deer population reached its historic low in 1920, officials began importing deer from nearby states such as North Carolina and Mississippi. Officials also imported larger northern subspecies of deer from Michigan, Montana, and Wisconsin. Other states often purchased deer from private herds or utilized remnant populations for their restocking programs.

DISTRIBUTION MAP FOR WHITETAIL DEER ENTRIES
1830 UP THROUGH 1939

During this time period, the majority of records-book whitetail deer came from the rugged fringes of the country where deer had not been extirpated—northern woodlands of Minnesota, Wisconsin, and Main, the brush country of southern Texas, and the mountains of Idaho and Montana.

DISTRIBUTION MAP FOR WHITETAIL DEER ENTRIES
1940 THROUGH 1949

0 ENTRIES
1-2 ENTRIES
3-5 ENTRIES
6+ ENTRIES

The top two counties during this decade were north Minnesota's Itasca County and southern Texas' Webb County. Deer had never been extirpated from these areas and the results are evident. The return of GIs at the end of this decade meant nearly twice as many hunters were taking to the field.

DISTRIBUTION MAP FOR WHITETAIL DEER ENTRIES

1950 THROUGH 1959

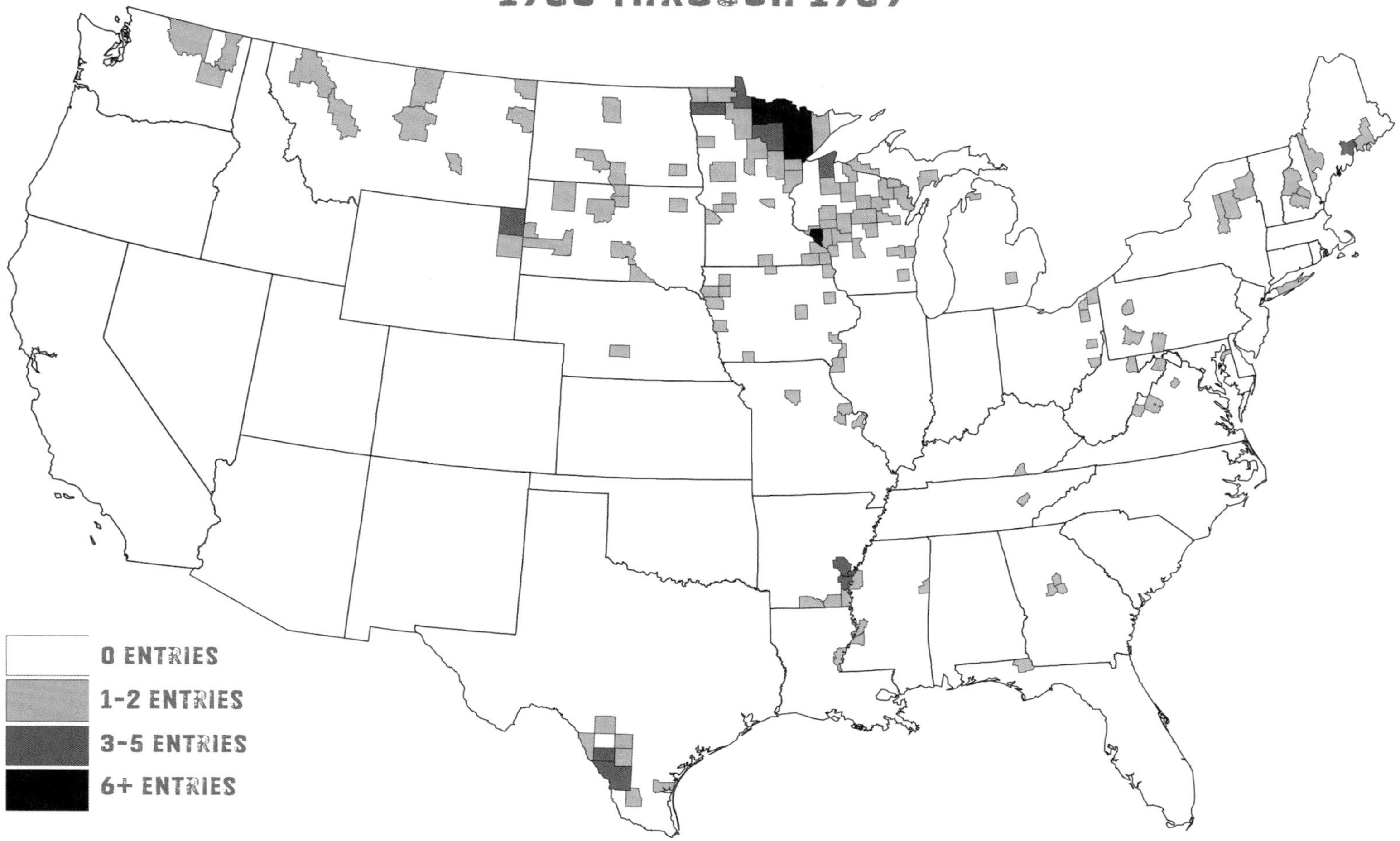

0 ENTRIES
1-2 ENTRIES
3-5 ENTRIES
6+ ENTRIES

The combined efforts to improve whitetail deer populations by hunters, conservation organizations, and government agencies were beginning to show results. By the end of this decade, the deer population in the U.S. was estimated at slightly over 5 million. Compare that the estimated population at the turn of the century of 500,000 whitetail deer.

Between 1939 and 1948, states would transplant over 17,000 whitetails.

Deer hunting during the 1940s was overshadowed by the war effort. Although many did continue to hunt, millions of men were overseas and license sales fell. Those hunters that remained supplied an estimated 54 million pounds of game meat, mainly whitetails, to their families during 1942. Hunters also donated over 200,000 deerskins during 1943-44 for military-issue gloves, jackets, and boots.

Following VJ Day in August of 1945, GIs began returning to the states in time for the fall deer season. Families were eager to rekindle relationships in the deer woods, or in many cases to mourn the loss of those who would never hunt again. License sales, which during the pre-war years had numbered about 7 million, quickly jumped to 12 million by 1947.

In most states, deer were still rare and protected. Buck-only regulations were the norm. Ohio held its first modern deer season in 1943, in only three counties. Hunters bagged a total of 168 bucks. In 1950, Missouri hunters tagged a mere 1,622 deer. The distribution of records-book entries reflects the status of the nation's deer herd. Most entries were still coming from those areas where deer were never extirpated. For example, the top two counties during the decade were northern Minnesota's Itasca County and southern Texas' Webb County.

1950-59

As the ink was drying on the newly patented Boone and Crockett Club scoring system, modern wildlife management was gaining momentum. Club member Aldo Leopold published his seminal work *Game Management* in 1933. Soon after its publication, the University of Wisconsin established a Department of Game Management, the first of its kind in the country, with Leopold as chair. During the next several decades universities across the country followed suit, establishing degree programs in wildlife management and active research programs in conservation. Using the G.I. Bill, former servicemen returned to college, and soon thousands of biologists, technicians, and conservation officers were actively working to restore habitat and wildlife. Of course, a significant portion of the funding for state personnel and programs came from hunters through taxes and license fees.

Not all the efforts were government led. In 1948, the Boone and Crockett Club established its Grants-In-Aid Program to support graduate-level research in wildlife management. Over the years this program had funded numerous projects focusing on big-game or habitat conservation. Other hunter-conservation organizations like Ducks Unlimited and the Izaak Walton League were also active in conservation. Many similar organizations would come in the next several decades.

The combined efforts of hunters, conservation organizations, and government agencies were beginning to show results. Mississippi had fewer than 4,600 deer in 1939, but by 1952 it had over 50,000. Virginia had only several hundred deer in 1939, but through restocking efforts the herd increased to 200,000 by 1960. By the late 1950s the nation's deer population was estimated at slightly over 5 million.

The records book mirrors these restoration successes. A sprinkling of entries is evident across Iowa and into northern Missouri. Additional clusters of entries can be seen in Georgia, southern Arkansas, and eastern Ohio. The best county was no longer in the north woods or in southern Texas. Buffalo County, Wisconsin, located along the Mississippi River, led the nation in entries during the 1950s. Located in the agricultural area of southwestern Wisconsin, it was a harbinger of the many Midwestern bucks that would flood the records book in years to come.

1960-69

For many, the 1960s represents the beginning of the environmental movement and widespread concern for our nation's natural resources. My

DISTRIBUTION MAP FOR WHITETAIL DEER ENTRIES

1960 THROUGH 1969

The records book reveals the rapid expansion of whitetails into the middle section of the country. Most states by now had at least one entry, and some, such as Wisconsin and Minnesota, had entries across the state.

university students are usually familiar with Earth Day, the Endangered Species Act, or Rachel Carson's *Silent Spring*. Although these are important, my concern is the ignorance most have of the role played by conservationists long before the 1960s, and more specifically the part hunters played in conserving America's wildlife, forests, parks, and wilderness areas.

As the environmental movement was emerging, hunters were enjoying the fruits of 60 years worth of effort. In Ohio, the state's deer population was now 20,000, while Illinois hunters tagged 1,000 deer in 1970. Archery hunting was gaining popularity, with the Pope and Young Club established in 1961. New technologies such as Gore-Tex and nylon ropes and tents made backcountry hunting easier. The newly completed interstate highway system made accessing hunting areas quicker and easier. Air travel became commonplace, and vehicles more reliable. The national economy was booming, resulting in more time and money to pursue nature and hunting.

The records book reveals the rapid expansion of whitetails into the middle section of the country. The agriculturally rich sections of the country that were cleared for agriculture were now beginning to show potential as deer habitat. Most states now had at least one entry, and some, such as Wisconsin and Minnesota, had entries across the state.

1970-79

By the time the time of the Club's 17th Awards Program in 1979, deer and deer hunting were again a firmly established facet of America's outdoors. Hunters were enjoying unprecedented opportunity that would only increase in the coming decades. The nation now had an estimated 12 million whitetails. Oklahoma's herd had increased from 500 in the 1920s to 94,000, while Ohio's had gone from zero to 100,000. In some areas managers were beginning to explore methods to slow deer population growth. Antlerless tags were increasingly common, as were longer seasons. Muzzleloader hunting was gaining in popularity, spurred by special primitive firearms seasons.

With more opportunity came the desire to shoot larger and more mature whitetail bucks. Since hunters could be assured of seeing numerous deer, they began to be more selective. This in turn led to more interest in the Club's records program. More hunters became aware of the "book," and the caliber of buck it took to meet the minimum.

The records-book distribution during this period actually matches closely the overall distribution of whitetails. Although several have no entries, most states have entries in numerous areas. Southern states, from Georgia across to Louisiana, began producing nice bucks, as did western Kentucky, southeastern Oklahoma, and areas of the western Great Plains.

Examining this series of maps makes one truly appreciate the whitetail hunting we presently enjoy. By comparing the early years of the Boone and Crockett Club's records book with the history of conservation, it also makes one proud to be a hunter-conservationist and Club member. We can see how the past efforts and resources of those before us assisted in restoring big game to this continent, and it encourages us to continue these efforts. Indeed, hunters and the Boone and Crockett Club are integral parts of the long and captivating history of whitetail deer and conservation in America.

It is equally important that we continue to be the vanguard of conservation in the future.

REFERENCES:

Dinsmore, James J. *A Country So Full of Game: The Story of Wildlife in Iowa* **(Iowa City: University of Iowa Press, 1994).**

Swift, Ernest. *A History of Wisconsin Deer* **(Madison: Wisconsin Conservation Department, 1946).**

Taylor, Walter P. Ed. *The Deer of North America: Their History and Management* **(Harrisburg: Stackpole Co., 1956).**

Trefethen, James B. *An American Crusade for Wildlife* **(New York: Winchester Press, Boone and Crockett Club, 1975).**

Reiger, John F. *American Sportsmen and the Origins of Conservation, 3rd Ed.* **(Corvallis: Oregon State University Press, 2001).**

Rue, Leonard Lee III. *The Deer of North America* **(New York: Crown Publishers, Inc., 1978).**

DISTRIBUTION MAP FOR WHITETAIL DEER ENTRIES

1970 THROUGH 1979

The nation now had an estimated 12 million whitetail deer. We can see how past efforts and resources of those before us assisted in restoring big game to this continent. And it encourages us to continued these efforts.

DEER

D E E R

LEFT
26 3/4"
4 1/4"
7 3/8"
9

PRIZE WINNING TROPHIES
Submitted for the
1948 NORTH AMERICAN
BIG GAME COMPETITION
of the
BOONE AND CROCKETT CLUB

B Circumference of main beam: Taken midway between t[...]
the first fork.

C Circumference of burr.

D Greatest spread: Measured between perpendiculars a[...]
horns at right angles to the center line of the skull.

Points: No point shall be counted unless it protrudes a[...]

Remarks: State whether the trophy has any charac[...]
from the normal for this species.

Please provide photographs showing front view and p[...]

Records of North American Big Game

A PUBLICATION OF
THE BOONE AND CROCKETT CLUB
IN CARE OF
AMERICAN MUSEUM OF NATURAL HISTORY
COLUMBUS AVENUE AND 77TH STREET
NEW YORK, N. Y.

COMMITTEE
ALFRED ELY, CHAIRMAN
HAROLD E. ANTHONY
R. R. M. CARPENTER

D E E R

SPECIES WHITE TAIL DEER

MEASUREMENTS

	RIGHT	LE[FT]
Length on outside curve A	26 1/2"	26
Circumference of main beam B	4 1/4"	4
Circumference of burr C	7 1/4"	7
Number of points on antler	9	9
Greatest spread: D	26 1/4"	

Exact locality where killed Saranac Lake

Date killed 1922

By whom killed William Barthman

Owner William Barthman

Address

Remarks: N.Y.C.

Photographs: Front view.............Profile.............
(Please place √ mark to indicate photographs furnished.

We hereby certify that we have measured the above described trophy on Jan. 9 1939, and that these measurements are correct and made in accordance with the directions overleaf.

Hansen Studio

3: THE EARLY YEARS

BY JOHN P. POSTON

From the beginning, members of the Boone and Crockett Club were interested in "trophy" hunting. At the First Annual Sportsmen's Exposition in New York City in 1891, Club members Theodore Roosevelt, George Bird Grinnell, and Archibald Rogers were the judges in a trophy competition. Unfortunately, there are no records of the winners or the standards by which the entries were judged. Theodore Roosevelt put it this way, "If it is morally right to kill an animal to eat its body, then it is morally right to kill it to preserve its head. A good sportsman will not hesitate as to the relative value he puts upon the two, and to get the one he will go a long time without eating the other."

One of the primary reasons for the formation of the Boone and Crockett Club were the concerns of its founding members, hunters all, about the unchecked destruction of the North American big game herds. Early on, the members sought to gather data and preserve specimens of all the various big game animals. It was believed that many species were going the way of the bison. Therefore, the collection of specimens were thought necessary for viewing by posterity should the species become extinct. This effort was institutionalized when, in 1895, the New York Zoological Society was organized by the Club with many of the Society's board members being Boone and Crockett Club members.

The Society created the New York Zoological Park and named as its Director Dr. William T. Hornaday, a renowned naturalist, hunter, and professional member of the Boone and Crockett Club. Under his leadership, the National Collection of Heads and Horns was created. Hornaday donated his own large personal collection, which became the core of the National Heads and Horns Collection.

In his remarkable 1904 text-book, *The American Natural History*, Hornaday dwelled on the supposition that it was just a matter of time before all big-game animals would become extinct or limited to small remnant herds, living in protected places like Yellowstone Park or in zoos. Hornaday opined that the whitetail would be the last of the big-game animals to become extinct. He called the whitetail "The Great Skulker." He described it thus: "When hiding, it crouches and carries its head low, and by clinging persistently to the friendly cover of brush or timber, saves itself under circumstances that would be fatal to any high-headed, open ground species."

In his book, Hornaday set forth "Rules for Measuring Mammals, Horn, Etc." to try to create a uniform system for recording data and making appropriate comparisons. Hornaday began ranking the Collection specimens in his regular reports beginning in 1910. Specimens were sought from many sources, such as sportsmen's clubs. This gave rise to competitions at various gatherings where sportsmen brought their trophies to be judged. If an exceptional trophy was brought in, the owner was solicited to donate it to the Collection. Some of the clubs kept permanent records, which were generously provided to the Collection.

Taxidermists were another source used in locating heads or horns to be included in the Col-

WAPITI

RECOR[D]

OF

North American Big Game

PRENTISS N. GRAY
EDITOR

Published under the auspices
of the

NATIONAL COLLECTION OF HEADS AND HORNS
NEW YORK ZOOLOGICAL SOCIETY

A BOOK OF
THE BOONE AND CROCKETT CLUB

NEW YORK
THE DERRYDALE PRESS
1932

NORTH AMERICAN BIG GAME

A BOOK OF THE BOONE AND CROCKETT CLUB
COMPILED BY THE COMMITTEE ON RECORDS
OF NORTH AMERICAN BIG GAME
ALFRED ELY, *Chairman*, H. E. ANTHONY
and R. R. M. CARPENTER

Published with the Cooperation of the National Collection of Heads and Horns of the New York Zoological Society and American Museum of Natural History

1939

The 1932 and the 1939 records books shown here both used the old scoring system, which only ranked by the length of one main beam.

lection. Commencing in 1892, Rowland Ward's Ltd., a British taxidermy business, began keeping records of the trophies of its customers. These records involved animals worldwide.

In 1930, Boone and Crockett Club President Madison Grant appointed a committee to review and organize records of heads and horns. Prentiss Gray was appointed the Committee Chairman. Members of the committee were Kermit Roosevelt, W. Redmond Cross, George Harrison, and E. Hubert Litchfield. The committee reported its work in 1931 and published it in 1932 under the title *Records of North American Big Game*.

All of the prior efforts to rank trophies, regardless of by whom, used only a single measurement. The 1932 book provided additional measurements and numbers of points but this data was not used in the ranking calculations. By using only one measurement—the length of the longest beam—these efforts were obviously flawed. For example, a trophy with one antler broken off opposite an intact antler that measured an inch more than a trophy with two intact antlers would be ranked higher. In the introduction to the 1932 book, Prentiss Gray acknowledged the problem:

"There is always the question of which measurements or combination of measurements should be regarded as constituting the record. We have not attempted to answer this question in this edition. Common usage has indicated the measurement which sportsmen generally look for first and according to this dimension we have listed the trophies in the schedules. We recognize fully that no one dimension is the controlling factor and we hope that eventually some fair method of 'scoring' a head may be devised which will be acceptable."

Prentiss Gray's personal effort to devise a fairer method of scoring trophies was halted by his untimely death. Prior to his death Mr. Gray had enlisted others to work with him to develop a better system; James L. Clark and Grancel Fitz were two of these individuals. Each, working independently, had commenced on developing what would become the basis of a more "fair" system of scoring trophies.

Addressing Gray's concern about a fair method, Grancel Fitz in the chapter on rating of trophies in the 1939 records book addressed the issue as follows:

"If the term 'record head' is to have much meaning, it is reasonable to assume that an ideal record list should give top ranking to the finest head in the world, and this might be defined as that trophy which the majority of informed sportsmen would choose as being the best of its species, all qualities being considered. The ranking of the other listed trophies also should be in the order of their general desirability, but no method of arriving at this ideal was available when Records of North American Big Game *was published. As an indication that the acceptable scoring system desired by Gray has not yet been evolved, it will be noted that, despite the passage of seven years since the above was written, no radical change has been made in this volume in the manner of listing trophies."*

Without the benefit of Gray's direction, the Club decided to publish the 1939 records book using the same method for scoring as the 1932 book. The criticism from sportsmen and writers in the field became more pronounced, with all pointing out flaws in the system. Aside from the criticism of the methodology of the scoring system, the basic idea of the book was almost universally accepted.

Due to the World War II, efforts in creating a fairer method of scoring were suspended. Commencing in 1947, the Club began holding annual competitions. Trophies were sought nationwide, with many trophy owners responding by sending in their trophies for judging. At each of the 1947, 1948, and 1949 competitions the single-measurement method was used by the judges. Each entrant was provided with a form and limited instructions on how to take the requested measurements. Controversy developed among the judges as to how to properly score the curvature of the main beams. In the end, a fair method of "scoring" the trophies had not been perfected through the 1949 competition.

OFFICIAL SCORING SYSTEM FOR NORTH AMERICAN BIG GAME TROPHIES

Records of North American Big Game and North American Big Game Competition

BOONE AND CROCKETT CLUB

% Am. Museum of Natural History
Central Park West at 79th Street
New York 24, New York

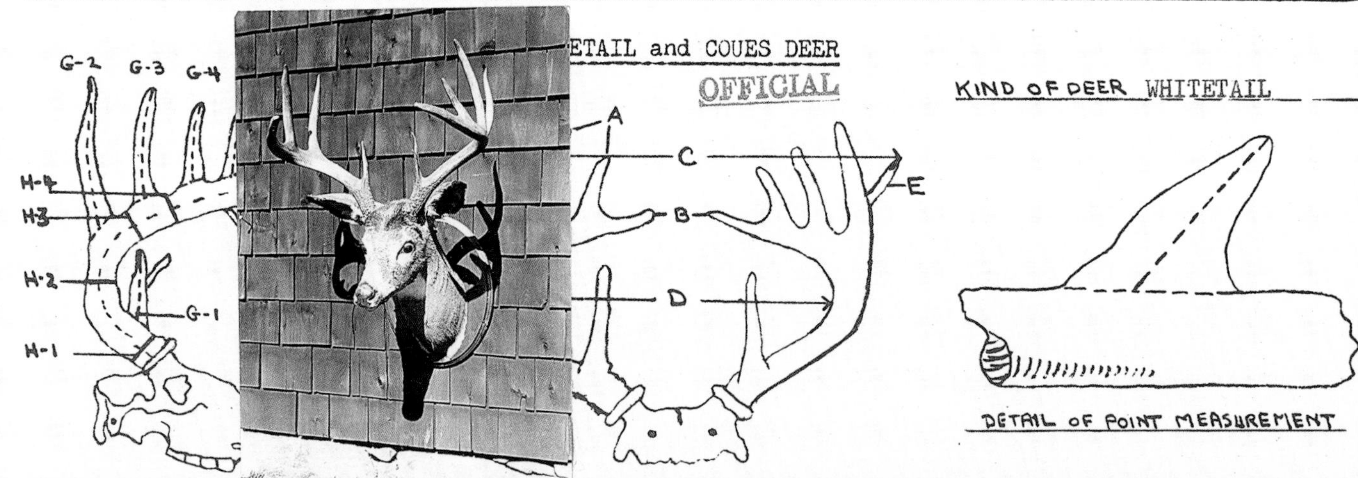

KIND OF DEER WHITETAIL

DETAIL OF POINT MEASUREMENT

SEE OTHER SIDE FOR INSTRUCTIONS	Supplementary Data R.	Supplementary Data L.	Column 1 Spread Credit	Column 2 Right Antler	Column 3 Left Antler	Column 4 Difference
A. Number of Points on Each Antler	5	6				
B. Tip to Tip Spread	13-3/8					
C. Greatest Spread	21-6/8					
D. Inside Spread of MAIN BEAMS 20 — Spread credit may equal but not exceed length of longer antler			20			
IF Inside Spread of Main Beams exceeds longer antler length, enter difference						-
E. Total of Lengths of all Abnormal Points						-
F. Length of Main Beam				24	24-4/8	4/8
G-1. Length of First Point, if present				4-4/8	5-1/8	5/8
G-2. Length of Second Point				9	7-4/8	1-4/8
G-3. Length of Third Point				8-4/8	8-4/8	-
G-4. Length of Fourth Point, if present				1-1/8	4-4/8	3-3/8
G-5. Length of Fifth Point, if present				-	-	-
G-6. Length of Sixth Point, if present				-	-	-
G-7. Length of Seventh Point, if present				-	-	-
H-1. Circumference at Smallest Place Between Burr and First Point				4-4/8	4-6/8	2/8
H-2. Circumference at Smallest Place Between First and Second Points				4-2/8	4-2/8	-
H-3. Circumference at Smallest Place Between Second and Third Points				4-4/8	4-3/8	1/8
H-4. Circumference at Smallest Place between Third and Fourth Points or half way between Third Point and Beam Tip if Fourth Point is missing				3-6/8	3-7/8	1/8
TOTALS			20	64-1/8	67-3/8	6-4/8

ADD	Column 1	20	Exact locality where killed HAMILTON COUNTY, N. Y.
	Column 2	64-1/8	Date killed 1885 By whom killed CHESTER DAY
	Column 3	67-3/8	Present owner J. W. WEBB
	Total	151-4/8	Address New York City
SUBTRACT	Column 4	6-4/8	Guide's Name and Address
012 FINAL SCORE		145.0	Remarks: (Mention any abnormalities) Head #15 on page 446 of 1939 Record Book.

VINTAGE PHOTOS*

THE EARLY YEARS

ABOVE: This Huntington County, Pennsylvania buck was taken in December 1946 by Leroy G. Kerr. Having that country lane off to the side seems to add something to this historic photo.

LEFT: Chester Day took this whitetail deer in 1885 in Hamilton County, New York. It was featured on page 446 of the 1939 edition of *Records of North American Big Game*. Note the classic taxidermy work for that time period.

*Many of the following photos are as stated, "vintage." The Boone and Crockett Club has carefully ushered in a new era with the advancement and availability of photographic equipment. Today, our expectations consist of presenting a blood-free trophy and hunter in an uncluttered, natural environment. These guidelines were born out of respect for the animal and its habitat.

B Greatest spread: Measured between parallels and at right angles to the center line of the skull.

C Circumference: Measured midway between the basal snag and the first fork.

Points: No point shall be counted unless it extends at least one inch.

D Circumference of burr.

Remarks: State whether the trophy has any characteristics which depart from the normal for this species.

ABOVE: This whitetail, taken by Alexander Cox in Webb County, Texas, in 1941, was submitted under the old scoring system. Its right main beam was 26 inches, good enough to receive an Honorable Mention at the Club's first competition.

RIGHT: It was December of 1913 when C.E. Sikes bagged this big buck from Wilson County, Texas. Before 1950, the original scoring system only counted the length of the main beams. This buck was never transitioned into B&C's current system. It looks as if it could possibly make the all-time typical minimum of 170.

LEFT: This is a great vintage photograph. Mansfield Royce Steidl is pictured holding his prized whitetail taken on November 22, 1947. He was hunting in the Laurentian Mountains in Quebec. Notes on the chart show a neck measurement of 31½ inches and 250-pound field-dressed weight.

1st Prize 1947

OFFICIAL

Boone and Crockett Club

RECORDS OF NORTH AMERICAN BIG GAME
AND
NORTH AMERICAN BIG GAME COMPETITION

IN CARE OF
AMERICAN MUSEUM OF NATURAL HISTORY
CENTRAL PARK WEST AT 79TH STREET
NEW YORK 24, N. Y.

UNDER THE AUSPICES
OF
THE NATIONAL MUSEUM
OF HEADS AND HORNS
OF THE
NEW YORK ZOOLOGICAL
SOCIETY

COMMITTEE

HAROLD E. ANTHONY, CHAIRMAN
R. R. M. CARPENTER
ALFRED ELY
KARL T. FREDERICK
A. C. GILBERT

Ace of Exhibition 1947

DEER

SPECIES .... WHITETAIL ....

MEASUREMENTS

	RIGHT	LEFT
Length of outside curve A	31-3/4	31 1/4 ~~32-7/8~~
Greatest spread B 23-1/8		
Circumference of main beam C	5	5-1/4
Number of points on antler	6	8
Circumference of burr D	8	7-7/8

Exact locality where killed .. Near Fredericton, N.B. ....

Date killed .... 1936 ....

By whom killed ... French Canadian farmer ....

Owner .... ~~Estate of Brooke Dolan~~ Acad. of Nat'l. Sciences Phila. Pa.

Address ....

Present location of trophy .. Academy of Natural Sciences

.... Philadelphia, Pa. ....

Remarks: Acad. Nat'l. Sciences # 20716

Pencilled measurements made by 1947 Judges.

We hereby certify that we have measured th[...]

on .... April 20, ... 1948, and th[...]

correct and made in accordance with the directions ove[...]

Measured by: ....

By ....

See: Wheeler 4/7/48
ANS 4/8/48

AWARD WINNERS

THE EARLY YEARS

FIRST PRIZE
1947 COMPETITION

This buck highlighted at left was taken by a French-Canadian farmer in New Brunswick in 1936. It was owned by the Academy of Natural Sciences of Philadelphia when it was originally measured. The original score chart of the 1947 Judges Panel is pictured on the opposite page.

Following is an excerpt from a letter from the Academy of Natural Sciences of Philadelphia to Harold E. Anthony of the American Museum of Natural History:

"It is a tremendously heavy head and I consider it an unfriendly freak of Mother Nature that one of those heavy beams did not reach forward just an inch further. As you will note, with the exception of one record from Michigan, this is the largest head recorded east of the Mississippi River."

The buck was remeasured under the new scoring system in 1951 with an official final score of 180-6/8 points. As of 2006, the buck still ranks as the second-largest whitetail taken from New Brunswick.

COMMITTEE
ALFRED ELY, CHAIRMAN
HAROLD E. ANTHONY
R. R. M. CARPENTER

Record of North American Big Game

IN CARE OF
AMERICAN MUSEUM OF NATURAL HISTORY
COLUMBUS AVENUE AND 77TH STREET
NEW YORK, N. Y.

UNDER THE AUSPICES OF
THE NATIONAL COLLECTION OF HEADS AND HORNS OF THE
NEW YORK ZOOLOGICAL SOCIETY
&
THE BOONE & CROCKETT CLUB

DEER

SPECIES .... Whitetail ....

MEASUREMENTS	RIGHT	LEFT
Length of outside curve A	$29\frac{3}{4}$"	$29\frac{1}{4}$"
Greatest spread B	$21\frac{1}{2}$"	
Circumference of main beam C	5"	5"
... points on antler	6	8
...ce of burr D	$7\frac{1}{2}$"	$7\frac{1}{2}$"

...y where killed .. one mile south of Hume, N. Y. Allegany Co.

... Nov. 25, 1939 ...

...d. Roosevelt Luckey

...osevelt Luckey

...me, N. Y.

... trophy .. At Garage in Hume, N. Y.

...eer had a very heavy set of horns..The beam betw een ...ures $6\frac{1}{2}$". There are six of the antlers that measure

... that we have measured the above described trophy ....194 0, and that these measurements are ...ce with the directions overleaf.

Roosevelt Luckey

By C. A. Landford

PRIZE WI...
NORTH
BIG GAM...
BOONE &...

SECOND PRIZE 1947 COMPETITION

Roosevelt Luckey's whitetail deer, highlighted at left, received a Second Prize at the 1947 Competition. The original score chart is shown opposite with a picture of Luckey holding the mounted buck.

Following is an excerpt from a letter from Clayton Seagears of the New York Conservation Department to Grancel Fitz, dated April 25, 1955:

"How would this plan work out to get those big New York heads measured officially? I'm having trucked down a live animal exhibit to the Kinsbridge Armory for the Boy Scout exposition May 6 and 7. I could send down the Roosevelt Luckey whitetail head – and possibly one or two other big ones not officially recorded – for display at the same time. Then either you or some other qualified person could take a look at them at the Armory during the exposition where I'll have them put on a wall panel.

I've measured them several times myself with a steel tape and I have never yet come out with precisely the same answer – so I'd sure like to have someone else do an official recording the heads."

The buck was indeed remeasured under the new scoring system that May by Fitz with a final score of 198-3/8 points. The buck still ranks as the largest typical whitetail taken in New York.

DEER

MAIN BEAM MEASUREMENT
FOR MULE AND BLACKTAIL
ble steel tape.
point on the main bean
and at right angles
basal snag and the firs

PRIZE WINNING TROPHIES
NORTH AMERICAN BIG GAME COMPETITION
Sponsored by
THE BOONE AND CROCKETT CLUB

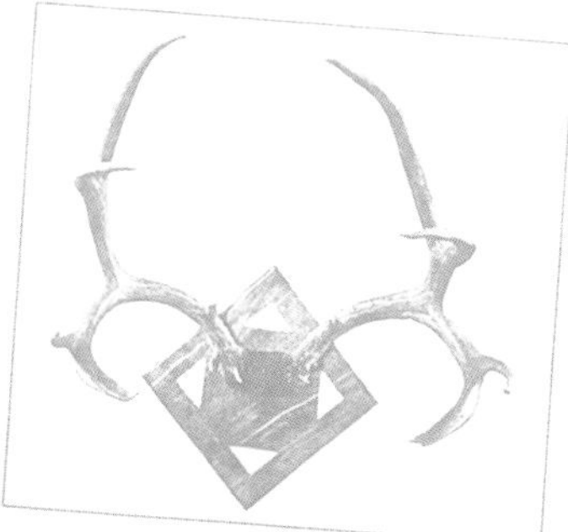

MULE DEER—1st Prize - 1949

STONE SHEEP—1st Prize - 1949

BIGHORN SHEEP—1st Prize - 1949

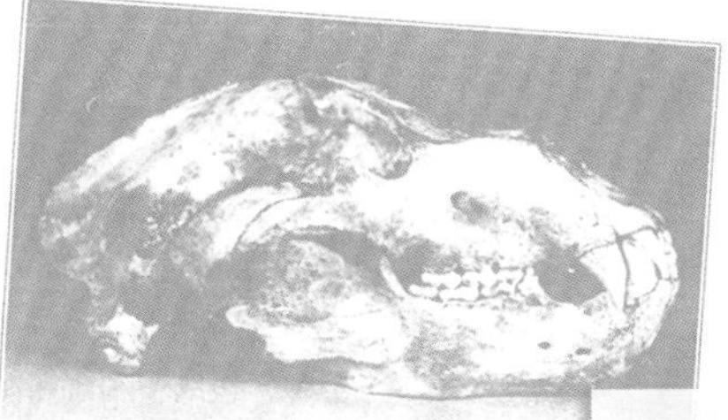

ALASKA BROWN BEAR—1st Prize - 1949

WHITETAIL DEER—1st Prize - 1949
Length—(R) 28-1/4 (L)30-1/8
Spread—24-7/8
Circumference (R) 5 (L) 5-7/8
Points—(R) 5 (L) 5
Locality—Cecil Co., Md. - 1948
Hunter—Roy F. Spies
Guide—None
Owner—Roy F. Spies

FIRST PRIZE
1949 COMPETITION

Tremendous beam lengths over 30 inches made this whitetail the First Prize winner at the 1949 Competition. Roy F. Spies was the successful hunter, punching his tag on this buck on December 6, 1948. Cecil County, Maryland, was the location of the hunt.

In the remarks section of the score chart, it states:

"Rack exceptionally heavy. Points very long. Four points better than 11 inches in length."

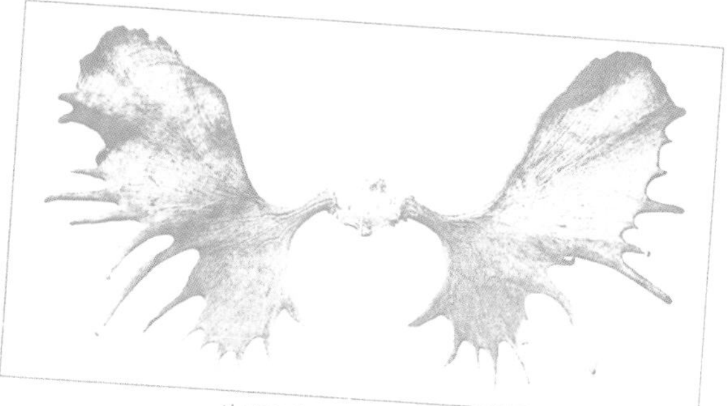

ALASKA MOOSE—1st Prize - 1949

Field & Stream – Jan. 1940

Record

Comparing the new world's record moose head with the former record-holder

(Left) The three-quarter view of the American head shows the "fold" on the under side of the palm. The same fold also appears in the same place on the right horn

(Below) Front view of the American head, showing weight and remarkable symmetry

(Circle) Mountain goat head equaling the world's record. Shot by Carl Beal, 1936. Length of horn, 12 inches; base, 5⅞ inches

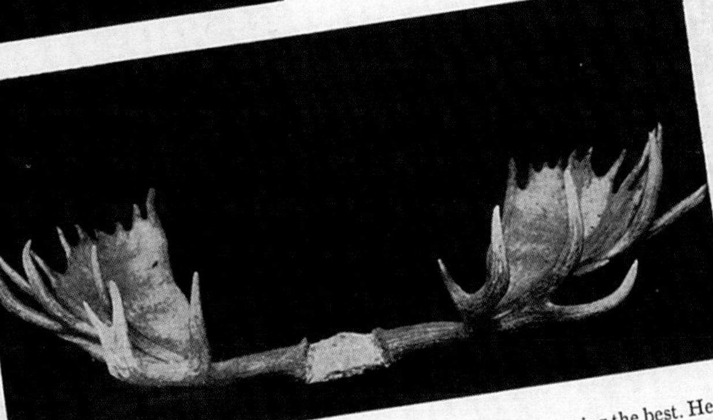

LATE last fall, sportsmen put their ears to the ground when they heard reports of a whopper of a moose head that not only was the biggest thing ever seen but shattered the world's record, which has been standing for thirty-seven years. And this fine head was found, and not shot!

Strange as it may seem, many of the world's record heads have not been shot, but found; "pick-ups," as we say, having come out of frontier lands, being passed from native to trapper, and trapper to trader until, falling into the hands of someone recognizing them as exceptional, they were brought to the knowledge of the sportsmen of the world. Such animals died of old age and the horns were found, or they were killed by some native for meat and the horns left or brought to some white man in trade for a little tobacco. A few of these record pick-ups with origin unknown are interesting to recall.

There is that magnificent world's record *Ovis poli* head, with one horn measuring as much as 6 feet 2 inches around its outer curve, while the other horn measured just short of that, making about 12 feet of horns on one sheep.

The last world's record moose head, which stood for long as No. 1 at the Field Museum in Chicago, was also a pick-up.

The world's largest pair of elephant tusks, of which one weighing 226 pounds was spared after the first was cut up for ivory, was taken by a native hunter. The longest elephant tusk (11 feet 5½ inches) is one of a pair which together weighed 296 pounds. They are now in the National Collection of Heads and Horns at the New York Zoological Park, and were probably found, for there are no records to show that a white man or a native was in on the taking.

The origin of some of our very best American heads is still unknown, and so we may go down the list of record trophies and find many with origin a blank. The best barren-ground caribou I have ever seen was picked up in Labrador by my friend, Charlie Peck. He was hunting with an Indian guide, who finally sensed he was looking for large heads and told him of two big ones he had shot for meat the year before. As one lay not too far away, Peck asked the guide to take him to it. When he saw it, it was so exceptional that he brought it home, only to find it to be a world's record. The Indian further told him that it was not as big as the other he had killed, which was too far away to go after.

There are many other interesting stories spun around record heads, and sportsmen of today should always be conscious of the possibility that on any one of their prospective trips they may yet bring back a trophy equaling or topping the best. Heads are growing as big today as they ever grew, and there is no reason why they shouldn't grow as big. Animals are living as long and are still dying of old age. Some of those old and wise ones, which always hold back and don't come out in the open until after dusk, may yet fall to the gun of the careful and conscientious hunter.

My good friend, Kermit Roosevelt, while in Central Asia, saw what looked to be two good ibex on the sky-line. He suc-

World's record Arizona deer. Shot by Laurance S. Rockefeller, 1937. Length of beam, 24½ inches; spread, 18⅜; points, 9

20

tory and a well-known big-game hunter, selected the Alaskan Moose Group as his major donation to the new Hall of North American Mammals, which was conceived as a hall of large and colorful habitat groups similar to those very beautiful groups in African Hall. It was his plan to organize an expedition to collect this

PUBLICITY

THE EARLY YEARS

Trophies

By

JAMES LIPPITT CLARK

(Right) The Field Museum head. Spread, 76½ inches. This head stood as the world's record moose for thirty-seven years

(Below) The American Museum head. Spread, 77⅝ inches—breaking the long-standing record of the Field Museum head

(Circle) The world's record Stone sheep, which was shot by R. S. Chadwick, 1936. Length on curl, 51⅝ inches; base, 15⅛

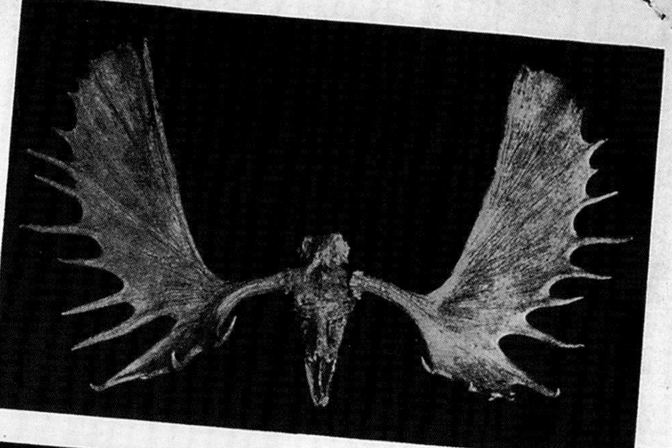

ssfully stalked and shot them both. Going up to the best, he found it had a fine pair of horns measuring just short of the world's record. The second best—as he thought—then took his attention, and he measured this, only to find the horns beat the world's record by over an inch. So you can never tell.

Outstanding among new world's records which have fallen to the sportsman's gun is the fine big Stone sheep shot by R. S. Chadwick, which jumped the Stone sheep record several inches in one stroke. Not only is it the top Stone sheep head, but it is the best North American sheep head of any kind on record. It was a truly beautiful head in all respects, and what interested me particularly was that it was only four inches short of equaling the best *Ovis poli* head that I got on my Central Asia Expedition.

...d's record barren ground caribou (Labrador). Pick-up by Charles Peck, 1932. Length of beam, 57¾; spread, 60; points, 55

When Mr. Chadwick got this head, he was out looking for meat, not for heads. But, of course, when he saw such a fine pair of horns before him, he shot, little knowing when he pulled the trigger that he was looking down his gun barrel at the biggest American sheep head in all the world.

It seems incredible that massive horns like those of the moose can grow to their enormous size in four or five months. Biggest of all the deer tribe, carrying antlers surpassed only by the great Irish elk, the moose grows its gigantic, spreading antlers each year between April and September, renewing them annually after the early-winter shedding at a swift rate of growth that is amazing.

There is a most thrilling story connected with the new world's record moose antlers. Actually seen and touched by two of the hunter's own guides, these antlers remained to be discovered by another guide later, who likewise touched them but, with more time or curiosity, found them worth bringing in, and the story of this interesting find runs as follows:

Mr. Wilton Lloyd-Smith, a trustee of the American Museum of Natural History and a well-known big-game hunter, selected the Alaskan Moose Group as his major donation to the new Hall of North American Mammals, which was conceived as a hall of large and colorful habitat groups similar to those very beautiful groups in African Hall. It was his plan to organize an expedition to collect this group and spend all the time he could in search of the biggest and best head he could find, but he never dared hope that Lady Luck would smile on him so sweetly as to put in his collector's bag the world's largest and, I think we can safely say, finest set of moose antlers ever brought to the knowledge of civilized man.

It was nearing the end of a long, hard day for two of the expedition's guides. They were cold and tired, with but one thought—to get to their objective before dark. Going downstream, they were forced into a narrow current where, to guide the canoe, they clutched a stump protruding from the water. As they swung by they noticed it was not a stump, but the prongs of a submerged moose head. On they passed, never quite forgetting that strange experience of the submerged moose horns. *(Continued on page 50)*

21

Boone and Crockett Club member and Director of the American Museum of Natural History in New York, James L. Clark, authored this article that appeared in the January 1940 issue of *Field & Stream*. Most recognizable of the trophies mentioned in Chadwick's World's Record Stone's sheep, which still stands as number one today. The Club would not resume any records-keeping activities until 1947, when the nation could once again focus on efforts other than the war.

the time he could in search of the biggest and best head he could find, but he never dared hope that Lady Luck would smile on him so sweet-

Courtesy American Museum of Natural History

IT'S ALL IN THE GAME IN

Long before he invented the airplane or the wheel, or found that fire would cook his food and warm his body, man was what essentially he is today—a hunter. Then, it was nakedly simple: a man hunted—or he starved.

But there was more to hunting than a struggle to survive: the wind in the huntsman's face, the crystal dawn as he waited for his game to search out a water hole, the comradeship of men in the chase, the clean thrill of the kill. All this remains for the adroit, knowing modern man who hunts big game.

In theory, hunting is simple: to propel something from the business end of a gun at a desirable target. In practice, it doesn't work out so easily. The rules are basic but not necessarily simple.

The wise hunter learns all he can about his quarry, its feeding times, its sleeping hours, the paths it takes. He ponders maps of game-lively districts, locating each salt lick. Even so he employs the best native guide. He realizes it can take years to become familiar with hunting grounds.

The hunter knows the wind must be in his face; else the game scents the man, and the chase is off. This applies to stalking and to still-hunting. And the hunter moves on his prey silently.

He stalks antelope, caribou, goats; he still-hunts most deer, bear, elk and moose. Usually, animals living in timber are still-hunted, those in open areas are stalked.

A good hunter knows his equipment as he knows his quarry. He realizes that good binoculars can save him many an exhausting mile, because Nature has given some game built-in, long-range eyesight.

One of the most popular game rifles is the 30/30 with a 170 grain soft-nosed bullet. Next comes the 30/06. Deer loads should be 180 grain; 220 grain bullets are used for elk, bear and moose. For brute power, a .375 with a 270 grain bullet delivers a knockout blow.

A good hunter may be recognized by the way he kills. A brain or neck vertebrae shot is considered humane and efficient, but a surer aim is at the heart or between the neck and shoulder. An expanding bullet which strikes with great shocking power is used. And, remember, a good hunter gets his game.

NORTH AMERICAN BIG GAME WORLD RECORD TROPHIES

From the Official Records of the Boone and Crockett Club

WHITETAIL DEER Length of outside curve: (R) 31¾″ (L) 31¼″ Greatest spread: 23⅛″ Killed by Canadian farmer in 1936 at Fredericton, New Brunswick	**BARREN GROUND CARIBOU** Length of outside curve: (R) 67⅝″ Greatest spread: 48½″ Killed at Hudson Bay in 1903	**DESERT SHEEP** Length of front curve: (R) 44″ (L) 43½″ Greatest spread: 23⅞″ Killed in Lower California
MULE DEER Length of outside curve: (R) 34″ Greatest spread: 37¼″ Killed in Wyoming in 1886	**CANADA MOOSE** Greatest spread: 73″ Length of palm: (R) 37¼″ Killed in 1922 in Alberta	**ROCKY MOUNTAIN GOAT** Length of front curve: (R) 12¼″ (L) 12½″ Greatest spread: 7″ Killed by A. Bryan Williams in British Columbia
COLUMBIAN BLACKTAIL DEER Length of outside curve: (R) 30½″ Greatest spread: 23⅛″ Killed by Gus Nordquist in 1927 in California	**ALASKA MOOSE** Greatest spread: 77⅝″ Length of palm: (R) 43″ (L) 45⅜″ Killed in 1938 in Alaska	**PRONG HORN** Length of outside curve: (R) 20 5/16″ Greatest spread: 16 3/16″ Killed by Wilson Potter in 1899 in Arizona
COUES DEER Length of outside curve: (R) 19¾″ (L) 22″ Greatest spread: 16⅞″ Killed by Rene Stallings in 1938 in Tyrone, New Mexico	**WYOMING MOOSE** Greatest spread: 58⅜″ Length of palm: (R) 35⅞″ (L) 36¼″ Killed by S. N. Benjamin in 1941 in Wyoming	**ALASKA BROWN BEAR** Greatest overall length of skull: 19⅛″ Killed by Donald S. Hopkins in 1940 on Kodiak Island, Alaska
WAPITI Length of outside curve: (R) 64¾″ Greatest spread: 49⅝″ Killed by Col. Archibald Rogers in Wyoming	**BIGHORN SHEEP** Length of front curve: (R) 49½″ (L) 48¼″ Greatest spread: 23⅞″ Killed by James Simpson in 1920 at Sheep Creek, British Columbia	**BLACK BEAR** Greatest overall length of skull: 14⅛″ Killed by E. O. McDonnell in 1933 at Kupreanof Bay, Alaska
MOUNTAIN CARIBOU Length of outside curve: (R) 65⅛″ (L) 62¼″ Greatest spread: 54½″ Killed by D. W. Bell in 1923 in Cassiar, British Columbia	**STONE SHEEP** Length of front curve: (R) 50⅛″ (L) 51⅝″ Greatest spread: 31″ Killed by L. S. Chadwick in 1936 in British Columbia	**MOUNTAIN LION—PUMA—COUGAR** Greatest overall length of skull: 9 5/16″ Killed by Theodore Roosevelt in 1901 at Meeker, Colorado
WOODLAND CARIBOU Length of outside curve: (R) 50″ Greatest spread: 44⅝″ Killed in Newfoundland	**WHITE SHEEP** Length of front curve: (R) 47½″ (L) 47″ Greatest spread: 26″ Killed by Patsey Henderson in 1927 in Alaska	**JAGUAR** Greatest overall length of skull: 11″ Killed in 1894 in San Andres, Mexico

CREDITS—*Esquire wishes to express its appreciation to Abercrombie & Fitch Company and Stoeger Arms Corporation, both in New York City, for their assistance in preparing this hunting section.*

Big Game Shrinking In Size, Experts Find

World-Telegram Photo by Palumbo.

William M. Chanler (left) and Samuel B. Webb judging a deer head at the American Museum of Natural History.

Big game hunting is running into the law of diminishing returns in North America, Harold E. Anthony, chairman of the Department of Mammals of the American Museum of Natural History, noted today as final judging of the Boone and Crockett Club's big game competitioins got under way.

His comment was made as a committee of sportsmen-judges began measuring 32 big game heads and skulls at the museum with steel tapes and calipers. There was considerable disagreement among the experts as to the relative importance of curvature of antlers as opposed to length, and vice versa, and much consulting of records.

Mr. Anthony estimated it would take the experts two or three weeks to reach a decision on the heads and also in two other classifications: still and motion pictures of big game in their natural habitats.

Mr. Anthony said the heads, on the whole, were smaller than they once were because hunters go after the biggest of the big game they can find. This selective shooting, he explained, has resulted in the survival of the breeding of smaller and smaller big game.

A unique exception, however, caused considerable excitement among the judges. One entry—the head of a white tailed deer shot in New Brunswick, Canada—set a new record for length and curvature of antlers. The left antler, 31¾ inches long, and the right antler, 31¼ inches, broke a record set in 1905.

The 32 surviving entries of the 450 brought to the attention of the club since 1939, included five bear skulls and four puma skulls. The other heads included those of deer, moose, caribou, Rocky Mountain goats and wapiti, a form of elk.

N.Y. Times
Wed. Apr. 28, 1948

EDNESDAY, APRIL 28, 1

BIG GAME CONTEST BEGINS IN MUSEUM

Panel of Experts Will Bestow Medals Upon Competitors With Best Entries

The judging of a big game competition began yesterday in a sunny workroom in the American Museum of Natural History, Central Park West and Seventy-ninth Street.

With steel measuring tapes and blank pads for notes, a panel of experts moved slowly from table to table inspecting about forty stuffed entries. These had been appraised earlier as the best of the 450 heads submitted in the competition being conducted by the Boone and Crockett Club, an organization of sportsmen founded sixty years ago by Theodore Roosevelt and some of his friends.

Among the heads and horns on display in the quiet room behind the scenes at the museum were several that are expected to set new records. A pair of many-pronged antlers from a white-tailed deer was one of these.

"You can hang your hat there all right," a judge murmured as he took out his tape. The outer curve of this deer's left antler measured 31¾ inches and of the right 31¼.

Other animals represented included moose, caribou, Rocky Mountain goats and big-horned sheep. Altogether thirteen different classes were covered in the competition, which was restricted to North American species.

However, no specimens of puma, jaguar or walrus were entered and many of the other animals were judged on the basis of photographs.

The competition, which is thought to be the first of its kind here, will probably be conducted annually from now on, Dr. Harold E. Anthony, chairman of the project and of the museum's department of mammals, said.

He added that although the aim to foster interest in North American big game there is no thought increasing the number of animals shot each year. On the contrary, he said, special awards will given to sportsmen who submit photographs as their only trophies.

Announcement of the winners will be made in two or three weeks, when the prize heads will be put on public view in one of the museum halls.

Prizes will be bronze medals decorated with portraits of Daniel Boone and Davy Crockett on one side and a powder horn on the other.

The Club received quite a bit of media coverage in the late 1940s. *Esquire* magazine (opposite) ran this one-page article featuring the winners of the first-ever Big Game Competition. Two more articles about the Competition appeared in New York newspapers, the *New York World Telegram* (above) and *The New York Times*.

Walkerville, Michigan
Route 1
January 31, 1947

Boone and Chrockett Club
Remington,
Bridgeport
c/o Henry P. Davis. Conn.

Dear Sirs;

Charles Andrus has white tail deer horns with thirty three points, taken from a deer he shot. The prongs are especially beautiful. Mr Andrus's address is same as the above one.

Yours Truly
Barbara E. Andrus.

CORRESPONDENCE FROM THE VAULTS

CHARLIE ANDRUS – 1947

February 11, 1947

Miss Barbara E. Andras
Route 1
Walkerville, Michigan

Dear Miss Andrus:

Mr. Davis of the Remington Arms Company has turned your letter of January 31st over to us for reply.

In 1939 this Committee published a book entitled North American Big Game in which the measurements of over 2000 trophies were recorded. In March 1940, due to the war, the office was closed and it has just been reopened. We are once again engaged in gathering together data on good trophies.

Enclosed you will find a chart upon which we would very much appreciate your having the data recorded concerning Mr. Andrus' trophy. Directions for measuring are to be found on the back of the blank.

Very sincerely yours,

Secretary to the Committee

Enc:1

Boon & Crockett Club Walkerville Mich 10-[illegible]

New york N.Y.

Gentlemen

Inclosed find picture of a deer Antlers which I think has Been over looked By your club.

This deer was killed in Newaygo. Co. Mich. We have all the data on the horns. By the way - it has 33 points and - 27 are over 1 inch.

If interested in these antlers please send blanks Etc. for specifications And I will fill them out at once

Truly yours

S.R. Andrus

Walkerville Mich

Please return picture if not needed.

On October 18, 1948, the Club responded to Mr. S.R. Andrus:

Dear Mr. Andrus:

Receipt is acknowledged of your letter of October 14th (shown at left) which arrived this morning together with the snapshot of your trophy.

We are enclosing a measurement blank for the data on the head and would like to keep the photographs to attach to that blank.

Thank you very much for your interest and cooperation in this work.

Very Sincerely Yours,
Secretary to the Committee

Before the advent of the new scoring system, it was very common for trophy owners to measure their own trophies. Records keeping was in its infancy, constantly evolving in knowledge, and growing in public interest, but the official measurer program was barely fledgling.

Taken in 1893, this fine buck is one of the oldest trophies ever entered into B&C's Records Program.

3-4-49

Boone And Brockett Club
New York. N.Y-

Walkerville Mich

Gentlemen:
I had given up sending the specifications in of the great set of Antlers we have as I know you have much larger ones.
But this set is a stand out. Of any I have ever see.
The points And circumference of burr seems to be unusual Also the 2 Palms. One has 3 Pts the other 2 points.
But am sending this just for the records.
My Brother was offered $50.00 for them before he took deer out of the woods
Inclose specifications Etc
I also wish to Thank you for what you are doing along this line

Truly yours

S.R. Andrus
Walkerville Mich

I sent snap shot of deer head some time Ago.

Ack. by card 3/15/49

1949

Boone and Crockett Club

RECORDS OF NORTH AMERICAN BIG GAME
AND
NORTH AMERICAN BIG GAME COMPETITION
IN CARE OF
AMERICAN MUSEUM OF NATURAL HISTORY
CENTRAL PARK WEST AT 79TH STREET
NEW YORK 24, N. Y.

UNDER THE AUSPICES OF THE NATIONAL MUSEUM OF HEADS AND HORNS OF THE NEW YORK ZOOLOGICAL SOCIETY

DEER

SPECIES White Tail Deer - Mich -

MEASUREMENTS	RIGHT	LEFT
Length of outside curve A	23	23
Greatest spread B	23	
Circumference of main beam C	6	
Number of points on antler	12	15
Circumference of burr D	7	6 1/2

Exact locality where killed Sec 33. 16-14. Newaygo Co Mich

Date killed Nov. 17 - 1893

By whom killed C L Andrus

Owner C L Andrus

Address Walkerville Mich

Present location of trophy C L Andrus
Walkerville Mich

Remarks The odd thing of these antlers is the 2 palms which are real thin R. 3 points on them and L 2 points.

We hereby certify that we have measured the above described trophy on Oct 20 1948, and that these measurements are correct and made in accordance with the directions overleaf.

C L Andrus

By L. R. Andrus
Walkerville Mich

In the remarks section of this score chart it says, "Largest Deer killed in Nebraska's first deer season." We sometimes take hunting and bountiful wildlife populations for granted today. In 1945 in Nebraska, they felt very fortunate to hunt at all.

Note the greatest spread on this spectacular whitetail. Unfortunately, no photo accompanied this entry.

1947

COMMITTEE
ALFRED ELY, CHAIRMAN
HAROLD E. ANTHONY
R. R. M. CARPENTER

Records of North American Big Game

IN CARE OF
AMERICAN MUSEUM OF NATURAL HISTORY
COLUMBUS AVENUE AND 77TH STREET
NEW YORK, N. Y.

UNDER THE AUSPICES OF
THE NATIONAL MUSEUM OF HEADS AND HORNS OF THE NEW YORK ZOOLOGICAL SOCIETY
&
THE BOONE & CROCKETT CLUB

DEER

SPECIES White Tail.

MEASUREMENTS	RIGHT	LEFT
Length on outside curve A	24	23
Circumference of main beam B	5 1/8	4 1/4
Circumference of burr C	6 3/4	6 1/8
Number of points on antler	5	7

Greatest spread D 32 1/16

Exact locality where killed Halsey National Forest, Nebr.

Date killed Dec. 8, 1945

By whom killed H E Burchfield

Owner H E Burchfield

Address McGrew, Nebr.

Remarks: Largest killed in Nebraska's first deer season.

Photographs: Front view ✓ Profile ✓
(Please place ✓ mark to indicate photographs furnished.)

We hereby certify that we have measured the above described trophy on May 6 1947, and that these measurements are correct and made in accordance with the directions overleaf.

H E Burchfield

By

Measurement of "D" can be verified at State Game Commission, Lincoln, Nebr.

Ack. by card 5/9/47

SCORE CHARTS

INTERESTING CHARTS FROM THE EARLY YEARS

47

Records of North American Big Game

A PUBLICATION OF
THE BOONE AND CROCKETT CLUB
IN CARE OF
AMERICAN MUSEUM OF NATURAL HISTORY
COLUMBUS AVENUE AND 77TH STREET
NEW YORK, N. Y.

COMMITTEE
ALFRED ELY, CHAIRMAN
HAROLD E. ANTHONY
R. R. M. CARPENTER

UNDER THE AUSPICES OF
THE NATIONAL MUSEUM OF HEADS AND HORNS OF THE
NEW YORK ZOOLOGICAL SOCIETY

D E E R

SPECIES Arizona Whitetail

MEASUREMENTS	RIGHT	LEFT
Length on outside curve A	18 1/4	18 3/8
Circumference of main beam B		
Circumference of burr C	4 3/8	4 1/4
Number of points on antler	4	4

Greatest spread: D 19

Exact locality where killed Las Mochis Rg., Sonora, Mex.

Date killed 1937

By whom killed Lion

Owner Jack O'Connor

Address Tucson, Ariz.

Remarks:

Photographs: Front view........ Profile........
(Please place V mark to indicate photographs furnished.)

We hereby certify that we have measured the above described trophy on..........193 , and that these measurements are correct and made in accordance with the directions overleaf.

....

By ....

O'Connor 10.2.38

World-famous outdoor writer Jack O'Connor was an official measurer and trophy owner in the early years of the Records Program. This chart, very beautifully written, is for a lion-killed Coues' deer that Jack owned. They were often called Arizona Whitetail in that era.

A Hit for Babe Ruth—Runnerup With Deer B.

Belated Score Is Chalked Up

By DELOS W. LOVELACE,
Staff Writer.

Come Monday night, Babe Ruth, the home-run king, will receive belated honor as Babe Ruth, the hunter.

The exclusive and authoritative Boone and Crockett Club, at its annual meeting in the Museum of Natural History, will award a second prize to a trophy the late Bambino bagged back in 1940.

It's hard to rate the Babe second in any competition, but that's where he's landed with the head of a white-tailed deer shot in Novia Scotia. And maybe second place is fair enough.

Head Less Than Record.

The record head for a white-tailed deer, according to Dr. Harold E. Anthony, big game hunter, museum curator of Mammals and club chairman of records, spreads 33½ inches. The Babe's measures 10 less. But the horns are notably symmetrical, Dr. Doland Carter, assistant curator pointed out. They form a circle almost as complete as the circle the Bambino used to make of the bases in his diamond heyday.

The head was entered into competition by John F. Hansen, a taxidermist, 59 Lake St., Jersey City, the present owner.

Standards to Change.

The club, in advance of its third annual competitive awards, today made another announcement. It isn't one that will make any difference to the bears, bisons or any of the 28 species whose heads and horns win prizes. When all the tumult and the shooting dies they will be just as stone cold in the market place or in trophy halls.

The Babe in his heyday—both as hunter and ballplayer.

But it certainly will perk up the hundreds of hunters who vie yearly for records.

The club is changing the standards by which entries are judged. "Heretofore," Dr. Anthony explained, "the length of horns was all we bothered about, or in an animal lacking horns the length of skull. Now we measure skull width also, and in horns the greatest spread, the tip-to-tip spread, and the circumference at every quarter of the length, we consider symmetry, too."

One hundred eighty-four entries were received this year, 16 more than last, and a total of 38 first, second and third-class prizes will be awarded. One prize winner will be a woman, but none will be anywhere near as young as 11-year-old Michael Rusten of Minnesota, who took a first last year with the head of a Barren Ground caribou.

Entries From All Over.

Entries came from all over the United States and for the award ceremony and buffet supper guests will come from as far away as Florida, Texas and Alaska. Any big game hunter may send an entry if he guarantees the two-way cost of transportation. This can run into money. Sometimes $200 or more.

The Boone and Crockett Club (Boone for Kentucky's Dan'l and Crockett for Davey of Texas) is a 61-year-old organization limited to 100 dyed-in-the-wool and authenticated big game hunters.

T. R. Headed Club.

A club founder and president was the late Theodore Roosevelt. His sons, Archie and Kermit, were presidents, too. Theodore Jr. also was a member.

The most valued award Monday will be the Sagamore Hill prize for the best trophy regardless of category.

"We started the competition three years ago," Dr. Anthony said, "to stimulate grea crimination, and to indu ters to have a definite when they went out in just shooting at random target."

A Hit for Babe Ruth—Runn
Belated Score Is Chalked Up
By DELOS W. LOVELACE, Staff Writer.
The Babe in his heyday—both as hunter and

erup

plained,
all we
animal
of skull
width
greatest

SPECIAL TROPHY

BABE RUTH TAKES AWARD-WINNING BUCK IN 1940

COMMITTEE
ALFRED ELY, CHAIRMAN
HAROLD E. ANTHONY
R. R. M. CARPENTER

Record of North American Big Game

IN CARE OF
AMERICAN MUSEUM OF NATURAL HISTORY
COLUMBUS AVENUE AND 77TH STREET
NEW YORK, N. Y.

UNDER THE AUSPICES OF
THE NATIONAL COLLEC[TION] OF HEADS AND HORN[S] OF THE NEW YORK ZOOLOGIC[AL] SOCIETY & THE BOONE & CROCKET[T] CLUB

DEER

SPECIES: WHITE TAIL

MEASUREMENTS

	RIGHT	LEFT
Length of outside curve A	26 3/8"	26 1/2"
Greatest spread B	18 1/2"	
Circumference of main beam C	5 1/16"	5 3/8"
Number of points on antler	5	6
Circumference of burr D	6 3/4"	7"

Exact locality where killed: FREDERICTON N.S.

Date killed: NOV. 1940

By whom killed: LATE – GEO. HERMAN "BABE" RUTH.

Owner: JOHN F. HANSEN

Address: JERSEY CITY N.J.

Present location of trophy: ABOVE

Remarks: A TYPICAL HEAD, HEAVY WITH LONG TINES. MAIN BEAMS MEET IN FRONT.

We hereby certify that we have measured the above described trophy on 11/19/48 194 , and that these measurements are correct and made in accordance with the directions overleaf.

Hansen Studios

By John F. Hansen

1950.

World Tel – 2/28/50

Hooks and Bulle[ts]

Big Game Hun[ters] Get Trophy A[wards]

—by Ray Trullinger

The head hunters collected their rewards last night. No, no. Let's have no confusion about this. Refe[rence is not] to missionary-stewing Jivaros, but to the winners in th[e Boone and] Crockett Club's third annual North American Big Ga[me competi]tion, who were awarded medals and certificates last [night at the] American Museum of Natural History.

A total of 184 big-game trophies were entered ar[d] Messrs. Samuel Webb, Robert Waters and Grancel Fit[z of New] York City, and of that number, 41 were honored and on[e singled] out as outstanding and a possible new world's record.

This great head was a mountain goat, shot by E. C. Haase of Ney, Ohio, in the Babine Mountains of British Columbia last season, and it was the judges' unanimous selection for the Sagamore Hill Award. This special honor is awarded annually in the memory of Theodore Roosevelt, first president of the Boone and Crockett Club; Theodore Roosevelt Jr., and Kermit Roosevelt, for the best trophy entered in the competition.

Under the revised scoring method, it is believed this mountain goat will take over top position in the official records, notwithstanding the fact the present world's record holder, a female, incidentally, carries 12½-inch horns, against the Haase trophy's 12 inches. The difference lies in the fact the Haase entry, a male, carries heavier horns.

Four hunters from the New York metropolitan area, including one who's no longer with us, received two first and two second prizes. Walter Geismer, Ridgefield, N. J., took the top award in the Canada moose division with a 65-inch bull, shot in the Pine Lake country of Quebec last season, and Fairman R. Dick, New York City, entered the best Stone sheep, shot in the Cassiar.

Best White Tail Comes From Surprise Locale.

Sheldon Wollman, NYC, was the place winner in the Rocky Mountain goat classification, with a fine head shot in Idaho three years ago, and John F. Hansen of Jersey City, also won a second award for a pretty whitetail buck, which Babe Ruth killed in New Brunswick 10 years ago.

Strangely enough, the best [...]

bucks, such as Brit[ish] Maine, Minnesota, o[r] wick. The '49 win[ner] in Cecil County, Mc ago by Roy F. Spies This big buck carr[ies] rack, with a sp[read] inches, and with fi[ve] and left. The grea[test] outside curve is 28 30⅛ inches left. of the best heads tourney.

The prize-winni[ng] in Idaho five yea[rs] Holes, of Gran[d] George D. Ballard entered the best r[...] in his home stat[e] Dixon, Marietta, with the top Al carries a 69¾-i[n] was downed last Rainy Pass coun[try] Oregon yielded horn. It was County by Ern[...] Bonanza, Oreg. [...] bear award wer[e] R. Stewart of [...] bear honors we[re] J. Van De Car, [...] and C. F. Gig[...] received a me[...] shot by Alan ton, B. C., two

Presentation followed by a some excellent movies.

Boone and Crockett Club

RECORDS OF NORTH AMERICAN BIG GAME
AND
NORTH AMERICAN BIG GAME COMPETITION
IN CARE OF
AMERICAN MUSEUM OF NATURAL HISTORY
CENTRAL PARK WEST AT 79TH STREET
NEW YORK 24, N. Y.

December 26, 1950

Mr. John F. Hansen
59 Lake Street
Jersey City, New Jersey

Dear Mr. Hansen:

For some time the Committee on Records of North American Big Game has realized that the system used by the Boone and Crockett Club for measuring trophies and the basis for judging them has left something to be desired.

About a year ago, recognizing the need for a single standard system of accepted authority, an independent committee was appointed for the purpose of developing an Official Scoring System for North American big game trophies. The Committee was made up of Milford Baker, Frederick K. Barbour, Dr. James L. Clark, Grancel Fitz, Samuel B. Webb, as Chairman, and myself.

Before adopting a new system and publishing the final results the measurement charts, as devised by the Scoring Committee were circulated to more than 200 qualified sportsmen, guides, authors, taxidermists, game officials and scientists for constructive criticism and approval. This new scoring system is now the official pattern for the Boone and Crockett Club and it is hoped will come into rather general usage throughout the country.

It is now the desire of the Committee on Records of North American Big Game to have the twenty top trophies in each category listed in our records measured so that we may determine their standing according to this permanent system of measurements.

Your 26-1/2 inch Whitetail which won 2nd Prize in the 1949 Competition and your 11-1/2 inch Goat which placed 5th in NORTH AMERICAN BIG GAME are in this group.

Will you therefore record the requested data on the enclosed sheets, have them witnessed, sign the blanks and return them to us. Your prompt cooperation will be very much appreciated by the Committee.

Very sincerely yours,

Harold E. Anthony
Chairman
CS

Oct. 19, 1953

Mr. Ernst Von Lengerke
688 Mosswood Avenue
Orange, N. J.

Dear Ernst:

Very confidentially, we haven't been able to successfully train John Hansen in taking careful measurements. Enclosed are two charts of trophies in Hi Blauvelt's Museum at Oradell. As I recall, the whitetail deer was just a fair head and I imagine the interest in it was due to the fact that it was killed by Babe Ruth. However, the goat is another story. If John's measurements are correct?? it ranks #2. From the chart you can see that it is very symmetrical. Sometime, at your convenience, would you be good enough to check the goat and if you have time, check the whitetail, merely because I know Hi is interested in records.

Incidentally, we are counting on you as a judge for the 1953 Competition. And you will remember that the judges meet around the 20th of February and the Awards Dinner is around the 25th of March. I do not know the exact dates at this time but can I count on you to be present or are you comtemplating a trip to Mexico or some other remote area?

I hope you had a nice summer and that I will see you soon.

Sincerely yours,

SBW:H

Samuel B. Webb

Encl.

P. S. If you see any other fine North American big game trophies in the Museum, would you be good enough to check on those also? Thanks.

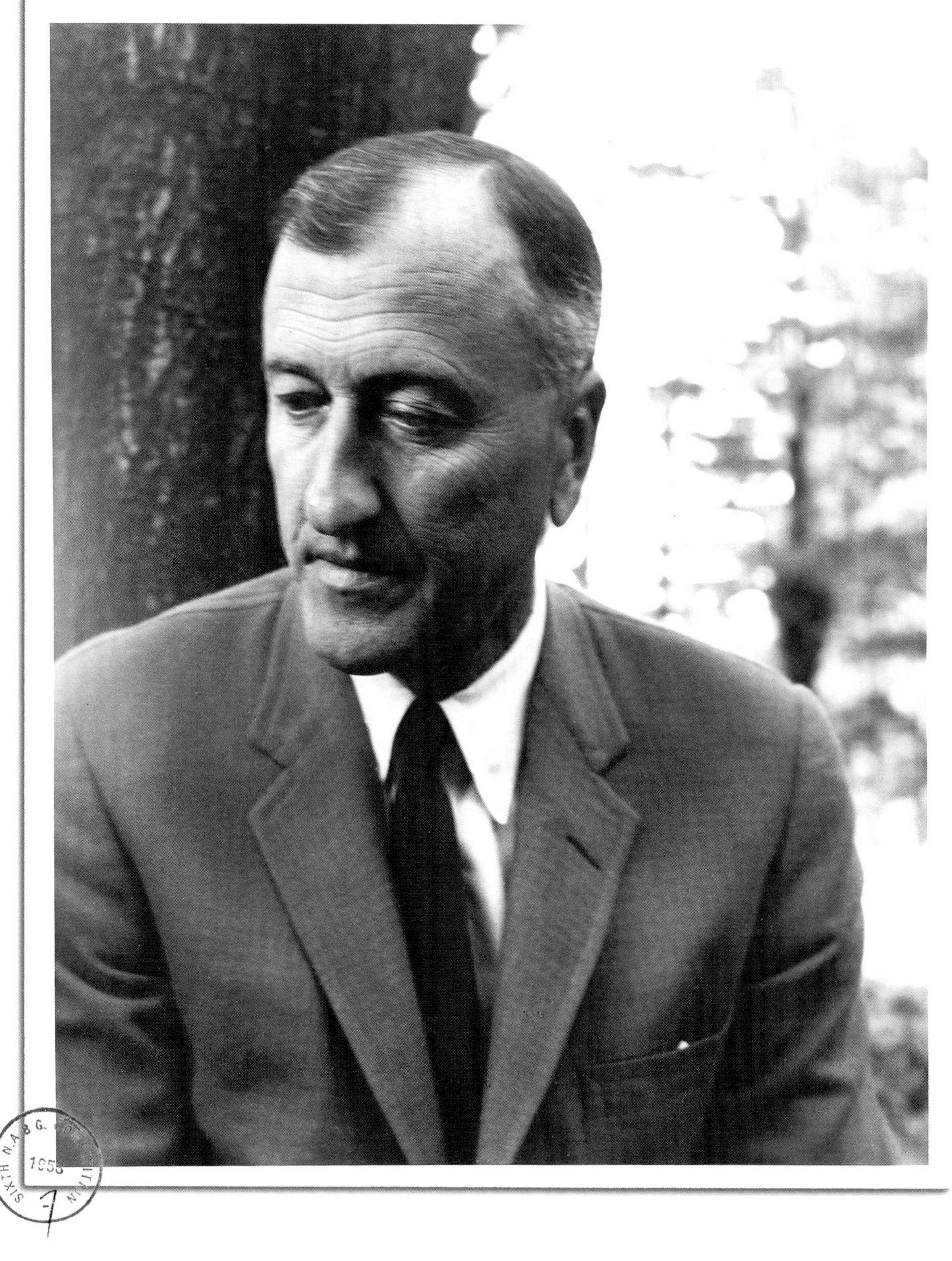

4: A NEW SYSTEM

BY FREDERICK J. KING

As the 1950s began, there were two events that had already taken place in the 1930s and 1940s that set the stage for major positive consequences on the future of wildlife management in North America.

The first event took place on September 2, 1937, when the Pittman-Robertson Federal Aid in Wildlife Restoration Act became law. In addition, any states that became involved with the use of this Federal PR money had to pass an enabling act. The enabling act meant that all funding generated by state wildlife agencies would have to be used for wildlife management, wildlife research, and wildlife habitat-acquisition programs. This Federal excise tax on sporting arms and ammunition, which is still in existence today, gave state wildlife agencies the financial backing and political strength that was necessary for successful implementation of broad-based wildlife management programs.

The second event that had a major impact on the future of wildlife came on September 2, 1945. The surrender of Japan and the end of World War II marked a new beginning for wildlife programs in the nation. This new beginning could only be positive. Returning veterans were eager to go hunting as soon as they got home, and they did. At the focal point of interest for hunting opportunity was a game animal that can be easily described as a "blue collar trophy that has nationwide appeal." Whitetail deer were quite available to the returning hunters due, in part, to the additional funding from the Pittman-Robertson Act before and, to a limited extent, during World War II. During this time there had been an effort of trapping and transplanting all North American big-game species, and this effort increased substantially after World War II. In the mid-western, eastern and southern states, great emphasis was given to not only trap and reestablish whitetail deer into adequate habitat, but also to purchase habitat for future wildlife and for hunting opportunities. Success of these efforts was immediate.

LEFT: Samuel B. Webb was chosen to chair the 1949 committee charged with designing a new system for measuring scoring North American big game. Webb's main role in the committee was mediator between Grancel Fitz and James L. Clark, who had already developed rival scoring systems. Webb's committee was successful in combining the best of both systems into the current system used by B&C.

To carry the momentum of hunting, wildlife management, and wildlife habitat acquisition into the future, the end of World War II also gave the opportunity for continued interest for participation or continuation in college careers for professional wildlife management positions. Also, the end of World War II brought the beginning of the "Baby Boom Generation." In a few years the opportunity to hand down this new tradition of wildlife management and hunting to a new generation of girls and boys would be complete.

In the late 1940s, there was also renewed interest for the Boone and Crockett Club to direct attention to design a new system for measuring and scoring North American big game. In 1949, Samuel B. Webb, well-known to major

OFFICIAL SCORING SYSTEM FOR NORTH AMERICAN BIG GAME TROPHIES

Records of North American
Big Game and North American
Big Game Competition

BOONE AND CROCKETT CLUB

% Am. Museum of Natural History
Central Park West at 79th Street
New York 24, New York

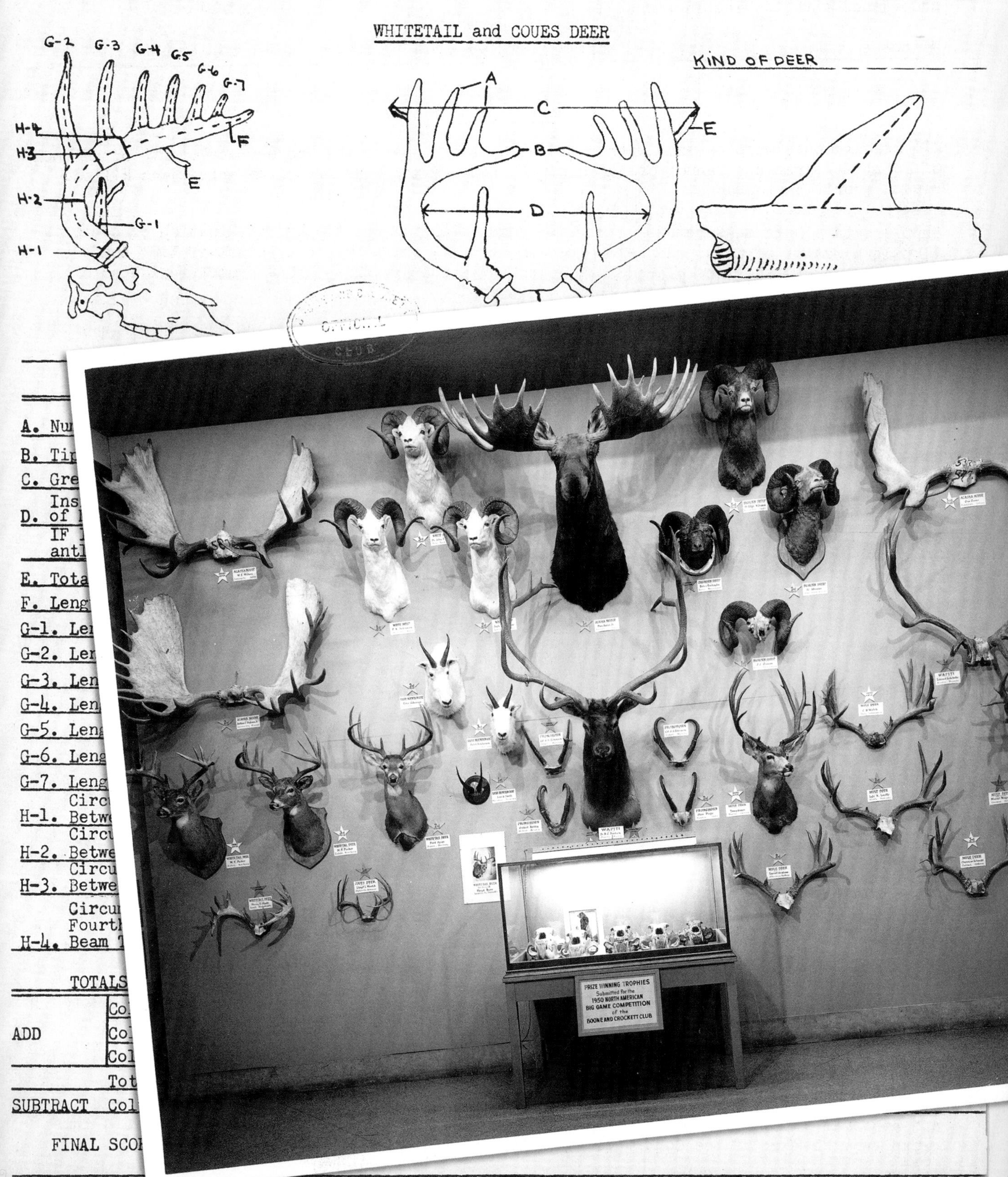

Club members and a close friend of both Grancel Fitz and Dr. James L. Clark, was chosen to chair a special committee of the Club to devise an equitable system for the big game of North America. In addition to Webb, Fitz, and Clark, the committee members included Dr. Harold E. Anthony, Milford Baker, and Frederick K. Barbour. All were experienced big-game hunters with strong interest in giving recognition to exceptional big-game trophies. The committee worked during the year to arrive at the system adopted by the Boone and Crockett Club in 1950. Prior to publication, the system was circulated to 250 sportsmen, biologists, and other interested parties for their comments. Once adopted, the system quickly became established as the universally accepted standard for measuring native North American big game.

The 4th Competition of North American Big Game was the first Competition to use the newly devised system of scoring by this committee. Whitetail deer, at this time, generated an elevated amount of interest. A minimum score for entry for a typical whitetail deer was established at 140 points. Because of the interest in hunting whitetails, and the number of entries recorded, the minimum score for typical whitetail deer was increased quickly to 150 points in 1953 and then increased again to 160 points in 1963. The non-typical category for whitetail deer started at 160 points in 1950 and then later was raised to 180 points in 1963. Interestingly enough, all the Competitions from the 4th through the 10th were held at the American Museum of Natural History in New York City. The 11th Competition would bring a change to that location.

LEFT: The 4th Competition, held in New York City at the American Museum of Natural History in 1950, was the first Competition featuring the results of the new scoring system developed by the Boone and Crockett Club. Grancel Fitz served as the competition Chairman, and was joined on the panel of judges by Milford Baker, James H. Bond, Frank H. Schramm, and Ernst von Lengerke. A total of five whitetail deer were at the competition—three received Awards.

The whitetail deer as a North American trophy stands high among all hunters. As the Boone and Crockett scoring system has been revised throughout the years, great interest has always been generated around this species. But more than what the animal represents as a trophy status is what it represents as a model of success for modern wildlife management programs that we now enjoy in North America. The efforts of those early organizers of the Boone and Crockett Club in 1887, Roosevelt, Grinnell, Hornaday, and others centered on not only appreciating the larger (trophy) animals but more on just trying to save and protect for future generations the variety of species, including whitetail deer, that were fast becoming destroyed.

Conditions were still so bad for wildlife that William T. Hornaday wrote in an introduction to his book, *A Wild Animal Roundup*, on July 1, 1925, *"The most and the best of the abundant wild life of yesterday is gone! Much of it you will never see nor hear of again… Honestly, I am glad that I will not be alive to see the tattered remnants of "picturesque* America" *as they will appear fifty years from today."* Theodore Roosevelt passed away in 1919, George Bird Grinnell passed away in April 1938, and William T. Hornaday passed away in March of 1937, approximately six months before the Pittman-Robertson Act was signed into law. None of these early conservationists lived long enough to witness the reality of their dream for the future of wildlife for the generations ahead. If they could be around for a brief time for this coming hunting season and look at the abundance, variety and availability of wildlife, they would have to feel personally satisfied that they gave their best efforts and that their best efforts have become a reality on this modern-day landscape of North America.

I certify that I have measured the above trophy on Dec. 25 1951
at (address) City Cohocton State New York
and that these measurements and data are, to the best of my knowledge and belief, made in accordance with the instructions given.

Witness: Signature: T. Donald Carter

INSTRUCTIONS

All measurements must be made with a flexible steel tape to the nearest one-eighth of an inch. Official measurements cannot be taken for at least sixty days after the animal was killed. Please submit photographs.

Supplementary Data measurements indicate conformation of the trophy. Evaluation of conformation is a matter of personal preference. Excellent, but nontypical Whitetail Deer heads with many points shall be placed and judged in a separate class. The symmetrical head will be given preference.

A. Number of Points on each Antler. To be counted a point, a projection must be at least one inch long AND its length must exceed the length of its base. All points are measured from tip of point to nearest edge of beam as illustrated. Beam tip is counted as a point but not measured as a point.

B. Tip to Tip Spread measur[...]rs.

C. Greatest Spread measured [...]ht angles to the center line of the skull at widest part whe[...]nts.

D. Inside Spread of Main Be[...] the center line of the skull at widest point between main be[...]again in "Spread Credit" column if it is less than or equal[...]r.

E. Total of Lengths of all [...]nts are generally considered to be those nontypical in shape o[...]

F. Length of Main Beam meas[...] of burr over outer curve to the most distant point of what [...]n beam.

G-1-2-3-4-5-6-7. Length of [...] project from main beam. They are measured from nearest edge [...] to tip.

H-1-2-3-4. Circumferences [...]ake H-1 and H-2 at smallest place between burr and second po[...]

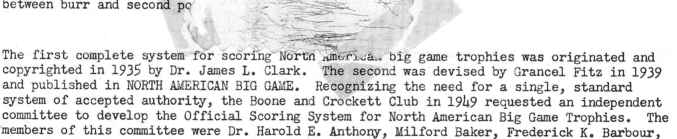

The first complete system for scoring North American big game trophies was originated and copyrighted in 1935 by Dr. James L. Clark. The second was devised by Grancel Fitz in 1939 and published in NORTH AMERICAN BIG GAME. Recognizing the need for a single, standard system of accepted authority, the Boone and Crockett Club in 1949 requested an independent committee to develop the Official Scoring System for North American Big Game Trophies. The members of this committee were Dr. Harold E. Anthony, Milford Baker, Frederick K. Barbour, Dr. James L. Clark, Grancel Fitz and Samuel B. Webb, Chairman.

This Official System is basically a consolidation of the best points in the two previously existing systems. In the process, some new points have been developed, errors corrected, and needed simplification has been achieved.

Before publication, these charts were circulated to more than 250 qualified sportsmen, guides, authors, taxidermists, game officials, and scientists for constructive criticism and approval. The Boone and Crockett Club gratefully acknowledges the contribution of this group and the work of the Committee.

4: VINTAGE PHOTOS*

A NEW SCORING SYSTEM

ABOVE: Francis Buckley holds his 1955 trophy from Cedar Lake, Ontario.The deer scores 160-3/8 points as a typical. What a great old-time photo! The rifle is a Winchester Model 71 in .348 caliber. ▲

RIGHT: Maurice E. Rowe balances his 189-1/8 non-typical from 1957. Vinton County, Ohio, was where Mr. Rowe was hunting when he brought home this 27-4/8-inch-wide buck. ▲

LEFT: This buck, taken by Asher McDowell in Steuben County, New York, was entered in 1951 with an entry score of 149-2/8 points. Since the Records Program was just beginning, the minimum entry score was 140 points. Now at 160, this buck no longer qualifies but remains part of the archives. ▲

*Many of the following photos are as stated, "vintage." The Boone and Crockett Club has carefully ushered in a new era with the advancement and availability of photographic equipment. Today, our expectations consist of presenting a blood-free trophy and hunter in an uncluttered, natural environment. These guidelines were born out of respect for the animal and its habitat.

▲ DENOTES UNOFFICIAL SCORE OR TROPHY IS BELOW CURRENT MINIMUM SCORE

ABOVE: A November 1957 hunt near Mandan, North Dakota, produced this 200-7/8 non-typical buck for Virgil Chadwick.

RIGHT: W.E. Brown was hunting in Perkins County, South Dakota, in December of 1957 when he harvested this buck. The non-typical has a final score of 207-7/8 points..

LEFT: Robert Smith holding his 1953 prized deer. His 181-3/8 typical from Portage Co., Ohio, was, at that time, the second-largest in the state.

Please submit photograph...

Supplementa... valuation of conformation is a m... tetail Deer heads
with many p... ymmetrical head will
be given pre...

A. Number of ... must be at least
one inch lon... ints are measured
from tip of ... ounted as a point
but not meas...

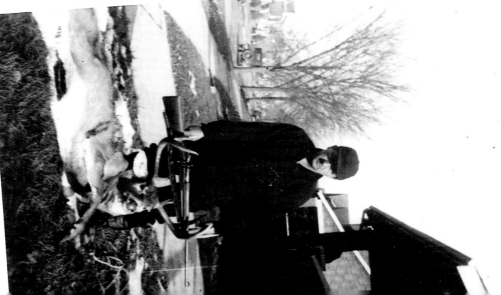

B. Tip to Ti...

C. Greatest S... center line of
the skull at

D. Inside Spr... e of the skull at
widest point ... "Credit" column
if it is less

E. Total of Lengths of all Abn... considered to be
those nontypica...

F. Length of Ma... curve to the
most distant po...

G-1-2-3-4-5-6-7, ... eam. They are
measured from ne...

H-1-2-3-4. Circu... allest place
between burr and

The first complet... ginated and
copyrighted in 19... F tz in 1939
and published in ... standard
system of accepte... independent

ABOVE: Lack of an identifiable typical frame makes this buck unscorable. It was taken by Ernest C. Davis in December of 1956 in Wyoming County, West Virginia. The deer had a reported weight of 325 pounds.

RIGHT: This Grass River, Manitoba, buck fell to E.A. Hoehn in 1949. Scoring 187-6/8 as a non-typical, this heavy deer had approximately 45-4/8 inches of mass measurements. ▲

LEFT: A 1949 hunt in Mackinac County, Michigan, resulted in this 160-7/8 typical trophy for John J. Wiznak. The rifle is a sporterized 1903 Springfield in .30-06. ▲

▲ DENOTES UNOFFICIAL SCORE OR TROPHY IS BELOW CURRENT MINIMUM SCORE

ABOVE: This buck is nothing short of giant considering the location. William Candler was hunting his home state of Florida (Polk County) when he downed this trophy in November of 1953. It was measured incorrectly, so no score is available. ▲

LEFT: Leon Richards was bowhunting in 1955 on Howland Island in New York, when he downed this fine buck. This 6x5 scores 164-2/8 points. It had a reported dressed weight of 203 pounds. ▲

▲ DENOTES UNOFFICIAL SCORE OR TROPHY IS BELOW CURRENT MINIMUM SCORE

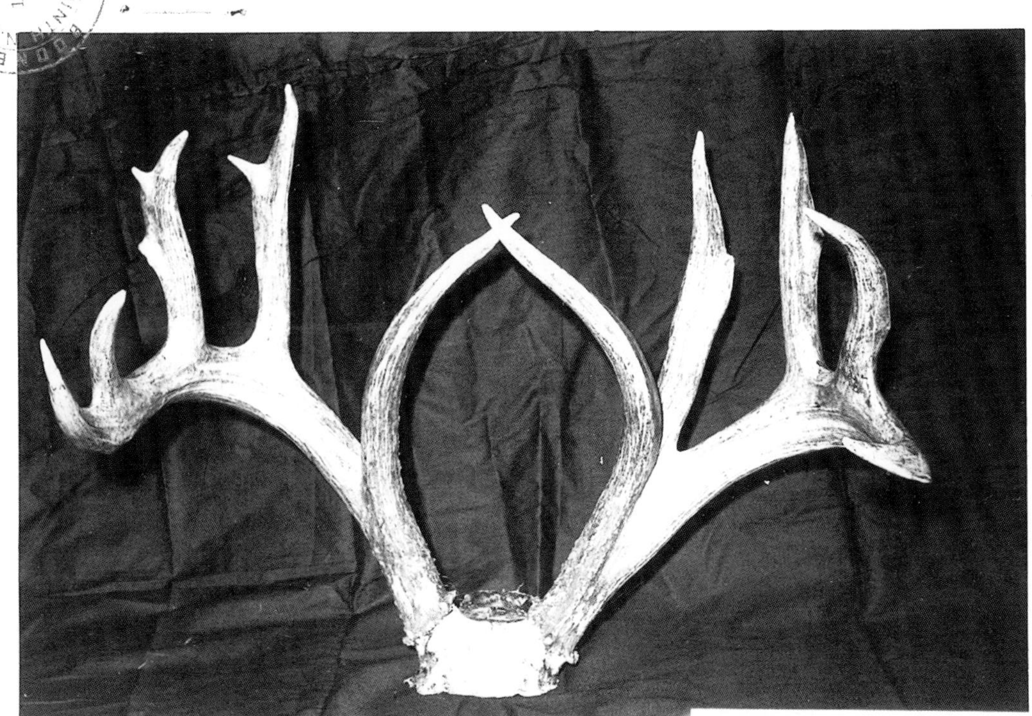

• FEB • 60

ABOVE: Crossing eye guards are certainly a rare occurrence, and one that makes this trophy all the more fascinating. Jerry May was the lucky hunter. This 178-6/8 typical lived just south of Elkhorn, Manitoba.

RIGHT: This 204-6/8 giant, taken by Brooks Reed in Gilmer County, West Virginia, in 1960, was the state record for many years. It currently stands fourth on West Virginia's state list.

LEFT: Ralph Klimek took this great 204-7/8 point non-typical in Trempealeau County, Wisconsin, in 1960. Mr. Klimek's deer was an entry in the 10th Competition.

ess: Harry D. Olcott   Signature: Otto Lyon (by Harry D. Olcott)

INSTRUCTIONS

neasurements must be made with a flexible steel tape to the nearest one-eighth of an in
cial measurements cannot be taken for at least sixty days after the animal was killed.
se submit photographs.

lementary Data measurements indicate conformation of the trophy. Evaluation of conform
is a matter of personal preference. Excellent, but nontypical Whitetail Deer heads
many points shall be placed and judged in a separate class. The symmetrical head will
iven preference.

umber of Points on each Antler. To ... at least
inch long AND its length must exceed ... measured
tip of point to nearest edge of bea... as a point
not measured as a point.

ip to Tip Spread measured between ti...

reatest Spread measured between perp... line of
skull at widest part whether across ...

nside Spread of Main Beams measured ... he skull at
st point between main beams. Enter ... " column
t is less than or equal to the lengt...

otal of Lengths of all Abnormal Poi... idered to be
nontypical in shape or location.

ength of Main Beam measured from low... ve to the
distant point of what is, or appear...

2-3-4-5-6-7. Length of Normal Point... They are
ured from nearest edge of main beam ...

2-3-4. Circumferences - If first poi... lest place
een burr and second point.

ACK...

first complete system for scoring N... inated and
righted in 1935 by Dr. James L. Cla... itz in 1939
published in NORTH AMERICAN BIG GAM... tandard
em of accepted authority, the Boone ... independent
ittee to develop the Official Scori... ophies. The
ers of this committee were Dr. Harold E. Anthony, Milford Baker, Frederick K. Barbour,
James L. Clark, Grancel Fitz and Samuel B. Webb, Chairman.

Official System is basically a consolidation of the best points in the two previously
ing systems. In the process, some new points have been developed, errors corrected,
needed simplification has been achieved.

e publication, these charts were circulated to more than 250 qualified sportsmen,
s, authors, taxidermists, game officials, and scientists for constructive criticism
approval. The Boone and Crockett Club gratefully acknowledges the contribution of this
and the work of the Committee.

RIGHT: Grace C. Elliott had a successful hunt in 1956 when she took this whitetail in Valley County, Montana. The buck had a final score of 153 points. ▲

LEFT: Otto Lyon stands next to his 1942 trophy from the Kingston, New Brunswick, area. It is one of thousands of trophies in B&C's Archive that is below the current minimum score. ▲

▲ DENOTES UNOFFICIAL SCORE OR TROPHY IS BELOW CURRENT MINIMUM SCORE

ABOVE: It was on a 1935 hunt in Lincoln County, Montana, when Ray Baenen encountered this amazing whitetail. Scoring 224 points, this is one of Montana's finest non-typicals. The greatest spread on this 16x12 point buck is 32 inches.

RIGHT: This huge 8-point buck, scoring 174-2/8 points, was taken by an unknown hunter near Cerralvo, Mexico, circa 1900.

LEFT: In December 1950, C.P. Howard shot what would become one of the highest-scoring whitetails in Texas. This Dimmitt County buck, with a 7x6 typical frame, scores 190 points.

I certify that I have measured the above trophy on Mar 10 1952
at (address) 1330 E Brice City Phx State Arizona
and that these measurements and data are, to the best of my knowledge and belief, made in accordance with the instructions given.

Witness: Jarris Ellington Signature: Bob Housholder

INSTRUCTIONS

STUBS ARE NOT 1" LONG

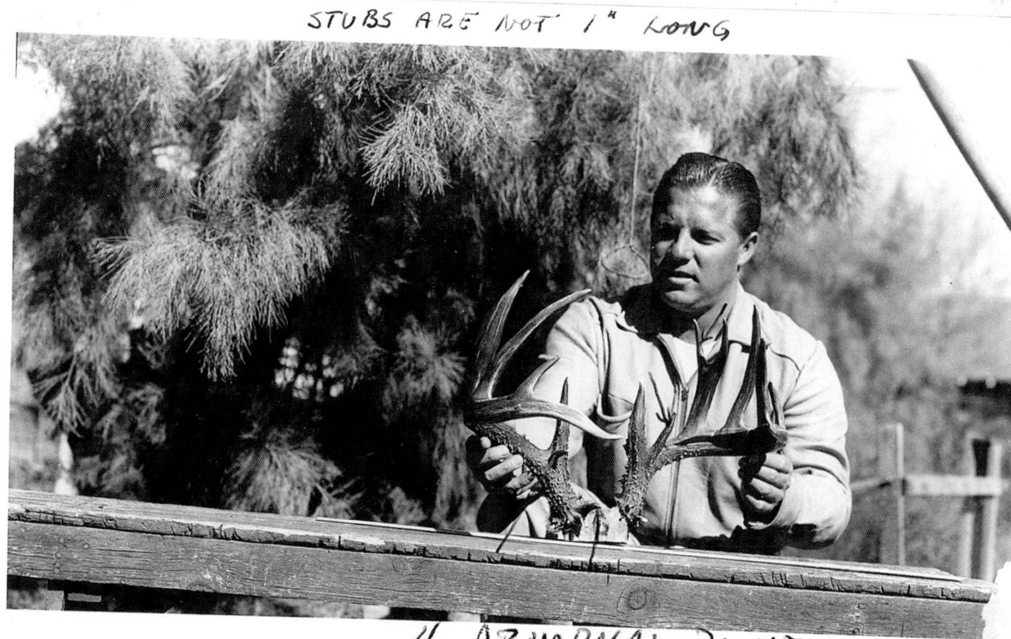

All m ... th of an inch.
Offic ... as killed.
Pleas

Suppl ... of conforma-
tion ... er heads
with ... l head will
be gi

A. Nu ... at least
one i ... measured
from ... s a point
but n

B. T

C. G ... line of
the

D. I ... he skull at
wide ... t" column
if i

4 ABNORMAL POINTS

E. To ... idered to be
those

F. Le ... e to the
most

G-1-2 ... They are
measu

H-1-2 ... est place
betwe

The ... nated and
copy ... tz in 1939
and ... tandard
syst ... independent
comm ... ophies. The
memb ... K. Barbour,
Dr.

6 POINTS

This ... previously
existing systems. ... corrected,
and needed simplification has been achieved.

Before publication, these charts were circulated to more than 250 qualified sportsmen, guides, authors, taxidermists, game officials, and scientists for constructive criticism and approval. The Boone and Crockett Club gratefully acknowledges the contribution of this group and the work of the Committee.

ABOVE: W.J. Closs poses with his 1953 whitetail. Closs was hunting near Long Lake on the Allagash River in Maine that November. This 53-year-old photograph meets today's high standards of photographic expectations of a hunter and his trophy. ▲

RIGHT: Edward Foss harvested this typical scoring 162-1/8 points. The buck was taken near Harrison, Michigan, in 1936. ▲

LEFT: S.M. Brown took this buck near Spokane, Washington, in 1923. At 147-2/8 points, it falls below the necessary minimum score for entry into the Records Program. Bob Housholder, who was an official measurer for a number of years, holds a trophy. ▲

▲ DENOTES UNOFFICIAL SCORE OR TROPHY IS BELOW CURRENT MINIMUM SCORE

ABOVE: O.C. Brown with his 1956 whitetail taken near North Canonto Township, Ontario. The deer's entry score was 153-5/8 points, just shy of qualifying for the Records Program. ▲

RIGHT: Dorchester County, Maryland, was the location of kill on this 192-5/8 non-typical. Mark R. Stewart was the hunter, taking the buck on a December hunt in 1954. Note the long abnormal point coming off the base of the left antler. ▲

OPPOSITE: Henry Mordan holds up the results of a successful hunt in Ontonagon County, Michigan. This entry was submitted at 152-6/8 points. ▲

▲ DENOTES UNOFFICIAL SCORE OR TROPHY IS BELOW CURRENT MINIMUM SCORE

ABOVE: William F. Cruff was hunting near Valley City, North Dakota, in 1955 when he bumped into this buck-of-a-lifetime. The final score on this non-typical is 204-3/8 points.

RIGHT: Double-double, drop-tine buck — J.V. Parker was hunting near Griswold, Manitoba, in 1946 when he harvested this tremendous 208-1/8 non-typical.

LEFT: This eye-catching non-typical, which scores 214-7/8 points, seems to have as many points facing down as he does facing up. The deer was taken near Aweme, Manitoba, in 1954. The hunter, from an older score chart, is listed as Criddle Bros.

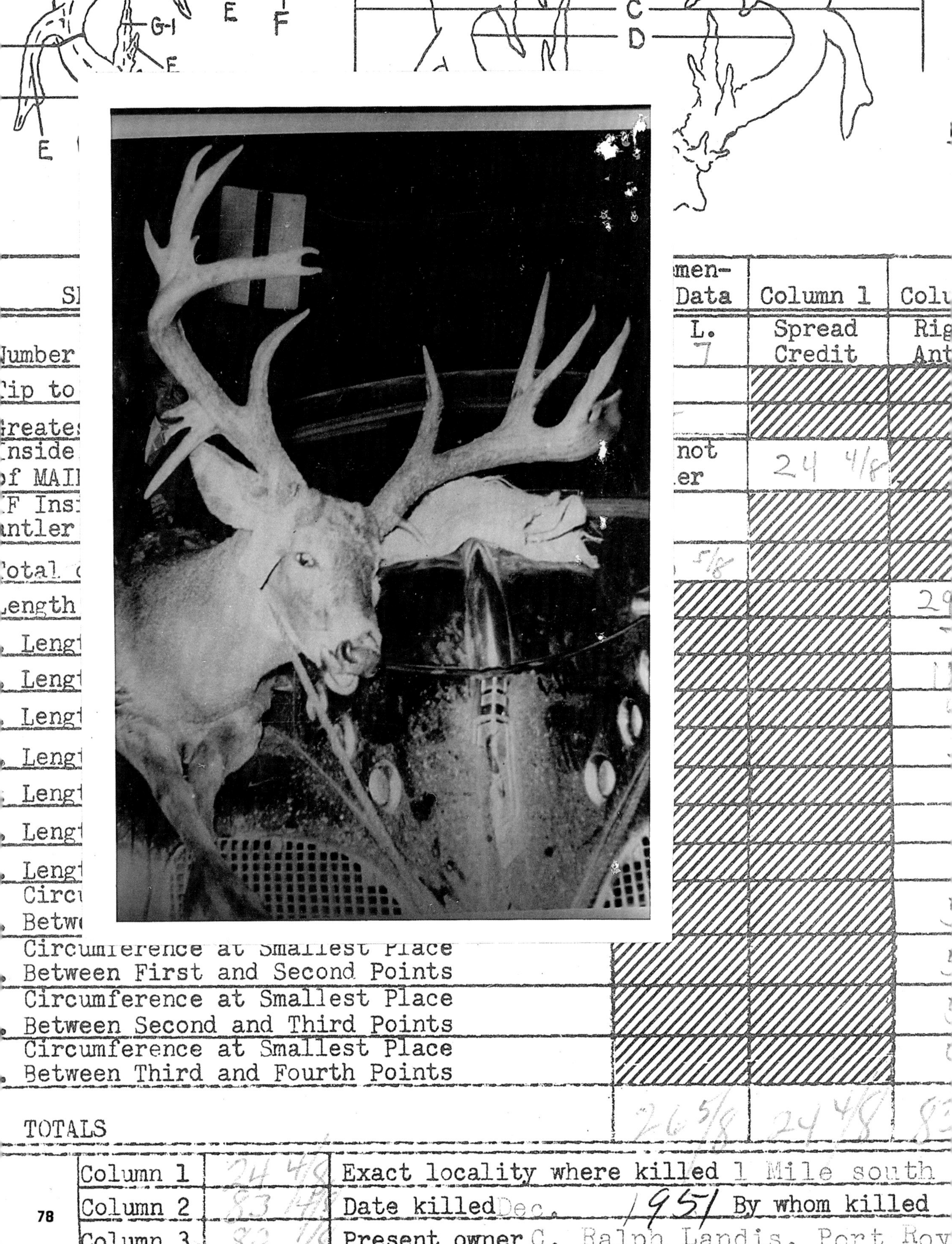

G-1
E
F
C
D
E

S...	...men- Data	Column 1	Colu...
Number ...	L. 7	Spread Credit	Rig... Ant...
Tip to ...			
Greates...			
Inside ... of MAI...	not ...er	24 4/8	
IF Insi... antler ...			
Total ...	5/8		
Length ...			29
. Lengt...			
. Lengt...			
. Lengt...			
. Lengt...			
. Lengt...			
. Lengt...			
. Lengt...			
Circu... . Betwe...			
Circumference at Smallest Place . Between First and Second Points			
Circumference at Smallest Place . Between Second and Third Points			
Circumference at Smallest Place . Between Third and Fourth Points			
TOTALS	26 5/8	24 4/8	83...

Column 1	24 4/8	Exact locality where killed 1 Mile south
Column 2	83 4/8	Date killed Dec. 1951 By whom killed
Column 3	80 1/8	Present owner C. Ralph Landis, Port Roy

ABOVE: This phenomenal 197 non-typical was taken by Sam Henry near the Oak River in Manitoba in 1946. The number and size of these drop-tines make this deer one of North America's most impressive whitetails.

RIGHT: Erwin Klaassen was hunting in Roseau County, Minnesota, when he and this buck met. Klaasen's 1955 non-typical whitetail scores 205-4/8 points. It was entered into the 8th Competition.

LEFT: This 207-7/8 non-typical was taken by C. Ralph Landis in Juniata County, Pennsylvania, in 1951. It is Pennsylvania's third-largest non-typical.

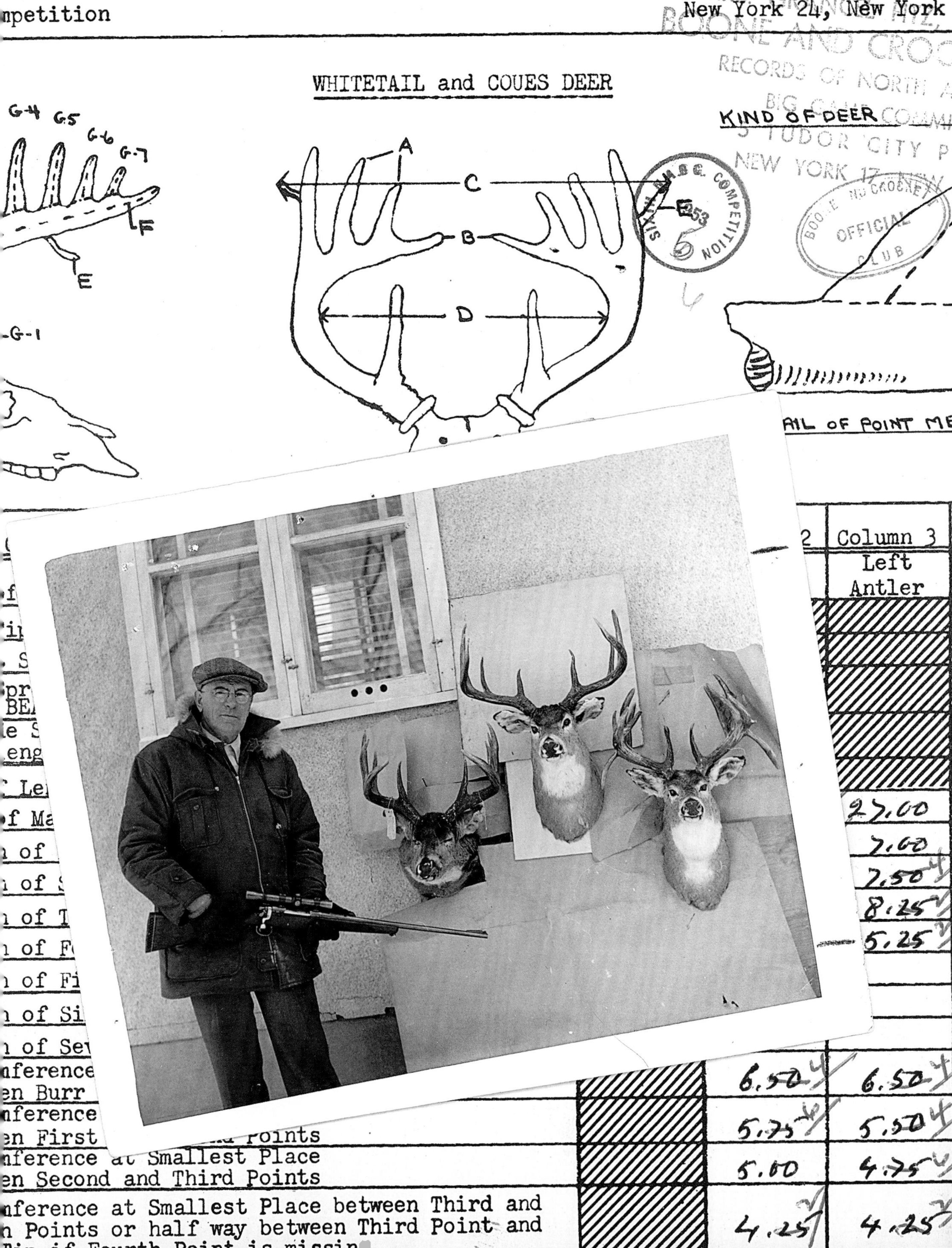

mpetition
New York 24, New York
BOONE AND CROC
RECORDS OF NORTH A
KIND OF DEER
NEW YORK 17
WHITETAIL and COUES DEER
G-4
G-5
G-6
G-7
F
E
A
C
B
D
G-1
AIL OF POINT ME
Column 3
Left Antler
27.00
7.00
7.50
8.25
5.25
nference
en Burr
6.50
6.50
nference
en First
Points
5.75
5.50
nference at Smallest Place
en Second and Third Points
5.00
4.75
nference at Smallest Place between Third and
n Points or half way between Third Point and
Tip if Fourth Point is missin
4.25
4.25

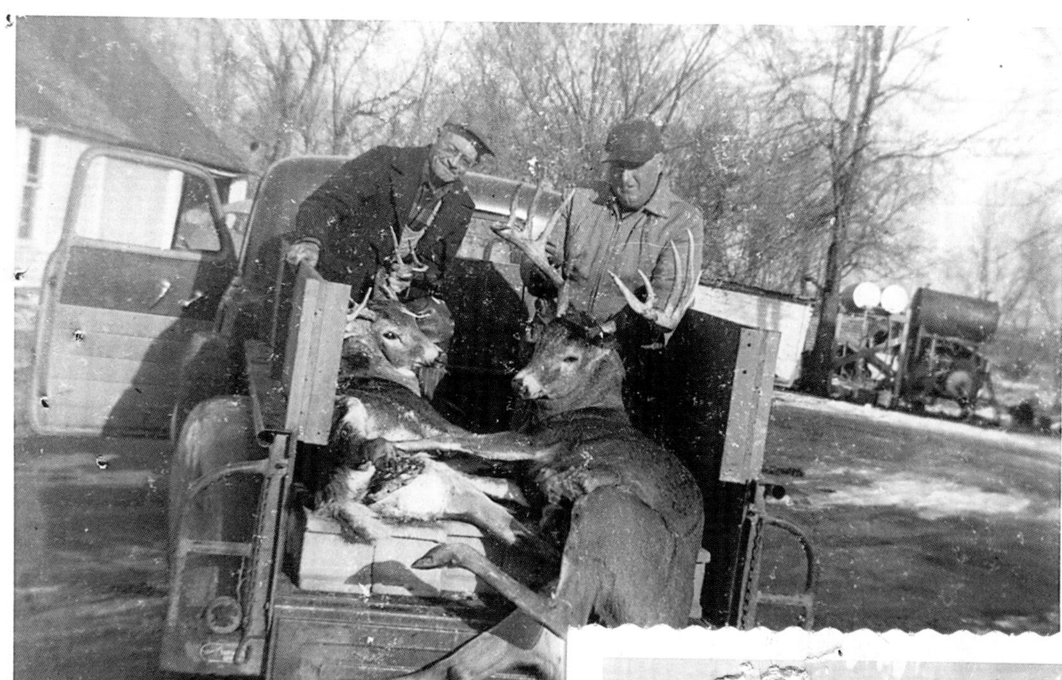

ABOVE: Harlan Francis (right) and an unidentified man hold up their deer from a 1956 hunt in Faribault County, Minnesota. Francis' big typical scores 170-1/8 points and was an entry in the 8th Competition.

RIGHT: Augusta County, Virginia, was the location of David H. Wolfe's hunt that produced this 173-4/8 typical. In the remarks section of the score chart, it states, "Virginia State Champion for 1957 season."

LEFT: Jessie Byer shows a most impressive run of luck he had while hunting whitetails in Manitoba in the 1950s. From left to right: Byer's buck scoring 157 points taken in 1952, his 170 typical taken in 1951 and entered in the 6th Competition, and his 9x12 scoring 182-4/8, taken in 1950.

THIRD PRIZE – TYPICAL 1950 COMPETITION

The 4th Competition was the first one that used the new scoring system. The Records Program was also still in the process of building public recognition. As such, entries trickled in at a much slower rate than today. At that time, the minimum score for entry of whitetail deer was 140 points. It was raised to 150 points in 1953.

This nice whitetail, scoring 154-5/8 points, was the Third Prize winner that year. The Competition was held at the American Museum of Natural History in New York City. The deer was taken by M.T. Parker near Enfield, Nova Scotia.

4: AWARD WINNERS

A NEW SCORING SYSTEM

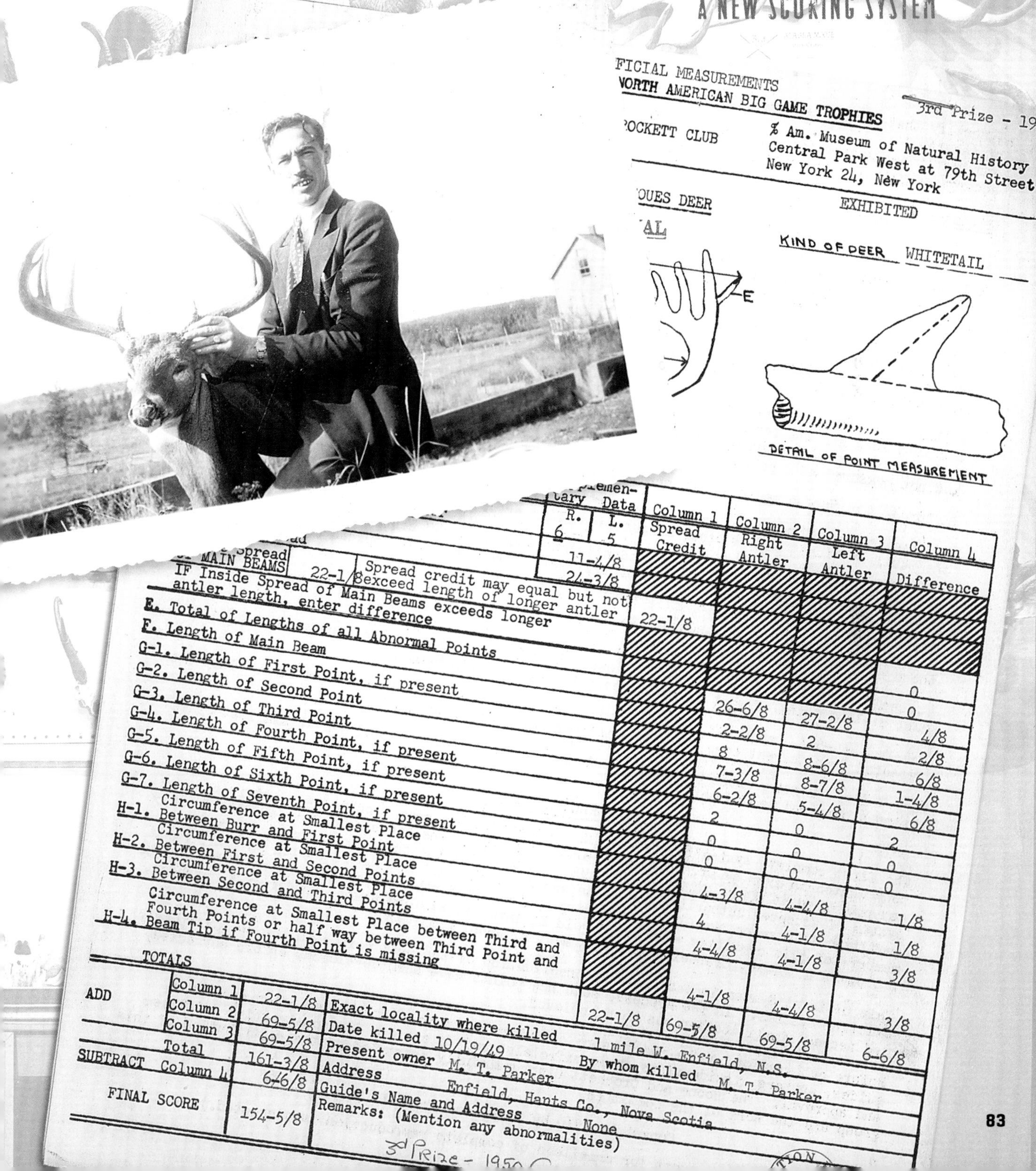

FICIAL MEASUREMENTS
NORTH AMERICAN BIG GAME TROPHIES — 3rd Prize - 1950

ROCKETT CLUB — % Am. Museum of Natural History, Central Park West at 79th Street, New York 24, New York

OUES DEER — EXHIBITED

AL

KIND OF DEER WHITETAIL

DETAIL OF POINT MEASUREMENT

	Supplementary Data R.	L.	Column 1 Spread Credit	Column 2 Right Antler	Column 3 Left Antler	Column 4 Difference
Number of Points on Each Antler	6	5				
Tip to Tip Spread	11-4/8					
Greatest Spread	24-3/8					
Inside Spread of MAIN BEAMS 22-1/8 — Spread credit may equal but not exceed length of longer antler			22-1/8			
IF Inside Spread of Main Beams exceeds longer antler length, enter difference						0
E. Total of Lengths of all Abnormal Points						0
F. Length of Main Beam				26-6/8	27-2/8	4/8
G-1. Length of First Point, if present				2-2/8	2	2/8
G-2. Length of Second Point				8	8-6/8	6/8
G-3. Length of Third Point				7-3/8	8-7/8	1-4/8
G-4. Length of Fourth Point, if present				6-2/8	5-4/8	6/8
G-5. Length of Fifth Point, if present				2	0	2
G-6. Length of Sixth Point, if present				0	0	0
G-7. Length of Seventh Point, if present				0	0	0
H-1. Circumference at Smallest Place Between Burr and First Point				4-3/8	4-4/8	1/8
H-2. Circumference at Smallest Place Between First and Second Points				4	4-1/8	1/8
H-3. Circumference at Smallest Place Between Second and Third Points				4-4/8	4-1/8	3/8
H-4. Circumference at Smallest Place between Third and Fourth Points or half way between Third Point and Beam Tip if Fourth Point is missing				4-1/8	4-4/8	3/8
TOTALS			22-1/8	69-5/8	69-5/8	6-6/8

ADD	Column 1	22-1/8	Exact locality where killed 1 mile W. Enfield, N.S.
	Column 2	69-5/8	Date killed 10/19/49 By whom killed M. T. Parker
	Column 3	69-5/8	Present owner M. T. Parker
	Total	161-3/8	Address Enfield, Hants Co., Nova Scotia
SUBTRACT	Column 4	6-6/8	Guide's Name and Address None
FINAL SCORE		154-5/8	Remarks: (Mention any abnormalities)

3rd Prize - 1950

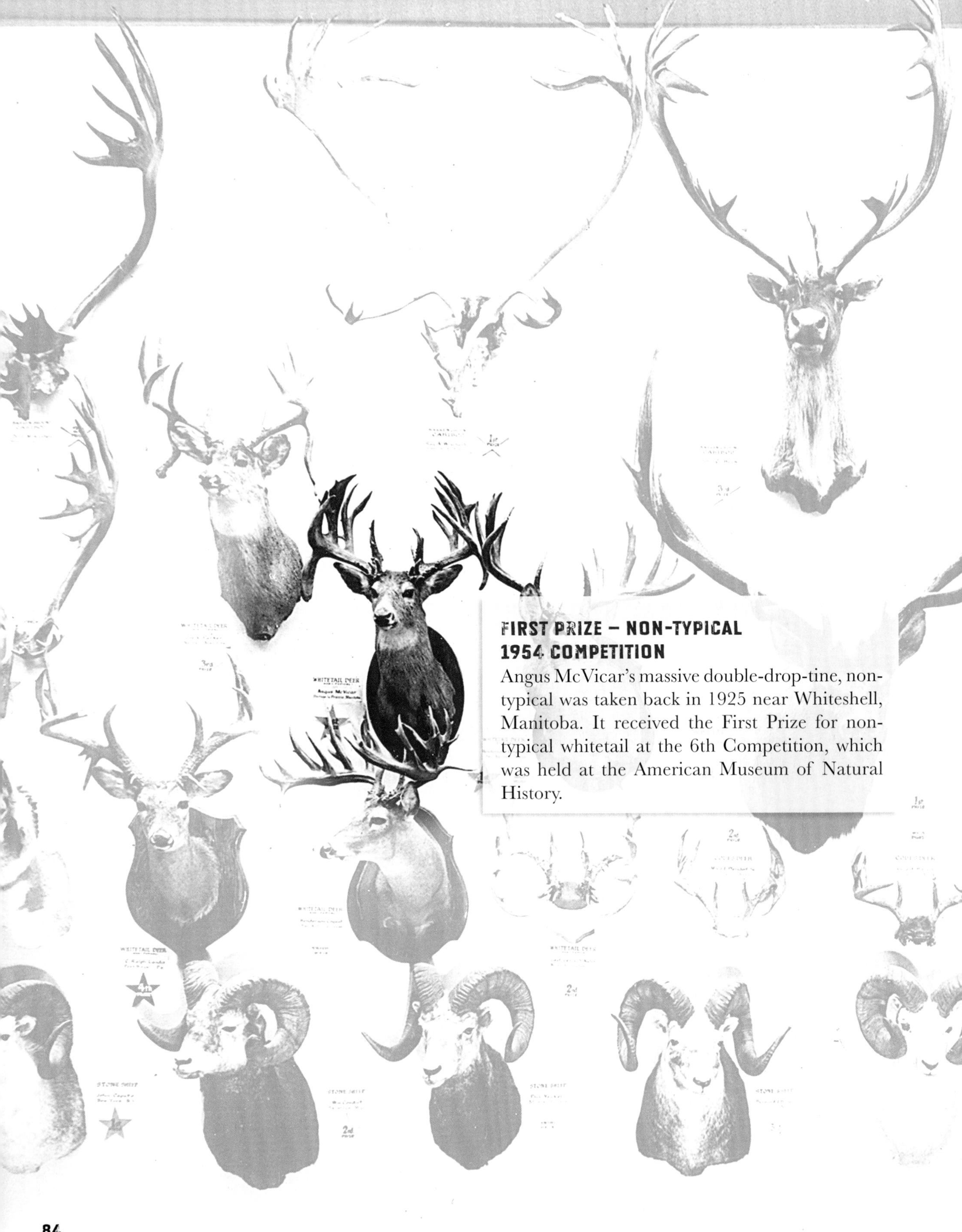

FIRST PRIZE – NON-TYPICAL 1954 COMPETITION

Angus McVicar's massive double-drop-tine, non-typical was taken back in 1925 near Whiteshell, Manitoba. It received the First Prize for non-typical whitetail at the 6th Competition, which was held at the American Museum of Natural History.

SYSTEM FOR NORTH AMERICAN BIG GAME TROPHIES

BOONE AND CROCKETT CLUB

Address Correspondence to:
Mrs. Grancel Fitz, Secretary
5 Tudor City Place, NYC 17, N

N-TYPICAL WHITETAIL DEER

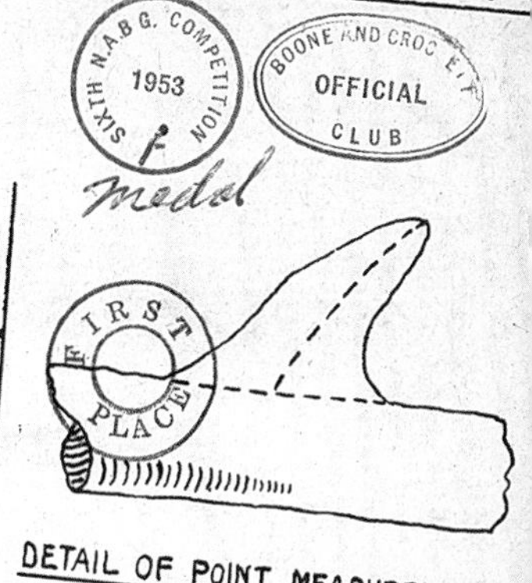

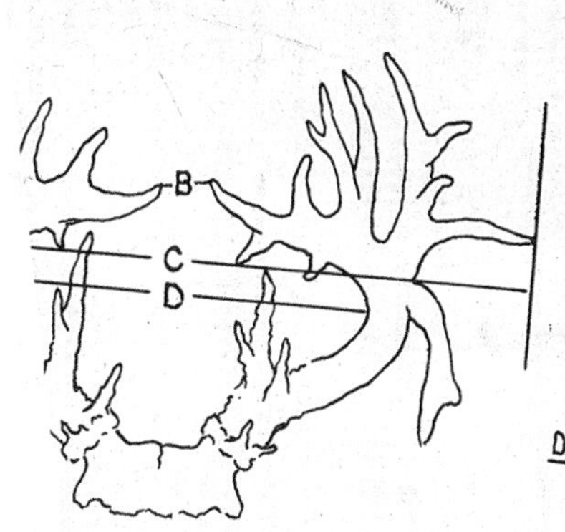

	Supplementary Data R. 12	Supplementary Data L. 16	Column 1 Spread Credit	Column 2 Right Antler	Column 3 Left Antler	Column 4 Difference
	12 6/8					
	25 6/8					
… but not … antler			20 2/8			
	59 1/8					—
				24 2/8	23 7/8	3/8
				6 4/8	6 1/8	3/8
				10 7/8	11 1/8	2/8
…resent				11 —	11 2/8	2/8
…oint, if present				6 —	7 —	1
…ngth of Sixth Point, if present				—	—	
G-7. Length of Seventh Point, if present				—	—	
Circumference at Smallest Place H-1. Between Burr and First Point				—	—	
Circumference at Smallest Place H-2. Between First and Second Points				5 4/8	5 4/8	—
Circumference at Smallest Place H-3. Between Second and Third Points				5 —	5 —	—
Circumference at Smallest Place H-4. Between Third and Fourth Points				5 5/8	5 4/8	1/8
				6 1/8	5 1/8	1
TOTALS	59 1/8		20 2/8	80 7/8	80 4/8	3 3/8

ADD	Column 1	20 2/8
	Column 2	80 7/8
	Column 3	80 4/8
	Total	181 5/8
SUBTRACT Column 4		3 3/8
	Result	178 2/8
Add Line E Total		59 1/8
FINAL SCORE		237 3/8

Exact locality where killed Whiteshell, Manitoba, Canada
Date killed 1925 By whom killed Angus McVicar
Present owner Angus McVicar
Address Portage la Prairie, Manitoba
Guide's Name and Address None
Remarks: (Mention any abnormalities)

690

BOONE AND CROCKETT CLUB

RECORDS OF NORTH AMERICAN
BIG GAME COMMITTEE

SAMUEL B. WEBB, CHAIRMAN
99 JOHN ST., N. Y.

MILFORD BAKER
285 MADISON AVE., N. Y.

FREDERICK K. BARBOUR
575 PARK AVE., N. Y.

ALFRED ELY
41 BROAD ST., N. Y.

ALFRED C. GILBERT
NEW HAVEN, CONN.

ADDRESS CORRESPONDENCE
MRS. GRANCEL FITZ, SECRET.
5 TUDOR CITY PLACE
NEW YORK 17, NEW YORK

Official

Jan. 6, 1954

Mr. Jim Sinclair
Neepawa
Manitoba, Canada

2 prize
not at show
172

Dear Sir:

It appears from our records that the fine Whitetail deer you entered in the North American Big Game Competition is one of the top trophies in its class. For this reason it is necessary to have the Board of Judges inspect it, measure it officially and compare it with other entries in its class. The trophy will then be hung in a temporary exhibit at the American Museum of Natural History, which will open shortly after the trophies have been judged.

We will greatly appreciate it if you will send your trophy to the American Museum of Natural History, Central Park West at 79th Street, New York 24, N. Y. The Committee requires that heads and horns sent to them be labeled with the name and complete address of the owner; be shipped and insured at the expense of the owner. These items will be given careful handling by the Committee and every precaution will be exercised against possible damage, but neither the Boone and Crockett Club nor the Committee can accept any responsibility for trophies either in transit or while in their possession. The return of the entries will be at the owner's expense for transportation and insurance.

...card is enclosed and we will appreciate ...the data requested and place it in the ...livery of trophies to the Museum is

...u upon such a fine trophy and thank you ...ion with these North American Big Game

Sincerely yours,

Samuel B. Webb

Chairman

SBW:H

SECOND PRIZE – TYPICAL
1954 COMPETITION

Jim Sinclair's typical buck, which scores 172 points, received the Second Prize at the 6th Competition despite the fact he did not send it in. This policy changed many years ago – only trophies sent to the Judges Panel are eligible for Place Awards and other recognition. Sinclair's handsome 5x5 was taken near Neepawa, Manitoba, in 1947.

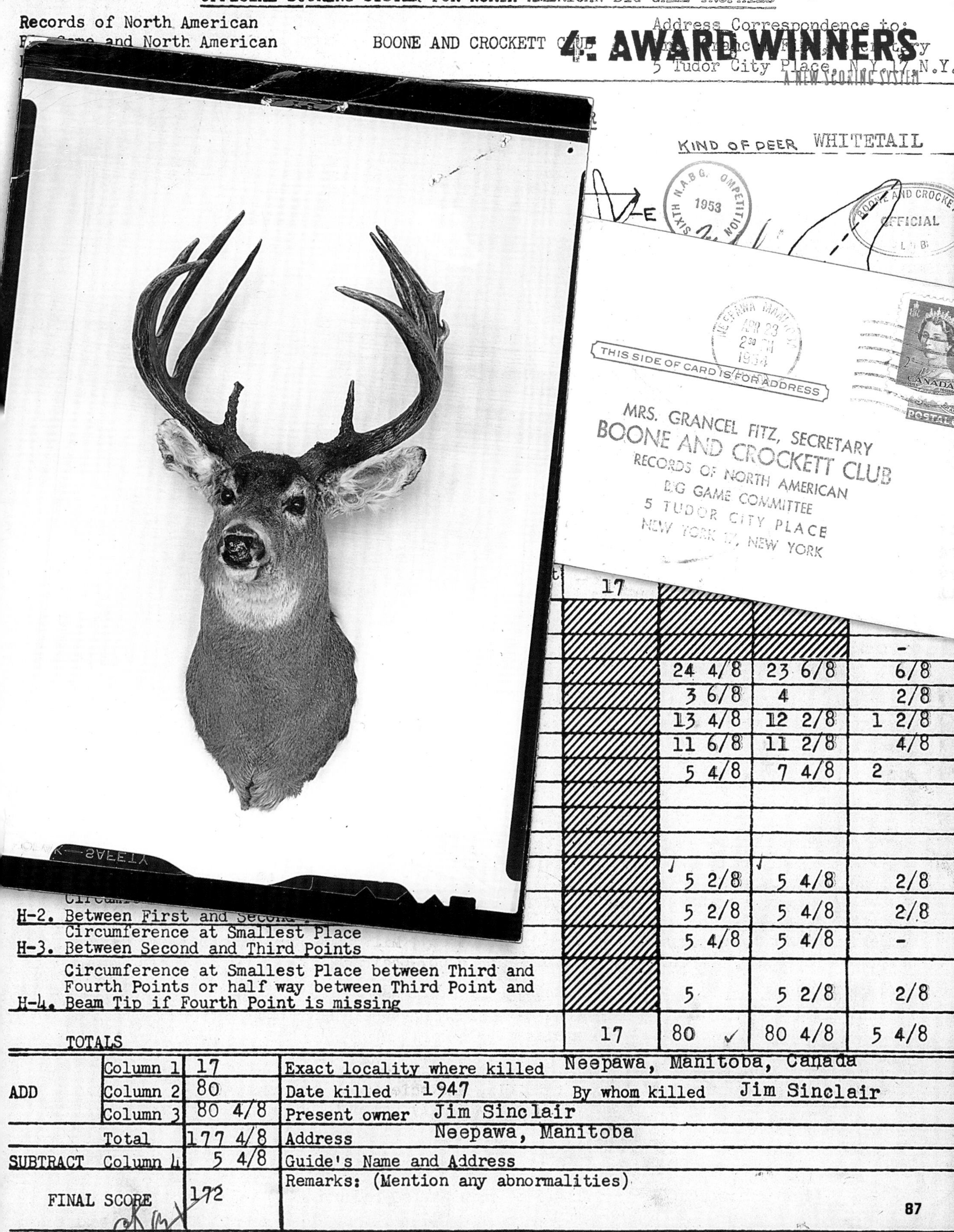

OFFICIAL SCORING SYSTEM FOR NORTH AMERICAN BIG GAME TROPHIES

Records of North American Big Game and North American

BOONE AND CROCKETT CLUB

Address Correspondence to:
5 Tudor City Place, N.Y. 17 N.Y.

KIND OF DEER WHITETAIL

	Column 1	Column 2	Column 3	Column 4
	17			
				-
		24 4/8	23 6/8	6/8
		3 6/8	4	2/8
		13 4/8	12 2/8	1 2/8
		11 6/8	11 2/8	4/8
		5 4/8	7 4/8	2
Circum...		5 2/8	5 4/8	2/8
H-2. Between First and Second ...		5 2/8	5 4/8	2/8
Circumference at Smallest Place H-3. Between Second and Third Points		5 4/8	5 4/8	-
Circumference at Smallest Place between Third and Fourth Points or half way between Third Point and H-4. Beam Tip if Fourth Point is missing		5	5 2/8	2/8
TOTALS	17	80	80 4/8	5 4/8

ADD	Column 1	17	Exact locality where killed	Neepawa, Manitoba, Canada
	Column 2	80	Date killed 1947	By whom killed Jim Sinclair
	Column 3	80 4/8	Present owner	Jim Sinclair
	Total	177 4/8	Address	Neepawa, Manitoba
SUBTRACT	Column 4	5 4/8	Guide's Name and Address	
FINAL SCORE		172	Remarks: (Mention any abnormalities)	

FIRST PRIZE – NON-TYPICAL
1956 COMPETITION

Richard I. Goble's tremendous non-typical, which scores 221-2/8 points, won the First Prize at the 7th Competition. It was taken in Itasca County, Minnesota, on November 24, 1955. His deer has a total of 27 points, and 63-5/8 inches of abnormal points.

WHAT MAY BE A PRIZE-WINNING DEER HEAD is displayed by Richard Goble of Dora Lake.

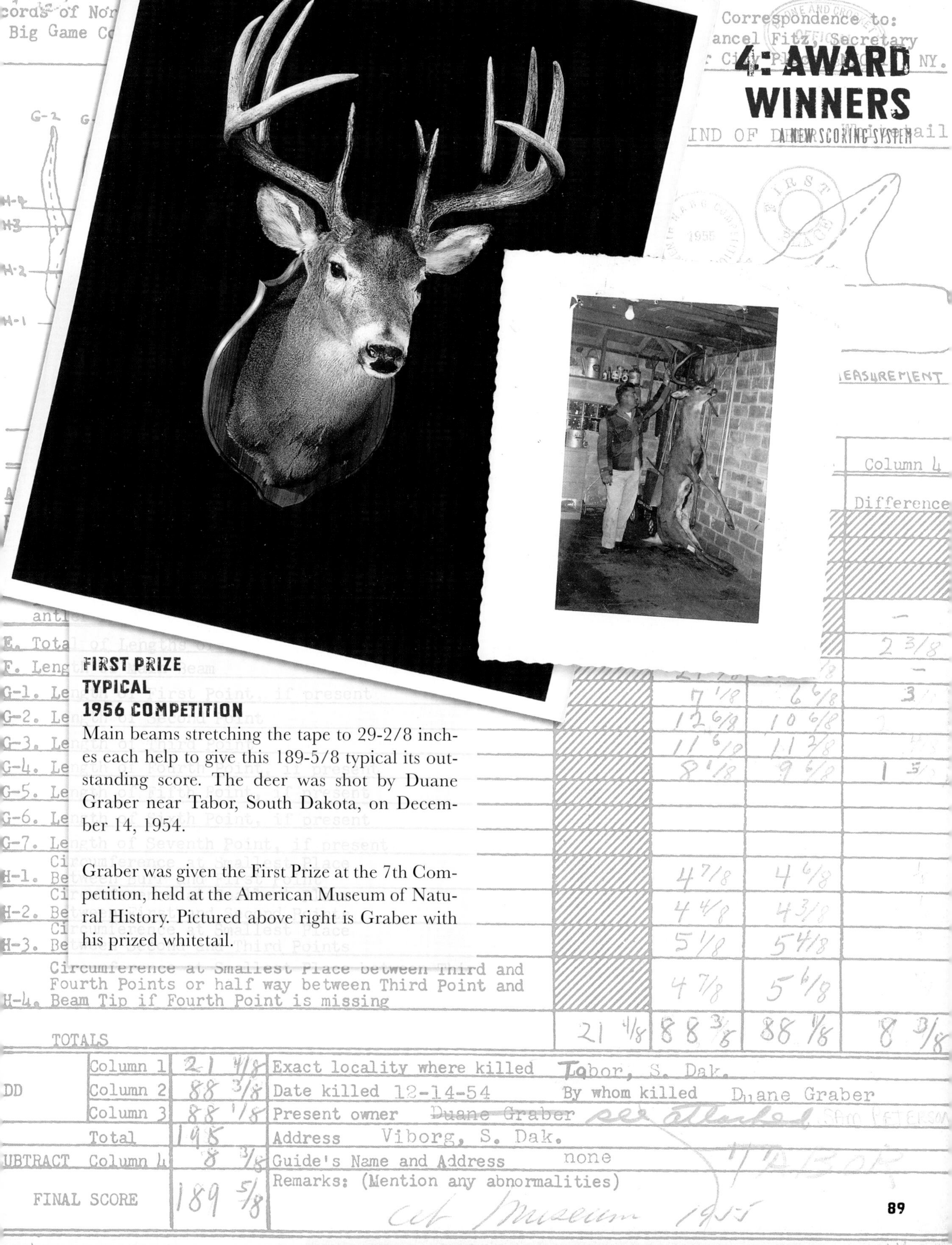

Correspondence to:
Column 4
Difference
Exact locality where killed Tabor, S. Dak.
Date killed 12-14-54
By whom killed Duane Graber
Present owner Duane Graber
Address Viborg, S. Dak.
Guide's Name and Address none
Remarks: (Mention any abnormalities)
FINAL SCORE 189 5/8

FIRST PRIZE
TYPICAL
1956 COMPETITION

Main beams stretching the tape to 29-2/8 inches each help to give this 189-5/8 typical its outstanding score. The deer was shot by Duane Graber near Tabor, South Dakota, on December 14, 1954.

Graber was given the First Prize at the 7th Competition, held at the American Museum of Natural History. Pictured above right is Graber with his prized whitetail.

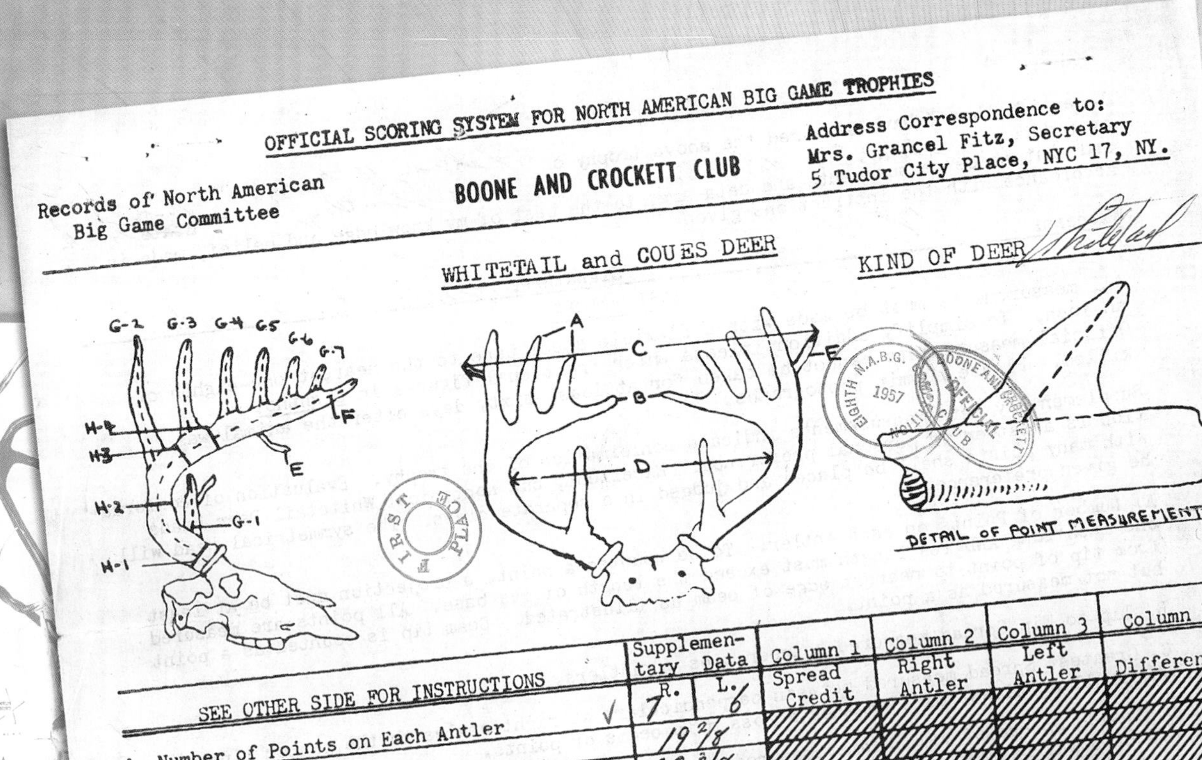

OFFICIAL SCORING SYSTEM FOR NORTH AMERICAN BIG GAME TROPHIES

Records of North American Big Game Committee

BOONE AND CROCKETT CLUB

Address Correspondence to:
Mrs. Grancel Fitz, Secretary
5 Tudor City Place, NYC 17, NY.

WHITETAIL and COUES DEER

KIND OF DEER Whitetail

SEE OTHER SIDE FOR INSTRUCTIONS	Supplementary Data R.	Supplementary Data L.	Column 1 Spread Credit	Column 2 Right Antler	Column 3 Left Antler	Column 4 Difference
A. Number of Points on Each Antler	7	6				
B. Tip to Tip Spread	19 2/8					
C. Greatest Spread	23 3/8					
D. Inside Spread of MAIN BEAMS	21 2/8	Spread credit may equal but not exceed length of longer antler	21 2/8			—
IF Inside Spread … exceeds longer antler length …						
E. Total … l Points						1 1/8
				25 2/8	24 3/8	7/8
				6 1/8	6 7/8	6/8
… ent				10 5/8	11 2/8	5/8
				8 6/8	9	2/8
				7 2/8	6 4/8	6/8
… t				2 3/8	1 2/8	1 1/8
				5 6/8	5 6/8	—
				5 3/8	5 1/8	1/8
				7 4/8	6 2/8	1 2/8
… Third and … oint and				6 4/8	5 7/8	5/8
			21 2/8	85 3/8	82 2/8	7 4/8

Sask.

… killed Southey, Sask

By whom killed A K Hamann

… Hamann … Sask … SAM PETERSON

… ormalities) see attached

FIRST PRIZE – TYPICAL
1958 COMPETITION

A.K. Flaman's massive typical, which scores 181-3/8 points, was the First Prize winner at the 8th Competition held in 1958. A total of 48 inches of circumference measurements help this great deer attain its high score.

Flaman was hunting near Southey, Saskatchewan, in 1955, when he tagged this huge deer.

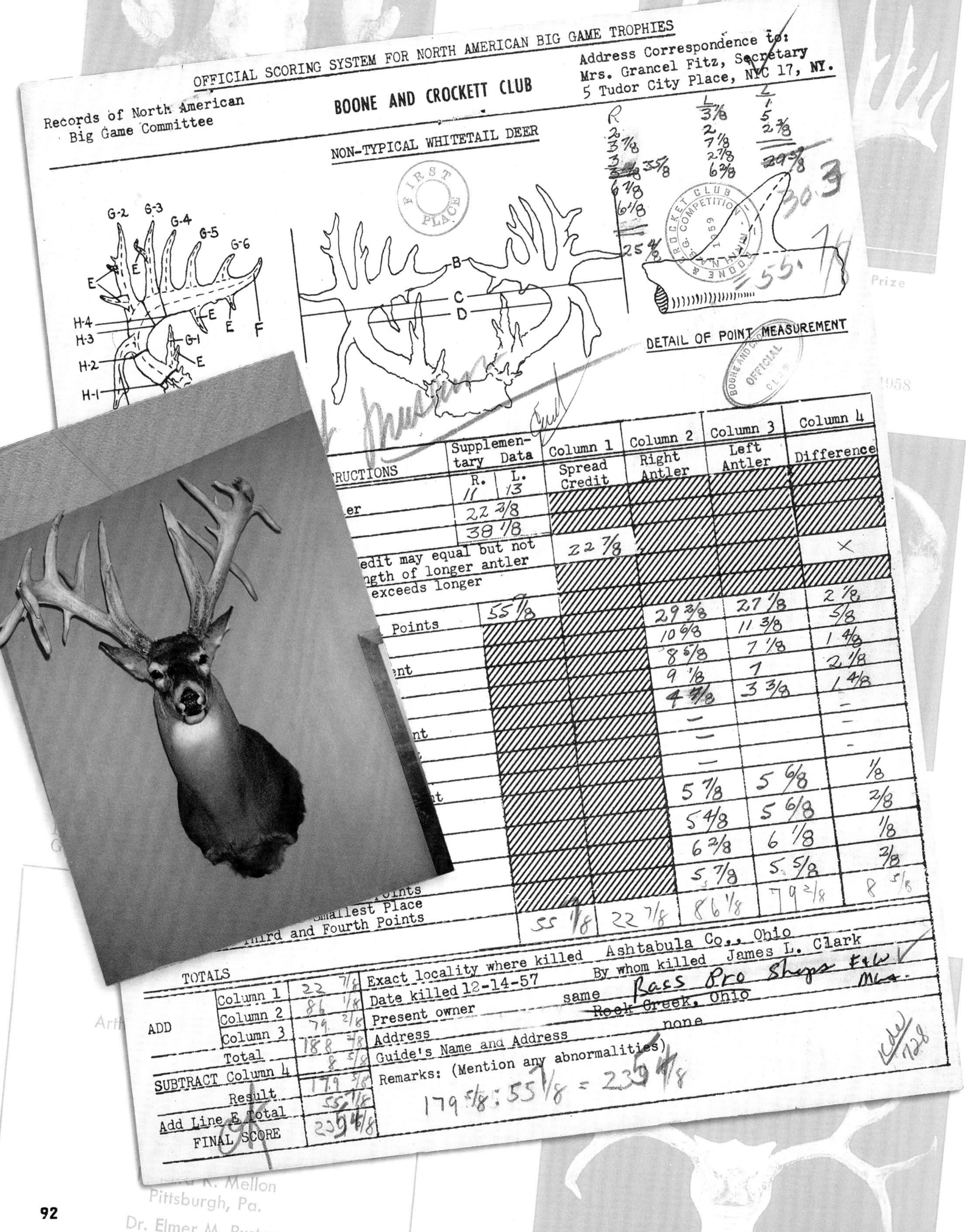

OFFICIAL SCORING SYSTEM FOR NORTH AMERICAN BIG GAME TROPHIES

Records of North American Big Game Committee

BOONE AND CROCKETT CLUB

Address Correspondence to: Mrs. Grancel Fitz, Secretary 5 Tudor City Place, NYC 17, NY.

NON-TYPICAL WHITETAIL DEER

DETAIL OF POINT MEASUREMENT

...RUCTIONS	Supplementary Data R.	Supplementary Data L.	Column 1 Spread Credit	Column 2 Right Antler	Column 3 Left Antler	Column 4 Difference
	11	13				
...er	22 2/8					
	38 1/8					
...edit may equal but not ...ngth of longer antler ... exceeds longer			22 7/8			X
	55 1/8			29 2/8	27 1/8	2 1/8
... Points				10 6/8	11 3/8	5/8
				8 5/8	7 1/8	1 4/8
...ent				9 1/8	7	2 1/8
				4 7/8	3 3/8	1 4/8
				—		—
...nt				—		—
				—		—
...nt				5 7/8	5 6/8	1/8
				5 4/8	5 6/8	2/8
				6 2/8	6 1/8	1/8
				5 7/8	5 5/8	2/8
...oints ...mallest Place ...hird and Fourth Points						8 5/8
			55 1/8	22 7/8	86 1/8	79 2/8

TOTALS		
ADD	Column 1	22 7/8
	Column 2	86 1/8
	Column 3	79 2/8
	Total	188 7/8
SUBTRACT Column 4		8 5/8
Result		179 5/8
Add Line E Total		55 1/8
FINAL SCORE		235 4/8

Exact locality where killed Ashtabula Co., Ohio

Date killed 12-14-57 By whom killed James L. Clark

Present owner same Bass Pro Shops

Address Rock Creek, Ohio

Guide's Name and Address none

Remarks: (Mention any abnormalities) 179 5/8 + 55 1/8 = 235 4/8

Owner—Utah Fish & Game Dept.

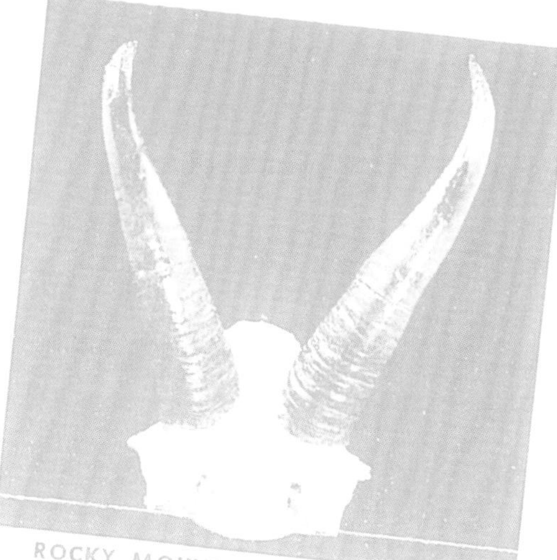

ROCKY MOUNTAIN GOAT—1st Prize
Score—54-6/8
Length—(R) 10-5/8 (L) 11-3/8
Basal Circumference—(R) 6-2/8 (L) 6-2/8
Locality—Coquihalla Mts., B. C.—1959
Hunter—Fred D. Fouty

DESERT SHEEP—1st Prize
Score—176-2/8
Length—(R) 35-6/8 (L) 36-6/8
Basal Circumference—(R) 14-3/8 (L) 14-3/8
Locality—Clark Co., Nev.—1957
Hunter—F. Lorin Ronnow
Guide—E. W. Arnold

FIRST PRIZE – NON-TYPICAL 1960 COMPETITION

The most outstanding feature on this world-class deer is its eye guards, measuring 10-6/8 inches and 11-3/8 inches. In combination with heavy mass, long main beams, and an exceptional inside spread, this deer's score of 235-4/8 points is easy to believe.

James L. Clark harvested this breathtaking non-typical in Ashtabula County, Ohio, in 1957. It received a First Prize at the 9th Competition, held at the American Museum of Natural History in New York City.

WHITETAIL DEER (non-typical)—1st Prize
Score—179-5/8 : 55-7/8 = 235-4/8
Length—(R) 29-2/8 (L) 27-1/8
Circumference—(R) 5-7/8 (L) 5-6/8
Points—(R) 11 (L) 13
Inside Spread—22-7/8
Locality—Ashtabula Co., Ohio—1957
Hunter—James L. Clark

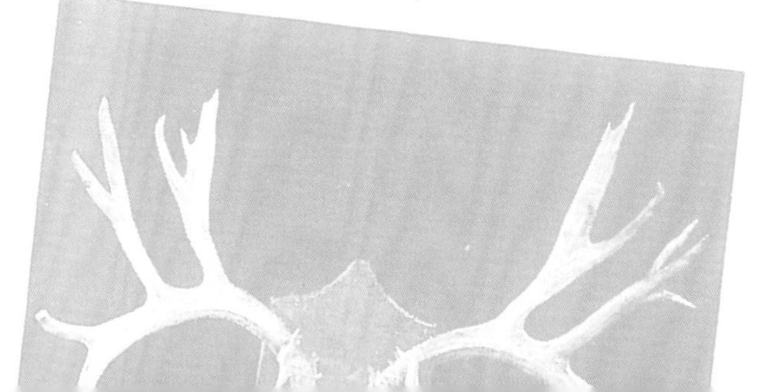

New Big Game Trophy Scoring Method May Give Ohio Hunter Record for Rocky Mountain Goat

By Edmund Gilligan

THE new system for scoring North American big game trophies, which was issued last week by the Boone and Crockett Club at the Museum of Natural History, may give to E. C. Haase, the Ohio, hunter, the honor of having taken a world's record Rocky Mountain goat. Mr. Haase received first prize in the club's 1947-'48-'49 awards for the heading measuring 12 inches in the front curves, 6½ inches in circumferences at base, 9½ in greatest spread, and 9 tip to tip.

The head will now be measured according to the new system. The club will then undertake a revision of the records listed in North American Big Game, 1939 edition, and it will also revise records filed since the publication. The newly adopted measurements will be added to the records and the final score will determine the re-allocation of each trophy under the new system. The result will be a ranking of trophies in accordance with their over-all excellence rather than one measurement, as in the present edition. I understand that Mr. Haase's trophy may be judged a world's record because of the higher score given to such horns for large bases than to length of the horn itself.

The first complete system for scoring such trophies was set up in 1935 by Dr. James L. Clark. A second system was devised by Grancel Fitz four years later, obviously because of a feeling that the first system could be improved. I don't know what the differences are. In any event, the Boone and Crockett Club came to recognize the need for a single standard by an authority that would be generally accepted. This was last year. The club appointed the following committee to develop the standard: Dr. Clark, Mr. Fitz, Dr. Harold E. Anthony, curator of mammals at the museum, Milford Baker, Frederick K. Barbour, and Samuel B. Webb, chairman. The new system is a consolidation of the old ones. The charts were sent to 200 qualified persons for criticism. After minor changes, the system was approved. The committee hopes that it will be accepted by the big game hunters as official.

The charts contain a sheet of instructions for each animal, moose, wapiti, mountain goat, sheep, etc. On the back of the sheet is a sketch of the head with key letters to indicate where the measurements are to be made with a flexible steel tape to the nearest one-eightieth of an inch. It is provided that the measurements may not be taken for at least sixty days after the kill. Photographs of the head are also required.

On the other side of the sheet are directions for the measurements. In the case of goats, the greatest spread is to be measured between perpendiculars at right angles to the center line of the skull. The next measurement is the tip-to-tip spread measured between tips of horns. The length of the horn is to be measured from the lowest point in front over the outer curve, to a point in line with the tip. The circumference of the base is to be measured at right angles to the axis of the horn. I believe that the new system will give a higher score to the base of the horn than to the length of the horn itself. The last measurements are the circumferences at the first, second and third quarter, which are to be determined by dividing the length by four, and marking both horns at these quarters.

Other parts of the instructions require the exact locality where the animal was killed, the date, the hunter's name and the guide's. In those cases where the head has passed into other hands, the name of the present owner is required.

The purpose of the new system is to carry on the work started by Theodore Roosevelt, a founder of the club, who hoped that by the award of trophies, hunters would pass up shots until a record head appeared.

4: PUBLICITY

A NEW SCORING SYSTEM

OPPOSITE: This article appeared in the *New York Times* in 1950. After several years of measuring, the Boone and Crockett Club had made the announcement introducing its new and much improved system for measuring North American big game. This comprehensive system quickly became the standard for which all trophies would be judged.

RIGHT: John E. Crew's exceptionally wide whitetail has a greatest spread of 29-4/8 inches. It was taken in Itasca County, Minnesota, in 1953. It measures 180-5/8 points as a non-typical (below the 185 minimum entry score) but remains part of the archives.

Biggest 'Rack'? The horns on this deer measure 29½ inches, probably a new United States record, as Carl Scherer, Oak Knoll taxidermist, proves. The deer, estimated at 260 pounds, was shot by John E. Crew, 3237 Eighteenth avenue S., who was hunting north of Grand Rapids, Minn. The listed United States record is an antler spread of 27⅞ inches, while the world record whitetail head, 33½ inches, came from British Columbia.—Sunday Tribune Photo.

Bisbee, Arizona, Thursda

ANTLERS OF TWO STATES DEER KILLS SET RECORD

NEW YORK, March 14 (AP)—Antlers of two deer killed in Arizona were announced tonight as world records by the Boone and Crockett Club at its biennial awards meeting in the American Museum of Natural History.

The hunters whose kills were recognized as new records are Horace T. Fowler, 1829 W. Lewis Ave. Phoenix, and Ed Stickwell, 3234 N. Dodge, Tucson.

A new record for mule deer antlers was established by Fowler's kill in North Kaibab Forest in 1938. The antlers were given a point total of 208 6-8. They had 6 and 5 points; a spread of 30 inches; the length of the main beam of the right antler was 27 6-8 inches and of the left 26 7-8 inches.

The previous record was held by Edison A. Pillmore, whose kill in Colorado in 1949 had a point total of 203 7-8.

Stockwell's kill in the Santa Rita Mountains in 1953 set a new record for desert white tail deer. Its antlers had a point total of 143. They had 6 and 5 points; a spread of 17 6-8 inches; the length of the main beam of the right antler was 20 2-8 inches and of the left 20 5-8 inches.

The old record was held by Gerald Hawes of Tucson with a deer killed at Arivaca in 1953. Its point total was 125 4-8.

The record set of antlers on Fowler's mule deer had gone unnoted for 17 years until Bob Housholder of Phoenix, state representative of the Boone and Crockett Club, noticed them on the wall of Fowler's cleaning shop.

Big game trophies may be entered in the club competition only once but there is no restriction on the year in which the game is killed.

The club was organized by Theodore Roosevelt at a dinner at his Sagamore Hill home in Oyster Bay, N. Y., after a hunting dinner in December, 1887. The club was to create interest in North American big game and in 1894 it organized the New York Zoological Society which now owns one of the continent's biggest and most valuable collection of big game heads.

Among the prize winners were Lt. Gen. James Doolittle, who entered a grizzly skull that was only 2 3-16 points less than the Columbus skull.

Warren, Arizona

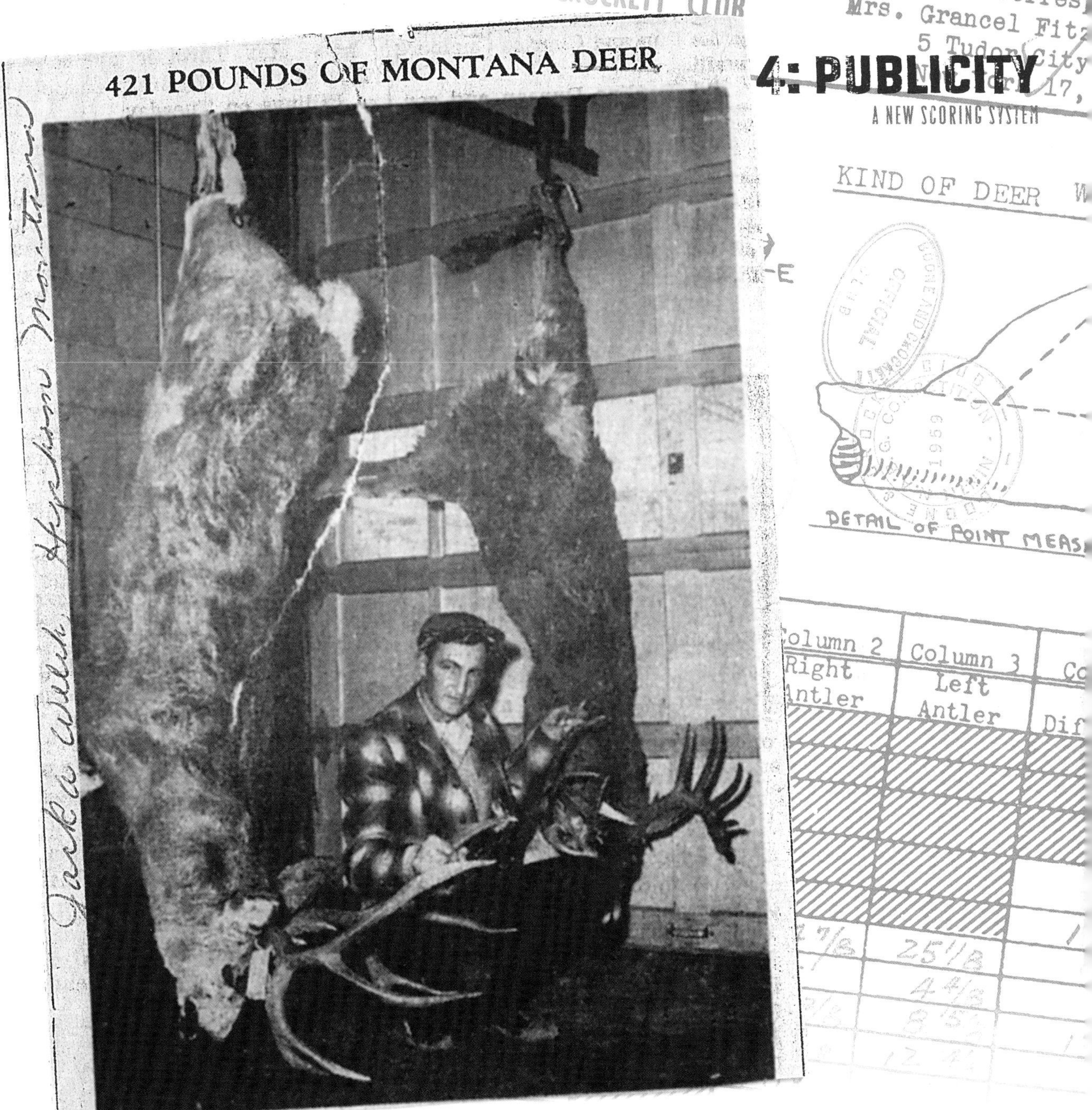

421 POUNDS OF MONTANA DEER

OPPOSITE: This clipping in an Arizona newspaper in 1956 announced two new World's Records from Arizona. One was Ed Stockwell's giant Coues' deer, the other Horace T. Fowler's typical mule deer. Stockwell's typical Coues' is still the World's Record, at 144-1/8 points. Fowler's mule deer has since been surpassed.

ABOVE: It may be hard to notice because of the giant mule deer in the way, but in the back is a magnificent typical whitetail deer, which scores 180-5/8 points. It was taken by Jack Welch in Treasure County, Montana, in 1958. No word on the score of the mule deer, which also looks to be record-class.

THE BIGGEST AND BEST

THIS SILENTLY ELOQUENT gallery in New York's Museum of Natural History drew outdoorsmen from across the continent last week—86 trophies in 25 North American categories representing the best of the big-game bag of the last two years. The occasion was the biennial awards dinner of the Boone and Crockett Club, official scorekeepers of North American game records.

Three of the prizes set new world records: a polar bear taken off Point Hope, Alaska by Tom F. Bolack of New Mexico; a white-tail deer shot in his home state by John A. Breen of Minnesota; and a mule deer with a mysterious past—it was discovered in a saloon by a Wyoming taxidermist, history and hunter forgotten. But the top excitement and the top award, the Sagamore Hill Medal, were for an elk shot by Fred C. Mercer of Montana. With right and left antler lengths totaling 10 feet, it was judged "the elk of the century." After a month's display in New York, the trophies will be taken off museum walls and shipped to their proud owners. Boone and Crockett experts find trophy hunting increasing, believe that even better trophies still await the hunter.

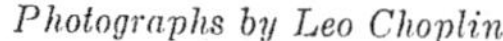

Photographs by Leo Choplin

"ELK OF CENTURY" (*above*) won top award among trophies (*opposite*) in Boone and Crockett Club competition.

OFFICIAL SCORING SYSTEM FOR NORTH AMERICAN BIG GAME TROPHIES

Records of North American
Big Game Committee

BOONE AND CROCKETT CLUB

Address Correspondence to:
Mrs. Grancel Fitz, Secretary
5 Tudor City Place, NYC 17, NY.

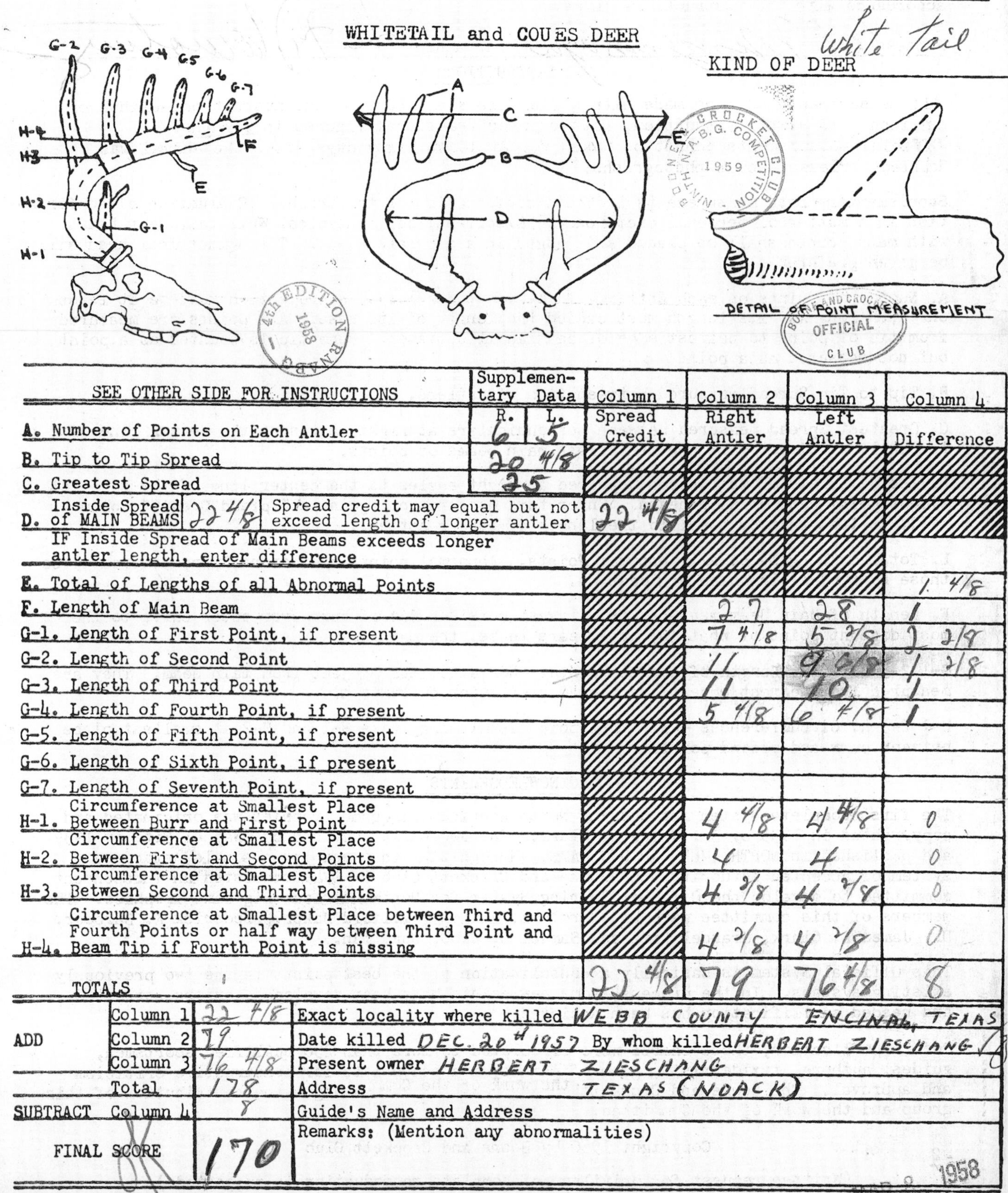

WHITETAIL and COUES DEER

KIND OF DEER: White Tail

SEE OTHER SIDE FOR INSTRUCTIONS	Supplementary Data R.	Supplementary Data L.	Column 1 Spread Credit	Column 2 Right Antler	Column 3 Left Antler	Column 4 Difference
A. Number of Points on Each Antler	6	5				
B. Tip to Tip Spread	20 4/8					
C. Greatest Spread	25					
D. Inside Spread of MAIN BEAMS 22 4/8 — Spread credit may equal but not exceed length of longer antler			22 4/8			
IF Inside Spread of Main Beams exceeds longer antler length, enter difference						
E. Total of Lengths of all Abnormal Points						1 4/8
F. Length of Main Beam				27	28	1
G-1. Length of First Point, if present				7 4/8	5 2/8	2 2/8
G-2. Length of Second Point				11	9 6/8	1 2/8
G-3. Length of Third Point				11	10	1
G-4. Length of Fourth Point, if present				5 4/8	6 4/8	1
G-5. Length of Fifth Point, if present						
G-6. Length of Sixth Point, if present						
G-7. Length of Seventh Point, if present						
H-1. Circumference at Smallest Place Between Burr and First Point				4 4/8	4 4/8	0
H-2. Circumference at Smallest Place Between First and Second Points				4	4	0
H-3. Circumference at Smallest Place Between Second and Third Points				4 2/8	4 2/8	0
H-4. Circumference at Smallest Place between Third and Fourth Points or half way between Third Point and Beam Tip if Fourth Point is missing				4 2/8	4 2/8	0
TOTALS			22 4/8	79	76 4/8	8

ADD	Column 1	22 4/8	Exact locality where killed	WEBB COUNTY ENCINAL, TEXAS
	Column 2	79	Date killed DEC. 20th 1957 By whom killed	HERBERT ZIESCHANG
	Column 3	76 4/8	Present owner	HERBERT ZIESCHANG
	Total	178	Address	TEXAS (NOACK)
SUBTRACT	Column 4	8	Guide's Name and Address	
FINAL SCORE		170	Remarks: (Mention any abnormalities)	

OK

MAR 8 1958

ZIESCHANG

RECORD DEER? — Herbert Zieselang hold an 11-point deer he bagged at Encinal. The white tail was shot with a 30.06 rifle. The spread measured 26 inches … tai…

United Press Telephoto

PREVIOUS PAGE: This spread, featured in the March 28, 1960, issue of *Sports Illustrated*, showcased the Boone and Crockett Club's 9th Competition held in New York City. Among other highlights, it announced John Breen's new World's Record typical whitetail, which scores 202 points. More details on the Breen buck are on the pages 138-143.

LEFT & ABOVE: Webb County, Texas, was where Herbert Zieschang brought down this big typical, which scores 170 points. This clipping appeared in a local paper shortly after the hunt, which took place on December 20, 1957.

Outdoor Life *First Choice of Discriminating Sportsmen*

353 FOURTH AVENUE · NEW YORK 10, N.Y.

April 20, 1 9 5 4

SHOOTING DEPARTMENT
JACK O'CONNOR, EDITOR

Dear Grancel:

My pal Mike Rudeen of Troy, Idaho, who had a hell of a big whitetail in the contest that I measured is all of a dither because his head did not win a prize. He had card from Betty saying his head scored 188 2/8 and was non-typical. No photo was sent with the measurements I sent in, but Mike now has had a photo taken and I am enclosing it. Mike thinks his head should be classed as typical, not non-typical. I tell Mike I don't even work there, that it is up to the committee.

I have also suggested that Mike take his head up to Don Hopkins and have Don look at it.

Please thank Betty for sending me the list for the last competition. Brother, you really got some trophies this last time! Herb Klein got a nice Stone this last fall, quite long but slender. He just got back from a tfip to India and Iran.

My best,

Jack

Box 382
Lewiston
Idaho

I got a fine kudu and one hell of a sable when I was in Africa

Conservation Pledge

I GIVE MY PLEDGE AS AN AMERICAN TO SAVE AND FAITHFULLY TO DEFEND FROM WASTE THE NATURAL RESOURCES OF MY COUNTRY—ITS SOIL AND MINERALS, ITS FORESTS, WATERS, AND WILDLIFE

IN OUR SCHOOLS – IN ALL ASSEMBLIES OF AMERICANS – LET THIS PLEDGE RING OUT!

4: CORRESPONDENCE FROM THE VAULTS

MIKE RUDEEN BUCK – JACK O'CONNOR LETTER

Colorful outdoor writer Jack O'Connor was also a Boone and Crockett Club Official Measurer. The preceding page shows a rare chance to read some more private and personal correspondence, written to Grancel Fitz. Several tidbits in this letter reference a few things that O'Connor fans will recognize. The main topic of the letter was Mike Rudeen's whitetail deer from Idaho, which is pictured at right.

The remaining correspondence can be found on the following two pages.

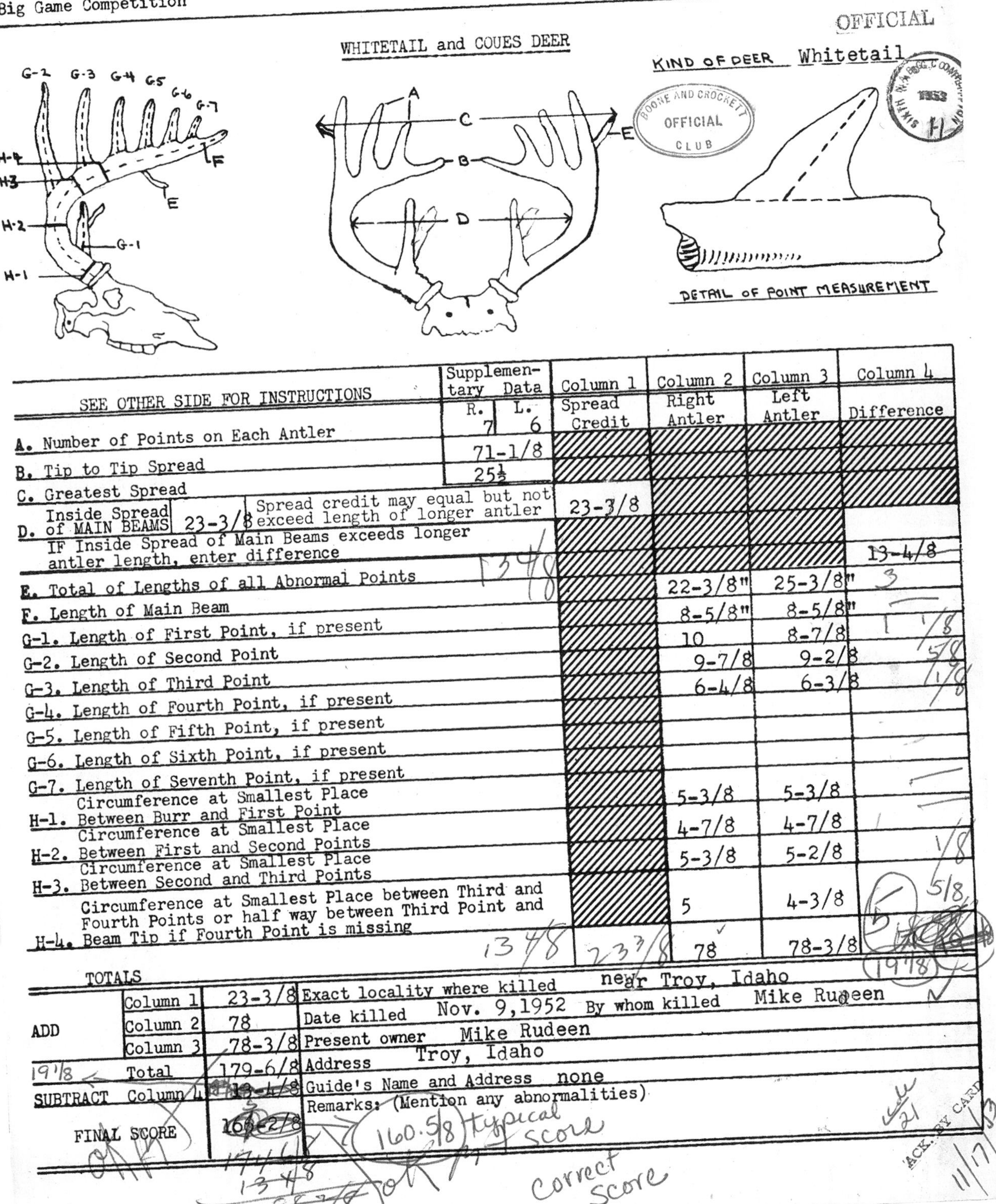

OFFICIAL SCORING SYSTEM FOR NORTH AMERICAN BIG GAME TROPHIES

Records of North American Big Game and North American Big Game Competition

BOONE AND CROCKETT CLUB

Address Correspondence to: Mrs. Grancel Fitz, Secretary 5 Tudor City Place, N.Y.17, N.Y.

OFFICIAL

WHITETAIL and COUES DEER

KIND OF DEER Whitetail

SEE OTHER SIDE FOR INSTRUCTIONS	Supplementary Data R.	Supplementary Data L.	Column 1 Spread Credit	Column 2 Right Antler	Column 3 Left Antler	Column 4 Difference
A. Number of Points on Each Antler	7	6				
B. Tip to Tip Spread	71-1/8					
C. Greatest Spread	25½					
D. Inside Spread of MAIN BEAMS 23-3/8 — Spread credit may equal but not exceed length of longer antler			23-3/8			
IF Inside Spread of Main Beams exceeds longer antler length, enter difference						13-4/8
E. Total of Lengths of all Abnormal Points				22-3/8"	25-3/8"	3
F. Length of Main Beam				8-5/8"	8-5/8"	
G-1. Length of First Point, if present				10	8-7/8	1 1/8
G-2. Length of Second Point				9-7/8	9-2/8	5/8
G-3. Length of Third Point				6-4/8	6-3/8	1/8
G-4. Length of Fourth Point, if present						
G-5. Length of Fifth Point, if present						
G-6. Length of Sixth Point, if present						
G-7. Length of Seventh Point, if present						
H-1. Circumference at Smallest Place Between Burr and First Point				5-3/8	5-3/8	
H-2. Circumference at Smallest Place Between First and Second Points				4-7/8	4-7/8	
H-3. Circumference at Smallest Place Between Second and Third Points				5-3/8	5-2/8	1/8
H-4. Circumference at Smallest Place between Third and Fourth Points or half way between Third Point and Beam Tip if Fourth Point is missing				5	4-3/8	5/8
TOTALS			23 3/8	78	78-3/8	19 1/8

ADD	Column 1	23-3/8	Exact locality where killed near Troy, Idaho
	Column 2	78	Date killed Nov. 9,1952 By whom killed Mike Rudeen
	Column 3	78-3/8	Present owner Mike Rudeen
19 1/8	Total	179-6/8	Address Troy, Idaho
SUBTRACT	Column 4	13-4/8	Guide's Name and Address none
FINAL SCORE		166-2/8	Remarks: (Mention any abnormalities)

160 5/8 typical score

Correct Score

ACK. BY CARD

April 26, 1954

Dear Jack:

In re your note on the Rudeen whitetail, let's first have a look at how the Scoring System works. The question of whether a head is typical or non-typical is solved quite automatically, without the need of any personal judgment. The scores for questionable specimens are easily computed for both classes, and the head is then ranked in the class in which it rates the higher place.

The Rudeen trophy shows a non-typical score of 174 6/8:13 4/8= 188 2/8, and this, of course, is good but by no means startling. On the other hand, if it were scored as a typical head, the 13 4/8 which is the total of the abnormal point lengths would be deducted from the 174 6/8, leaving a net score of 161 2/8. There were 22 typical heads with higher scores entered in the Competition, which was won by a new world record scoring 183 7/8, although several heads we asked for were not sent in to the show. In the non-typical class, the lowest score of the five exhibited was 15 points ahead of the Rudeen trophy.

While the Rudeen buck is unquestionably large for an Idaho specimen, it hardly stacks up with the really big ones. For instance, it has beam lengths of 22 3/8 and 25 3/8. Compare this with the 29 5/8 and 31 1/8 beams of the Pennsylvania buck which won only 4th prize in the non-typical class. Actually, these two trophies are alike in that they are too freakish to get far in the typical class -- which emphasizes normal conformation -- and they are not nearly freakish enough to stack up with the real non-typicals such as this year's winner, which shows 28 antler points and a score of 178 2/8: 59 1/8 = 237 3/8. I hope that this will clarify the picture for your friend.

All best wishes, and congratulations on your fine African trophies.

Yours sincerely,

Grancel Fitz

GF:H

Mr. Jack O'Connor
Box 382
Lewiston, Idaho

OFFICIAL SCORING SYSTEM FOR NORTH AMERICAN BIG GAME TROPHIES

Records of North American
Big Game Committee

BOONE AND CROCKETT CLUB

Address Correspondence to:
Mrs. Grancel Fitz, Secretary
5 Tudor City Place, NYC 17, NY.

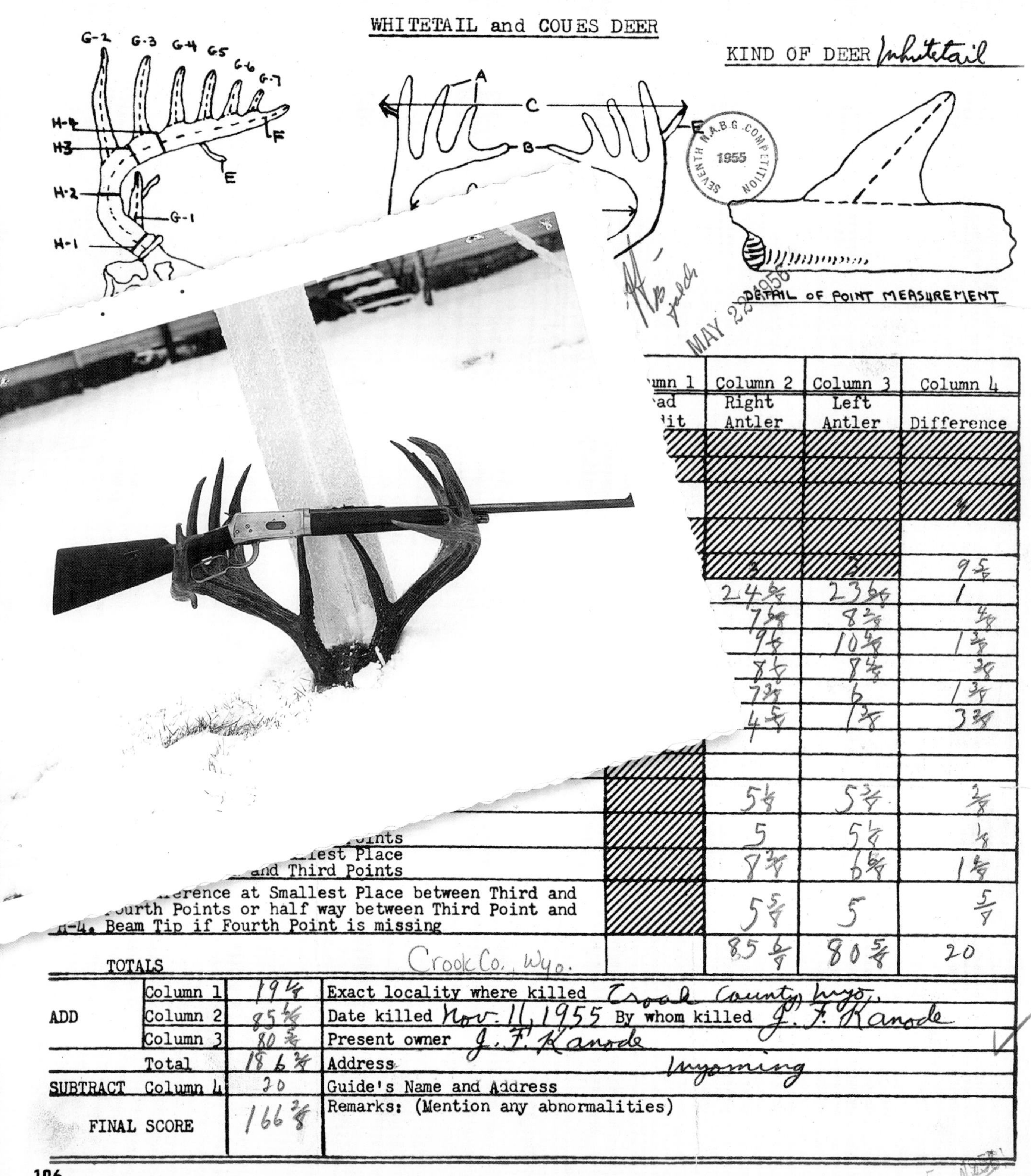

WHITETAIL and COUES DEER

KIND OF DEER Whitetail

	Column 1 Spread Credit	Column 2 Right Antler	Column 3 Left Antler	Column 4 Difference
				4
		2	2	9 5/8
		24 6/8	23 6/8	1
		7 6/8	8 2/8	4/8
		9 1/8	10 4/8	1 3/8
		8 1/8	8 4/8	3/8
		7 3/8	6	1 3/8
		4 5/8	1 3/8	3 3/8
		5 1/8	5 3/8	2/8
...oints		5	5 1/8	1/8
...llest Place ... and Third Points		8 3/8	6 5/8	1 6/8
H-4. Circumference at Smallest Place between Third and Fourth Points or half way between Third Point and Beam Tip if Fourth Point is missing		5 5/8	5	5/8
TOTALS	Crook Co., Wyo.	85 6/8	80 5/8	20

ADD	Column 1	19 7/8	Exact locality where killed Crook County, Wyo.
	Column 2	85 6/8	Date killed Nov. 11, 1955 By whom killed J. F. Kanode
	Column 3	80 5/8	Present owner J. F. Kanode
	Total	186 2/8	Address Wyoming
SUBTRACT	Column 4	20	Guide's Name and Address
FINAL SCORE		166 2/8	Remarks: (Mention any abnormalities)

4: CORRESPONDENCE FROM THE VAULTS

J.F. KANODE – DEER AND RIFLE

Sundance, Wyoming
November 14, 1955

Mrs. Grancel Fitz
5 Tudor City Place, New York 17, N.Y.

Dear Mrs. Fitz:

On November 11th I took a whitetail deer the antlers of which I would like to enter in the Big Game Competition. I would like to know when the best time to send it would be. Also I am not having the head mounted but plan to put the antlers on a board for hanging on a wall. Would it be best to put them on this board before or after sending to you? Would also appreciate any other pertinent information you can give me.

Sincerely
J. F. Kanode

BH 74

Gun and antler enthusiasts could argue over which object in this photo deserves more attention. The antlers were from a deer taken by J.F. Kanode in Crook County, Wyoming, in 1955. The rifle he used to bag the buck is a Winchester Model 1894 takedown, and most likely a .30-30.

OFFICIAL SCORING SYSTEM FOR NORTH AMERICAN BIG GAME TROPHIES

Records of North American Big Game and North American Big Game Competition

BOONE AND CROCKETT CLUB

% Am. Museum of Natural History
Central Park West at 79th Street
New York 24, New York

SEVENTH N.A.B.G. COMPETITION 1955

KIND OF DEER *Whitetail*

DETAIL OF POINT MEASUREMENT

	Column 1	Column 2 Right Antler	Column 3 Left Antler	Column 4 Difference
		//////	//////	//////
		//////	//////	//////
		//////	//////	//////
		//////	//////	—
		//////	//////	1 1/8
		26 [illegible]/8	27 1/8	~~4/8~~ 2/8
	//////	5 3/8	4 7/8	4/8
[...] of Second Point	//////	7 2/8	5 3/8	1 7/8
G-3. Length of Third Point	//////	8 4/8	7 3/8	1 1/8
G-4. Length of Fourth Point, if present	//////	6 7/8	5 7/8	1 0
G-5. Length of Fifth Point, if present	//////	–	–	–
G-6. Length of Sixth Point, if present	//////	–	–	–
G-7. Length of Seventh Point, if present	//////	–	–	–
H-1. Circumference at Smallest Place Between Burr and First Point	//////	5 4/8	5 7/8	3/8
H-2. Circumference at Smallest Place Between First and Second Points	//////	5.0	5.0	0
H-3. Circumference at Smallest Place Between Second and Third Points	//////	4 6/8	4. 6/8	0
H-4. Circumference at Smallest Place between Third and Fourth Points or half way between Third Point and Beam Tip if Fourth Point is missing	//////	4 6/8	4 4/8	2/8
TOTALS	23 4/8	74 7/8	70 6/8	6 4/8

ADD	Column 1	23 4/8	Exact locality where killed (Saddle Hill) MELROSE, Guys, Co. N. S.
	Column 2	74 7/8	Date killed 1917, By whom killed C. W. McKeen
	Column 3	70 6/8	Present owner C.W.McKeen,
	Total	169 1/8	Address Kapuskasing, Ont. Canada.
SUBTRACT	Column 4	6 4/8	Guide's Name and Address C. W. McKeen.
	FINAL SCORE	162 3/8	Remarks: (Mention any abnormalities) *Scar on inside of right beam at the base of the 3rd point. Abnormal point projects dorsally from burr of left antler. Otherwise remarkably symmetrical.*

4: CORRESPONDENCE FROM THE VAULTS

CLARENCE W. MCKEEN

To whom it may concern.

The following items are in connection with a very large red deer killed by this writer during the first open hunting season for deer in the Province of Nova Scotia, Canada,during the year of 1917, The history of red deer in that Province is understood to have began in 1888 when a sportsman of that time liberated three deer at one trip and fouror five were liberated from a ship a second trip. Prior to that time red deer were unknown to exist in that Province. Today and this since a few years,Nova Scotia has got to be reputed by many as being the worlds greatest deer hunting, it has not been determined why they have thrived so well there, is it the favourable climate or,on account of there being no wolves known in the Province, It is admitted wild cats (bob cat) are an enemy but their kills are only noticed during heavy deep snows, undoubtly cats would not be the equal of wolves.

Immediately following the liberation of those few deer in Nova Scotia, the Game and Fisheries Department enacted what was known as the heaviest fine ever levied for molesting or the killing of a deer which was $300.00. The day following when they were liberated,one of these well marked and taged deer was shot by a sea Captain from the deck of his ship while it was swimming across Isaacs Harbour and he paid the first and only fine known for many years after. The next one of these liberated deer to be accounted for was found by moose hunters near Goldenville badly decomposed but the markings and silver ear tag were observed, the later removed as a souvenir. The third of these liberated deer to be accounted for and which this inclosed has reference to, was killed by this writer during the first open season 1917 at Saddle Hill which is about two miles from Melrose in Guysboro County. It is noted here that all three of these liberated deer were accounted for in Guysboro County which indicate that red deer probably spend their entire lives near the same locality. Another point comes to notice and is proven in regard to this third deer, this buck deer was at least 29 years old from the date when liberated, now he could and must at least somewhat a few years older before being captured. How old do deer usually get or has anything been established about them.

The weight of this deer was 272 lbs. head, hide and legs were detached before being weighed, Thersworn testimony papers signed by a few of the witnesses cover this adequately,including the observations of the ear markings when same was liberated during 1888 or 29 years previous.

Box # 127
Kapuskasing Ont.

June 4 1954

American Museum of Natural History
Miss Grancel Fitz. Secretary,
5 Tudor City Place,
NEW YORK
N. Y. U. S. A.

Dear Miss Fitz:

It will be sometime after July 1st before before both red deer and moose measurements charts wil be along on the way to you for your findings.

Already I have the moose chart and picture of same back from Neenah Wisconsin completed, while this moose is well up amongst the large ones already known on account of known actual weight (sworn testimony) by a group of non-intereated persons who had actually done the scales weighing job,has been in the possession of Mr. Randolph Peterson, at the Toronto Museum since the year I had got this moose in 1947, its suggested your findings will place this trophy well up, while it may not quite make a record, a lot is expected about the red deer trophy.

As per your Club instructions, I took the red deer antlers to the Chief Game Warden of this District, Mr. Lewis, let him examine the deer chart and read over the Club regulations and instructions which you forwarded me, and Mr. Lewis after reading up and examining the antlers suggested, This antlers looks so much like the possibilities of an all time record large red deer, you might as well send all this to Mr. Randolph Peterson, Toronto, Ontario right now, as he is the proper authority and will be the final its clear to him enough. I wrote Mr. Peterson and have his reply as follows.-

Dear Mr. McKeen;

I will be away from the office until after July Ist, I suggest you ship the specimen about then. I will be most interested in having all the information you have available, especially where and when collected and so on. I will be pleased to measure this specimen on your behalf of the Boone and Crockett Club.

Along about Aug. 1st, its hoped to have all this information in your possession. Again thanking you. I remain.

Yours very Truly,
C W McKeen
Clarence W. McKeen

TO WHOM IT MAY CONCERN.

This is to certify that, in the case of any person or persons, Whom, may now or any time in the future, become interested, in any of the claims or statements made below relating to a distinctively marked and taged red deer libereted during 1888, which was shot at Saddle Hill between Melrose and Country Harbour, during the first deer hunting season of 1917 by, Clarence W. McKeen of, Aspen, Guysboro County, in the Province of Nova Scotia, are true and correct, and that we, in the case of our signatures were, eye witnesses of this well marked and tagged trophy.

This mentioned large red deer had very distinct markings on both its ears consisting of, four clean made knife slits, one slit on the top side of each ear, and one slit on the bottem side of each ear, each of these four slits were about two inches long, in addition, the right ear had a three quarter inch punch hole about two inches from its bottom side, in which was inserted a silver band which was worn to a feather thin from the years same was being carried, while skinning the head out after arriving home, a 22 caliber mushroomed bullet surrounded by heavy gristle was imbedded above the left eye apparently lodged there some years previous.

This mentioned red deer was properly skinned from both knees and both hock joints to the neck behind the head and all was severed from the body, hide, head and legs.

This mentioned red deer was weighed on accurate scales, and found to weigh two days after the kill, to weigh exactly two hundred and seventy two pounds of properly dressed venison, with no hide, head, leg or anything other being attached.

We the undersigned here below place our hands, our signatures and testify, that the above statements ar true and correct.

Sworn before me,

Witnesses.

[signature] ... Justice of the Pease

Marshall McKeen

John W. McKeen

At Aspen, Municapility of St Marys.
In the Province of Nova Scotia.
This day of 17 Day of June 1954.

ROYAL ONTARIO MUSEUM OF ZOOLOGY AND PALAEONTOLOGY
100 QUEEN'S PARK TORONTO 5, CANADA
TELEPHONE WAlnut 3-6641

June 25th, 1954

Boone and Crockett Club,
c/o American Museum of Natural History,
Central Park West at 79th Street,
New York City 24.

Dear Sirs:

Mr. Clarence W. McKeen, of Kapuskasing, Ontario, has forwarded to me a specimen of white-tailed deer taken in 1917 in Guys County, Nova Scotia, which he has asked me to measure for official entry in the competition and records of the Boone and Crockett Club. This specimen has a fine set of antlers which proves, according to its score (162 3/8) to be worthy of listing among the record heads. I enclose the score sheet for this specimen.

Yours very truly,

R. L. Peterson

R. L. Peterson, Curator,
Division of Mammalogy.

RLP:E

encl.

July 2, 1954

Dr. R. L. Peterson
Division of Mammalogy
Royal Ontario Museum of Zoology and Palaentology
100 Queen's Park
Toronto 5, Canada

Dear Dr. Peterson:

Thank you very much for sending in the chart of Mr. McKeen's whitetail deer. Thanks also for the data, which is very interesting.

For future correspondence in re records, our address is 5 Tudor City Place, New York 17, N. Y. However, any mail sent to the Museum will be forwarded to us.

We enclose a copy of a form latter we have sent out and there is a possibility that a couple of hunters may get in touch with you.

Your interest in the work we are doing is greatly appreciated.

Yours sincerely,

Samuel B. Webb

SBW:h

Encl.

OFFICIAL SCORING SYSTEM FOR NORTH AMERICAN BIG GAME TROPHIES Cert. only ✓

Records of North American
Big Game Committee

BOONE AND CROCKETT CLUB

Address correspondence to:
Mrs. Grancel Fitz, Secretary
5 Tudor City Place
New York 17, N. Y.

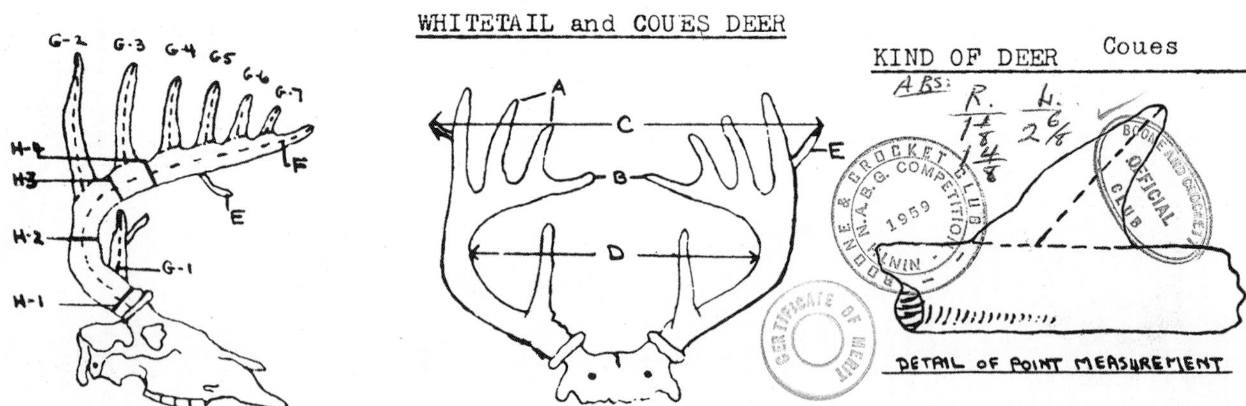

SEE OTHER SIDE FOR INSTRUCTIONS	Supplementary Data R.	Supplementary Data L.	Column 1 Spread Credit	Column 2 Right Antler	Column 3 Left Antler	Column 4 Difference
A. Number of Points on Each Antler	7	5				
B. Tip to Tip Spread	19 3/8					
C. Greatest Spread	25 2/8					
D. Inside Spread of MAIN BEAMS 23 6/8 — Spread credit may equal but not exceed length of longer antler			23 6/8			
IF Inside Spread of Main Beams exceeds longer antler length, enter difference						
E. Total of Lengths of all Abnormal Points						5 3/8
F. Length of Main Beam				23 2/8	24.0	6/8
G-1. Length of First Point, if present				1 6/8	2 3/8	5/8
G-2. Length of Second Point				7 6/8	11 1/8	3 3/8
G-3. Length of Third Point				10 —	9 5/8	3/8
G-4. Length of Fourth Point, if present				5 6/8	—	5 6/8
G-5. Length of Fifth Point, if present						
G-6. Length of Sixth Point, if present						
G-7. Length of Seventh Point, if present						
H-1. Circumference at Smallest Place Between Burr and First Point				4 4/8	4 3/8	1/8
H-2. Circumference at Smallest Place Between First and Second Points				4 —	4 —	0
H-3. Circumference at Smallest Place Between Second and Third Points				4 3/8	4 4/8	1/8
H-4. Circumference at Smallest Place between Third and Fourth Points or half way between Third Point and Beam Tip if Fourth Point is missing				3 6/8	2 3/8	1 3/8
TOTALS			23.6	65 1/8	63 3/8	17 7/8

ADD	Column 1	23 6/8	Exact locality where killed	Burro Creek, Ariz.
	Column 2	65 1/8	Date killed 11-2-50	By whom killed Noel Scott
	Column 3	63 3/8	Present owner ~~Buckeye, Ariz.~~	SAME
	Total	152 2/8	Address	~~Buckeye, Ariz.~~
SUBTRACT	Column 4	17 7/8	Guide's Name and Address	none
FINAL SCORE		134 3/8	Remarks: (Mention any abnormalities) 3 Abnormal points	

OK

4: CORRESPONDENCE FROM THE VAULTS

NOEL SCOTT COUES' DEER OR MULE DEER?

This and the following eight pages tell the story of a questionable Coues' deer. At one point, it was ranked as #2 in the World, until it was pointed out by a few concerned individuals. The ensuing reevaluation proved both interesting and convoluted.

BOONE AND CROCKETT CLUB

RECORDS OF NORTH AMERICAN BIG GAME COMMITTEE

ROBERT S. WATERS, CHAIRMAN
218 FRANKLIN STREET
JOHNSTOWN, PA.

MILFORD BAKER
285 MADISON AVENUE
NEW YORK 17, N. Y.

DUNCAN M. HODGSON
523 ARGYLE AVE.
WESTMOUNT 6, P. Q., CAN.

DONALD S. HOPKINS
1201 OLD NATL. BANK BLDG.
SPOKANE 1, WASH.

LAWRENCE C. WOODS, JR.
ONE GATEWAY CENTER
PITTSBURGH, PA.

Mr. Noel Scott
Box 380
Buckeye, Ariz.

Dear Sir:

It appears from our records that the fine Coues Deer you entered in the North American Big Game Competition is one of the top trophies in its class. For this reason it is necessary to have the Board of Judges inspect it, measure it officially, and compare it with the other entries in the Competition.

We, therefore, will greatly appreciate it if you will send your trophy to:

Mr. Edward McGuire
American Museum of Natural History
Central Park West at 79th Street
New York 24, N. Y.

The Committee requires that heads and horns sent to the Museum be clearly marked with the owner's name and complete address - and that the owner pay all insurance and shipping charges.

The trophy will be hung in a temporary exhibit at the American Museum of Natural History, which should be open shortly after the trophies have been judged. Trophies, meriting medal awards, will only receive medals if they are sent to the Competition in response to this request.

The trophies will be given careful handling by the Committee, and every precaution will be exercised against possible damage, but neither the Boone and Crockett Club nor the Committee can accept any responsibility for trophies either in transit or while in their possession. The return of the entries will be at the owner's expense for transportation and insurance.

A self-addressed postcard is enclosed and we will appreciate it if you will please fill in the data requested and place it in the mail immediately. The deadline date for delivery of trophies to the Museum is February 3rd.

We congratulate you upon obtaining a fine trophy, and thank you for your cooperation in connection with these North American Big Game Competitions.

Sincerely yours,

Robert S. Waters

Chairman

RSW:BF

SAMUEL P. GODDARD JR.
Governor

Commissioners

RALPH MORROW, *PORTAL, CHAIRMAN*
ROBERT J. SPILLMAN, *PHOENIX*
MARTIN JOHNSON, *KINGMAN*
MILTON G. EVANS, *FLAGSTAFF*
O. M. SIZER, *CLIFTON*

ARIZONA GAME & FISH DEPARTMENT

2211 West Greenway Rd. *Phoenix, Arizona 85023* *942-3000*

WENDELL G. SWANK *Director* PHIL M. COSPER *Assistant Director*

May 13, 1966

Mrs. Grancel Fitz, Secretary
Boone and Crockett Club
5 Tudor City Place
New York 17, N. Y.

Dear Mrs. Fitz:

Several days ago I had an opportunity to examine the 1964 edition of Records of North American Big Game. When I turned to the section on Coue's deer, a species of much interest to me, the photo of the No. 2 head drew me up short. As I stared at it, marveling at such an unusual rack on a Coue's deer, it suddenly hit me -- this was not a Coue's deer.

Frankly, the idea was rather disturbing. I read through the front part of the book seeking a possible explanation. I also checked a copy of the 1958 edition and found this head was not listed then even though the animal was apparently shot in 1950. I found no mention of how this most unusual head suddenly was given the No. 2 spot.

On page 41 I learned that top heads must be sent to a Judge's Committee for final scoring so clearly the inclusion of this animal was not solely the result of an error in identification on the part of one of the local sources.

Now for my reasons for concluding that this is not a Coue's deer: This rack has all of the characteristics of a mule deer or Columbian blacktail and none of the features of a Coue's whitetail. No other rack listed has a spread of as much as 18 inches, this one is one-eighth short of 24 inches. On both antlers it has forked antlers typical of mule deer instead of having the points coming off one main beam. Diameter is not commensurate with spread or other measurements. It lacks the tight inward curl typical of whitetail. Eye guards (brow tines) are too small for a whitetail although large ones are not found on all whitetails. The tips of the main beams turn upward as typical of mule deer; they usually don't on whitetails. Several of the points have a slight zig-zag appearance, also fairly characteristic of mule deer and seldom seen on whitetail.

Any one or even two of the above could perhaps be disregarded since all characteristics are not usually found on an animal. Taken all together, however, they constitute what I would consider irrefutable evidence that this

Mrs. Grancel Fitz, Secretary May 13, 1966

is a rack from some race of O. hemionus not of O. virginianus couesi. And if further evidence is needed the locality Burro Creek, from which the deer is reported to have come, is some distance removed from the nearest whitetail habitat.

The only feature about this head which does appear to be characteristically whitetail is the cape. This, of course, need not have come off the same animal that sported the antlers.

As a check against my judgment I have shown the photo to others in the Arizona Game Department who are familiar with both species. Without exception they agreed with me. In fact, when I covered the caption and head and asked some to identify the species of deer illustrated by the rack, the answer was unfailingly "mule deer".

I personally have hunted and taken 6-8 heads of both mule deer and whitetails over the past 20 years. I have collected probably 50 others of both species in connection with my work. In addition I have had the opportunity to examine and measure hundreds of both species at checking stations on various study areas. There is absolutely no doubt in my mind that this is not a whitetail.

If in spite of the above the Judge's Committee is convinced this is in fact the animal it is purported to be I would be most interested in learning what criteria were used in making the determination of species.

Sincerely,

Steve Gallizioli

Steve Gallizioli, Chief
Research Division

SG:rb

RECD JUN 13 1966

RECD JAN 20 1967

JAN. 16, 1966.
Box 121
Sonoita, Ariz.

Xerox CC to McGuire — orig sent Rusten 1/24/67 — ET

Dr. Elmer M. Rusten
4400 Forbes Ave.
Pittsburg, Penn.

Dear Dr. Rustin,

I am sorry that you had to send this back to me. I guess that I did not make it clear that this deer was an Arizona White-Tail or Coues Deer. I must further add that the hunter who killed the deer was not available to sign the statement on the bottom of the back side of the form. I was asked to send this entry in because it is a new classification for the coues deer and your representative in Tucson (John Doyle) asked if I knew of any non typical Coues Deer in my area. I am with the Arizona Game and Fish Dept and hope that this letter will help in putting this trophy in the record book.

While I am writing you I would like to say that I have serious doubts about the number 2 Coues deer you have pictured in your new addition.

I have Lived in Arizona all my Life, and have hunted for the past 20 years. Mostly for the Coues Deer. Since I have been with the Game & Fish Dept I have worked in one of the Prime Coues Deer Areas. The Santa Rita Mts, Canelo Hills & the Huachuca Mts. These areas have produced many fine Coues Deer Records including the Number One Taken by Stockwell. I have never seen a Coues Deer which would even come close to a 23 inch spread. The Largest I have seen has been about 18 inches. The Location of where this Number Two was taken is not Coues Deer Country. This Deer appears to be a Typical below average Desert Mule Deer. Several people have mentioned this to me and they also are in doubt about it being a Coues Deer. I believe it should be looked into.

If you ever get a chance to come to Arizona to hunt the Coues Deer look me up I may be able to point you in the right direction.

Best Regards -

John N Carr

JOHN N. CARR
WILDLIFE MANAGER

OFFICE MA 4-4951

A June 10, 1966, letter from Elmer M. Rustsen, M.D., the chairman of the Records Committee at that time, states:

"...Enclosed is a letter from Mr. Steve Gallizioli, Research Division for the Arizona Fish Department. He feels that the #2 Deer is not a Coues Deer. I remember we had some correspondence about this. This of course was prior to your time but you could contact Edd McGuire and see whether he has any information or recalls the incidents leading up to such a decision."

Edd. McGuire responded to Rusten's letter on January 31, 1967. This letter is reproduced in its entirety on the facing page.

On October 30th of that year Chairman Rusten sent a letter to the trophy owner, Mr. Noel Scott requesting that he ship his Coues' deer to the Boone and Crockett Club, in care of the Carnegie Museum. There a Panel of Judges would review the trophy. Rusten went on to inform Scott that the Club would pay for the shipping expense.

Below is Scott's response to the inquiry by Chairman Rusten to send in the Coues' deer trophy to the Panel of Judges.

File ✓ at Pgh - in file.

November 19, 1967

Dear Mr. Rusten:

The coues deer head scoring 133-3/8 along with several other of my trophies were destroyed by fire when the O.S. Stopley Hardware & Sporting Good store here in Buckeye burned to the ground in 1965.

If I can be of any further help to you please let me know.

Noel Scott
212 3rd Avenue
Buckeye, Arizona

BOONE AND CROCKETT CLUB

RECORDS OF NORTH AMERICAN BIG GAME COMMITTEE
OFFICE OF SECRETARY
C/O CARNEGIE MUSEUM
4400 FORBES AVE.
PITTSBURGH, PA. 15213

Scott, Coues Deer

1November 22, 1967

Dear Dr. Rusten:

I am enclosing a letter to Steve Gallizioli for your approval - perhaps it would be better to have one of our measurers verify this information from Noel Scott about the fire at the O.S.Stopley Hardware and Sporting Goods Store completely burning up.

It could be that you do not want any more information - it appears Mr. Scott is not trying to get out of anything - his letter seems very sincere, but you most certainly would be able to judge that better than I - so many crazy things have been attempted - and I guess I always more or less take it for granted all people are honest.

Happy Thanksgiving!

Emily T.

Immediately after receiving the news of the fire from Scott, Chairman Rusten sent a letter to Steve Gallizioli asking him to verify that the O.S. Stopley Hardware and Sporting Goods store did indeed burn to the ground. At left is a note from Rusten's secretary regarding this letter. An undated handwritten note in the file states:

"Delete – Mule deer rather than Coues. Trophy gone, burned in fire – cannot be judged as requested for verification and reevaluation."

But, the saga of the Scott buck didn't end there...

January 31, 1967

Scott -
Coues Deer -
1959 -

Elmer M. Rusten, M.D.,
18420 D Eighth Avenue North
Wayzata, Minnesota 55391

Dear Dr. Rusten:

In answer to Steve Gallizioli's letter of May 13, 1966, I do not remember any discussion as to the credibility of this trophy not being a Coues deer at the 1958-59 judging. As you can see, it was measured originally by Jonas Brothers in Seattle, Washington, and remeasured by Don Hopkins and the late Grancel Fitz.

After doing a thorough research job on the geographical distribution of the Coues deer, it seems to me we are in error. I also went over this situation with Dr. Doutt and he is of the same opinion because Burro Creek seems to be too far west of the marginal range for this species.

Upon looking the photograph over carefully, we were both inclined to believe that the formation of the antlers is more characteristic of the mule deer. What can be done about the situation at this late date is a bit difficult. The only thought I can offer, for what it is worth, is to have the specimen checked by the Committee and whatever decision they reach pass on to the owner so the photograph and listing could be deleted from the next printing.

I trust you are back in the groove and feeling better after your trip.

Best regards,

Edd. McGuire

et

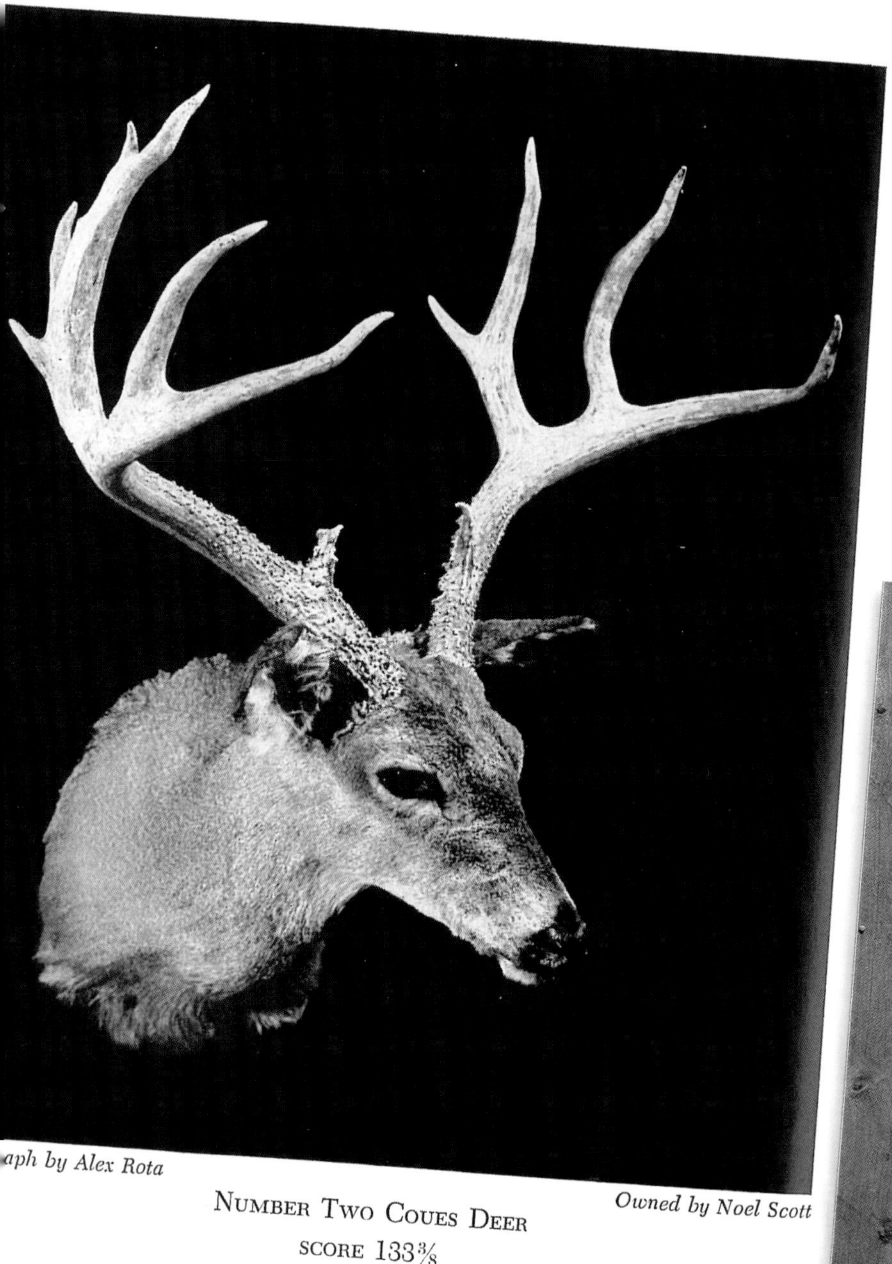

aph by Alex Rota

Owned by Noel Scott

NUMBER TWO COUES DEER

SCORE 133⅜

Montana Department of Fish, Wildlife & Parks

8695 Huffine Lane
Bozeman, MT 59715

July 11, 1986

RECEIVED
JUL 15 1986
BOONE & CROCKETT CLUB

Mr. William H. Nesbitt
Boone & Crockett Club
205 South Patrick St.
Alexandria, VA 22314

Dear Mr. Nesbitt:

Enclosed is a picture of a buck deer that I personally took at the Altimus Taxidermy Shop in Ennis, MT. This deer is the one which you and I had a phone conversation about in mid-May.

I took the picture at pretty much the same angle that shows up in the record book as a Coues Deer. I hope this picture helps you out and consider it yours for your necessary record keeping.

I have misplaced the name of the biologist in Arizona that you said determined this buck to be a Mule Deer. Could you possibly send me his name?

If I can be of any further assistance in this matter, please contact me.

Sincerely,

Fred

Fred J. King
Wildlife Area Manager

FJK:jtb

Enc.

Reportedly burned up in a fire, the buck made an amazing "come back." Records Committee member Fred King took this photo (opposite page on right) in 1986, 21 years after it was reported destroyed. Believe it or not, this is just one of a few cases B&C has had that involved a trophy supposedly burned up in a fire that actually did not. Why this story was concocted may never be known. What we do know is that this trophy was correctly removed from the Coues' whitetail listings, helping to keep our historical records more correctly documented.

T
E
X
A
S
78 POINTS

4: SPECIAL TROPHY

LONE STAR BREWING "78-POINTER"

The non-typical pictured at left would ultimately prove to be a set of shed antlers off the buck pictured on page 128.

Jan. 11, 1955

Mrs. Norma Freidrich Ward
&
Mr. Milton A. Friedrich
Buckhorn Curio Store
400 W. Houston St.
San Antonio, Texas

Dear Mrs. Ward and Mr. Friedrich:

About ten days ago my husband, Grancel Fitz, and I had the pleasure of seeing your fine collection of trophies. We were sorry to have been there at a time when you were not in; however, Mr. Kent was most gracious to us and we had the pr ivilege of scoring two of your fine trophies.

We took the measurements on the large non-typical whitetail (referred to as the 78-point Texas deer) and also on the next largest non-typical whitetail. This trophy is the one above the bar register - left hand side as you face the trophies. I shall refer to these trophies as #1 and #2, and enclose two charts with the hope that you gan give us the data as to where killed, date, etc. I've marked this part of the chart with red. We can fill in the score from the measurements we took while there.

These two magnificent trophies should have been included in the past issues of the record book and it is our desire to secure the necessary information before the next record book is published. A circular of the last edition is enclosed. A self-addressed envelope is enclosed for your use in returning to me the two chart, and your kind assistance will be most appreciated.

Yours sincerely,

bsf

(Mrs. Grancel Fitz)
Secretary to the
Records Committee

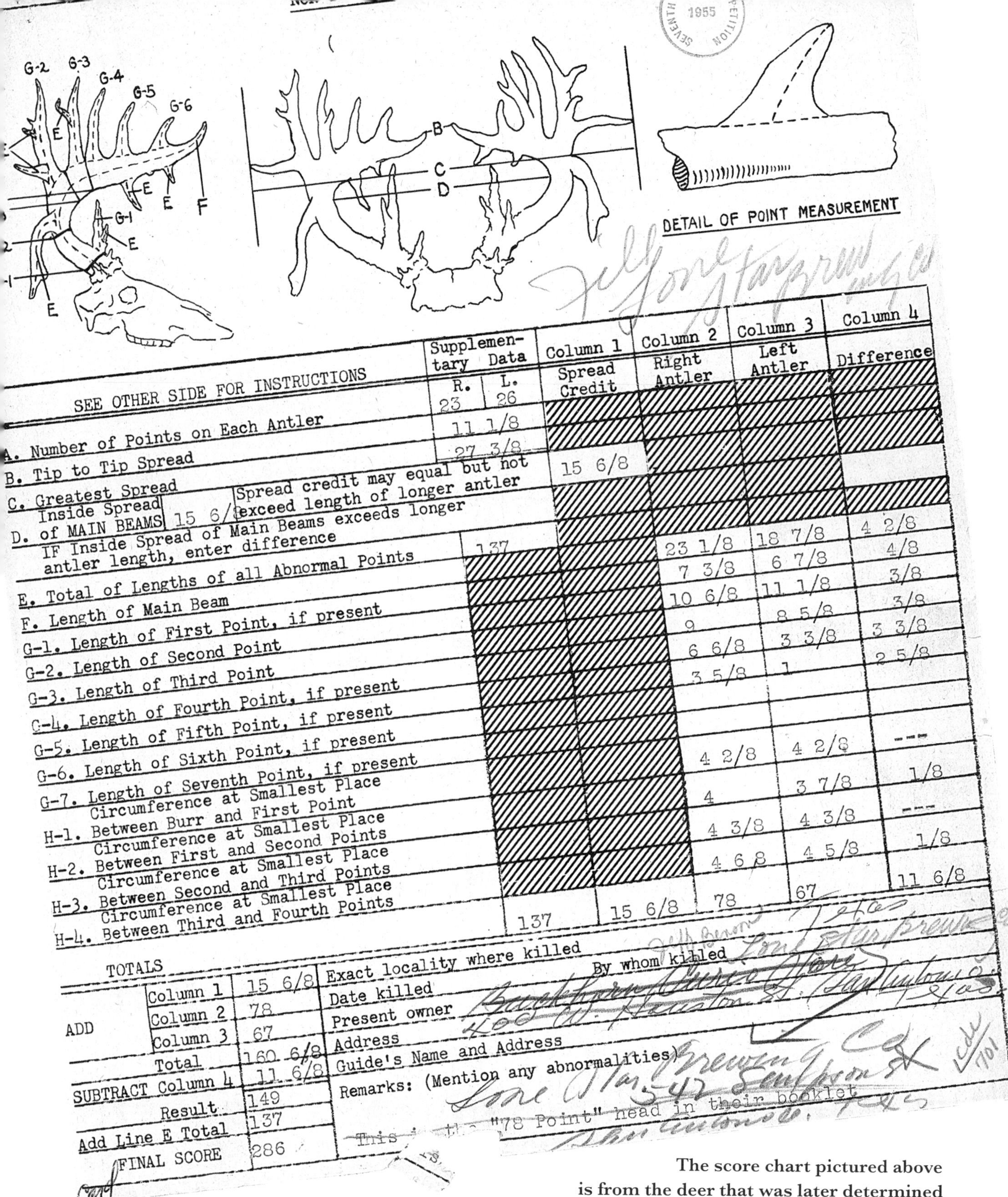

SEE OTHER SIDE FOR INSTRUCTIONS	Supplementary Data R.	Supplementary Data L.	Column 1 Spread Credit	Column 2 Right Antler	Column 3 Left Antler	Column 4 Difference
A. Number of Points on Each Antler	23	26				
B. Tip to Tip Spread	11 1/8					
C. Greatest Spread	27 3/8					
D. Inside Spread of MAIN BEAMS 15 6/8 — Spread credit may equal but not exceed length of longer antler			15 6/8			
IF Inside Spread of Main Beams exceeds longer antler length, enter difference						
E. Total of Lengths of all Abnormal Points	137					
F. Length of Main Beam				23 1/8	18 7/8	4 2/8
G-1. Length of First Point, if present				7 3/8	6 7/8	4/8
G-2. Length of Second Point				10 6/8	11 1/8	3/8
G-3. Length of Third Point				9	8 5/8	3/8
G-4. Length of Fourth Point, if present				6 6/8	3 3/8	3 3/8
G-5. Length of Fifth Point, if present				3 5/8	1	2 5/8
G-6. Length of Sixth Point, if present						
G-7. Length of Seventh Point, if present						
H-1. Circumference at Smallest Place Between Burr and First Point				4 2/8	4 2/8	---
H-2. Circumference at Smallest Place Between First and Second Points				4	3 7/8	1/8
H-3. Circumference at Smallest Place Between Second and Third Points				4 3/8	4 3/8	---
H-4. Circumference at Smallest Place Between Third and Fourth Points				4 6 8	4 5/8	1/8
TOTALS	137		15 6/8	78	67	11 6/8

ADD	Column 1	15 6/8
	Column 2	78
	Column 3	67
	Total	160 6/8
SUBTRACT Column 4		11 6/8
	Result	149
Add Line E Total		137
FINAL SCORE		286

Exact locality where killed

By whom killed

Date killed

Present owner Lone Star Brewing Co

Address

Guide's Name and Address

Remarks: (Mention any abnormalities)

~~This is the "78 Point" head in their booklet~~

The score chart pictured above is from the deer that was later determined to be shed antlers – from page 124.

LONE STAR BREWING COMPANY
★ 542 SIMPSON STREET . . . P.O. BOX 2060
TELEPHONE CAPITOL 6-8301

San Antonio 6 · TEXAS

March 4, 1958

Mrs. Grancel Fitz, Secretary
5 Tudor City Place
New York 17, N.Y.

Dear Mrs. Fitz:

In a post card to Mr. Auld in Kerrville, Texas you asked for information regarding some of our white-tail deer.

As you may have heard, we purchased this entire Buckhorn Collection, and have built a new: BUCKHORN HALL OF HORNS on our property. It is a beautiful new building, built especially for this world famous collection. As yet, we have not had time to fully record, and make measurements of all horns.

We do send you two pictures of white-tail deer, killed in Texas, which we believe to be near records, if not world records, at least from the standpoint of number of points.

The one has 78 points, and the other 72. We have many, many horns with unusualy large spreads, both in white tail and mule deer, but if your book goes to press on the 10th of this month, we are perhaps too late for this edition. Please keep me advised and I will supply the information requested.

You may rest assured we are greatly interested in your work, and in the work of the Boone and Crocket Club, and we want to cooperate to the fullest measure.

With kindest personal regards.

Sincerely yours,

Fritz A. Toepperwein

Fritz A. Toepperwein, Buckhorn Historian

OFFICIAL SCORING SYSTEM FOR NORTH AMERICAN BIG GAME TROPHIES

Records of North American
Big Game Committee

#2

BOONE AND CROCKETT CLUB

Address Correspondence to:
Mrs. Grancel Fitz, Secretary
5 Tudor City Place, NYC 17, NY.

NON-TYPICAL WHITETAIL DEER

7th Comp.

SEVENTH N.A.B.G. COMPETITION 1955

BOONE AND CROCKETT CLUB OFFICIAL

G-2 G-3 G-4 G-5 G-6 E E H-4 H-3 E E F H-2 G-1 E H-1 E B C D

DETAIL OF POINT MEASUREMENT

SEE OTHER SIDE FOR INSTRUCTIONS	Supplementary Data R.	Supplementary Data L.	Column 1 Spread Credit	Column 2 Right Antler	Column 3 Left Antler	Column 4 Difference
A. Number of Points on Each Antler	21	26				
B. Tip to Tip Spread	13 4/8					
C. Greatest Spread	26 2/8					
D. Inside Spread of MAIN BEAMS 16 2/8 — Spread credit may equal but not exceed length of longer antler. IF Inside Spread of Main Beams exceeds longer antler length, enter difference			16 2/8			
E. Total of Lengths of all Abnormal Points	134 3/8					
F. Length of Main Beam				21 4/8	19 6/8	1 6/8
G-1. Length of First Point, if present				8 2/8	8 4/8	2/8
G-2. Length of Second Point				10 6/8	9 3/8	1 3/8
G-3. Length of Third Point				8 7/8	6 7/8	2
G-4. Length of Fourth Point, if present				6 4/8	5 1/8	1 3/8
G-5. Length of Fifth Point, if present						
G-6. Length of Sixth Point, if present						
G-7. Length of Seventh Point, if present						
H-1. Circumference at Smallest Place Between Burr and First Point				4 4/8	4 4/8	--
H-2. Circumference at Smallest Place Between First and Second Points				4	4 1/8	1/8
H-3. Circumference at Smallest Place Between Second and Third Points				4 5/8	4 4/8	1/8
H-4. Circumference at Smallest Place Between Third and Fourth Points				4 4/8	5	4/8
TOTALS	134 3/8		16 2/8	73 4/8	67 6/8	7 4/8

ADD	Column 1	16 2/8
	Column 2	73 4/8
	Column 3	67 6/8
	Total	157 4/8
SUBTRACT	Column 4	7 4/8
	Result	150
	Add Line E Total	134 3/8
	FINAL SCORE	284 3/8

Exact locality where killed Texas
Date killed — By whom killed
Present owner Buckhorn Curio Store
Address 400 W. Houston St. San Antonio, Tex.
Guide's Name and Address
Remarks: (Mention any abnormalities)
Lone Star Brewing Co.

CONTROVERSY EMERGES

In October of 1977, Director of Big Game Records Jack Reneau put down in writing the summary of a telephone conversation he had with Mr. Robert Rogers, author of the book *Big Rack.*

RE: Trophy non-typical whitetail deer (284-3/8) owned by the Lonestar Brewing Company that appeared in the 1958 edition of the records book but not in the 1964 or 1971 editions.

As per a telephone conversation relative to the above, Mr. Robert Rogers stated that he understands the rack in question is a shed set of antlers of the non-typical whitetail deer (286) which is currently the World's Record. He further indicated that he believes the smaller antlers were found by Jeff Benson (the hunter that took the world's record), and that they were apparently shed the year before Mr. Benson took his trophy. Mr. Rogers believes that this explains the reason the non-typical whitetail deer scoring 284-3/8 was dropped from the records books published after 1958.

The newspaper clipping from 1959 shown here details the history about the two whitetails.

The story about these two incredible sets of antlers doesn't end here. Following is a three-page letter, dated 1996, from John Stein, a B&C Official Measurer.

The Houston Press THURSDAY, DEC. 10, 1959

TEXAS OUTDOORS

By ZANE CHASTAIN and KEITH OZMORE

Houstonian Disputes Story

How 'Record' Rack Was Found on River

By ZANE CHASTAIN
Press Outdoor Editor

Houston police lieutenant A. W. Rainey, who spent his boyhood days hunting big whitetail bucks near Jacksonville, revealed today that Texas can't possibly claim the second place standing it holds in the Boone and Crockett Club for whitetail deer with non-typical (freak) antlers.

"Simply because that deer was never killed," he said. "So how can they claim second place among world records?

"You see, the rack they measured is the same one now in the old Buckhorn Saloon collection which the Lone Star Brewery of San Antonio owns . . . and back in January of 1896, Mr. Marion Stewart and Will Miller, with whom my dad hunted, each found one side of those antlers laying in the woods just outside [illegible]

Press Staff Photo by Jim Cox
A. W. RAINEY — CHARLIE BENGE
Their fathers were on the record hunt.

Sold Them to Buckhorn

Those two men—who found one side in Cherokee County and the other across the Neches River in Anderson County—then sold the points to owners of the Buckhorn Saloon, in Palestine at that time.

"They, in turn, had the two sides mounted," the 68-year-old police officer continued, "and to this day, folks up there swear they came off the same buck claiming the world record that was killed in that locale."

Rainey, who inspected the Boone and Crockett record book, was surprised and disappointed that the publication didn't list where the record deer in that category was killed, nor by whom it was killed. He quickly cleared up that mystery.

Three Hunters Bagged Him

"Three hunters were responsible for that deer's death," he said, "Samuel Benge, Brice Burrett and James Arnwine. All three of them are dead now.

"They were chasing deer with dogs near the Dunica Bend area on the Cherokee County side of the Neches River when they jumped it. Mr. Burrett wounded it first with a shotgun, breaking the deer's leg. Then Mr. Benge hit it with an old Winchester .32, and the deer fell in Pails Creek. That's when Mr. Arwine finished off that buck."

This, he said, was in the fall of 1896, and after leaving the deer antlers at James Arnwine's home, Mr. Burrett learned he could sell the rack.

"Got $25 from the owners of the Buckhorn Saloon," Rainey recalled his father's recollection of the incident. "They kept it, along with the other rack, there in the saloon at Palestine."

The two racks stayed there in Palestine until the county became dry. Then the owners moved the saloon to San Antonio, taking the racks with them. That was the last Rainey had heard of them, except for the tales told time and time again by his father of the hunt that produced them.

Where in San Antonio, the racks gathered much notice from tourists.

Finally, when the Lone Star Brewery of San Antonio bought out the world-famous collection in 1956, officials of that firm had the racks measured for possible consideration as records. They weren't disappointed when the Boone and Crockett Club notified them they were the top two.

The racks had gone virtually unnoticed for 60 years.

Now, though, one must possibly drop from the ranks following the revelation of an innocent human error on everyone's part.

P.O. Box 460104
San Antonio, TX 78246-0104
(210) 377-3648
Fax (210) 377-3756

BOONE AND CROCKETT RECORDS COMMITTEE
Old Milwaukee Depot
250 Station Drive
Missoula, MT 59801

May 31, 1996

Dear Sirs:

I would like to bring a situation that I have discovered to your attention. A top ranking whitetail non-typical trophy listed in Boone and Crockett since the 1958 Records Book is actually a set of shed antlers. However, the true antlers of this very deer also exist and were once listed in the 1958 Record Book.

I will try to explain the chain of events as briefly as possible. Albert Friedrich started collecting antlers in 1881. In 1887 he opened his own establishment called the "Buckhorn Saloon." He continued his collecting efforts until the day he died Nov. 27, 1928. On January 3, 1955, Grancel Fitz had measured both of these whitetails at the old Buckhorn Saloon in San Antonio, Texas, my home town. His two final scores were 286 and 284 3/8 non-typical. This put these two trophies in the #1 and #2 spots in the 1958 Record Book. In 1956, the Lone Star Brewery bought the Albert Friedrich collection from his son and daughter and put it in storage. In August of 1957 the collection was moved to the brewery grounds and opened up as the "Buckhorn Hall of Horns."

In 1958 both trophies were sent for remounting. It was discovered that one of these was the sheds to the other. In the 1964 Records Book the lesser scoring trophy (284 3/8) was dropped. Only the 286 NT remained. At this time the 286 was changed from an unknown hunter and date in the 1958 book to Jeff Benson and 1892. Unfortunately, I understand the B&C records of these trophies from this era are no longer available. This world record non-typical held its title for 26 years before the "Missouri" and the "Hole-in-the Horn" "pick-up" bucks displaced it to #3.

I am an official B&C measurer and take this position very seriously. I have previously assisted the B&C office in clarifying and correcting several trophies in the past. I am continuing this practice.

About a year ago, I became a measurer for the "North American Shed Hunters Club" who record and catalogue shed antlers. I have measured many trophies for B&C at the Buckhorn Hall of Horns where the two deer in question still reside. Last March I went to measure the 284 3/8 B&C, thought to be "sheds", for the NASHC. Upon doing this, I felt there was a possibility they were not actually sheds.

I had heard the 286, #1 Texas trophy had loose antlers. This would not be too unusual since it had been 41 years since Mr. Fitz had measured it and also considering the fact it had been in storage and relocated and remounted. I was able to photograph the 286 next to a replica of it that had been made since the 1989 remount. I too felt loose antlers.

The 284 3/8 "sheds" felt very "solid" on the 1958 mount. I needed to know for sure. I talked with the museum curators and offered to have the trophy remounted at my own expense.

This I did. I discovered the 284 3/8 were not sheds but a true skull cap. It was however cracked and wired back together.

I now wanted to know for sure what lay under the hide of the "286" buck. I could not officially measure the 286 for the NASHC unless I knew they were sheds. It had been remounted in 1989. I could not offer to do this again since it still looked very good. I went to the taxidermist who did the work in 1989 and questioned him. He said he was required to do the job at the brewery in front of an audience. He was unsure what the truth was. He did say the antlers were loose but there was a skull plate. That is all he could tell me.

I made arrangements to have the 286 trophy, along with five others, X-rayed at my expense. This had to be done at the brewery itself since it is opened to the public seven days a week. An industrial X-ray company did this for me after hours with portable equipment. It took three men several hours to complete the process.

Sure enough, these were the sheds. Screws were turned through a replacement skull plate and up into the bases of the shed antlers. The wrong trophy was dropped from the 1958 Record Book! If that error had not been done, I suppose there would be no need for this letter to you. More often than not, old heads that are discovered cracked 41 years after they were officially measured are repaired and acceptably left untold. I am convinced the 284 3/8 NT skull plate was cracked after Grancel Fitz officially measured it.

If we look at the ancient mount it possessed in the 1958 record book, we can only imagine the way it was secured to the primitive deer form. Modern day foam forms did not exist at the turn of the century. In fact, nails instead of screws were commonly used. When taxidermist Jose Salinas, who worked at Lin Nowotny's Taxidermy Studio, removed the rusty screws or nails from the brittle skull plate in 1958, there is a very good chance the skull was cracked at that time. Another possibility was when it was moved to or out of storage from 1956 to 1957. I suspect this is when antler points on the other head scoring 286 were broken. Grancel Fitz's score chart reflects that three points currently broken and glued back on were actually in place and measurable on January 3, 1955 when both heads were scored. The photo taken by Grancel Fitz used in later B&C Record Books, starting in 1981, shows these points "broken." We don't know the date he took his second published photo showing broken points but it was between 1958 and May of 1963 when he passed away. I suspect it was near 1963 since the mount looks aged in this photo. A newspaper clipping I saw taken in 1956 when the brewery bought the collection, shows the oldest mount.

The 284 3/8 is pristine and perfectly in tact except for the cracked skull plate. Not a point is broken, much less haphazardly glued on. It seems a much more fitting example to hold a top spot in B&C. There are actually six broken points on the 286. Three that were broken and gone in the 1958 Record Book photo and three more glued back in place in the 1981 book's photo. I have earlier photos of the 286 showing all six points in place.

I firmly believe the skull on the 284 3/8 deer was cracked after Grancel Fitz measured it. I feel Mr. Lin Nowotny, also a late B&C measurer, found the fact one was sheds and reported it. The racks are so close together in appearance, who is to say how the wrong one was dropped in the 1964 book. If Mr. Nowotny reported that one was sheds at that time, I am confident he would have mentioned the condition of the other head if there was something unknown to tell. Maybe the 284 3/8 was still intact then. Or maybe Jose Salinas broke it while trying to remove the brittle 66 year old rack. Maybe the skull was already cracked from the 1956 storage and move and the condition was discussed with the records committee in 1963 in Pittsburgh PA. I cannot help but believe any contrary condition discovered years after Grancel Fitz measured these two heads was already addressed somehow, somewhere. Unfortunately, the early records of these events are not available to us now.

I feel no cover-up of any kind was schemed on either trophy. These antlers have been around way longer than our scoring system has. We can look at the photos of both heads in the 1958 book and see they were very old. They were certainly mounted before any scoring system was around to scrutinize trophy conditions.

I am satisfied to know a set of sheds that held the World's Record is now displaced and dropped from the archives. I would like to see the 284 3/8 true whitetail rack simply take the place of the 286 NT. When I measured the 284 3/8 on the Nowotny mount, it had a 3/8 inch less inside spread measurement than the one Grancel Fitz took in 1955. No other trophy in the record book falls between 286 and 284 3/8. If the mix-up had never occurred, the rejection of a mediocre rack measured by Grancel Fitz 41 years ago would most probably not be considered. I would hate to imagine the turmoil trying to clarify skull conditions of old mounts that may be discovered broken decades later.

Both of these non-typical mounts were arm in arm since Grancel Fitz measured them. We know they were in storage from 1956 to 1957. We also know three points were broken off the 286 after 1955. We know the ancient heads were remounted since Grancel Fitz measured them. Both of these occasions could easily have been the time the skull was cracked.

Being a Texan and the person to discover this situation, I obviously want the 284 3/8 to carry on in the Boone and Crockett archives as the current #3 in the world, replacing the innocent yet erroneous 286. Knowing this situation required the attention of the records committee, I promptly reported my discoveries to the B&C office, continued my investigation, and followed up with this letter and pictures for your consideration and final decision. Please be satisfied with the replacement of the true whitetail rack being ascertained. A much graver iniquity than what has historically occurred with the wrong trophy holding top honors, would be the denial of an equally impressive and ardent set of antlers from a truly magnificent whitetail. After all, these two sets of antlers are 99.9% assuredly off the same animal.

Sincerely,

John Stein

A FINAL DECISION IS MADE

In a November 13, 1996, letter to the Buckhorn Hall of Fame, Jack Reneau informs them of the final decision on the two non-typical whitetails they have in their collection. Ultimately, the buck that was removed from the records book decades earlier (scoring 284-3/8) was in fact the hunter-taken trophy, not the shed antlers and therefore was reinstated in the records books.

On a side note, B&C's Official Measurers are the true eyes and ears of the Records Program. The lengths that Official Measurer John Stein took to find the truth is commendable. Luckily, many of B&C's Official Measurers are equally diligent and dedicated.

OFFICIAL SCORING SYSTEM FOR NORTH AMERICAN BIG GAME TROPHIES

Records of North American Big Game Committee

BOONE AND CROCKETT CLUB

Address Correspondence to:
Mrs. Grancel Fitz, Secretary
5 Tudor City Place, NYC 17, NY.

WHITETAIL and COUES DEER

KIND OF DEER Whitetail

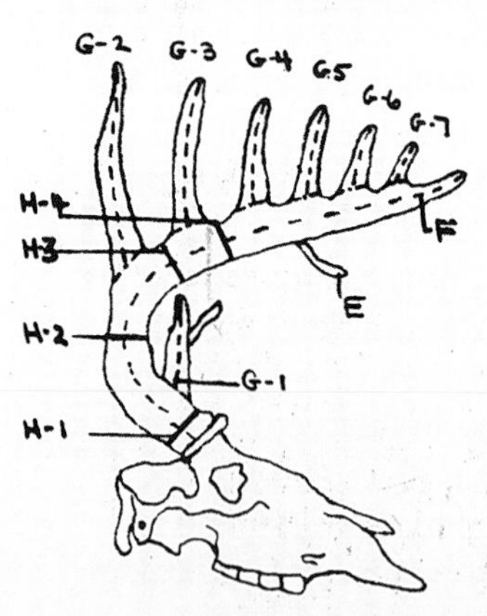

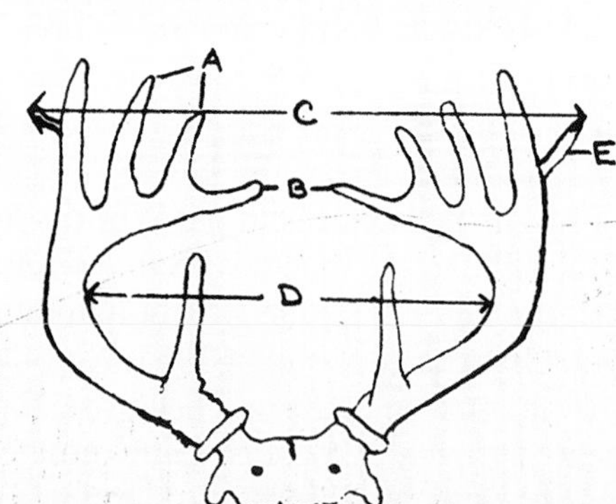

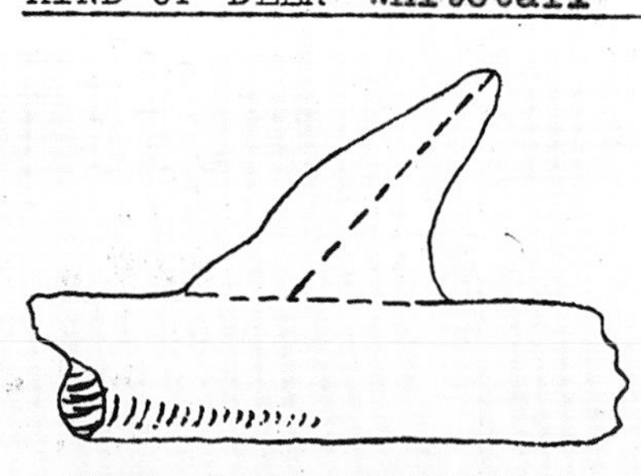

SEE OTHER SIDE FOR INSTRUCTIONS	Supplementary Data R.	Supplementary Data L.	Column 1 Spread Credit	Column 2 Right Antler	Column 3 Left Antler	Column 4 Difference
A. Number of Points on Each Antler	7	6				
B. Tip to Tip Spread	27 2/8					
C. Greatest Spread	30 2/8					
D. Inside Spread of MAIN BEAMS 27 — Spread credit may equal but not exceed length of longer antler			25 6/8			
IF Inside Spread of Main Beams exceeds longer antler length, enter difference						~~1 2/8~~
E. Total of Lengths of all Abnormal Points						1 3/8
F. Length of Main Beam				25 6/8	25 3/8	3/8
G-1. Length of First Point, if present				7	6 5/8	3/8
G-2. Length of Second Point				10 5/8	9 5/8	1
G-3. Length of Third Point				9 3/8	9 6/8	3/8
G-4. Length of Fourth Point, if present				9 1/8	7 4/8	1 5/8
G-5. Length of Fifth Point, if present				5 6/8	4	1 6/8
G-6. Length of Sixth Point, if present						
G-7. Length of Seventh Point, if present						
H-1. Circumference at Smallest Place Between Burr and First Point				5	4 6/8	2/8
H-2. Circumference at Smallest Place Between First and Second Points				4 4/8	4 2/8	2/8
H-3. Circumference at Smallest Place Between Second and Third Points				5 1/8	4 4/8	5/8
H-4. Circumference at Smallest Place between Third and Fourth Points or half way between Third Point and Beam Tip if Fourth Point is missing				6 2/8	4 3/8	1 7/8
TOTALS			25 6/8	88 4/8	80 6/8	~~11 1/8~~

ADD	Column 1	25 6/8	Exact locality where killed	Webb Co., Texas - Apache Ranch
	Column 2	88 4/8	Date killed Dec. 1949	By whom killed Henderson Coquat
	Column 3	80 6/8	Present owner	Henderson Coquat
	Total	195	Address	San Antonio, Texas
SUBTRACT	Column 4	11 1/8	Guide's Name and Address	
FINAL SCORE		183 7/8	Remarks: (Mention any abnormalities)	NEW WORLD'S RECORD 1953

BOONE AND CROCKETT CLUB OFFICIAL

185-1/8

4: SPECIAL TROPHY

NEW WORLD'S RECORD TYPICAL WHITETAIL - 1953

Texas Hunting Gains New Honors With a

WORLD RECORD WHITETAIL

Henderson Coquat of San Antonio tells his own story of how he bagged the new world record white-tailed deer trophy and how this majestic buck lived and grew in South Texas' brushland.

Grancel Fitz from Boone & Crockett Club

New World Record from Texas

Every boy in North America who ever carried a gun into the woods has dreamed of killing the biggest buck in the world. The ghost-like big whitetail buck can and does slip out of his sight, but he cannot slip out of his mind. And so I dreamed, but it took half a hundred years of consistent hunting before I became the proud possessor of the world record whitetail deer head.

"Where did you take that trophy," you ask? Well, there is a strip of country 200 miles long and about a hundred miles wide on the Texas side of the Rio Grande, where many people say the biggest whitetail deer in Texas grow. Through years of hunting competition, these claims have been substantiated. In this wild, hard, brushy country, these old bucks develop a body, a spirit, a majesty, that is supreme. Personally, I have hunted the wary whitetail in several states of the Union, and in many foreign countries, but the old moss heads of Southwest Texas stand out as distinct and majestic in comparison to other deer as the mighty Longhorn of Texas stood out as a trail leader in a herd of cattle.

I own two fine ranches in this hunter's paradise in Southwest Texas. It was on one of these, the old Apache ranch, that I killed this world record whitetail.

The old Apache is located on the east bank of the Rio Grande about 50 miles north of Laredo. It was part of a government bombing range during World War II, and thousands of empty 50-caliber machine gun shells are on every hill and in every valley of its rugged surface. When I bought the place in 1948, I had doubts that much game had survived the mighty bombardments of our eager young pilots. But I had not given full credit to the cunning and the courage of the whitetail. Not only had a goodly number of them survived, but they had learned what a man with a gun meant, and how to outwit him.

I saw only tracks for a while, but what tracks they were. I watched from tree tops, and from the tops of the Little Apache and the Big Apache mountains, trying to locate the deer that made them. Sure enough, there were great grey ghosts with rocking chair-like heads. I permitted my friends to hunt, but most of them came away with tales of enchanted bucks that stared them into inaction, or caused them to look wide-eyed at the deer and forget the gun sights as they fired away. One seasoned hunter shot up the dirt half way to the deer, while another pumped all the shells out of his gun without firing a shot. It looked as though the super natural, which makes up so much of the border folklore, had a hard core of reality in the lives of those mighty whitetail bucks.

Like most confirmed hunters, I studied the game records of the world as part of my light and heavy reading. I learned by heart most of what was recorded by the Boone and Crockett Club and by the American Museum of Natural History. To my dismay the great State of Texas played a sorry part in showing off its game. Not one of our lordly bucks was recorded in the top ten record holders. I was ashamed and felt honor-bound to do something to correct such a condition. On December 28, 1949, I got my chance to set the record right.

• Continued on Page 21

WORLD'S RECORD TYPICAL 1953

Henderson Coquat's whitetail, which scores 185-1/8 points, hangs to the right of Angus McVicar's 237-3/8 point non-typical, showing great contrast between the two categories. Coquat's deer was declared the new World's Record at the 6th Competition held in 1953.

On the opposite page, Coquat holds up his impressive, wide-spread whitetail from the 1949 hunting season.

Sunday, April 4, 1954

Dallas Texas

7 World's Records Shattered In 1953 Big Game Competition

Texas Deer and Hunter Break Whitetail Mark

Perhaps wild animals on the continent were bigger in the exaggerated "good old days," but seven new world's records were hung up in the 1953 competition of the Boone and Crockett Club of New York.

In doing so, some records that go back nearly a century were shattered.

Strangely, in a day of generally smaller deer in Texas, a Lone Star deer shattered the old record of a New Brunswick, Canada, deer, shot in 1937. The Texas deer was killed by Henderson Coquat of San Antonio in Webb County in 1949 and not previously entered in the contest. This new world's record animal, which tops eighty-four others in the trophy class running back to 1885, has 25-plus-inch long antlers, thirteen points, which is not excessive, but a 27-inch spread, which is.

Despite the occasional outdoor magazine story of giant bears, a new grizzly record shatters that hung up in 1890. The grizzly list runs back to one now in the United States National Museum and killed n 1866. The new record bear with 16 10/16-inch long skull and 11/16-inch width, was killed by o Indians last year at Slave ke, Alberta, Canada.

lmost as strange as a new rec- grizzly is the addition of five e grizzlies on the Boone and kett Club trophy list. Inci- ally, one was shot by Grancel Fitz, one of the indefatigable workers of the club.

There is also a new record for the biggest bear in the world, the Alaskan brown. This one with a 17 15/16-inch long and 12 13/16-inch wide skull was one of those accidental kills by a scientific expedition, that of the Los Angeles County Museum, on Kodiak Island. Five other Alaskan browns made the 1953 trophy list.

Other new records included a mule deer killed in Jackson County, Colorado, in 1949; both Wyoming and Alaska moose and a Coues deer shot near Arivaca, Ariz.

Ninety-one new trophy heads in all won prizes or honorable mentions in the 1953 competition. Six were supplied by Texans. San Antonian Coquat, in addition to breaking the whitetail record, made the whitetail non-typical honorable-mention list with one killed in Live Oak County in 1916.

Flat-country Texans seemed to run strong after those binocular-eyed dwellers of the cliffs, mountain sheep. Second prize for a desert sheep shot in Sonora, Mexico, in 1939, was won by Phil Yeckel of Midland. B. N. Lively of Lufkin in the vicinity of Jakey's Fork, Wyo., last year killed a bighorn that took third prize. Yeckel's 1950 stone sheep shot in British Columbia drew an honorable mention.

A Texas woman hunter, Mrs. Milroy Powell of Center Point, Kerr County, topped all other Texans in the non-typical mule deer category, winning second prize with a buck shot in the Kaibab Forest, Arizona, in company with her husband and her father, Dan Auld. A year ago her twin brother won Boone and Crockett Club honors.

Among the judges this year was Walter B. McClurkan, Denton big game hunter, who has a number of sheep and goat trophies. Chairman of the records committee in general charge was Samuel B. Webb of New York.

4: SPECIAL TROPHY

WORLD'S RECORD TYPICAL WHITETAIL - JOHN BREEN BUCK

Dec. 31, 1958

Mr. W. L. Cowden
Bemidji
Minn.

Dear Mr. Cowden:

Thank you very much for getting the Breen whitetail deer trophy scored by Dr. Rusten. We are very glad to have this record and in fact, you may have a new world's record whitetail deer. Before we can say it is a new world's record, however, it will be necessary to have the trophy rechecked by the committee in N. Y. This is a procedure we employ on all world record trophies so that at no time will the record be questioned.

The Competitions are held every two years and the closing date for entries for the current show is Dec. 31, 1959. I do know that the judges will want to see your trophy when they meet in the spring of 1960 and should it be a new world's record, naturally, we'd want to exhibit it at the American Museum with the other prize winning trophies. However, if you'd like to know before that time if you have a new world's record, you may ship the trophy to us at 5 Tudor City Place, New York 17, N. Y., and I'll see that the score is rechecked and a copy of our findings will be sent to you. If you do not want to go to the expense of shipping the trophy to N. Y. now and would rather wait until the show, we'll understand. We would appreciate some word from you as to your plans and don't let us lose track of you or the trophy as a world record or near world record whitetail deer is one of the rarest North American big game when you consider the number killed each year. If you know the history of the trophy, we'd be glad to have that for our files.

A pictorial folder showing the award winners in the last show is enclosed, which you may find interesting.

Yours sincerely,

(Mrs. Grancel Fitz)

Encl.

Copy to Dr. Elmer M. Rusten

When this great whitetail was submitted to B&C, it had the potential to shake up the entire whitetail world. Taken by John A. Breen in Beltrami County, Minnesota, in 1918, this buck had enormous main beam lengths of 31-2/8 and 31 inches.

R 1 2/8 1 4/8 L 2.0 1.3/8

OFFICIAL SCORING SYSTEM FOR NORTH AMERICAN BIG GAME TROPHIES

Records of North American
Big Game Committee

BOONE AND CROCKETT CLUB

Address correspondence to:
Mrs. Grancel Fitz, Secretary
5 Tudor City Place
New York 17, N. Y.

1 2/8 4.0 1.0 4 3/8

WHITETAIL and COUES DEER

KIND OF DEER Whitetail

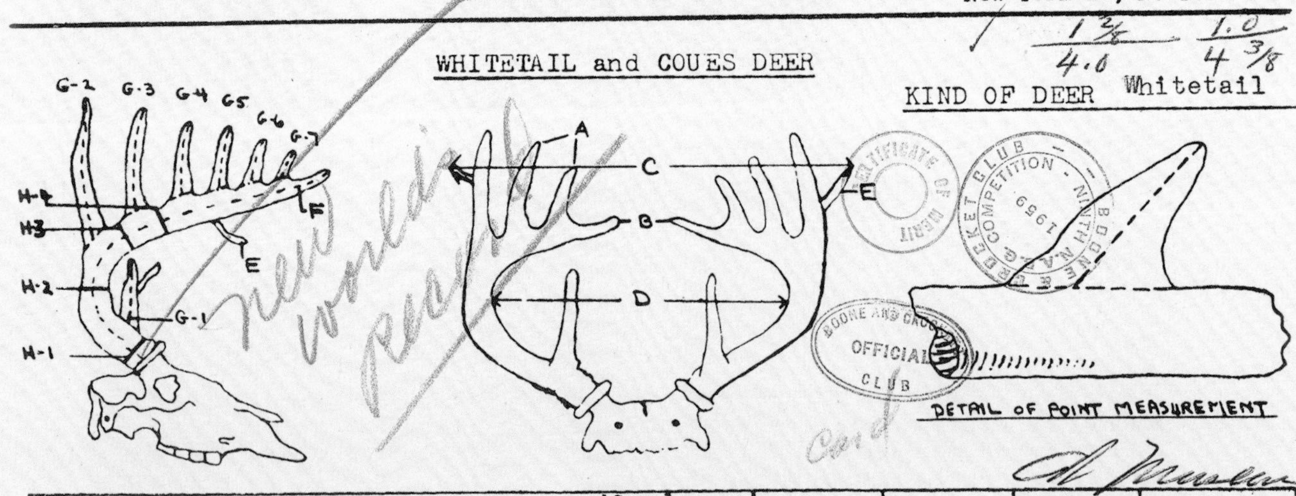

SEE OTHER SIDE FOR INSTRUCTIONS	Supplementary Data R.	Supplementary Data L.	Column 1 Spread Credit	Column 2 Right Antler	Column 3 Left Antler	Column 4 Difference
A. Number of Points on Each Antler	8	8				
B. Tip to Tip Spread	20 3/8					
C. Greatest Spread	26 7/8					
D. Inside Spread of MAIN BEAMS 23 5/8 — Spread credit may equal but not exceed length of longer antler			23 5/8			
IF Inside Spread of Main Beams exceeds longer antler length, enter difference						
E. Total of Lengths of all Abnormal Points						8 3/8
F. Length of Main Beam				31 2/8	31.0	2/8
G-1. Length of First Point, if present				5 6/8	6.3/8	5/8
G-2. Length of Second Point				12 4/8	11.6/8	6/8
G-3. Length of Third Point				12 4/8	13 2/8	6/8
G-4. Length of Fourth Point, if present				9 4/8	11 3/8	1 7/8
G-5. Length of Fifth Point, if present						
G-6. Length of Sixth Point, if present						
G-7. Length of Seventh Point, if present						
H-1. Circumference at Smallest Place Between Burr and First Point				5 7/8	6.0	1/8
H-2. Circumference at Smallest Place Between First and Second Points				5 6/8	5 5/8	1/8
H-3. Circumference at Smallest Place Between Second and Third Points				6 1/8	6 1/8	0
H-4. Circumference at Smallest Place between Third and Fourth Points or half way between Third Point and Beam Tip if Fourth Point is missing				5 3/8	5 2/8	1/8
TOTALS			23 5/8	94 5/8	96 6/8	13.0

ADD	Column 1	23 5/8	Exact locality where killed	Funkley, Minn.
	Column 2	94 5/8	Date killed Nov. 1918	By whom killed John A. Breen*
	Column 3	96 6/8	Present owner	Arthur, Harry & Ray Breen
	Total	215.0	Address	Bemidji, Minn.
SUBTRACT	Column 4	13.0	Guide's Name and Address	none
FINAL SCORE		202.0	Remarks: (Mention any abnormalities)	*deceased ~~Any award should be made in name of John A. Breen & mailed to Arthur Breen, Bemidji, Minn.~~

new world record

Card

"Where Sportsmen Serve Sportsmen"

★ ★ ★

Lakeland Sporting Goods

D. A. SCHEI - - W. L. COWDEN
215 THIRD STREET
Bemidji, Minnesota

July 14, 1959

Mrs. Grancel Fitz, Secretary
Boone and Crocket Club
5 Tudor City Place
New York 17, New York

Dear Mrs. Fitz:

Thank you for your letter of December 31, 1958 relative to the Breen whitetail deer trophy which we have had scored by Dr. Rusten. We were very pleased to hear from you.

At present we wish merely to inform you that arrangements have been made to ship the trophy to New York for official scoring this fall. We may wait until just after our local deer season which will be in early November since we like to have the head in our store at that time. As we understand, the trophy must be in your hands before the end of 1959 for entry inthe current show. When we do ship the head I will forward the complete history. If you desire, the head may then be held for the exhibit in the American Museum.

Thank you again for your interest in this trophy.

Yours very truly,

W. L. COWDEN

"Where Sportsmen Serve Sportsmen"

* * *

Lakeland Sporting Goods

D. A. SCHEI - - W. L. COWDEN

215 THIRD STREET

Bemidji, Minnesota

January 18, 1960

JAN 21 1960

Mrs. Grancel Fitz, Secretary
5 Tudor Place
New York 17, New York

Dear Mrs. Fitz:

You undoubtedly have received the card which I put in the mail the day we shipped the Breen Whitetail deer trophy to the Museum.

We recently received a form letter from Mr. Waters regarding this trophy. He asked particularly whose name should be used in the event that it should win an award. I have talked to the brothers who own the head (Arthur, Harry and Ray Breen) and they feel that it should be done in their father's name, John A. Breen. Should there be an award, it can be mailed to me or to Mr. Arthur Breen, Bemidji. John has been dead many years, but that shouldn't matter.

I believe you have the history of this head, but I will repeat the basic information. It was shot by John Breen in November, 1918 at Houpt, Minnesota. This was merely a railroad siding on what is now the Northern Pacific line, and is no longer in existance. The location is 33 miles northeast of Bemidji. The deer, when shot weighed 235 pounds, but was in extremely poor condition. We have displayed the head for the past three years. When it is returned please have it sent to us. We were the ones to promote its entrance in the competition and want to foot the bill for the transportation. Although it is the collective property of the Breen Brothers I am sure that they still wish us to display it in our store. Thank you for the help you have given us with this entry. Believe me, we have your fingers crossed that it will score high among the record heads.

Yours very truly,

W. L. COWDEN

John Breen's sons, Ray (left) and Art (right), pose with their dad's World's Record typical whitetail. Breen's buck was an entry in the 9th Competition, where it received not only a Certificate of Merit, but was also officially recognized as the largest typical whitetail in history.

While the buck stood as the World's Record for many years, it has since been surpassed. However, Breen's buck is still the top scoring B&C buck from Minnesota.

Breen's buck was big news when he shot it in 1918. He had to bring it back by train and then hired a horse and wagon to get it to his house. Once home, they hard a hard time getting it through the front door because the rack was so wide.

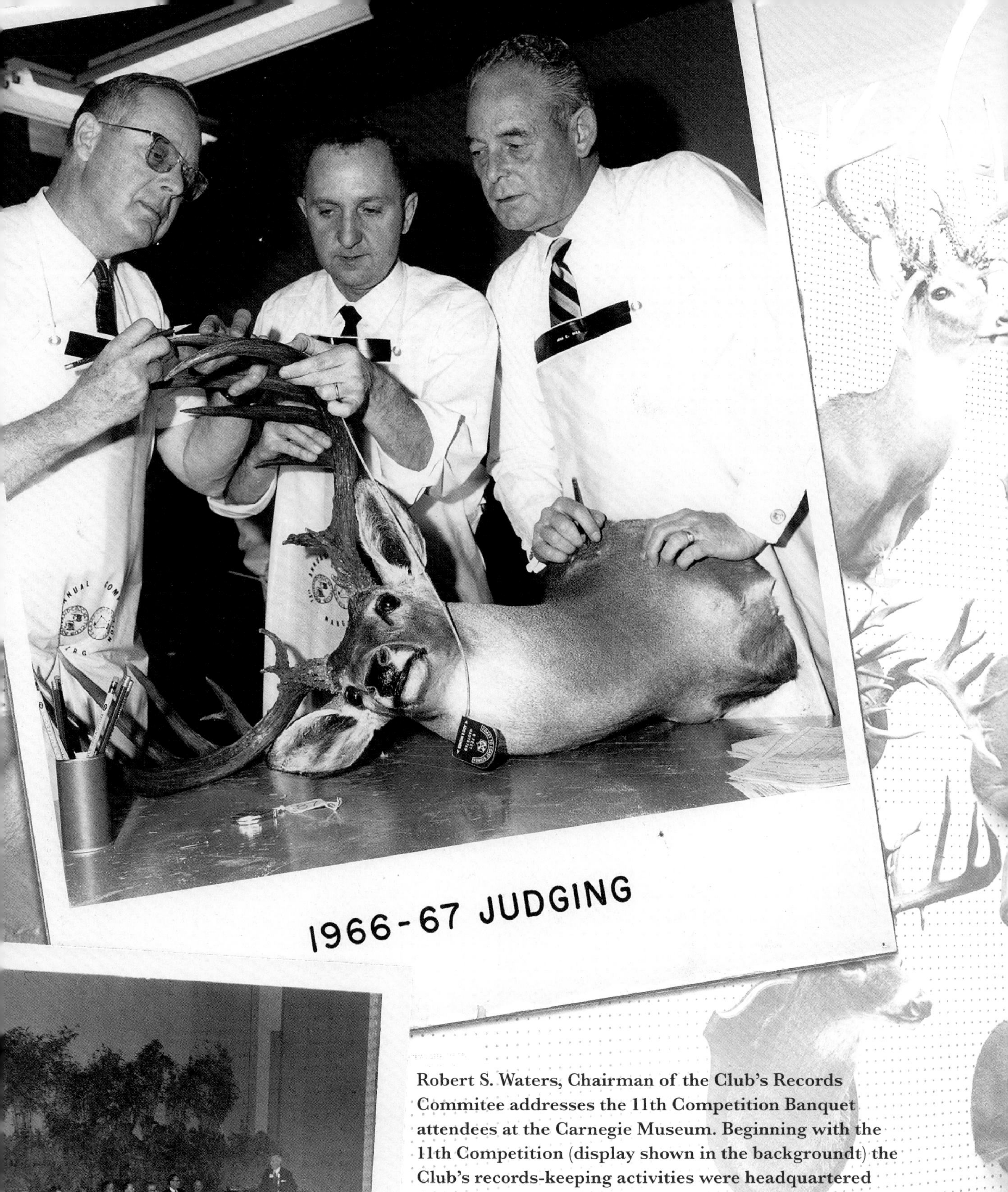

Robert S. Waters, Chairman of the Club's Records Commitee addresses the 11th Competition Banquet attendees at the Carnegie Museum. Beginning with the 11th Competition (display shown in the backgroundt) the Club's records-keeping activities were headquartered at the Carnegie Museum. Above, members of the 13th Competition's Judges Panel (John H. Batten, B.A. Fashingbauer, and Club President John E. Rhea) measure one of the whitetails submitted for judging.

5: CARNEGIE MUSEUM

BY GILBERT T. ADAMS

After 16 years at the American Museum of Natural History in New York City, the Club's records-keeping activities and competitions moved to the Carnegie Museum in Pittsburgh, Pennsylvania in 1964.

During this new time, referred to as the Carnegie Era (1964-71), the successes of some six decades of big-game conservation became dramatically evident. Not only did the Club have to make one broad revision of the minimum entry scores for deer effective for the 1963 Competition, but again five years later, the Club raised the minimum scores for entry for virtually all deer as well as many other species. Nothing similar has occurred either before or since.

The first of these dramatic increases for whitetail deer came in 1963. The Records Committee, chaired by Robert S. Waters, made the recommendation, adopted by the Club, that the typical whitetail minimum for entry be raised from 150 to 160 and that the minimum non-typical score be raised from 160 to 180.

In 1968, Dr. Elmer M. Rusten was the Records Committee chairman. Unprecedented in the Club's history, the Club again substantially raised the minimum requirements for whitetail deer to 170 for typical and 195 for non-typical, where they remain today. Clearly, this was a statement to the success of the big-game conservation management and the vibrant health of the species.

During this time, the Club's records-keeping system became overwhelmed with reports that extraordinary big-game animals were being harvested by hunters in previously unreported numbers. Additionally, the reports of exceptional animals were being recorded from states and areas that had not previously reported the occurrence and/or numbers of animals meeting the minimum score for entry into the records of the Club.

One noteworthy example during the Carnegie Era was the entry of a typical whitetail buck harvested by bowhunter Melvin J. Johnson in Peoria County, Illinois, in 1965. The report of the hunt and significance of this outstanding deer merited the award of the Sagamore Hill Medal. This is the highest recognition offered by Boone and Crockett Club, with concurrence and approval from the Roosevelt family.

During the Carnegie Era another of the greatest typical whitetail bucks of all time, the Jordan buck, turned up in a rummage sale. The reader will enjoy reading the hunting story and the subsequent sordid history of its possession, ownership, rediscovery and entering into the official records by someone claiming not to know the hunter. Turned out he did.

From 1964 through 1971, the Club did not have any semblance of the staff we have today. The records-keeping work was accomplished by the members and volunteers. Interestingly, at the 11th Competition held in 1965, a thoughtful man brought his nephew along to see the magnificent display of trophies at the Carnegie Museum. It turned out this young man was none other than Jack Reneau, whose distinguished history with the Club is still in the making. His roots with the Club are deep, indeed.

The Carnegie Era ended in 1971 when Club leaders Robert M. Ferguson, Sherman Gray, and Jack S. Parker negotiated an agreement with the National Rifle Association, and the headquarters of the Club were moved to the NRA headquarters in Washington, D.C.

5: VINTAGE PHOTOS*

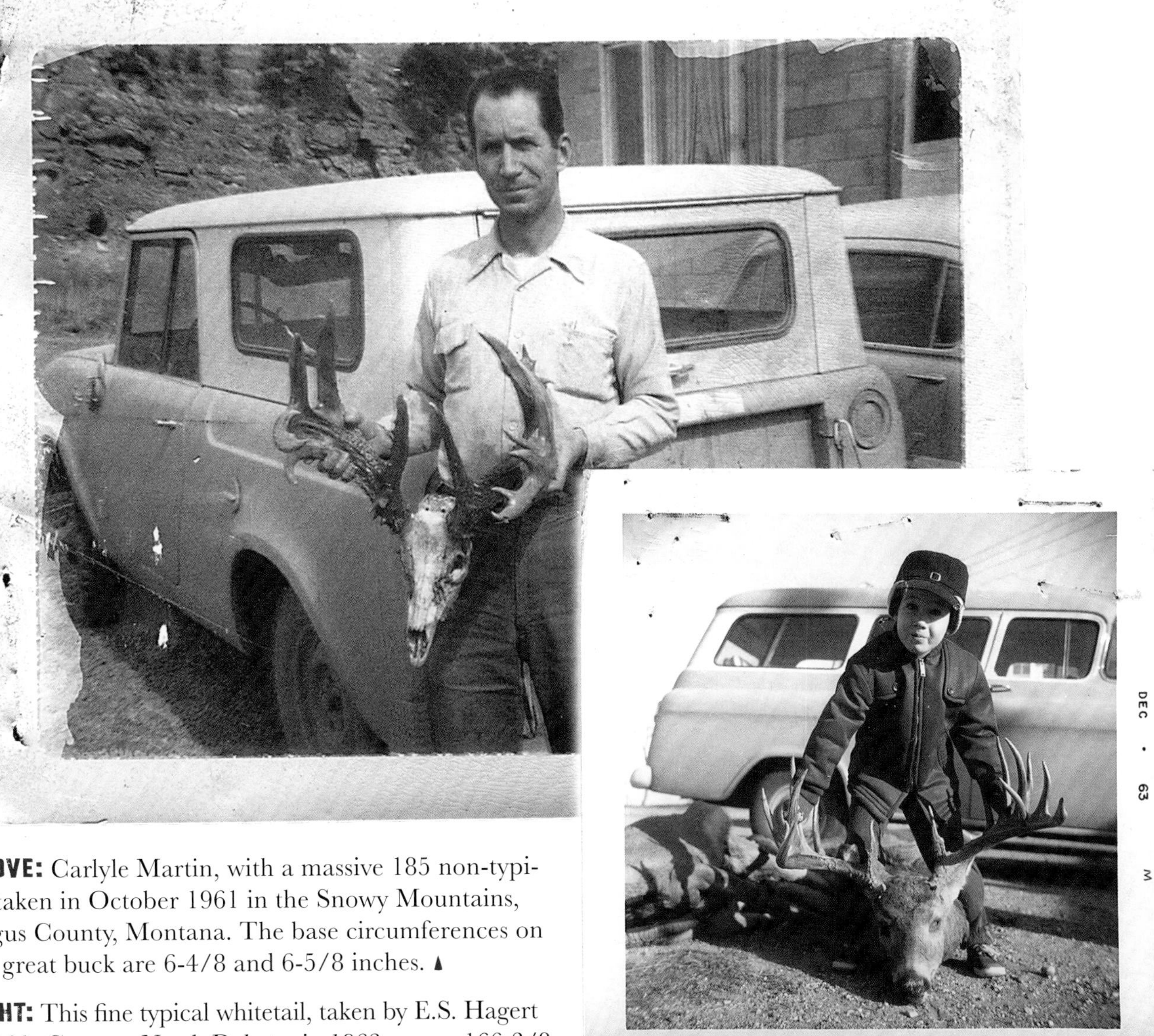

ABOVE: Carlyle Martin, with a massive 185 non-typical taken in October 1961 in the Snowy Mountains, Fergus County, Montana. The base circumferences on this great buck are 6-4/8 and 6-5/8 inches. ▲

RIGHT: This fine typical whitetail, taken by E.S. Hagert in Eddy County, North Dakota, in 1963, scores 166-3/8 points, with a greatest spread of 26 inches. ▲

LEFT: Karl Volz proudly displays his non-typical, which scores 187-5/8 points, taken in St. Genevieve County, Missouri, on November 15, 1964. Three tremendous drop tines make this a very intriguing trophy. ▲

▲ DENOTES UNOFFICIAL SCORE OR TROPHY IS BELOW CURRENT MINIMUM SCORE

***Many of the following photos are as stated, "vintage." The Boone and Crockett Club has carefully ushered in a new era with the advancement and availability of photographic equipment. Today, our expectations consist of presenting a blood-free trophy and hunter in an uncluttered, natural environment. These guidelines were born out of respect for the animal and its habitat.**

ABOVE: Buddy Wise displays his long- and sharp-tined typical whitetail, which scores 172 points, taken near Bearden, Arkansas, in November of 1962. This stunning buck has a 24-2/8-inch spread.

LEFT: Jay Kesner holds the result of a Jefferson County, Pennsylvania, hunt on November 28, 1965. This 7x7 scores 165-1/8 points. ▲

▲ DENOTES UNOFFICIAL SCORE OR TROPHY IS BELOW CURRENT MINIMUM SCORE

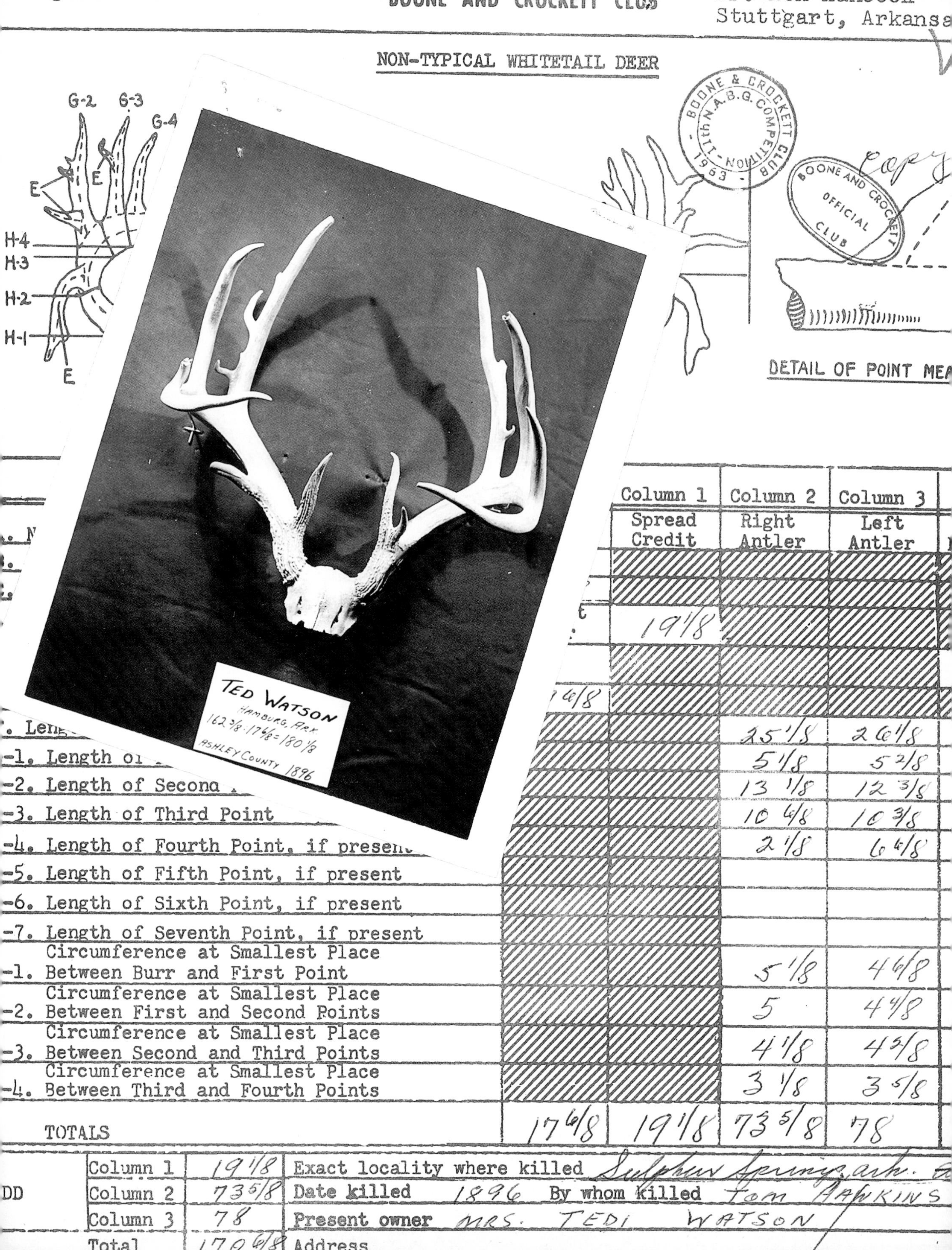

BOONE AND CROCKETT CLUB

Stuttgart, Arkansa

NON-TYPICAL WHITETAIL DEER

DETAIL OF POINT MEA

		Column 1	Column 2	Column 3
		Spread Credit	Right Antler	Left Antler
		19 1/8		
	17 6/8			
. Leng			25 1/8	26 1/8
-1. Length of			5 1/8	5 2/8
-2. Length of Second			13 1/8	12 3/8
-3. Length of Third Point			10 6/8	10 3/8
-4. Length of Fourth Point, if present			2 1/8	6 6/8
-5. Length of Fifth Point, if present				
-6. Length of Sixth Point, if present				
-7. Length of Seventh Point, if present				
Circumference at Smallest Place -1. Between Burr and First Point			5 1/8	4 6/8
Circumference at Smallest Place -2. Between First and Second Points			5	4 4/8
Circumference at Smallest Place -3. Between Second and Third Points			4 1/8	4 5/8
Circumference at Smallest Place -4. Between Third and Fourth Points			3 1/8	3 5/8
TOTALS	17 6/8	19 1/8	73 5/8	78

DD	Column 1	19 1/8	Exact locality where killed Sulphur Springs, Ark.
	Column 2	73 5/8	Date killed 1896 By whom killed Tom Hawkins
	Column 3	78	Present owner Mrs. Tedi Watson
	Total	170 6/8	Address

ABOVE: O.E. Martin holds his non-typical whitetail, which scores 192-6/8 points, taken in Concordia Parish, Louisiana, in 1963. This compact and impressive rack has base circumferences of 5-7/8 and 6 inches. ▲

RIGHT: This excellent non-typical Coues' deer, which scores 142-7/8 points, was one of the top specimens entered in the 13th Competition. It currently stands 16th on the All-time list. The original entry lists this buck being taken by a Native American, and is currently owned by the Arizona Department of Game and Fish.

LEFT: A nice non-typical scoring 180-1/8 points taken by Tom Hawkins near Sulphur Springs, Arkansas, in 1896. This deer is below B&C minimum entry score for non-typical whitetail of 185, but is nonetheless a historic trophy. ▲

▲ DENOTES UNOFFICIAL SCORE OR TROPHY IS BELOW CURRENT MINIMUM SCORE

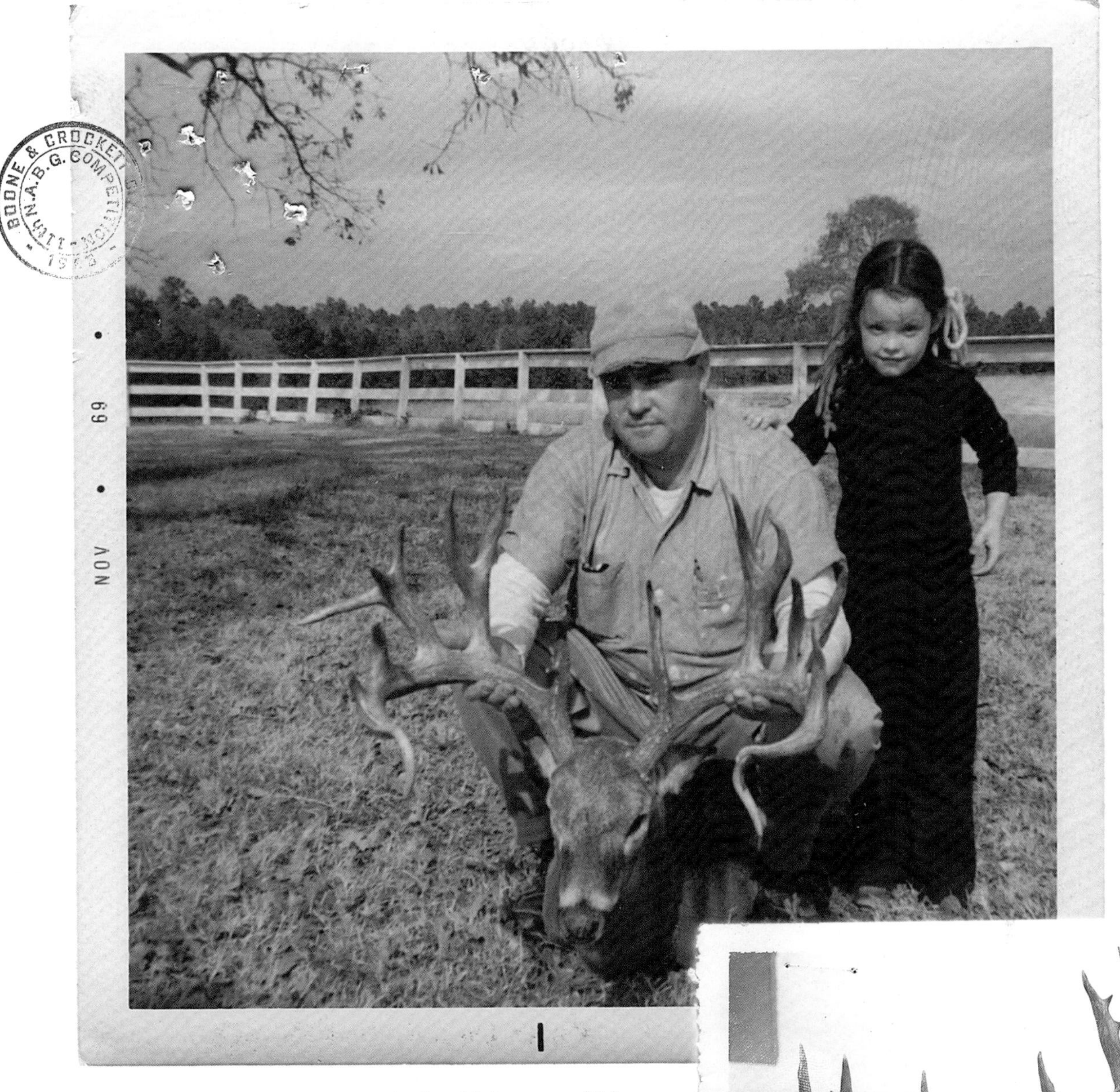

ABOVE: This fantastic non-typical, which scores 205-7/8 points, was taken by Gary Rogers in Houston County, Texas, in November of 1969.

RIGHT: This non-typical whitetail, taken by Joe Kunigiskis near Outlook, Saskatchewan, in 1965, scores 188-3/8 points. Its most outstanding feature may be its inside spread, which stretches the tape to 26-4/8 inches. ▲

LEFT: Raymond Cowan, with his non-typical, which scores 198-5/8 points. The buck was taken in Concordia Parish, Louisiana, in 1961.

▲ DENOTES UNOFFICIAL SCORE OR TROPHY IS BELOW CURRENT MINIMUM SCORE

ABOVE: With a greatest spread of 28-7/8 inches, this rack is nearly too wide for a rifle. Don Erickson bagged this trophy buck, which scores 165-6/8 points, in Otter Tail County, Minnesota, in 1954. The rifle is a Winchester Model 94 carbine, most likely in .30-30 caliber. ▲

RIGHT: This giant non-typical buck scores 238 points. Donald B. Phipps harvested this great trophy in Keya Paha County, Nebraska, on November 11, 1969. The two drop-tines measure 9-7/8 and 9-5/8 inches.

LEFT: Dave Delap harvested this typical, which scores 170 points, in Flathead County, Montana, on November 14, 1966.

▲ DENOTES UNOFFICIAL SCORE OR TROPHY IS BELOW CURRENT MINIMUM SCORE

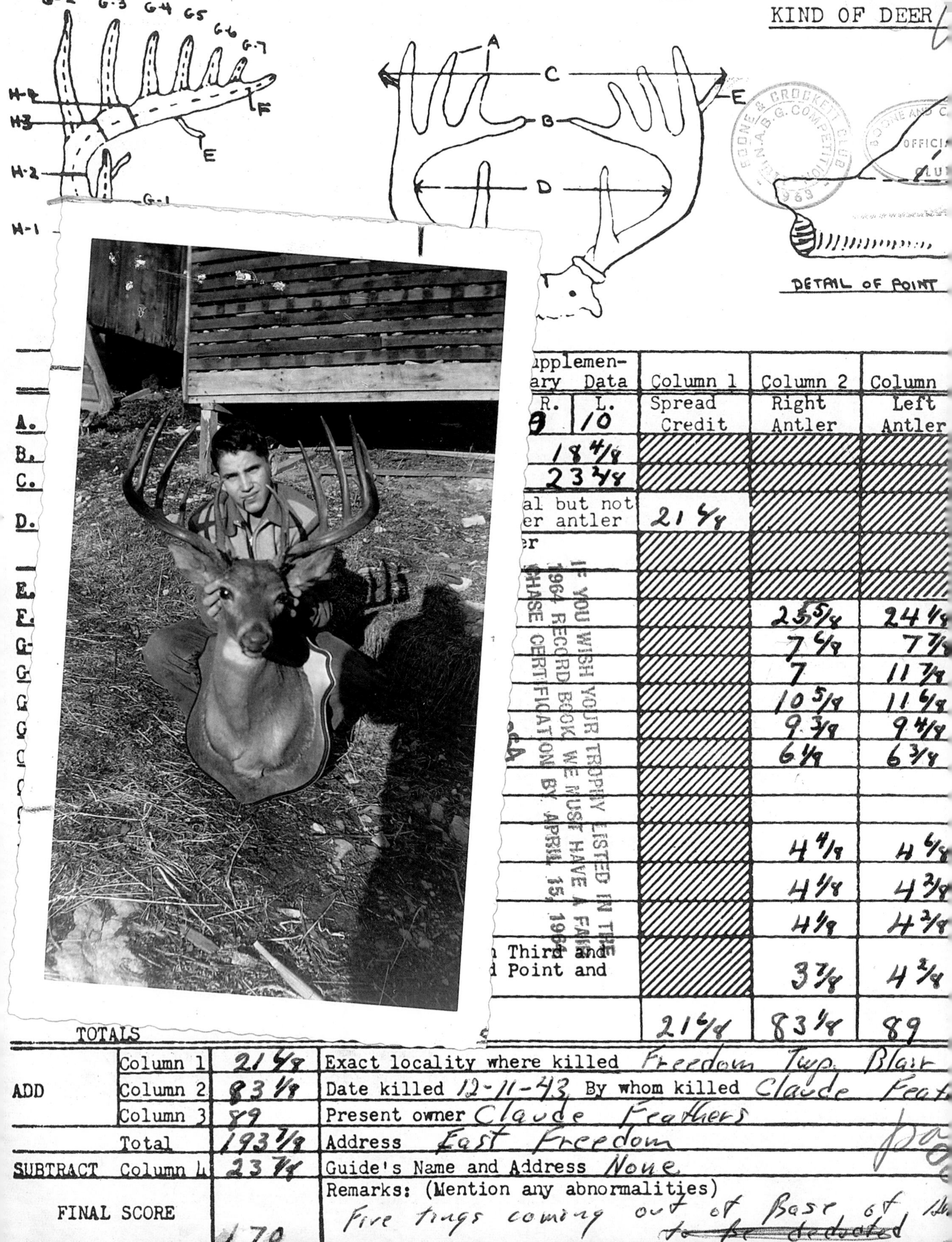

KIND OF DEER

	Supplementary Data R.	Supplementary Data L.	Column 1 Spread Credit	Column 2 Right Antler	Column 3 Left Antler
A.	9	10			
B.	18 4/8				
C.	23 2/8				
D. ...al but not ...er antler			21 6/8		
...er					
E.					
F.				25 5/8	24 1/8
G-				7 6/8	7 7/8
G				7	11 7/8
G				10 5/8	11 6/8
G				9 3/8	9 4/8
G				6 1/8	6 3/8
G					
G					
				4 4/8	4 6/8
				4 1/8	4 2/8
				4 1/8	4 2/8
...n Third and ...d Point and				3 7/8	4 2/8
TOTALS			21 6/8	83 1/8	89

ADD	Column 1	21 6/8	Exact locality where killed *Freedom Twp. Blair*
	Column 2	83 1/8	Date killed *12-11-43* By whom killed *Claude Feat...*
	Column 3	89	Present owner *Claude Feathers*
	Total	193 7/8	Address *East Freedom*
SUBTRACT	Column 4	23 7/8	Guide's Name and Address *None*
FINAL SCORE		170	Remarks: (Mention any abnormalities) *Five tings coming out of Base of ...* ~~*to be deducted*~~

ABOVE: Joe Schwegman stands next to his non-typical, which scores 197-4/8 points, taken in Pope County, Illinois, in December of 1961. This 10x9 buck has a greatest spread of 28-6/8 inches.

RIGHT: Four-wheel-drive pickups and ATVs were not the norm in 1967. Spotting a big buck in the trunk of a car was a common occurrence. This typical, which scores 172-3/8 points, was taken in Monroe County, Missouri, on November 21, 1967, by Clark E. Bray.

LEFT: Claude Feathers displays his typical whitetail, which scores 170 points, taken from Blair County, Pennsylvania, in December of 1943.

Sports Afield

59 EIGHTH AVENUE · NEW YORK, NEW YORK · 10019

March 29, 1965

This may be in 1964 folder.

Mrs. Gracel Fitz
5 Tudor Place
New York 17, New York

Dear Mrs. Fitz:

We are informed that Hugh Cox of Alton, Ohio shot with bow and arrow a 20-point, non-typical whitetail deer, thereby placing among the top five or six record holders "with gun or bow" in Ohio, by Boone and Crockett standards...

I do n...

six ...
Coul...
next ...

than ...
send t...

ABOVE: This 192-2/8 non-typical was found dead by John Kozyra near Heatherdown, Alberta, in December of 1962. John wrote, "This buck was killed by another buck during the rut." ▲

RIGHT: In 1969, Harold McKnight was hunting near Coronation, Alberta, when he harvested this typical buck scoring 179-4/8 points.

LEFT: This snapshot shows Hugh Cox with his non-typical whitetail, which scores 198-1/8 points. He arrowed the buck in Hocking County, Ohio, in 1964.

▲ DENOTES UNOFFICIAL SCORE OR TROPHY IS BELOW CURRENT MINIMUM SCORE

997

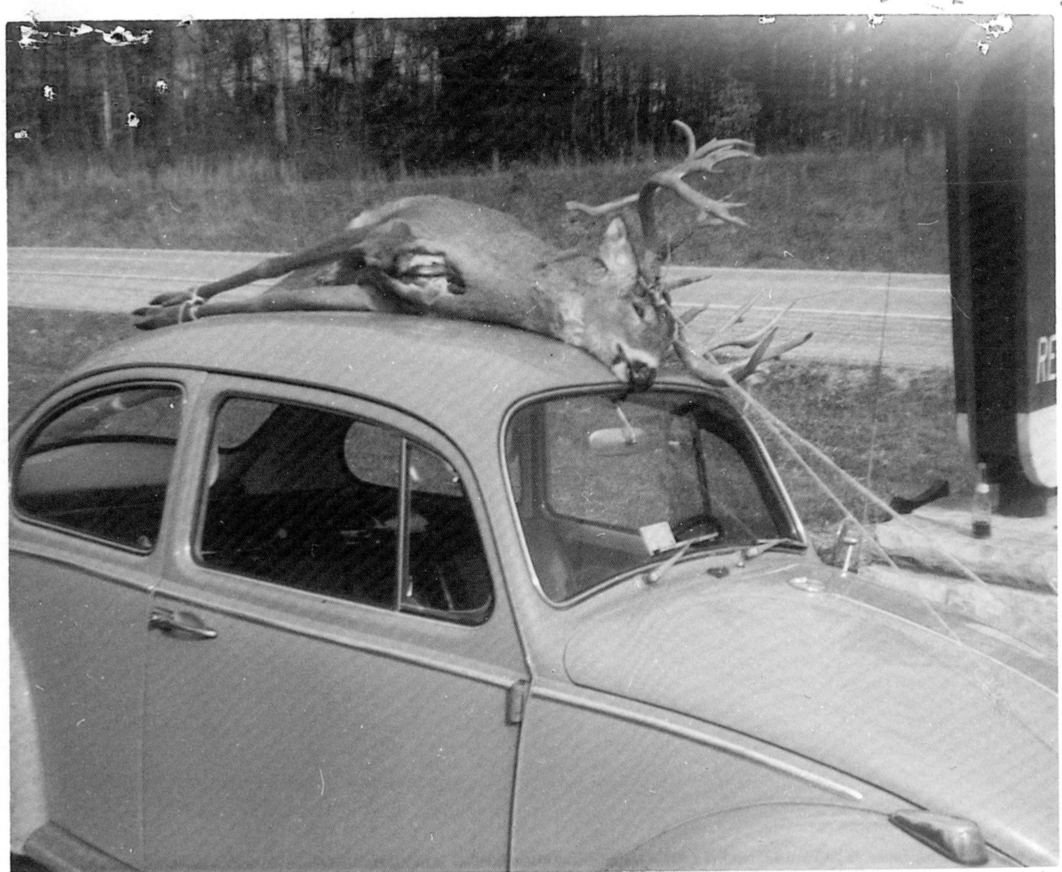

ABOVE: By today's standards, this would be unacceptable. Back then, it was both practical and commonplace. Richard G. Lohre harvested this outstanding non-typical buck in McCreary County, Kentucky, in November 1968. The final score on his trophy is 208-6/8 points – one of the finest of that era.

RIGHT: Clair W. Jensen with a huge buck from aptly-named Big Horn County, Montana. Taken in 1967, this typical scores 180 points. The body size of this buck is simply astounding.

LEFT: This typical, which scores 172-6/8 points, was taken in 1968 by Maurice Robinette in Spokane County, Washington. The buck currently ranks 10th All-time for that state.

REVISED FAIR CHASE STATEMENT FOR ALL ENTRIES IN BOONE AND CROCKETT CLUB COMPETITIONS AFTER DECEMBER 31, 1967

TROPHIES OBTAINED ONLY BY **FAIR CHASE** MAY BE ENTERED IN ANY BOONE AND CROCKETT CLUB BIG GAME COMPETITION

To make use of the following methods shall be deemed UNFAIR CHASE and unsportsmanlike, and any trophy obtained by use of such means is disqualified from entry in any Boone and Crockett Club big game competition:

I. Spotting or herding game from the air, followed by landing in its vicinity for pursuit;

II. Herding or pursuing game with motor-powered vehicles;

III. Use of electronic communications for attracting, locating or observing game, or guiding the hunter to such game.

* * * * * * * * * * *

not taken in UNFAIR CHASE as defined above by the Boone and

hunter from the air followed by landing in its vicinity for pursuit,
vehicles.

sed to attract, locate, observe, or guide the hunter to such game;
laws or regulations of the state, province or territory.

D

Ple

440

North American Big Game Committee, c/o Carnegie Museum,

F S DAVIDGE.

ABOVE: Jerry Loper is pictured with one of Louisiana's finest whitetails. This typical, taken in West Feliciana Parish, scores 170 points.

RIGHT: This non-typical, which scores 201-1/8, was harvested by Daniel B. Bullock in Arkansas County, Arkansas, in 1953. B&C received numerous entries from Arkansas during the 11th Competition, then saw no entries until the 19th Awards (1983-1985.)

LEFT: This phenomenal non-typical—a 13x15 scoring 238-1/8 points—was taken by Jack Davidge near Whitewood, Saskatchewan, on November 20, 1967. Davidge shot the buck with a .30-06 at 300 yards. This buck currently ranks 10th in Saskatchewan.

JUN • 61

ABOVE: This photo was included with Alvin Zimmerman's entry materials when his buck was entered in the spring of 1967. Zimmerman bagged this great typical, which scores 176-6/8 points, in Knox County, Nebraska, in November 1966.

RIGHT: It was November 23, 1960, when Ralph Duellman tagged this remarkable deer. Taken in Buffalo County, Wisconsin, this typical's final score is 172 points.

LEFT: Robert W. Newell and his wife, Sandy, pose with their deer from the 1960 season in Stevens County, Washington. Robert's 14x13 non-typical scores 201-4/8 points.

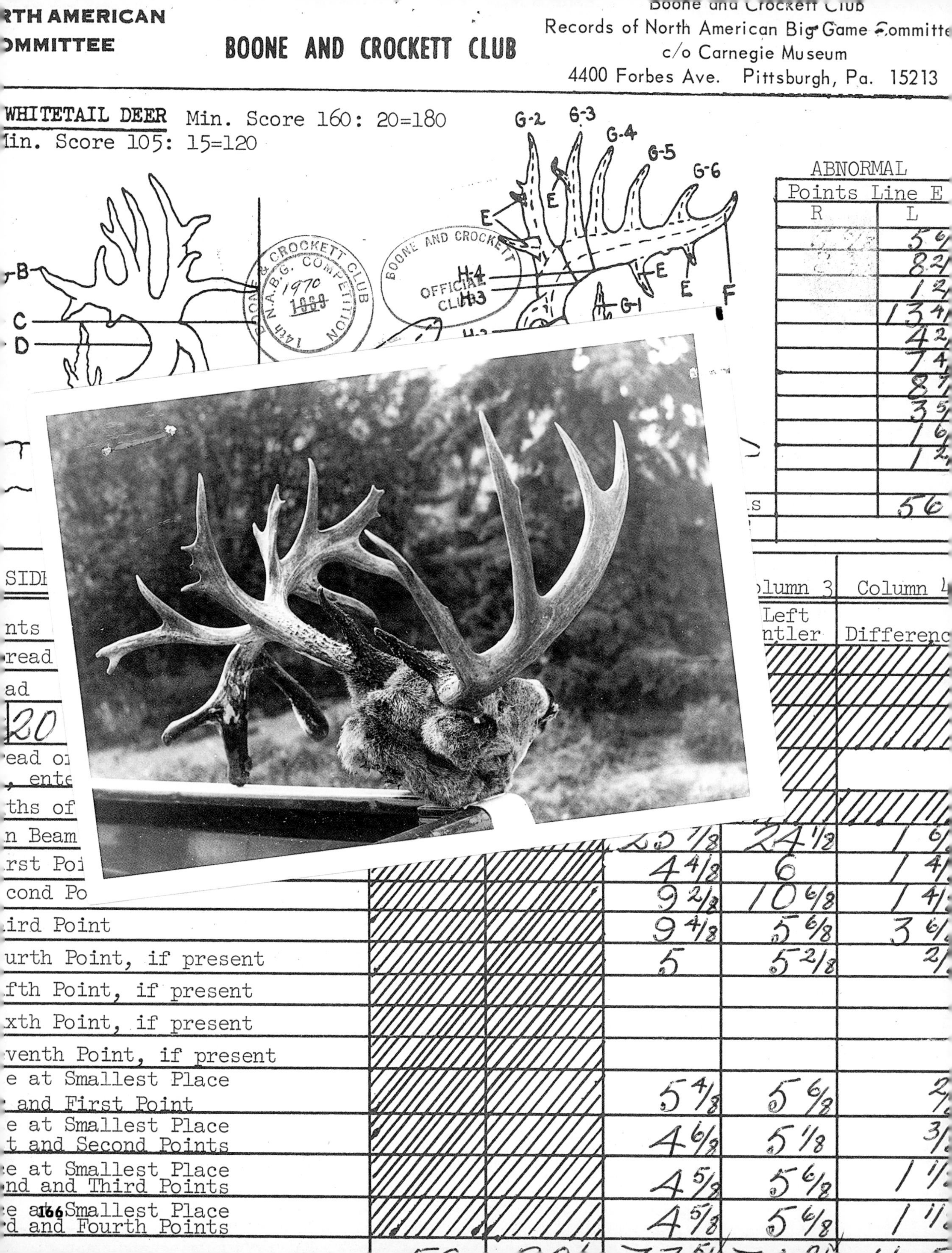
RTH AMERICAN
OMMITTEE
BOONE AND CROCKETT CLUB
Boone and Crockett Club
Records of North American Big Game Committe
c/o Carnegie Museum
4400 Forbes Ave. Pittsburgh, Pa. 15213
WHITETAIL DEER Min. Score 160: 20=180
Min. Score 105: 15=120
G-2 G-3 G-4 G-5 G-6
E E E E F
H-4 H-3 G-1
B C D
BOONE & CROCKETT CLUB 14th N.A.B.G. COMPETITION 1970 1969
BOONE AND CROCKETT OFFICIAL CLUB
ABNORMAL
Points Line E
R L
5 6/
8 2/
1 2/
13 4/
4 2/
7 4/
8 7/
3 5/
1 6/
1 2/
56
SIDE
Column 3 Column 4
Left Antler Difference
nts
read
ad
20
ead of
, ente
ths of
n Beam 25 1/8 24 1/2 1 6/
rst Point 4 4/8 6 1 4/
cond Point 9 2/8 10 6/8 1 4/
ird Point 9 4/8 5 6/8 3 6/
urth Point, if present 5 5 2/8 2/
fth Point, if present
xth Point, if present
venth Point, if present
e at Smallest Place and First Point 5 4/8 5 6/8 2/
e at Smallest Place t and Second Points 4 6/8 5 1/8 3/
e at Smallest Place nd and Third Points 4 5/8 5 6/8 1 1/
e at Smallest Place d and Fourth Points 4 5/8 5 6/8 1 1/

ABOVE: Four drop tines add a wealth of character to this non-typical, which scores 197-5/8 points. The deer was taken by James P. Borman in Sawyer County, Wisconsin, in November 1945.

RIGHT: W.R. Ingraham used a .30-06 to down this buck at 40 yards on a November 24, 1965, hunt in Adams County, Wisconsin. The final score on this 6x7 buck is 172-2/8 points.

LEFT: This unique non-typical, which scores 213 points, was taken by Jim Runzer near Rush Lake, Saskatchewan, during the 1966 season. Abnormal points on this 5x15 deer totaled 56 inches, all of which are formed on the deer's left side.

HUNTER, GUIDE AND HUNT INFORMATION

To be completed by hunter

BOONE AND CROCKETT CLUB

Records of North American
Big Game Committee

c/o Carnegie Museum
4400 Forbes Avenue
Pittsburgh, Pa. 15213

Hunter's name Marvin F. Lentz

Address Missouri

City P Zip

Guide's name None

Address

City

Location of hunt Miss

Date of arrival 11/16/68

Month Da

Date of departure 11/16/68

Month I

Mode of transportation Pickup

Were motor-powered vehicles used? No

and purpose

Date of kill November 16 1968

Month Day Year

Caliber of weapon .308 Winchester - Model 100

Weight of bullet 150 Grain

Pull of bow if bow and arrow used

Approximate distance from trophy 60 Feet

Marvin F. Lentz

Signature of Hunter

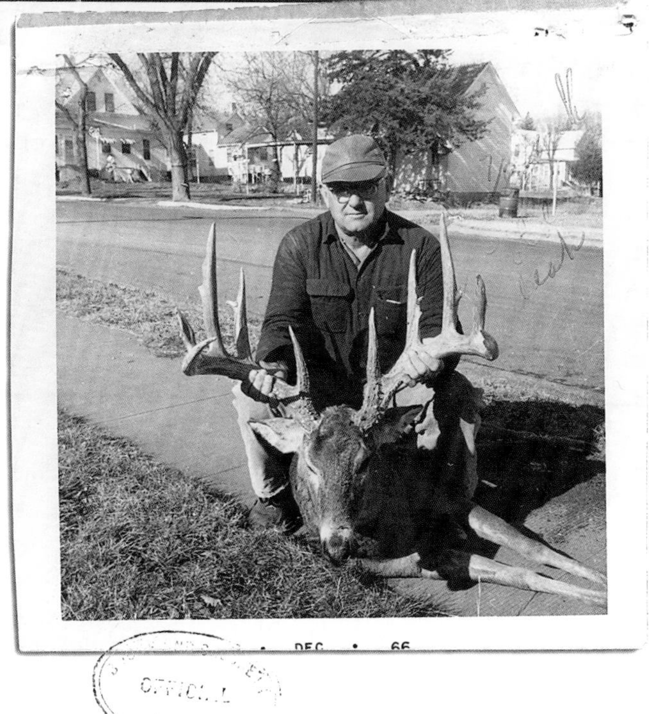

ABOVE: 1935 was the year Edward John encountered this amazing buck. Taken near Nelway, British Columbia, this non-typical scores 198-1/8 points.

RIGHT: Norman Anderson harvested this non-typical buck on December 12, 1966, in Waubaunsee County, Kansas. It scores 182-3/8 points.

LEFT: Marvin F. Lentz stands beside his buck-of-a-lifetime. Scoring 183-4/8 points, this typical buck is among Missouri's finest. Details of the hunt can be seen on the Hunter, Guide and Hunt Information form shown in the background.

HUNTER, GUIDE AND HUNT INFORMATION

To be completed by hunter

BOONE AN[illegible] CROCKETT CLUB

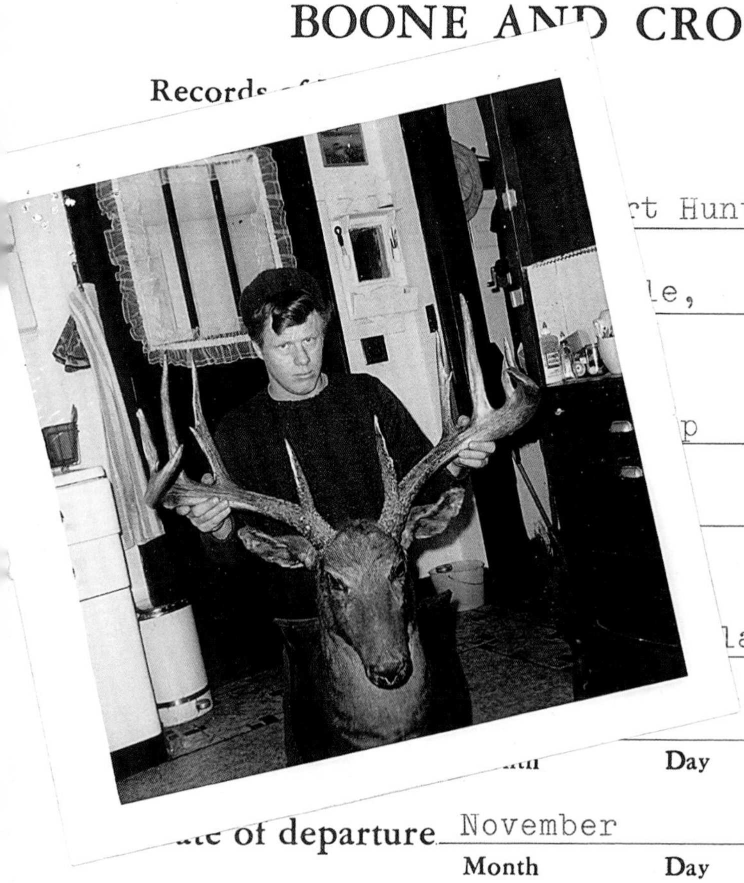

Records [illegible]

c/o Carnegie Museum
4400 Forbes Avenue
Pittsburgh, Pa. 15213

[illegible]rt Hunter

[illegible]le, Wisconsin
State Province Zip

[illegible]p

Wisconsin
State Province Zip

[illegible]las County, Wisconsin

1910
[illegible] Day Year

[illegible] of departure November 1910
Month Day Year

Mode of transportation Horse & Wagon Horse & Wagon
In Out

Were motor-powered vehicles used? No If so, specify type

and purpose

Date of kill November 1910
Month Day Year

Caliber of weapon 45-70

Weight of bullet 300gr

Pull of bow if bow and arrow used

Approximate distance from trophy 30 yd.

X May Docken, — Hunter Decease[illegible] Many Years Ag[illegible]

Signature of Hunter

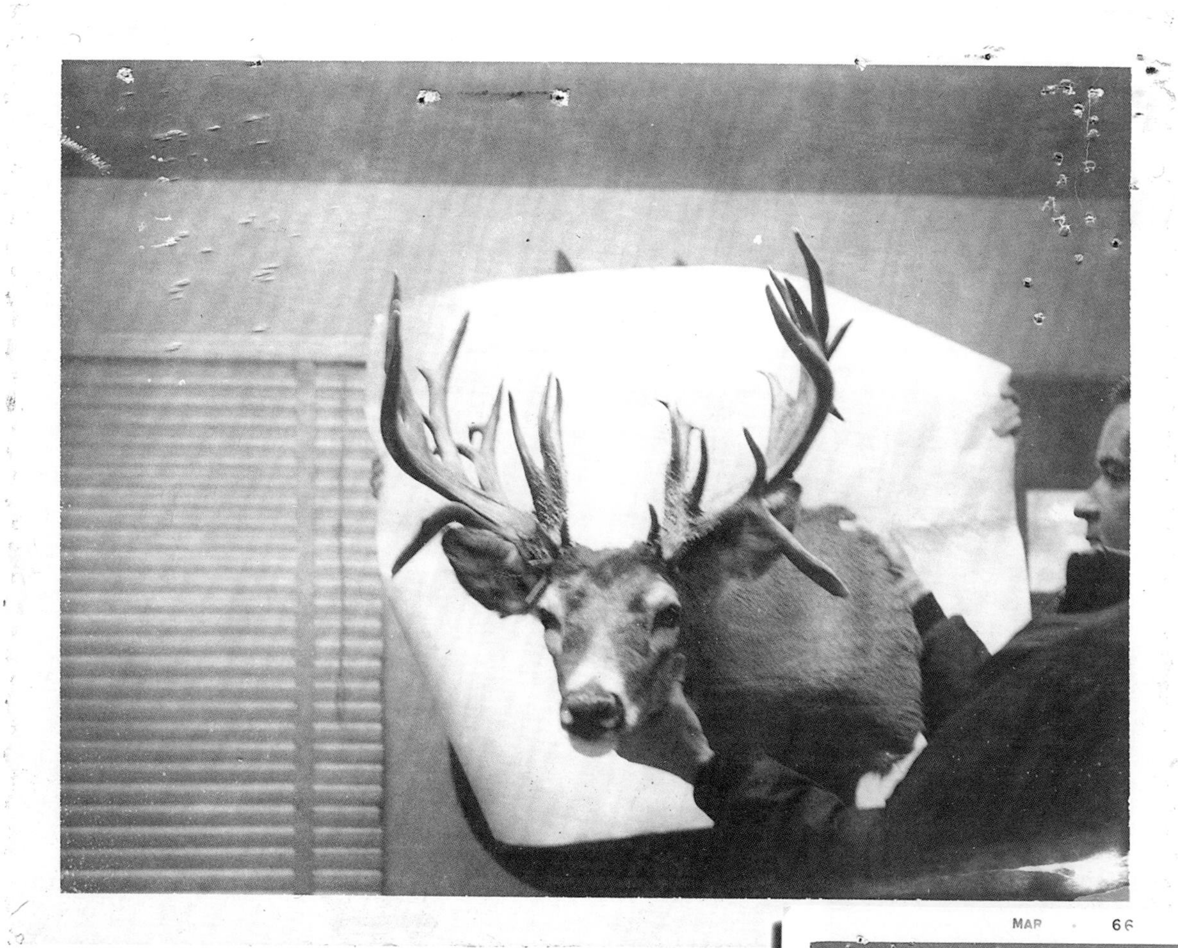

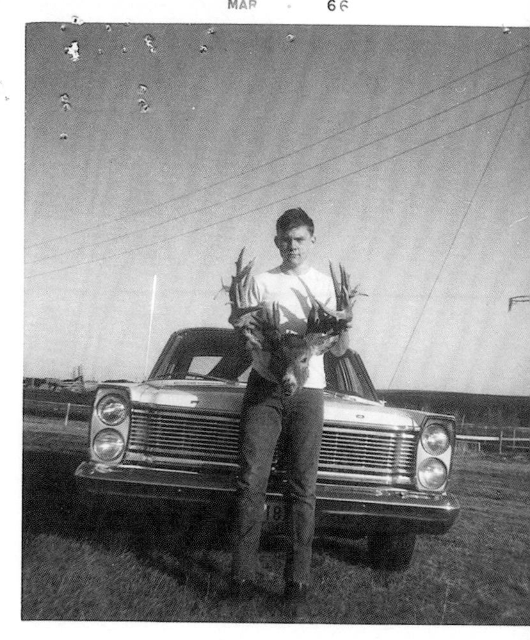

ABOVE: This giant 17x15 non-typical, scoring 238-7/8 points, is the second-largest whitetail ever recorded in Wyoming. The following note was in the entry materials: *Dear Mrs. Fitz, This non-typical whitetail was found by Mr. Petera two days after the season, with locked antlers. The other buck was a large typical head and when Mr. Petera released the two, the large typical deer was able to move away, but this fine non-typical deer was apparently paralyzed in the right side and was unable to move. — James Staley (Official Measurer)*

RIGHT: Jerry Roitsch holds his 249-1/8 non-typical, the third largest in South Dakota history. The 12x20 trophy, with a 201-3/8 typical frame, was taken near Lily, South Dakota, in 1965.

LEFT: Robert Hunter took this huge typical buck, which scores 191-3/8 points, in Vilas County, Wisconsin, in 1910. The greatest spread on this trophy is 30-2/8 inches. Almost 100 years later, this buck is still the fourth-largest whitetail from Wisconsin. Note the mode of transportation on the accompanying form.

ABOVE: Clarion County, Pennsylvania, was the location of the hunt that produced this fine typical scoring 173-3/8 points. While the photo was taken circa 1965, the deer was actually harvested in 1947 by Mead R. Kiefer.

RIGHT: This giant-framed typical was taken by Dwight E. Green in Warren County, Iowa, in 1964. This impressive deer has several outstanding features, including both main beams measuring over 30 inches, and the seventh-widest inside spread ever recorded at 30-3/8 inches. It received the First Award at the 13th Competition, and scores 187-2/8 points.

LEFT: A gentleman believed to be Peter Haupt (A B&C Official Measurer) holds a great typical buck taken by Lee F. Spittler in November 1953. This typical, which scores 183-5/8 points, was taken in Buffalo County, Wisconsin.

ABOVE: Dorsey O. Breeden holds Virginia's 15th-largest non-typical whitetail scoring 211-7/8 points. Breeden took this 10x12 in Rockingham County in 1966. This buck was one of the better entries in its category in the 13th Competition.

RIGHT: With a 25-7/8-inch inside spread, this great buck has a final score of 189-1/8 points. Van Shotzman was hunting in Nuckolls County, Nebraska, in 1968, when he harvested this buck. It currently stands as the fourth-largest typical ever recorded from Nebraska.

LEFT: Gary Littlejohn took this great typical buck (Georgia's 9th largest typical) with a 40-yard shot from his .303 in 1968. The final score is 179-2/8 points. Littlejohn (left) is pictured with Official Measurer Jack Crockford at the Georgia State Capitol, where the buck was officially measured.

To be completed by hunter

BOONE AND CROCKETT CLUB

Records of North American
Big Game Committee

c/o Carnegie Museum
4400 Forbes Avenue
...h Pa. 15213

Hunter's name Bill Metcalf

Address Wisc
City State Provir...

Guide's name

Address
City P...

Location of hunt Hayward, Sawyer

Date of arrival Nov ?
Month Day

Date of departure Nov ?
Month Day Year

Mode of transportation log train (In) log train (Out)

Were motor-powered vehicles used? no If so, specify type and purpose

Date of kill Nov ? 1924
Month Day Year

Caliber of weapon 38-40

Weight of bullet 250 gr

Pull of bow if bow and arrow used

Approximate distance from trophy 30 yd

ABOVE: H. Glenn Johnston downed this extremely massive New Brunswick whitetail in 1962. Even today this buck, which scores 243-7/8 points, stands as the second-largest ever recorded from that province. This buck sports 8-2/8-inch bases, and a phenomenal 56-3/8 inches of overall mass—one of the highest of such figures in B&C.

RIGHT: Ray Sadler harvested this fine whitetail in Clinton County, Mississippi, on November 25, 1963. The final score on this 12x11 is 176-6/8 points. It also would have scored 210-6/8 points as a non-typical, suggesting perhaps it should have been entered in the non-typical category instead. The final decision is always up to the trophy owner.

LEFT: Bill Metcalf shows his typical whitetail, which scores 174-6/8 points, from Sawyer County, Wisconsin. The deer was taken in 1924. Note the mode of transportation shown on the form. Mr. Metcalf's trophy was entered in the 14th Competition.

ABOVE: Gallia County, Ohio, was the location of this successful hunt in 1969. Jack Auxier displays his deer, which scores 175-3/8 points.

RIGHT: At 212 points, this huge non-typical is one of Michigan's finest. Ben Komblevicz downed the buck in Iron County in 1942.

LEFT: Extremely heavy base circumference measurements of 6-5/8 and 6-4/8 inches make this Butts County, Georgia, typical quite the trophy. Jack Hammond bagged this buck in 1963 with a .300 Savage. Its final score is 172 points.

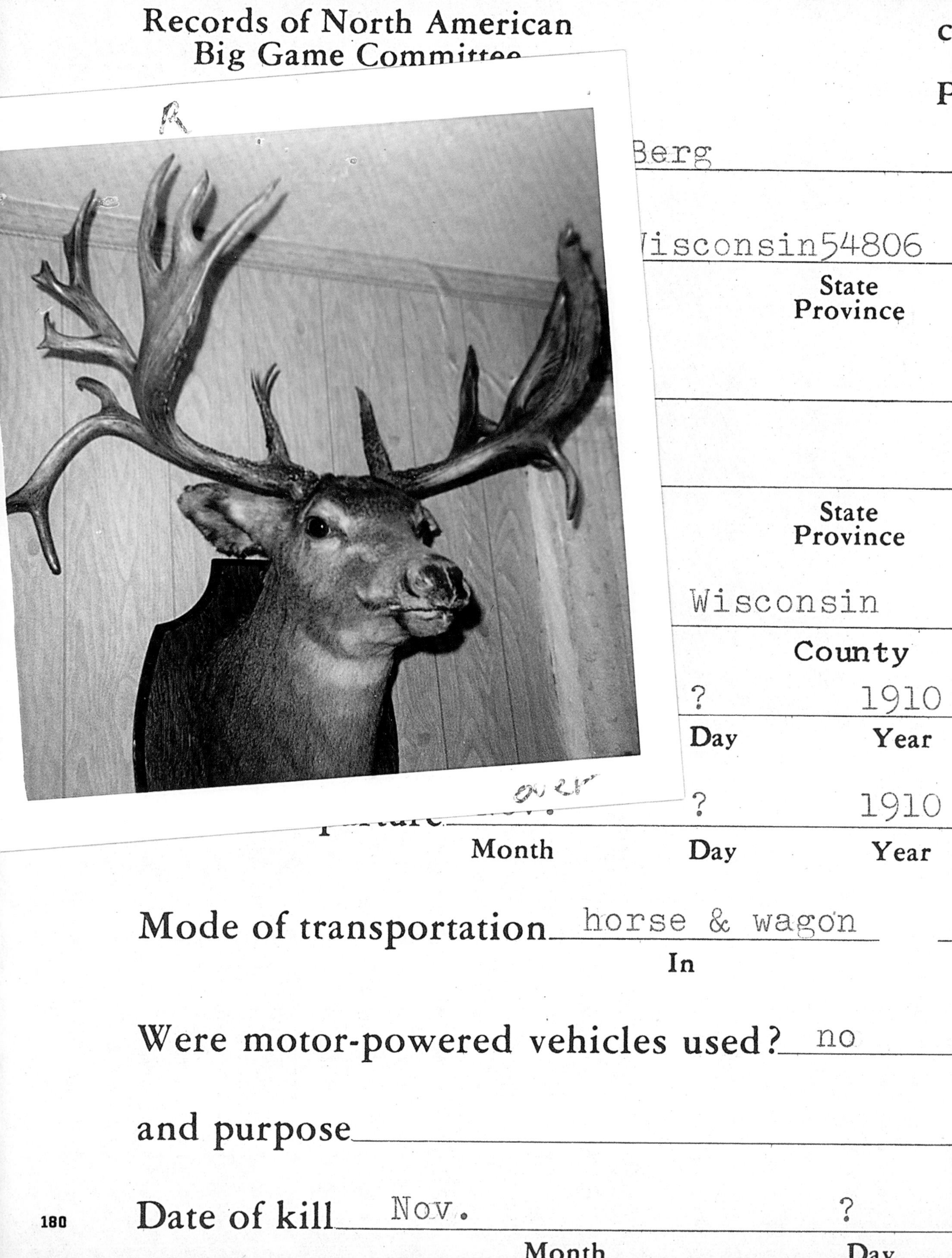

Records of North American
Big Game Committee

Berg

Wisconsin54806

State
Province

State
Province

Wisconsin

County

? 1910

Day Year

? 1910

Month Day Year

Mode of transportation horse & wagon

In

Were motor-powered vehicles used? no

and purpose

Date of kill Nov. ?

Month Day

ABOVE: Currently ranking number four on the Mississippi state list, this typical, which scores 180-4/8 points, is a tremendous trophy. W.F. Smith was the hunter, taking the buck on a 1968 hunt in Leflore County with a .257 Roberts out of a tree stand.

RIGHT: This non-typical, which scores 240 points, is the seventh largest ever recorded from Texas. Walter R. Schreiner was hunting in Kerr County in 1905 when he and this huge 15x11-point crossed paths.

LEFT: Horse and wagon was the mode of transportation Charles Berg used on the day he took this giant buck in 1910. He was hunting northeast of Cable, Wisconsin, when he encountered this 13x10 point non-typical scoring 228-2/8 points.

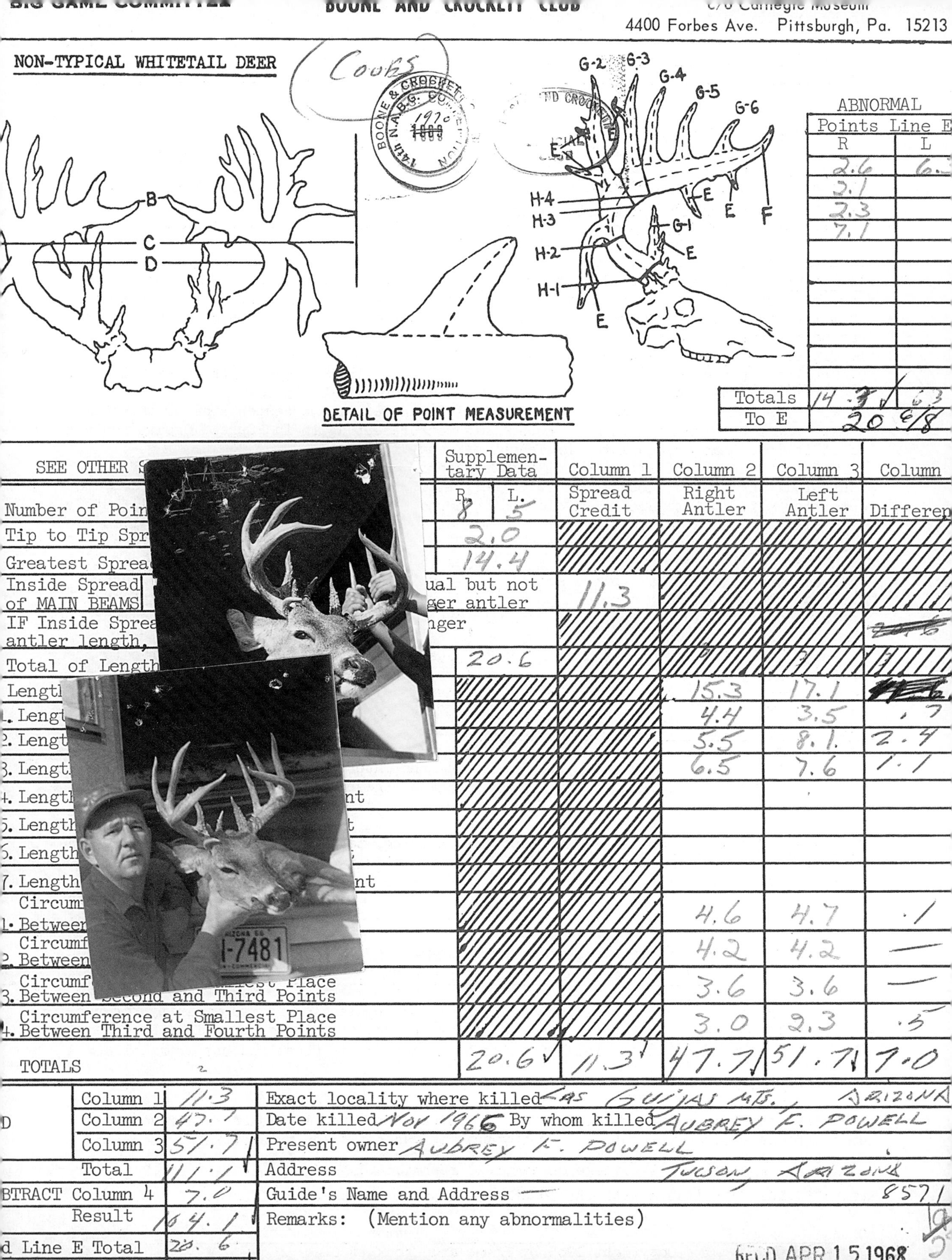

BIG GAME COMMITTEE — BOONE AND CROCKETT CLUB — c/o Carnegie Museum, 4400 Forbes Ave. Pittsburgh, Pa. 15213

NON-TYPICAL WHITETAIL DEER (Coues)

ABNORMAL Points Line E	R	L
	2.6	6.3
	2.1	
	2.3	
	7.1	
Totals	14.1 ✓	6.3
To E	20 6/8	

SEE OTHER S[IDE FOR INSTRUCTIONS]	Supplementary Data R.	Supplementary Data L.	Column 1 Spread Credit	Column 2 Right Antler	Column 3 Left Antler	Column 4 Difference
Number of Poin[ts on Each Antler]	8	5				
Tip to Tip Spr[ead]	2.0					
Greatest Sprea[d]	14.4					
Inside Spread of MAIN BEAMS [... may equ]ual but not [exceed lon]ger antler			11.3			
IF Inside Sprea[d ... exceeds lo]nger antler length,						~~20.6~~
Total of Length[s of Abnormal Points]	20.6					
Length [of Main Beam]				15.3	17.1	~~1.8~~
1. Lengt[h ...]				4.4	3.5	.9
2. Lengt[h ...]				5.5	8.1	2.4
3. Lengt[h ...]				6.5	7.6	1.1
4. Length [... Poi]nt						
5. Length [...]						
6. Length [...]						
7. Length [... Poi]nt						
Circum[ference ...] 1. Between [...]				4.6	4.7	.1
Circumf[erence ...] 2. Between [...]				4.2	4.2	—
Circumf[erence at Sma]llest Place 3. Between Second and Third Points				3.6	3.6	—
Circumference at Smallest Place 4. Between Third and Fourth Points				3.0	2.3	.5
TOTALS	20.6 ✓		11.3	47.7 ✓	51.7 ✓	7.0

Column 1	11.3	Exact locality where killed Las Guijas Mts., Arizona
Column 2	47.7	Date killed Nov 1966 By whom killed Aubrey F. Powell
Column 3	51.7	Present owner Aubrey F. Powell
Total	111.1	Address Tucson, Arizona 85711
[SU]BTRACT Column 4	7.0	Guide's Name and Address —
Result	104.1	Remarks: (Mention any abnormalities)
[Ad]d Line E Total	20.6	

ABOVE: The Tumacacori Mountains in Santa Cruz County, Arizona, produced this Coues' deer for Seymour H. Levy in 1967. At 116-7/8 points, this Coues' deer was the ninth-largest entered in the 14th Competition (1968-1970.)

RIGHT: Diego G. Sada was hunting in Sonora, Mexico, when he encountered this giant Coues' deer. This long-tined buck won the First Award at the 14th Competition, held at the Carnegie Museum in Pittsburgh. This deer, taken in 1969, scores 120-4/8 points.

LEFT: This non-typical Coues' whitetail was taken in 1966 by Aubrey F. Powell. The buck, taken in the Las Guijas Mountains of Arizona, has a final score of 124-7/8 points.

ABOVE: Earl H. Harris (far right) displays his trophy typical Coues' whitetail, which scores 116-3/8 points. The buck was taken near the Blue River in Arizona in 1965. Jason McPharlin (second from the left) was his hunting partner that day.

RIGHT: This great trophy taken by Bernard Tennant in 1960 has tremendous eye guards. The final score on this Jackson County, Ohio, buck is 204-4/8 points.

LEFT: A very pleased Richard E. Johndrow displays the NRA's Silver Bullet Award plaque he received for his typical whitetail taken near Schroon Lake, New York, in 1968. Scoring 171-4/8 points, Johndrow's Essex County deer was an entry in the 14th Competition (1968-1970.)

HUNTER, GUIDE AND HUNT INFORMATION

To be completed by hunter

BOONE AND CROCKETT CLUB

Records of North American
Big Game Committee

c/o Carnegie Museum
4400 Forbes Avenue
Pittsburgh, Pa. 15213

Hunter's name HENRY J. BREDAEL

Address GREEN BAY
City State Province Zip

Guide's name

AUG 68

State Province Zip

Oconto Co., Wis.

1939
Year

1939
Year

Automobile
Out

If so, specify type

Date of kill Nov. 24 1939
Month Day Year

Caliber of weapon 30/06

Weight of bullet 220 GR.

Pull of bow if bow and arrow used

Approximate distance from trophy 75 yds.

Henry J. Bredael
Signature of Hunter

RECD SEP 23 1968

ABOVE: Trempealeau County, Wisconsin, is where Dennis L. Ulberg harvested this non-typical buck scoring 205-3/8 points. The hunt took place on November 28, 1968. This trophy was an entry in the 14th Competition (1968-1970).

RIGHT: Rudy C. Grecar arrowed this fine non-typical buck with a 35-yard shot in 1969. This buck, from Geauga County, Ohio, scores 200-4/8 points.

LEFT: This 172-point typical was taken by Henry J. Bredael in Oconto County, Wisconsin, on a November 1939 hunt. Official Measurer Peter Haupt is shown holding the trophy.

HUNTER, GUIDE AND HUNT INFORMATION

T... e completed by hunter

...ND CROCKETT CLUB

c/o Carnegie Museum
4400 Forbes Avenue
Pittsburgh, Pa. 15213

R. HUGHES

ARIZONA

State Province — Zip

...NZ

State Province — Zip

LIBERTAD, MEXICO

11/1/67

...h Day Year

11/2/67

...th Day Year

...n JEEP — JEEP

In — Out

... vehicles used? NO If so, specify type

/1/67

Month Day Year

Caliber of weapon 30-30 WINCHESTER

Weight of bullet 150 GRAIN

Pull of bow if bow and arrow used

Approximate distance from trophy 150 YDS

Abe R Hughes

Signature of Hunter

ABOVE & RIGHT: Enrique C. Cicero had two consecutive amazing seasons in 1966 and 1967. The first year he harvested a 110-typical Coues' (right) in Sonora, Mexico. He returned in 1967 and bagged this non-typical shown above, which scores 125-3/8 points.

LEFT: While the date on this entry was 1967, the equipment and transportation used would have seemed appropriate many decades earlier. Abe R. Hughes took this outstanding Coues' deer, which scores 117-5/8 points, near Libertad, Mexico.

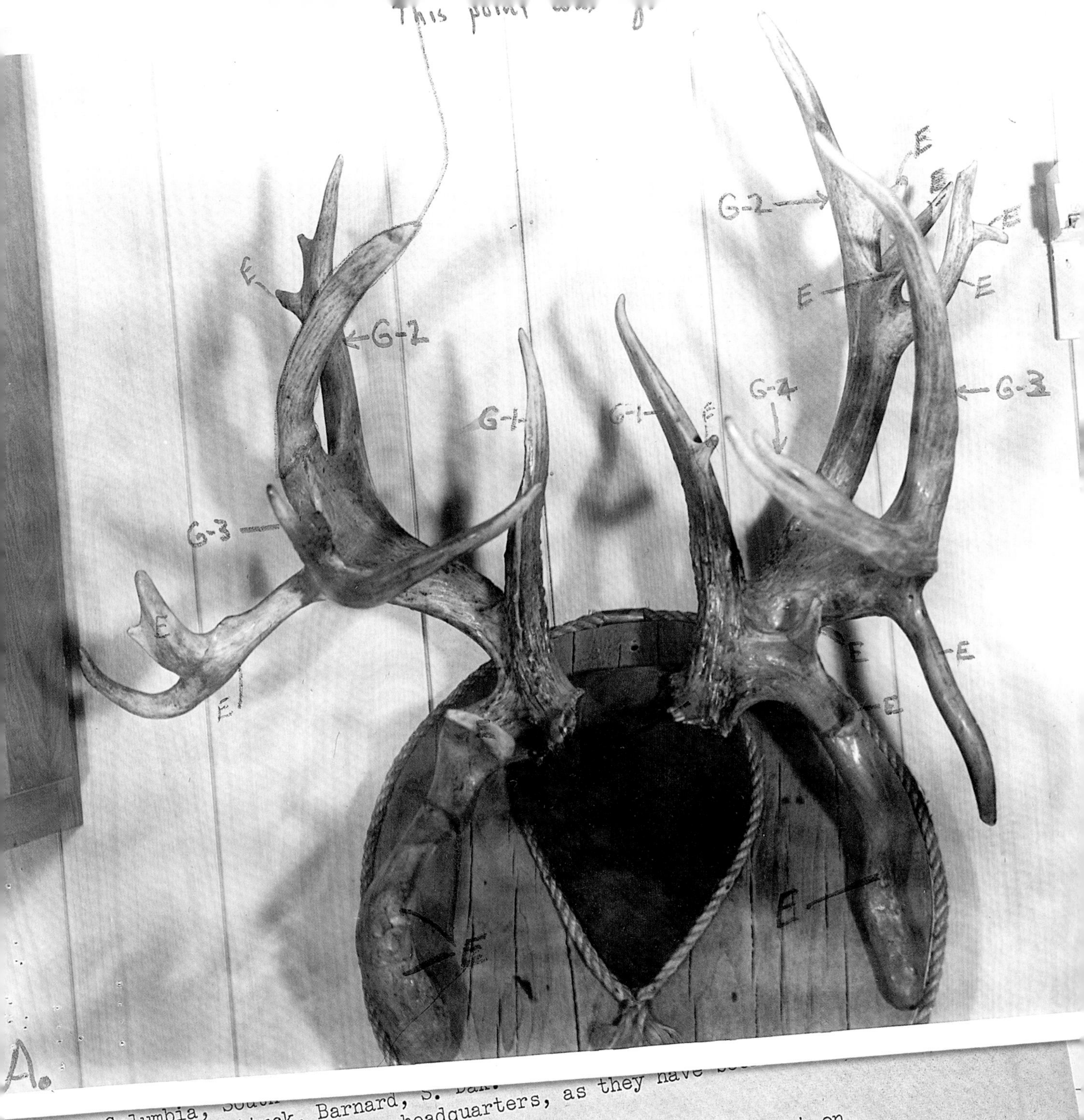

Columbia, South ... Francis Shattuck, Barnard, S. Dak. ... on display at the refuge headquarters, as they have been since 1961.

A fellow at the refuge some years ago attached a point on the right antler at a location where a point (location of G-3) apparently had been broken off (see photo A) before the deer was shot. I have a copy of the photo of the deer immediately after it was shot (see photo B) so that a comparison can be made. Although this original point would be E-3, it is 1-5/8" long, but over 2½" wide at the base. Consequently, it is not counted as a point.

...ional interpretation is needed. One of the ab- ... antler that is 2-6/8" (see score ... from the tip and glued ... total score

'NT INFORMATION
y hunter

CKETT CLUB

c/o Carnegie Museum
4400 Forbes Avenue
Pittsburgh, Pa. 15213

ı Dakota 57426
State Zip
rovince

State Zip
ovince

Wildlife Refuge, Brown Co., S

1960
Year

1960
Year

ɪs are allowed in refuge while
Out it is open
to deer hunting

If so, specify type

1960
Day Year

sed None

hy 25 yards

G. Shattuck
Signature of Hunter

ABOVE: Okanogan County, Washington, produced this outstanding non-typical, which scores 203-3/8 points, in 1961. Michael A. Anderson was the successful hunter.

LEFT: Francis Shattuck downed this incredible non-typical, scoring 216-7/8 points, in Brown County, South Dakota, in 1960 using a 12-gauge shotgun. The tremendous drop-tines measured 11-1/8 and 11-6/8 inches. Shattuck was hunting in the Sand Lake National Wildlife Refuge.

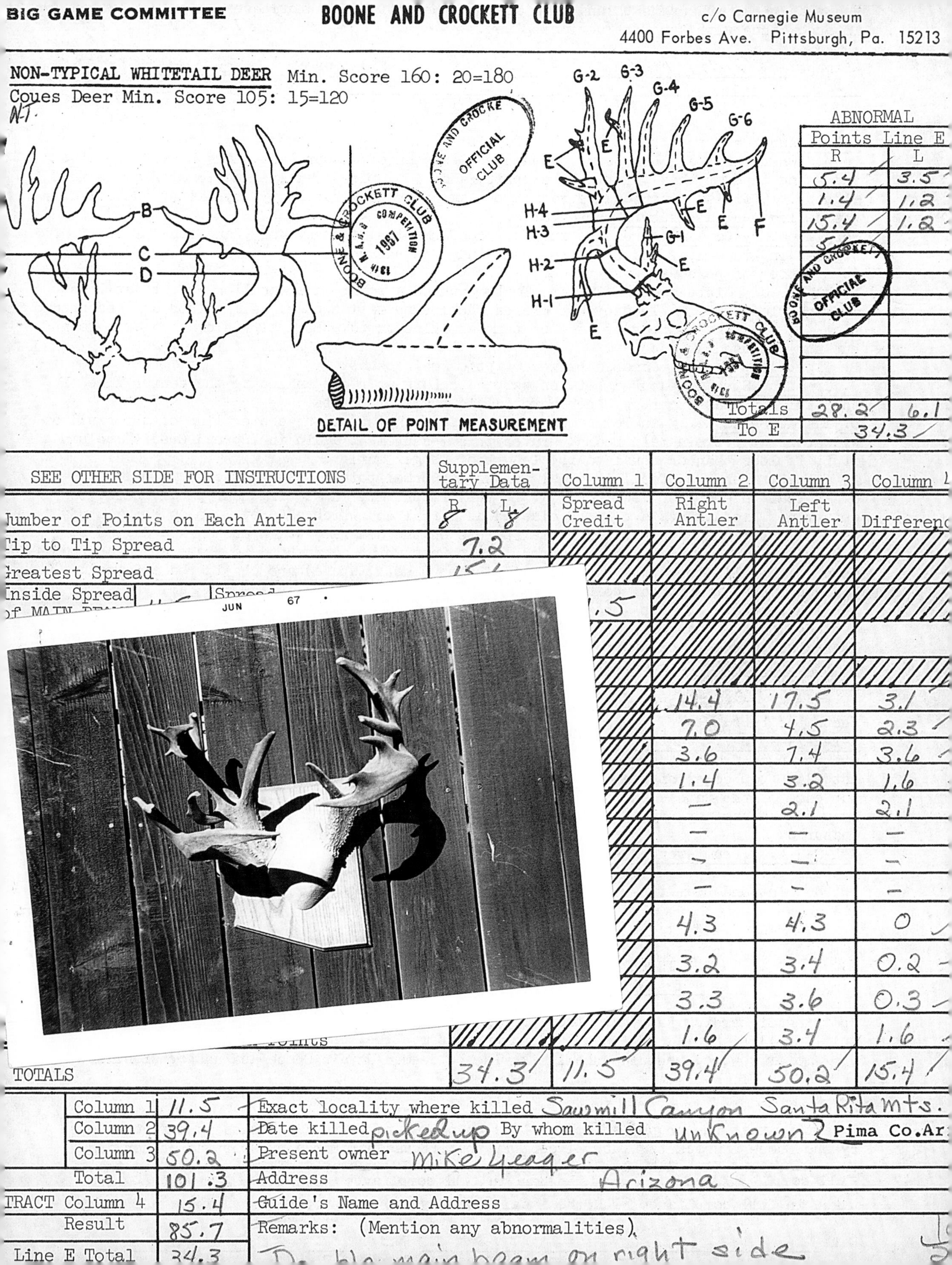

BIG GAME COMMITTEE **BOONE AND CROCKETT CLUB** c/o Carnegie Museum
4400 Forbes Ave. Pittsburgh, Pa. 15213

NON-TYPICAL WHITETAIL DEER Min. Score 160: 20=180
Coues Deer Min. Score 105: 15=120
N-T

ABNORMAL Points Line E	
R	L
5.4	3.5
1.4	1.2
15.4	1.2
5.[illegible]	
Totals 28.2	6.1
To E 34.3	

SEE OTHER SIDE FOR INSTRUCTIONS	Supplementary Data R	Supplementary Data L	Column 1 Spread Credit	Column 2 Right Antler	Column 3 Left Antler	Column 4 Difference
Number of Points on Each Antler	8	8				
Tip to Tip Spread	7.2					
Greatest Spread	15.[illegible]					
Inside Spread of MAIN BEAMS / Spread [illegible]	4.5		11.5			
				14.4	17.5	3.1
				7.0	4.5	2.3
				3.6	7.4	3.6
				1.4	3.2	1.6
				—	2.1	2.1
				—	—	—
				—	—	—
				—	—	—
				4.3	4.3	0
				3.2	3.4	0.2
				3.3	3.6	0.3
[illegible] Points				1.6	3.4	1.6
TOTALS	34.3		11.5	39.4	50.2	15.4

Column 1	11.5	Exact locality where killed Sawmill Canyon Santa Rita Mts.
Column 2	39.4	Date killed picked up By whom killed unknown Pima Co. Ar[illegible]
Column 3	50.2	Present owner Mike Yeager
Total	101.3	Address Arizona
[SUB]TRACT Column 4	15.4	Guide's Name and Address
Result	85.7	Remarks: (Mention any abnormalities)
Line E Total	34.3	Double main beam on right side

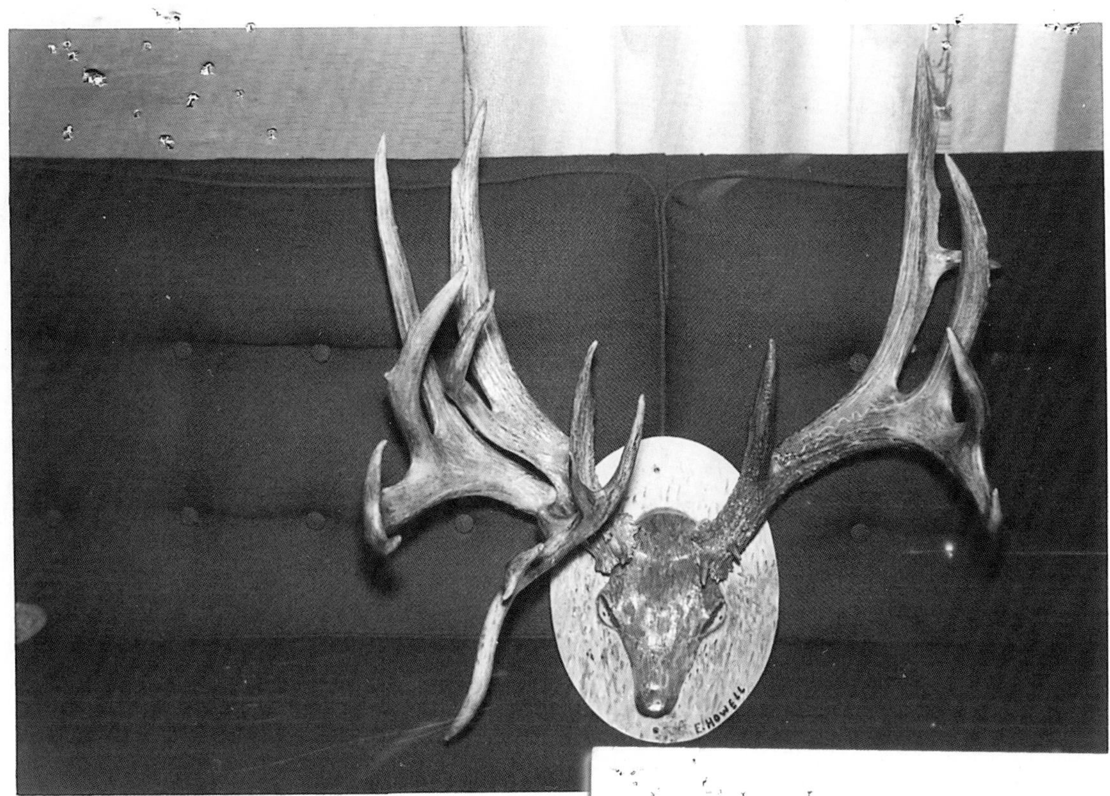

69

ABOVE: This great buck was taken by Steve Kapay. The non-typical, which scores 233 points, was taken near Punnichy, Saskatchewan, in 1968.

RIGHT: This fine 198-5/8 non-typical from Iron County, Mississippi, was taken in 1930 by Eino Macki.

LEFT: This amazing Coues' deer, owned by Mike Yeager, was taken by an unknown hunter prior to 1966, when it was entered. The final score on this unique and intriguing non-typical is 120-2/8 points.

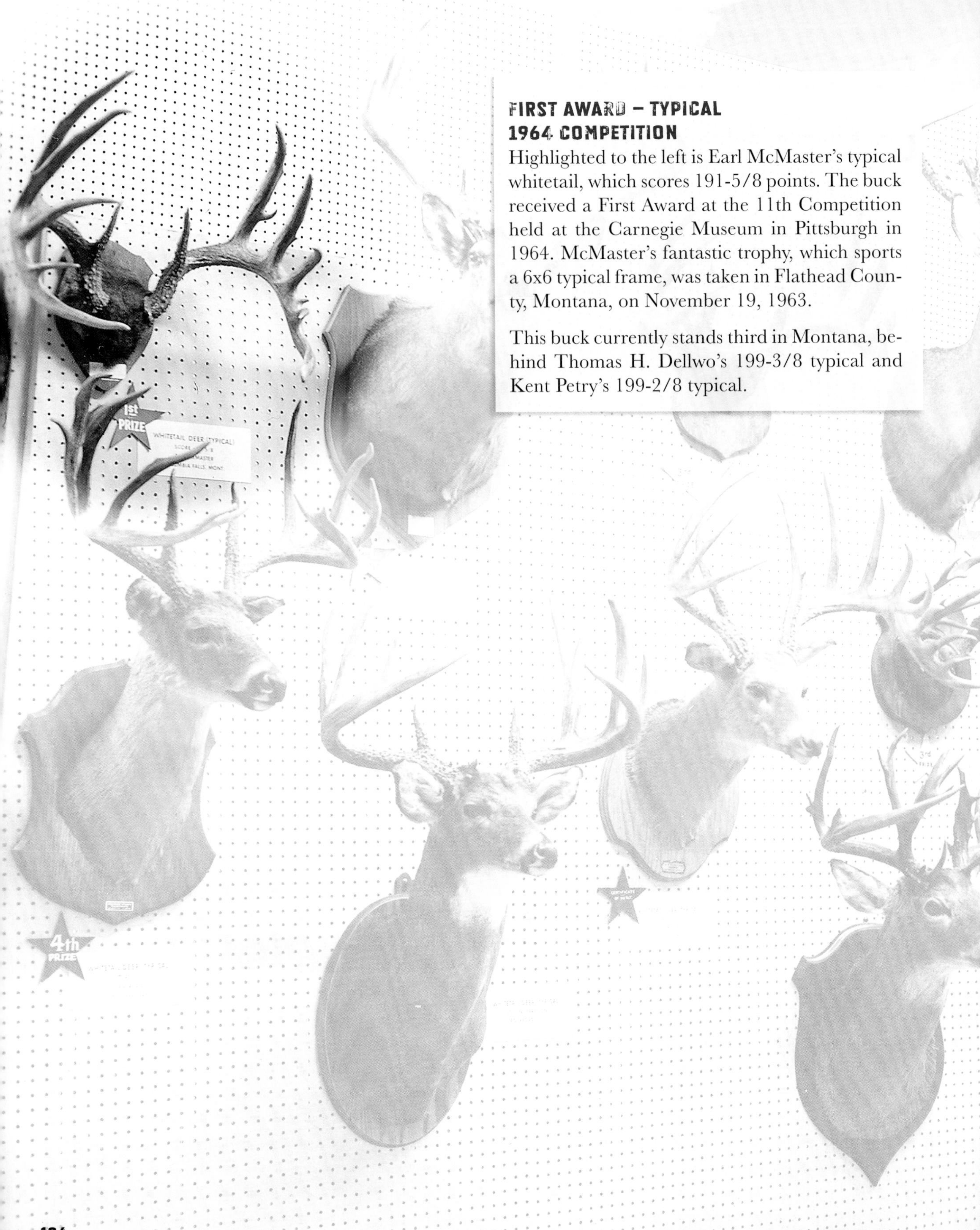

FIRST AWARD – TYPICAL 1964 COMPETITION

Highlighted to the left is Earl McMaster's typical whitetail, which scores 191-5/8 points. The buck received a First Award at the 11th Competition held at the Carnegie Museum in Pittsburgh in 1964. McMaster's fantastic trophy, which sports a 6x6 typical frame, was taken in Flathead County, Montana, on November 19, 1963.

This buck currently stands third in Montana, behind Thomas H. Dellwo's 199-3/8 typical and Kent Petry's 199-2/8 typical.

5: AWARD WINNERS

A MOVE TO CARNEGIE MUSEUM

E. T. McMaster

OFFICIAL SCORING SYSTEM FOR NORTH AMERICAN BIG GAME TROPHIES

RECORDS OF NORTH AMERICAN BIG GAME COMMITTEE

BOONE AND CROCKETT CLUB

Address Correspondence to:
Mrs. Grancel Fitz, Secretary
5 Tudor City Place, NYC 17,

#57

WHITETAIL and COUES DEER

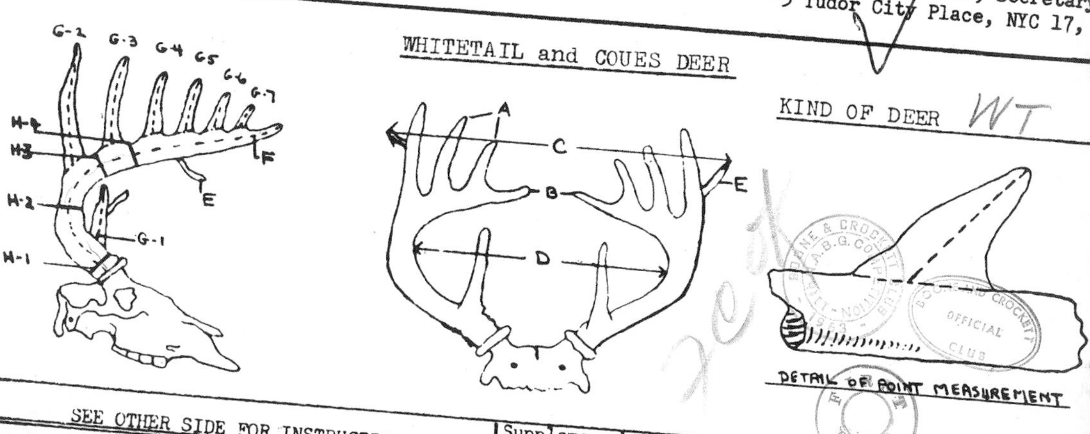

SEE OTHER SIDE FOR INSTRUCTIONS

	Supplementary Data R.	Supplementary Data L.	Column 1 Spread Credit	Column 2 Right Antler	Column 3 Left Antler	Column 4 Difference
A. Number of Points on Each Antler	6	7				
B. Tip to Tip Spread	13 3/8					
C. Greatest ...	21 5/8					
...dit may equal but not ...gth of longer antler			19			
...xceeds longer						
...Points						
				26 4/8	26 4/8	1 5/8
				4 6/8	4 6/8	3/8
				13 7/8	13 5/8	—
				12 2/8	11 7/8	4/8
				9 6/8	9 6/8	1 4/8
				4	4 5/8	—
						5/8
				5 1/8	5	1/8
				4 3/8	4 4/8	1/8
				4 4/8	4 3/8	1/8
... Third and ... Point and				4 5/8	4 5/8	2/8
			19.000 19	88.875 88 7/8	88.625 88 5/8	4.875 4 7/8

...re killed Greston, Flathead County, Montana

...3 By whom killed Earl McMaster

...l McMaster

...alls, Montana,

...ress

... abnormalities)

SECOND AWARD – TYPICAL 1964 COMPETITION

Arlee McCullough's typical whitetail, scoring 181-4/8 points, was taken from Licking County, Ohio, in 1962. The buck received the Second Award at the 11th Competition.

Today, this trophy would be quite far down the list of potential invited trophies. In the 1960s, however, this was a remarkable trophy. This is just one example of how much whitetail hunting has changed in 40 years.

Stephen Kish (left) and John Batten (right) measure the inside spread of McCullough's 181-4/8 typical at 22-7/8 inches.

McCullough

SYSTEM FOR NORTH AMERICAN BIG GAME TROPHIES

OONE AND CROCKETT CLUB

Address Corresp
Mrs. Grancel Fi
5 Tudor City Pl

ITETAIL and COUES DEER

KIND OF DEER

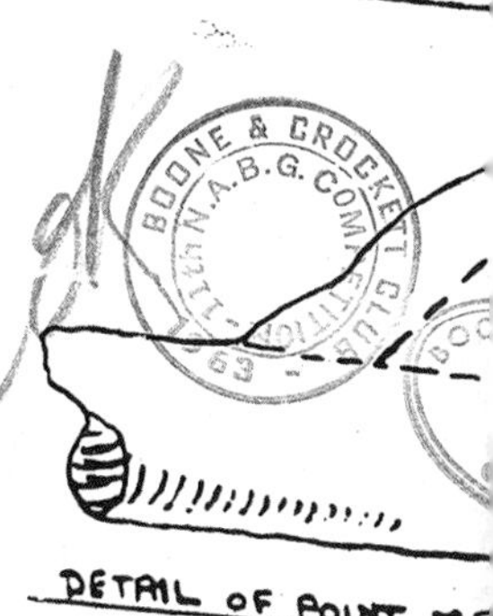

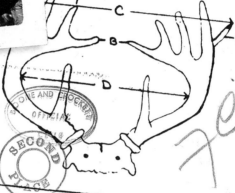

DETAIL OF POINT ME

SEE OTHER SIDE FOR INSTRUCTIONS

	Supplementary Data R.	Supplementary Data L.	Column 1 Spread Credit	Column 2 Right Antler	Column 3 Left Antler
A. Number of Points on Each Antler	7	7			
B. Tip to Tip Spread	21 3/8				
C. Greatest Spread	24 4/8				
D. Inside Spread of MAIN BEAMS 22 7/8 — Spread credit may equal but not exceed length of longer antler			22 7/8		
IF Inside Spread of Main Beams exceeds longer antler length, enter difference					
E. Total of Lengths of all Abnormal Points					
F. Length of Main Beam				24 4/8	25 3/4
G-1. Length of First Point, if present				5 7/8	4 4/8
G-2. Length of Second Point				6 3/8	7 6/8
G-3. Length of Third Point				8 6/8	10 7/8
G-4. Length of Fourth Point, if present				9 5/8	9 7/8
G-5. Length of Fifth Point, if present				5 2/8	5 5/8
G-6. Length of Sixth Point, if present					
G-7. Length of Seventh Point, if present					
H-1. Circumference at Smallest Place Between Burr and First Point				5 4/8	5 7/8
H-2. Circumference at Smallest Place Between First and Second Points				5	5 2/8
H-3. Circumference at Smallest Place Between Second and Third Points				5 1/8	5 4/8
H-4. Circumference at Smallest Place between Third and Fourth Points or half way between Third Point and Beam Tip if Fourth Point is missing				5	5 4/8
TOTALS			22.875	81.250	85.5[illegible]

R 25 2/8 L 25 6/8

ADD 81,150 | Column 1 22 7/8 | Exact localit

Medal x Certificate received at ... Trophy

OFFICIAL SCORING SYSTEM FOR NORTH AMERICAN BIG GAME TROPHIES

RDS OF NORTH AMERICAN
IG GAME COMMITTEE

BOONE AND CROCKETT CLUB

Boone and Crockett Club
Records of North American Big Game Committee
c/o Carnegie Museum
4400 Forbes Ave. Pittsburgh, Pa. 15213

DP17000461

WHITETAIL and COUES DEER

KIND OF DEER *Whitetail*

II

109 (62)

#62

G-2 G-3 G-4 G-5 G-6 G-7 F E G-1 A C B D E

BOONE & CROCKETT CLUB 1965

SECOND PLACE

DETAIL OF POINT MEASUREMENT

12th Competition

SEE OTHER SIDE FOR ...	Supplementary Data R.	Supplementary Data L.	Column 1 Spread Credit	Column 2 Right Antler	Column 3 Left Antler	Column 4 Difference
A. Number o...	*7*	*7*				
B. ...	*13 3/8*					
	20 6/8					
...ual but not ...er antler			*18 6/8*			
...onger						
						1/8
				25 2/8	*25 6/8*	*1 4/8*
				4 2/8	*3 3/8*	*2 6/8*
				6 1/8	*8 2/8*	*1 7/8*
				11	*9 6/8*	*5/8*
				10 4/8	*11 1/8*	*7/8*
				9 5/8	*9 7/8*	*3 3/8*
				2 3/8	*5 5/8*	
						1/8
				5 1/8	*5 2/8*	*2/8*
				4 6/8	*5*	*7/8*
				5 3/8	*5 5/8*	*2/8*
...and				*5 2/8*	*7 3/8*	*2 1/8*
			18 6/8	*90 6/8*	*97 5/8*	*12 5/8*

...	*...18*	Exact locality where killed *Monroe Co. Iowa*
Column 2	*90 6/8*	Date killed *12-2-62* By whom killed *LLOYD GOAD*
Column 3	*97 5/8*	Present owner *" ~~Lloyd Hoffman~~ KNOXVILLE IOWA*
Total	*207 1/8*	Address
SUBTRACT Column 4	*12 5/8*	Guide's Name and Address
		Remarks: (Mention any abnormalities)
FINAL SCORE	*194 4/8*	

406

**SECOND AWARD – TYPICAL
1966 COMPETITION**

Lloyd Goad took this tremendous 7x7 typical in Monroe County, Iowa, in 1962. At 194-4/8 points, Goad's buck received the Second Award at the 12th Competition held at Pittsburgh's Carnegie Museum. Only the new World's Record (later identified as being taken by James Jordan) and Melvin J. Johnson's Sagamore Hill Award-winning typical scoring 204-4/8 points, scored higher.

A few of the 1966 Judges Panel members are shown in the background, from left to right: John H. Batten, Dr. John Hammett, Frank Cook, and George Church.

OFFICIAL SCORING SYSTEM FOR NORTH AMERICAN BIG GAME TROPHIES — Trophy Rack

RECORDS OF NORTH AMERICAN BIG GAME COMMITTEE

BOONE AND CROCKETT CLUB

Boone and Crockett Club
Records of North American Big Game Committee
c/o Carnegie Museum
4400 Forbes Ave. Pittsburgh, Pa. 15213

WHITETAIL and COUES DEER

KIND OF DEER Whitetail

H.M.

SEE OTHER SIDE FOR INSTRUCTIONS

	Supplementary Data R.	Supplementary Data L.	Column 1 Spread Credit	Column 2 Right Antler	Column 3 Left Antler	Column 4 Difference
	10	7				
	11 6/8					
	20 6/8					
... but not ... antler			18 5/8			—
...iger						1
						2/8
				24 2/8	24 5/8	1 5/8
				4 2/8	6 4/8	—
				8 3/8	8 3/8	1 2/8
				12	10 6/8	4/8
				9 5/8	10 1/8	2/8
				3 5/8	4 7/8	1
				6 5/8	6 2/8	3/8
				4 6/8	4 5/8	1/8
				4 2/8	4 5/8	2/8
Third and ... Point and ...				4 4/8	4 5/8	1/8
			18 5/8	84 1/8	85 3/8	6 6/8 ~~6 4/8~~

H-4. Beam Tip if Tou...

TOTALS			
ADD	Column 1	18 5/8	Exact locality where killed Southern Pope Co. Ill. By whom killed Jack A. Higgs
	Column 2	84 1/8	Date killed
	Column 3	85 3/8	Present owner Jack A. Higgs
			Address
(6 6/8)	Total	188 1/8	Guide's Name and Address
SUBTRACT	Column 4	- 6 4/8	Remarks: (Mention any abnormalities)
		5/8	181 3/8

408

**HONORABLE MENTION
TYPICAL
1966 COMPETITION**

Jack A. Higgs' typical, which scores 181-3/8 points, is shown mounted at left, and in transit at right. It received an Honorable Mention at the 12th Competition. Higgs' trophy was taken in Pope County, Illinois, on November 30, 1963.

The entire 12th Competition Judges Panel in shown in the background. From left to right: Emily S. Toerge (secretary), Edd McGuire, Dr. J. Kenneth Doutt, John Andrews, George L. Norris, John H. Batten, Dr. John Hammett, Frank Cook, and George Church.

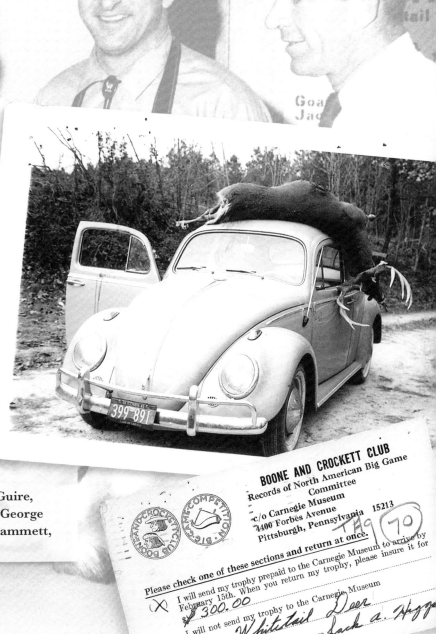

BOONE AND CROCKETT CLUB
Records of North American Big Game Committee
c/o Carnegie Museum
4400 Forbes Avenue
Pittsburgh, Pennsylvania 15213

TAG 70

Please check one of these sections and return at once.

(X) I will send my trophy prepaid to the Carnegie Museum to arrive by February 15th. When you return my trophy, please insure it for $300.00

( ) I will not send my trophy to the Carnegie Museum

Kind of trophy Whitetail Deer Signature Jack a. Higgs

Date 1/31/65

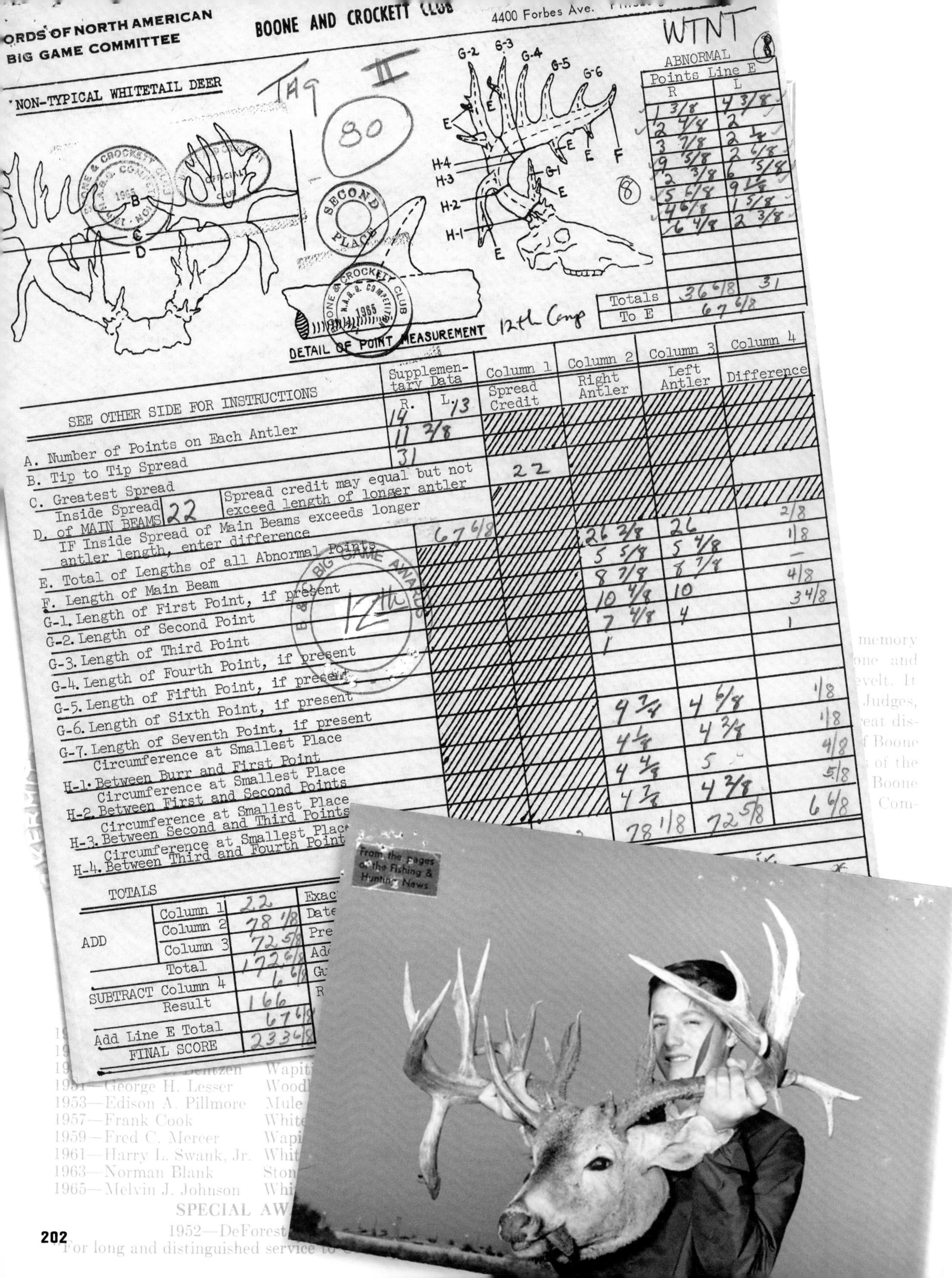

RECORDS OF NORTH AMERICAN BIG GAME COMMITTEE

BOONE AND CROCKETT CLUB

4400 Forbes Ave.

WTNT

NON-TYPICAL WHITETAIL DEER

TAG II

80

SECOND PLACE

BOONE & CROCKETT CLUB N.A.B.G. COMPETITION 1965

DETAIL OF POINT MEASUREMENT 12th Comp

ABNORMAL Points Line E R	L
1 3/8	4 3/8
2 4/8	2
3 7/8	2 1/8
9 3/8	2 6/8
2 3/8	6 5/8
5 6/8	9 2/8
4 6/8	1 5/8
6 4/8	2 3/8
Totals 36 6/8	31
To E 67 6/8	

SEE OTHER SIDE FOR INSTRUCTIONS	Supplementary Data R.	L.	Column 1 Spread Credit	Column 2 Right Antler	Column 3 Left Antler	Column 4 Difference
A. Number of Points on Each Antler	14	13				
B. Tip to Tip Spread	11 3/8					
C. Greatest Spread	31					
D. Inside Spread of MAIN BEAMS 22 — Spread credit may equal but not exceed length of longer antler			22			
IF Inside Spread of Main Beams exceeds longer antler length, enter difference						
E. Total of Lengths of all Abnormal Points			67 6/8			
F. Length of Main Beam				26 3/8	26	2/8
G-1. Length of First Point, if present				5 5/8	5 4/8	1/8
G-2. Length of Second Point				8 7/8	8 7/8	—
G-3. Length of Third Point				10 4/8	10	4/8
G-4. Length of Fourth Point, if present				7 4/8	4	3 4/8
G-5. Length of Fifth Point, if present				1		1
G-6. Length of Sixth Point, if present						
G-7. Length of Seventh Point, if present						
H-1. Circumference at Smallest Place Between Burr and First Point				4 7/8	4 6/8	1/8
H-2. Circumference at Smallest Place Between First and Second Points				4 1/8	4 2/8	1/8
H-3. Circumference at Smallest Place Between Second and Third Points				4 4/8	5	4/8
H-4. Circumference at Smallest Place Between Third and Fourth Points				4 7/8	4 2/8	5/8
TOTALS				78 1/8	72 5/8	6 6/8

ADD	Column 1	22
	Column 2	78 1/8
	Column 3	72 5/8
	Total	172 6/8
SUBTRACT Column 4		6 6/8
Result		166
Add Line E Total		67 6/8
FINAL SCORE		233 6/8

BIG GAME AWARDS 12th

1951—George H. Lesser Woodl
1953—Edison A. Pillmore Mule
1957—Frank Cook White
1959—Fred C. Mercer Wapi
1961—Harry L. Swank, Jr. Whit
1963—Norman Blank Ston
1965—Melvin J. Johnson Whi

SPECIAL AW

1952—DeForest

"For long and distinguished service to

AWARDS AND HONORABLE MENTIONS

WHITETAIL DEER

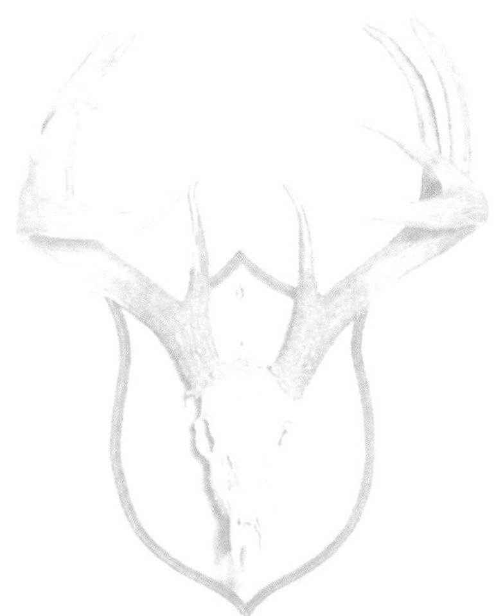

NEW WORLD'S RECORD

WHITETAIL DEER (Typical)
Certificate of Merit
Score — 206-5/8

Length—(R) 30 (L) 30
Circumference—(R) 6-2/8 (L) 6-1/8
Points—(R) 5 (L) 5
Inside Spread—20-1/8
Locality—Probably vicinity Sandstone, Minn. — Date killed unknown
Owner—Robert Ludwig

WHITETAIL DEER (Typical) — 2nd Award
Score — 194-4/8

Length—(R) 25-7/8 (L) 25-6/8
Circumference—(R) 5-1/8 (L) 5-2/8
Points—(R) 7 (L) 7
Inside Spread—18-6/8
Locality—Monroe Co., Iowa — 1962
Hunter—Lloyd Goad

WHITETAIL DEER (Typical) — 3rd Award
Score — 185-4/8

Length—(R) 30 (L) 29-2/8
Circumference—(R) 5-2/8 (L) 5-2/8
Points—(R) 8 (L) 8
Inside Spread—30-2/8
Locality—Todd Co., Elkton, Kentucky — 1964
Hunter—C. W. Shelton

WHITETAIL DEER (Typical) Honorable Mention
Score — 181-5/8

Length—(R) 24-7/8 (L) 24-5/8
Circumference—(R) 6-5/8 (L) 6-2/8
Points—(R) 6 (L) 7
Inside Spread—18-5/8
Locality—Southern Pope Co., Ill. — 1963
Hunter—Jack A. Higgs

WHITETAIL DEER (Non-Typical)

WHITETAIL DEER (Non-Typical) — 1st Award
Score — 178-6/8 + 62 = 240-6/8

Length—(R) 25-5/8 (L) 26-2/8
Circumference—(R) 5-2/8 (L) 5-1/8
Points—(R) 17 (L) 20
Inside Spread—17-2/8
Locality—Central Lakes, Minn. — 1964
Hunter—John Cesarek

WHITETAIL DEER (Non-Typical) — 2nd Award
Score — 166 + 67-6/8 = 233-6/8

Length—(R) 26-2/8 (L) 26
Circumference—(R) 4-7/8 (L) 4-6/8
Points—(R) 14 (L) 13
Inside Spread—22
Locality—Thompson Creek, Wash. — 1964
Hunter—George Sly, Jr.

WHITETAIL DEER (Non-Typical) — 3rd Award
Score — 186-6/8 +

Length—(R) 29-3/
Circumference—(R
Points—(R) 9 (L)
Inside Spread—23-
Locality—Licking
Hunter—Norman

MULE DE

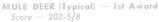

MULE DEER (Typical) — 1st Award
Score — 202-5/8

Length—(R) 26-3/8 (L) 25-5/8
Circumference—(R) 5-1/8 (L) 5
Points—(R) 5 (L) 5
Inside Spread—21-5/8
Locality—Ouray County, Colorado — 1965
Hunter—Louis V. Schlosser
Guide—Leon Comerer

MULE DEER (Typical) — 2nd Award
Score — 200

Length—(R) 29-6/8 (L) 29-7/8
Circumference—(R) 5-3/8 (L) 5-2/8
Points—(R) 6 (L) 6
Inside Spread—24-4/8
Locality—Unit 9 Mouqi, Arizona — 1964
Hunter—Tom Corey

MULE DEER (Typical) — 3rd Award
Score — 199-7/8

Length—(R) 24-1/8 (L) 24-7/8
Circumference—(R) 5 (L) 5-1/8
Points—(R) 5 (L) 5
Inside Spread—23-1/8
Locality—Uncompahgre National Forest, Colo. — 1963
Hunter—H. E. Gerhart

MULE DEER (Typical) — Certificate of Merit
Score — 209-4/8

Length—(R) 28-7/8 (L) 29-6/8
Circumference—(R) 5-7/8 (L) 5-7/8
Points—(R) 6 (L) 8
Inside Spread—28
Locality—Grizzly Ridge, Wallowa Co., Oregon — 1920
Hunter—Dr. John Calvin Evans
Owner—Budd Gronquist

MULE DEER (Typical) — Certificate of Merit
Score — 204

Length—(R) 27 (L) 27-3/8
Circumference—(R) 5-4/8 (L) 5-3/8
Points—(R) 5 (L) 5
Inside Spread—24
Locality—Muddy Creek, Pitkin Co., Colo. — 1950
Hunter—Jens. O. Solberg

MULE DEER (Non-Typical)

MULE DEER (Non-Typical) — 1st Award
Score — 204-4/8 + 64-7/8 = 269-3/8

Length—(R) 25-4/8 (L) 27-5/8
Circumference—(R) 6-1/8 (L) 6
Points—(R) 17 (L) 11
Inside Spread—23
Locality—Leroux Creek, Colo. — 1962
Hunter—Shirley Smith

MULE DEER (Non-Typical) — 2nd Award
Score — 217-3/8 + 46-5/8 = 264

Length—(R) 25-5/8 (L) 26-1/8
Circumference—(R) 6-2/8 (L) 5-7/8
Points—(R) 14 (L) 13
Inside Spread—22-7/8
Locality—Elko Co., Nev. — 1965
Hunter—Jimmy Stichter

SECOND AWARD - NON-TYPICAL 1966 COMPETITION

Second Award for non-typical whitetail at the 12th Competition went to George Sly, Jr.'s buck, scoring 233-6/8 points. The whitetail was taken on Thompson Creek in Washington in 1964. It is the third largest to ever come from that state. The greatest spread on this trophy is 31 inches.

Certificate receipt 5/18/66
Medal receipt 5/20/66

96A Trophy

OFFICIAL SCORING SYSTEM FOR NORTH AMERICAN BIG GAME TROPHIES

RECORDS OF NORTH AMERICAN BIG GAME COMMITTEE

BOONE AND CROCKETT CLUB

Boone and Crockett Club
Records of North American Big Game Committee
c/o Carnegie Museum
4400 Forbes Ave. Pittsburgh, Pa. 15213

WHITETAIL and COUES DEER

KIND OF DEER Coues

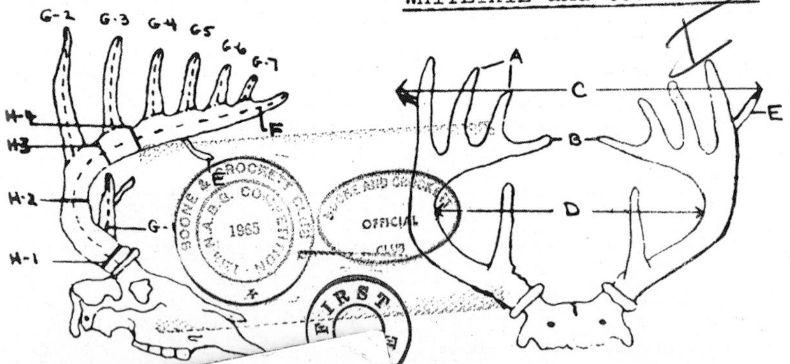

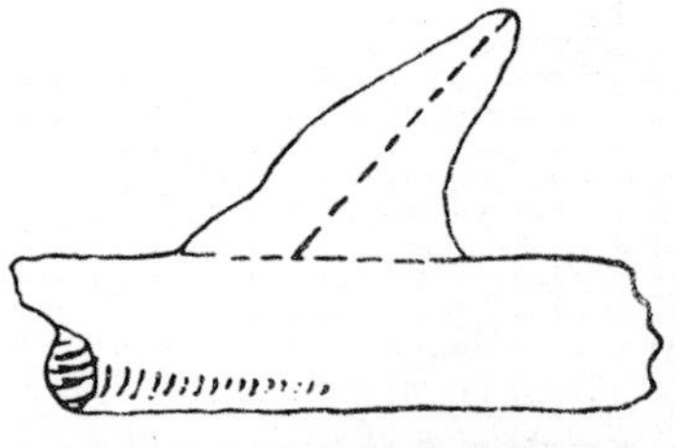

DETAIL OF POINT MEASUREMENT

...CTIONS	Supplementary Data		Column 1	Column 2	Column 3	Column 4
...er	R. 6	L. 6	Spread Credit	Right Antler	Left Antler	Difference
	5					
	13 1/8					
...t may equal but not ...h of longer antler			10 7/8			
... exceeds longer						—
... Points						
				16 1/8	17	7/8
...nt				4 1/8	2	2 1/8
				9 5/8	8	1 5/8
				7 7/8	8 2/8	3/8
...t				6 4/8	7 1/8	5/8
				1 6/8	2 5/8	7/8
...t						
				3 4/8	3 4/8	—
				3 2/8	3 2/8	—
				3	3 3/8	3/8
...een Third and ...ird Point and				3 2/8	3 4/8	2/8
			10 7/8	59	58 5/8	7 1/8

	10 7/8	Exact locality where killed Santa Rita Mts., Ariz.
Column 2	59	Date killed Oct 1964 By whom killed GEORGE SHAAR.
Column 3	58 5/8	Present owner George Shaar
Total	128 4/8	Address
SUBTRACT Column 4	7 1/8	Guide's Name and Address
FINAL SCORE	121 3/8	Remarks: (Mention any abnormalities)

202

Certificate receipt 5/18/66
Medal receipt 5/20/66

...ORING SYSTEM FOR NORTH AMERICAN BIG GAME TROPHIES   96 B.

...CLUB

Boone and Crockett Club
Records of North American Big Game Committee
c/o Carnegie Museum
4400 Forbes Ave. Pittsburgh, Pa. 15213

...S DEER

KIND OF DEER Coues

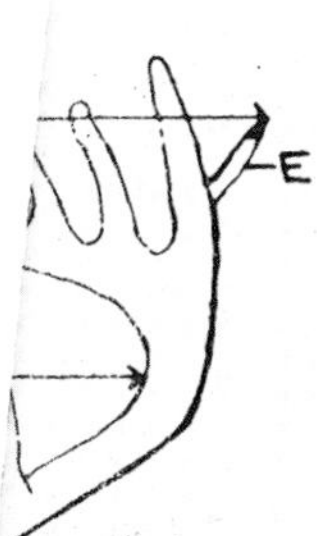

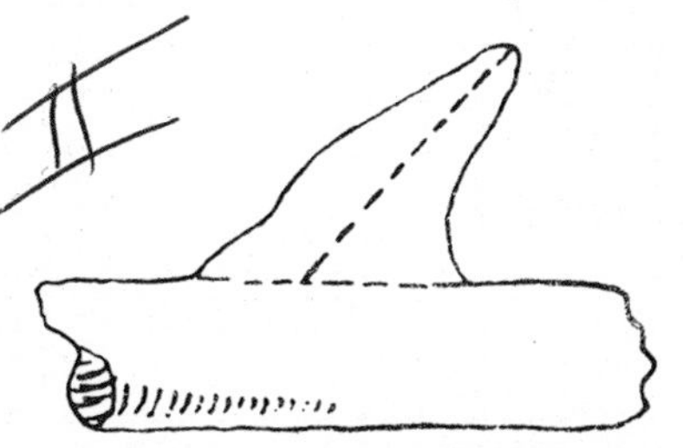

FIRST AND SECOND AWARD
TYPICAL COUES' DEER
1966 COMPETITION

George Shaar had not one, but two huge Coues' deer in the 12th Competition. His 121-3/8 typical (pictured at left) won the First Award. His 117-7/8 typical (pictured above) captured the Second Award. The two trophies were both taken in the Santa Rita Mountains in Arizona, in subsequent years beginning in 1964.

SEE OTHER SIDE FOR INSTRUCTIONS	Supplementary Data R.	L.	Column 1 Spread Credit	Column 2 Right Antler	Column 3 Left Antler	Column 4 Difference
A. Number of Points on Each Antler	6	5				
B. Tip to Tip Spread	14 2/8.					
C. Greatest Spread	14 1/8					
D. Inside Spread of MAIN BEAMS — Spread credit may equal but not exceed length of longer antler			12 3/8.			
IF Inside Spread of Main Beams exceeds longer antler length, enter difference						
E. Total of Lengths of all Abnormal Points						1 4/8
F. Length of Main Beam				19 5/8	19 4/8	1/8
G-1. Length of First Point, if present				4 5/8	3 2/8	1 3/8
G-2. Length of Second Point				8 5/8	8	5/8
G-3. Length of Third Point				7 4/8	7 2/8	2/8
G-4. Length of Fourth Point, if present				1 5/8	3 6/8	2 1/8
G-5. Length of Fifth Point, if present						
G-6. Length of Sixth Point, if present						
G-7. Length of Seventh Point, if present						
H-1. Circumference at Smallest Place Between Burr and First Point				4 1/8	3 7/8	2/8
H-2. Circumference at Smallest Place Between First and Second Points				3 5/8	3 5/8	—
H-3. Circumference at Smallest Place Between Second and Third Points				3 3/8	3 3/8	—
H-4. Circumference at Smallest Place between Third and Fourth Points or half way between Third Point and Beam Tip if Fourth Point is missing				3	3 1/8	1/8
TOTALS			12 3/8	56 1/8	55 6/8	6 3/8

ADD	Column 1	12 3/8	Exact locality where killed Santa Rita Mts., Ariz.
	Column 2	56 1/8	Date killed 10/29/65 By whom killed GEO SHAAR
	Column 3	55 6/8	Present owner George Shaar
	Total	124 2/8	Address
SUBTRACT Column 4		6 3/8	Guide's Name and Address
FINAL SCORE		117 7/8	Remarks: (Mention any abnormalities)

203

S-6-20 A C-21 Tag #88

C.M.

OFFICIAL SCORING SYSTEM FOR NORTH AMERICAN BIG GAME TROPHIES

RECORDS OF NORTH AMERICAN BIG GAME COMMITTEE

BOONE AND CROCKETT CLUB

Boone and Crockett Club
Records of North American Big Game Committee
c/o Carnegie Museum
4400 Forbes Ave. Pittsburgh, Pa. 15213

Minimum Score: Deer
Whitetail: Typical 160
Coues: Typical 105

WHITETAIL and COUES DEER

KIND OF DEER WHITETAIL

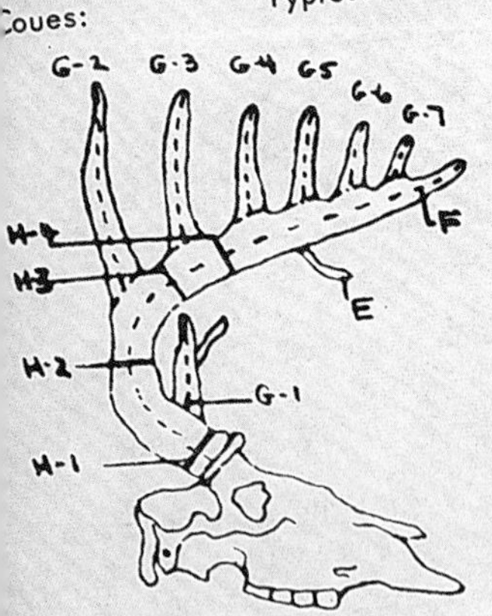

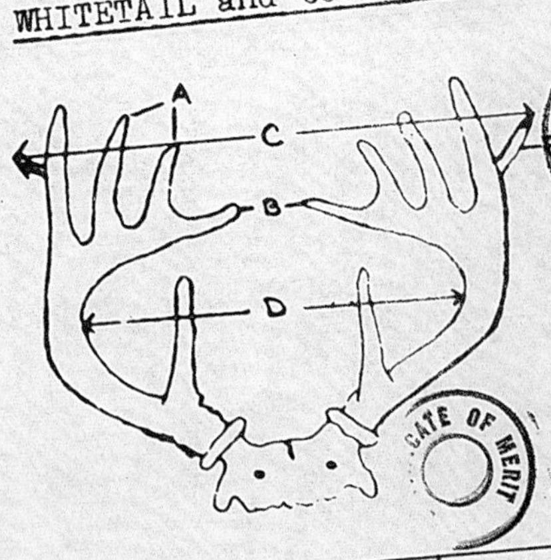

CERTIFICATE OF MERIT

SEE OTHER SIDE FOR INSTRUCTIONS	Supplementary Data R. 8	L. 9	Column 1 Spread Credit	Column 2 Right Antler	Column 3 Left Antler	Column 4 Difference
A. Number of Points on Each Antler	7 4/8					
B. Tip to Tip Spread	21 2/8					
C. Greatest Spread			19 2/8			—
D. Inside Spread of MAIN BEAMS 19 2/8 — Spread credit may equal but not exceed length of longer antler						9 6/8
IF Inside Spread of Main Beams exceeds longer antler length, enter difference						4/8
E. Total of Lengths of all Abnormal Points				27 4/8	28 —	2/8
F. Length of Main Beam				7 2/8	7 —	3 —
G-1. Length of First Point, if present				4 —	7 —	4/8
G-2. Length of Second Point				8 7/8	9 1/8	1/8
G-3. Length of Third Point				12 2/8	12 3/8	3/8
G-4. Length of Fourth Point, if present				10 3/8	10 —	—
G-5. Length of Fifth Point, if present				—	—	—
G-6. Length of Sixth Point, if present				—	—	
G-7. Length of Seventh Point, if present				4 6/8	4 6/8	—
H-1. Circumference at Smallest Place Between Burr and First Point				4 2/8	4 2/8	—
H-2. Circumference at Smallest Place Between First and Second Points				7 3/8	8 2/8	7/8
H-3. Circumference at Smallest Place Between Second and Third Points						5/8
H-4. Circumference at Smallest Place between Third and Fourth Points or half way between Third Point and Beam Tip if Fourth Point is missing				5 7/8	5 2/8	
TOTALS			19 2/8	92 4/8	96 —	15 6/8

ADD	Column 1	19 2/8	Exact locality where killed **Lyman County, South Dakota**
	Column 2	92 4/8	By whom killed **Bob Weidner**
	Column 3	96	Date killed **Nov. 1957**
	Total	207 6/8	Present owner **E. N. Eichler**
SUBTRACT Column 4		15 6/8	Address **South Dakota**
FINAL SCORE		192	Guide's Name and Address —
			Remarks: (Mention any abnormalities)

CERTIFICATE OF MERIT
1968 COMPETITION

E.N. Eichler, owner of Bob Weidner's trophy typical whitetail scoring 192 points, entered the buck in the 13th Competition held in 1968. The deer was harvested in Lyman County, South Dakota, in 1957. The buck received a Certificate of Merit. It was the highest-scoring typical present, but only trophies entered by the hunter and immediate family are eligible for Place Awards.

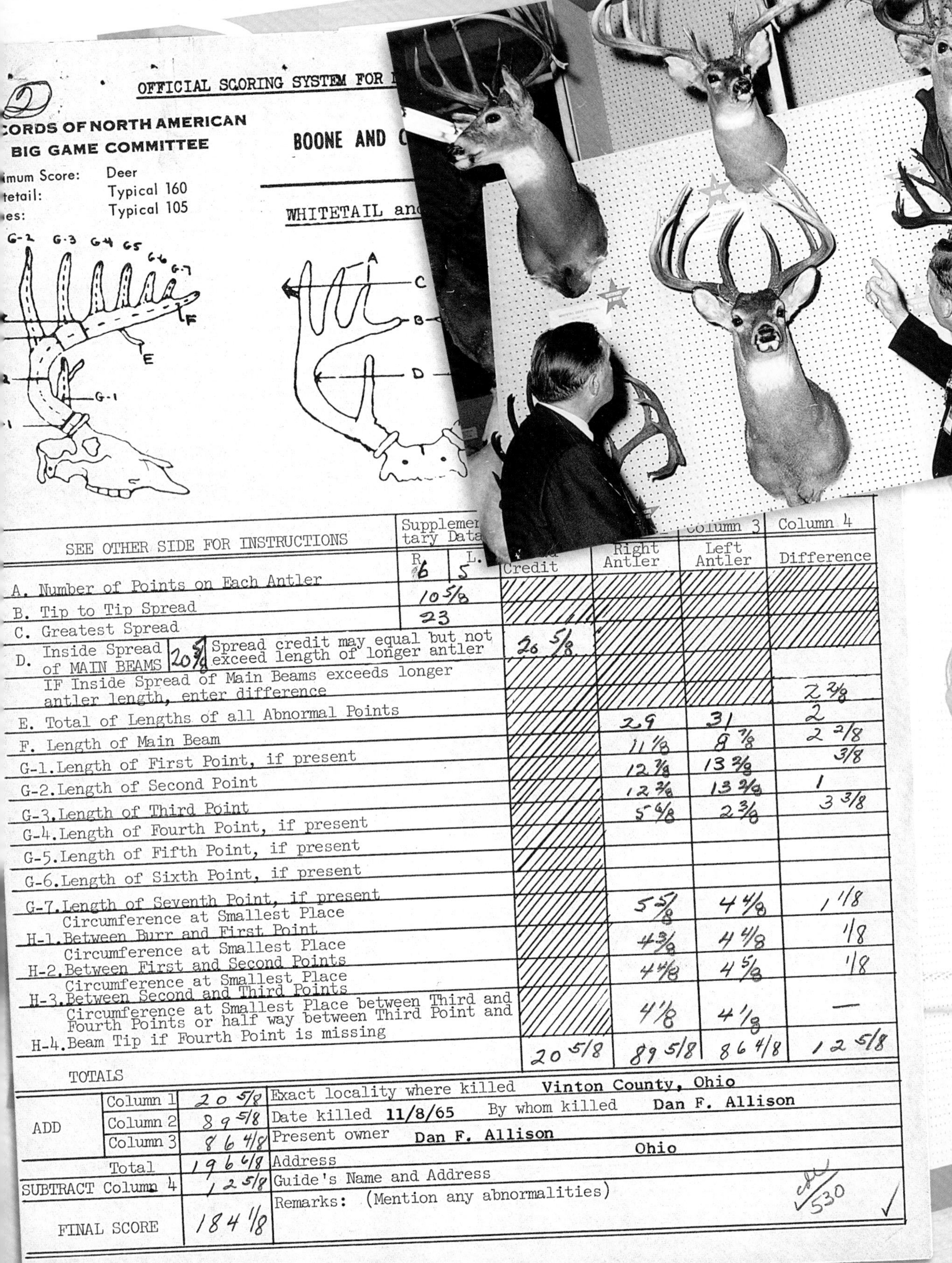

OFFICIAL SCORING SYSTEM FOR

CORDS OF NORTH AMERICAN BIG GAME COMMITTEE

BOONE AND C

imum Score: Deer
tetail: Typical 160
ies: Typical 105

WHITETAIL and

SEE OTHER SIDE FOR INSTRUCTIONS	Supplementary Data R.	L.	Credit	Right Antler	Column 3 Left Antler	Column 4 Difference
A. Number of Points on Each Antler	6	5				
B. Tip to Tip Spread	10 5/8					
C. Greatest Spread	23					
D. Inside Spread of MAIN BEAMS 20 5/8 Spread credit may equal but not exceed length of longer antler			20 5/8			
IF Inside Spread of Main Beams exceeds longer antler length, enter difference						2 2/8
E. Total of Lengths of all Abnormal Points				29	31	2
F. Length of Main Beam				11 1/8	8 7/8	2 2/8
G-1. Length of First Point, if present				12 7/8	13 2/8	3/8
G-2. Length of Second Point				12 3/8	13 3/8	1
G-3. Length of Third Point				5 6/8	2 3/8	3 3/8
G-4. Length of Fourth Point, if present						
G-5. Length of Fifth Point, if present						
G-6. Length of Sixth Point, if present						
G-7. Length of Seventh Point, if present				5 5/8	4 4/8	1 1/8
Circumference at Smallest Place H-1. Between Burr and First Point				4 3/8	4 4/8	1/8
Circumference at Smallest Place H-2. Between First and Second Points				4 4/8	4 5/8	1/8
Circumference at Smallest Place H-3. Between Second and Third Points				4 1/8	4 1/8	—
Circumference at Smallest Place between Third and Fourth Points or half way between Third Point and H-4. Beam Tip if Fourth Point is missing						
TOTALS			20 5/8	89 5/8	86 4/8	12 5/8

ADD	Column 1	20 5/8	Exact locality where killed Vinton County, Ohio
	Column 2	89 5/8	Date killed 11/8/65 By whom killed Dan F. Allison
	Column 3	86 4/8	Present owner Dan F. Allison
	Total	196 6/8	Address Ohio
SUBTRACT Column 4		12 5/8	Guide's Name and Address
FINAL SCORE		184 1/8	Remarks: (Mention any abnormalities) 530

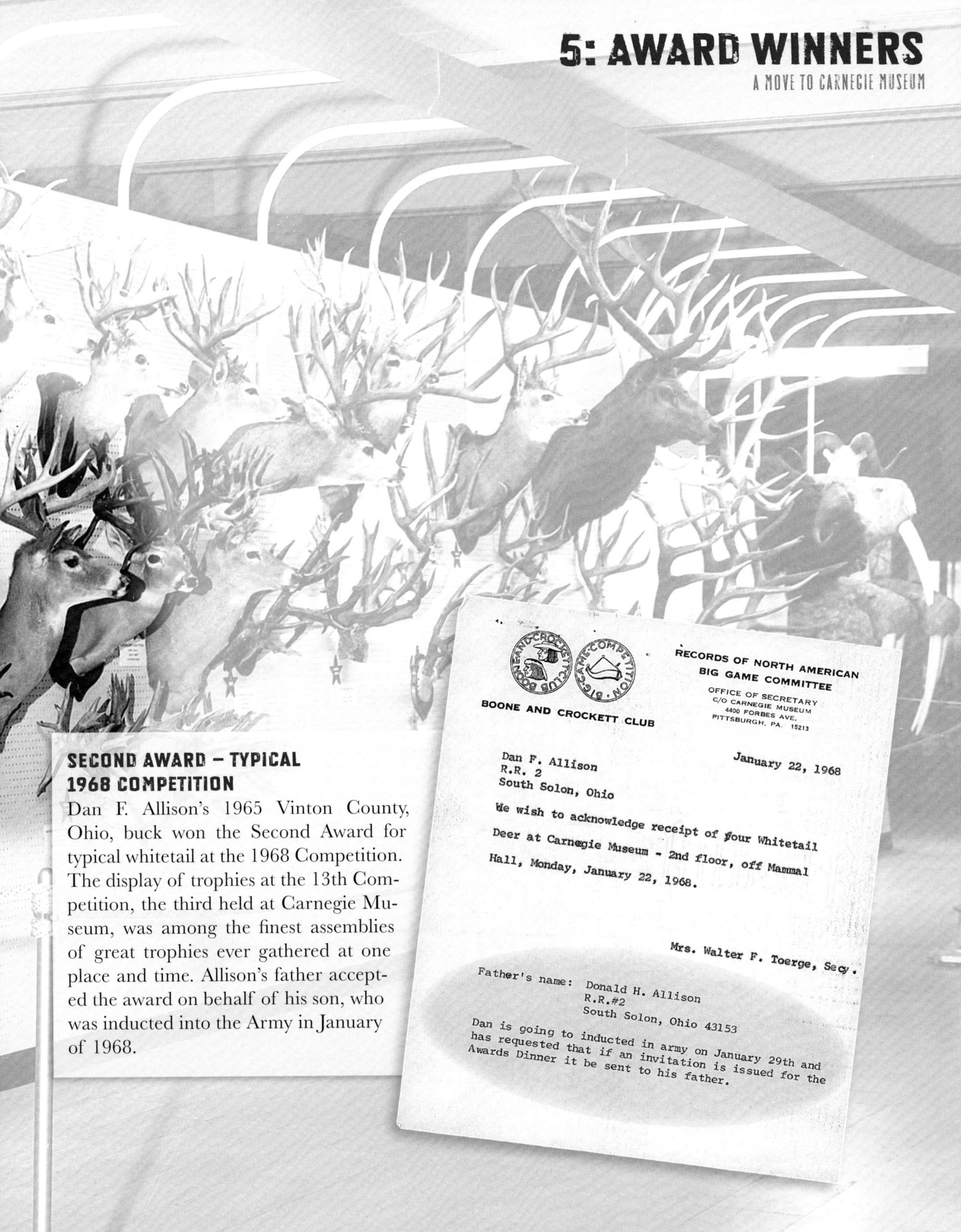

RECORDS OF NORTH AMERICAN
BIG GAME COMMITTEE

OFFICE OF SECRETARY
C/O CARNEGIE MUSEUM
4400 FORBES AVE.
PITTSBURGH, PA. 15213

BOONE AND CROCKETT CLUB

January 22, 1968

Dan F. Allison
R.R. 2
South Solon, Ohio

We wish to acknowledge receipt of four Whitetail Deer at Carnegie Museum - 2nd floor, off Mammal Hall, Monday, January 22, 1968.

Mrs. Walter F. Toerge, Secy.

Father's name: Donald H. Allison
R.R.#2
South Solon, Ohio 43153

Dan is going to inducted in army on January 29th and has requested that if an invitation is issued for the Awards Dinner it be sent to his father.

SECOND AWARD – TYPICAL 1968 COMPETITION

Dan F. Allison's 1965 Vinton County, Ohio, buck won the Second Award for typical whitetail at the 1968 Competition. The display of trophies at the 13th Competition, the third held at Carnegie Museum, was among the finest assemblies of great trophies ever gathered at one place and time. Allison's father accepted the award on behalf of his son, who was inducted into the Army in January of 1968.

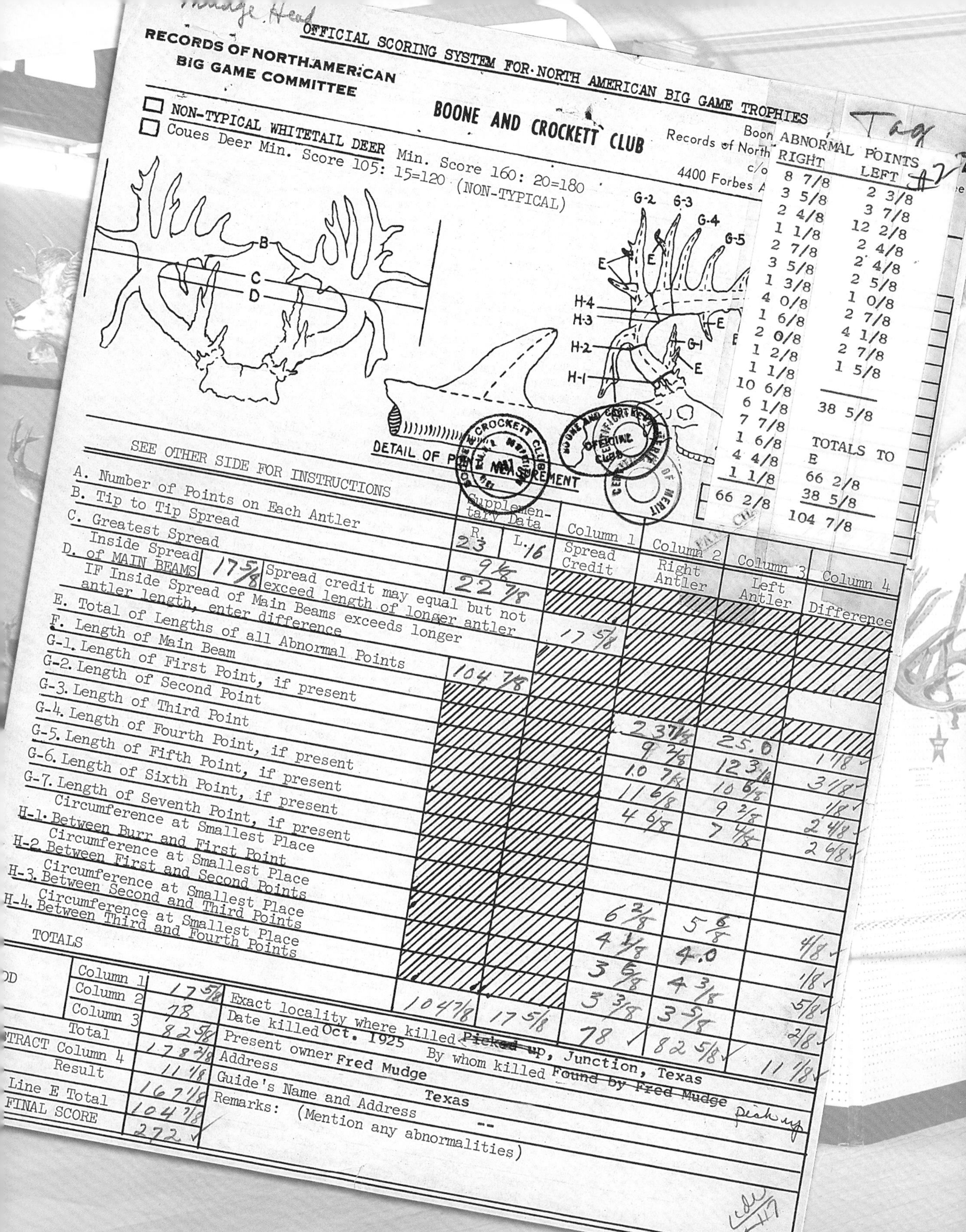

Mudge Head

OFFICIAL SCORING SYSTEM FOR NORTH AMERICAN BIG GAME TROPHIES

RECORDS OF NORTH AMERICAN BIG GAME COMMITTEE

BOONE AND CROCKETT CLUB

Boone ... Records of North ... c/o ... 4400 Forbes A...

☐ NON-TYPICAL WHITETAIL DEER Min. Score 160: 20=180
☐ Coues Deer Min. Score 105: 15=120 (NON-TYPICAL)

B
C
D

G-2 G-3 G-4 G-5
E E E E E
H-4 H-3 H-2 H-1 G-1

DETAIL OF POINT MEASUREMENT

Tag #7

ABNORMAL POINTS RIGHT	LEFT
8 7/8	2 3/8
3 5/8	3 7/8
2 4/8	12 2/8
1 1/8	2 4/8
2 7/8	2 4/8
3 5/8	2 5/8
1 3/8	1 0/8
4 0/8	2 7/8
1 6/8	4 1/8
2 0/8	2 7/8
1 2/8	1 5/8
1 1/8	
10 6/8	
6 1/8	38 5/8
7 7/8	
1 6/8	TOTALS TO E
4 4/8	
1 1/8	66 2/8
66 2/8	38 5/8
	104 7/8

SEE OTHER SIDE FOR INSTRUCTIONS

	Supplementary Data R.	Supplementary Data L.	Column 1 Spread Credit	Column 2 Right Antler	Column 3 Left Antler	Column 4 Difference
A. Number of Points on Each Antler	23	16				
B. Tip to Tip Spread	9 1/8					
C. Greatest Spread	22 7/8					
D. Inside Spread of MAIN BEAMS 17 5/8 — Spread credit may equal but not exceed length of longer antler			17 5/8			
IF Inside Spread of Main Beams exceeds longer antler length, enter difference						
E. Total of Lengths of all Abnormal Points	104 7/8					
F. Length of Main Beam				23 7/8	25.0	1 1/8
G-1. Length of First Point, if present				9 2/8	12 3/8	3/8
G-2. Length of Second Point				10 7/8	10 6/8	1/8
G-3. Length of Third Point				11 6/8	9 2/8	2 4/8
G-4. Length of Fourth Point, if present				4 6/8	7 4/8	2 6/8
G-5. Length of Fifth Point, if present						
G-6. Length of Sixth Point, if present						
G-7. Length of Seventh Point, if present						
H-1. Circumference at Smallest Place Between Burr and First Point				6 2/8	5 6/8	4/8
H-2. Circumference at Smallest Place Between First and Second Points				4 1/8	4.0	1/8
H-3. Circumference at Smallest Place Between Second and Third Points				3 6/8	4 3/8	5/8
H-4. Circumference at Smallest Place Between Third and Fourth Points				3 3/8	3 5/8	2/8
TOTALS	104 7/8		17 5/8	78	82 5/8	11 1/8

Column 1	17 5/8
Column 2	78
Column 3	82 5/8
Total	178 2/8
SUBTRACT Column 4	11 1/8
Result	167 1/8
Add Line E Total	104 7/8
FINAL SCORE	272

Exact locality where killed ~~Picked up~~, Junction, Texas
Date killed Oct. 1925 By whom killed Found by ~~Fred Mudge~~ picked up
Present owner Fred Mudge
Address Texas
Guide's Name and Address --
Remarks: (Mention any abnormalities)

CERTIFICATE OF MERIT
NON-TYPICAL
1968 COMPETITION

Fred Mudge's non-typical whitetail scoring 272 points received a Certificate of Merit. Mudge found this striking buck dead in October 1925 near Junction, Texas. It has 39 total points—too many to be recorded in the abnormal point box—so the Judges had to improvise. This awesome non-typical is one of only 18 bucks in the B&C Records Program to have over 100 inches of abnormal points.

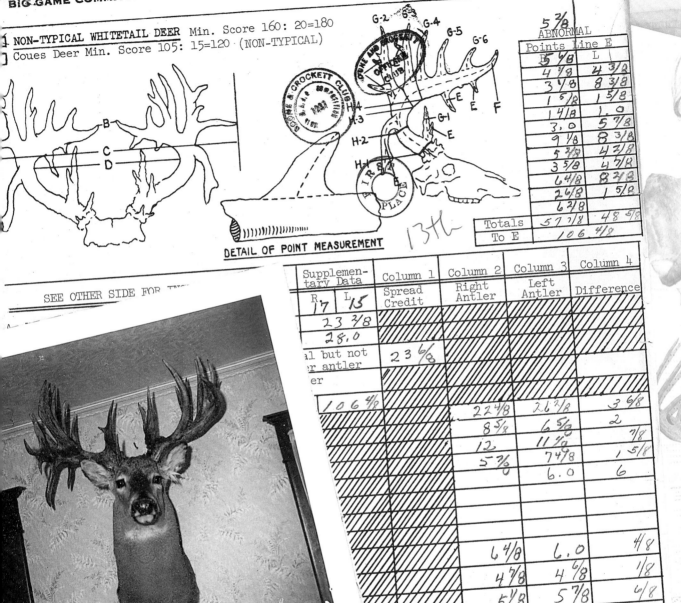

OFFICIAL SCORING SYSTEM FOR NORTH AMERICAN BIG GAME TROPHIES

RECORDS OF NORTH AMERICAN BIG GAME COMMITTEE

BOONE AND CROCKETT CLUB

Boone and Crockett Club
Records of North American Big Game Committee
c/o Carnegie Museum
4400 Forbes Ave. Pittsburgh, Pa. 15213

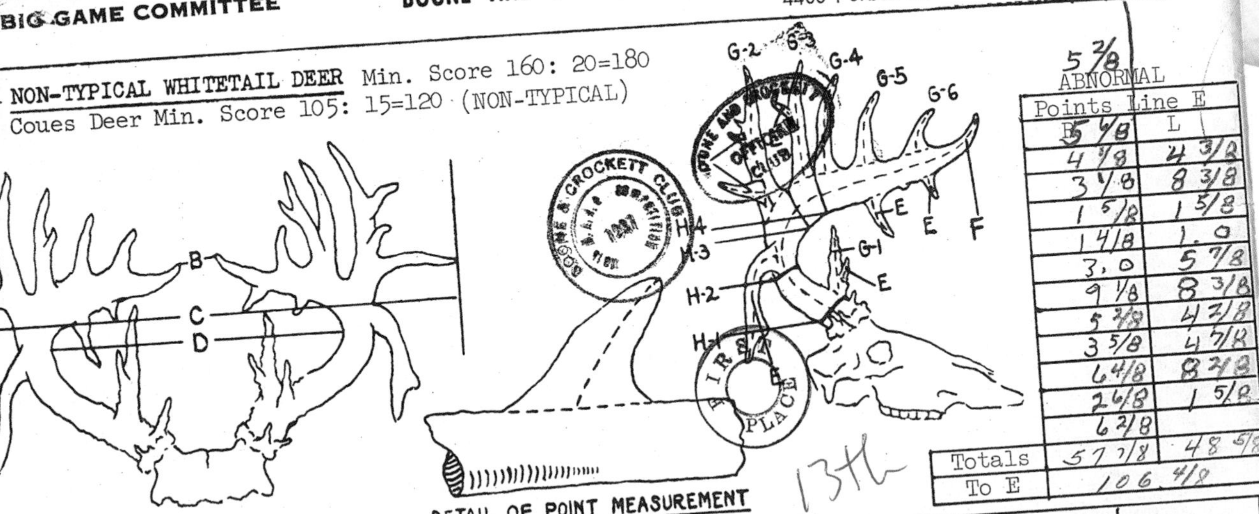

NON-TYPICAL WHITETAIL DEER Min. Score 160: 20=180
Coues Deer Min. Score 105: 15=120 (NON-TYPICAL)

5 2/8

ABNORMAL Points Line E	
R	L
5 4/8	
4 1/8	4 3/8
3 1/8	8 3/8
1 5/8	1 5/8
1 4/8	1.0
3.0	5 7/8
9 1/8	8 3/8
5 2/8	4 2/8
3 5/8	4 7/8
6 4/8	8 2/8
2 6/8	1 5/8
6 2/8	
Totals 57 7/8	48 5/8
To E 106 4/8	

SEE OTHER SIDE FOR ...

	Supplementary Data R / L	Column 1 Spread Credit	Column 2 Right Antler	Column 3 Left Antler	Column 4 Difference
	R 17 / L 15				
	23 2/8				
	28.0				
...al but not ...er antler		23 6/8			
...er					
	106 4/8				
			22 4/8	26 2/8	3 6/8
			8 5/8	6 5/8	2
			12	11 1/8	7/8
			5 7/8	7 4/8	1 5/8
				6.0	6
			6 4/8	6.0	4/8
			4 7/8	4 6/8	1/8
			5 1/8	5 7/8	6/8
			2 3/8	5 3/8	3
			67 6/8	79 3/8	18 5/8
	106 4/8	23 6/8			

ADD	Column 1	23 6/8	Exact locality where killed Republic, ~~Kansas~~ County
	Column 2	67 6/8	Date killed 12/12/65 By whom killed John O. Band
	Column 3	79 3/8	Present owner ~~John O. Band~~
Total		170 7/8	Address ~~Kansas~~
SUBTRACT Column 4		18 5/8	Guide's Name and Address None
Result		152 2/8	Remarks: (Mention any abnormalities) Bass Pro Shops
Add Line E Total		106 4/8	
FINAL SCORE		258 6/8	

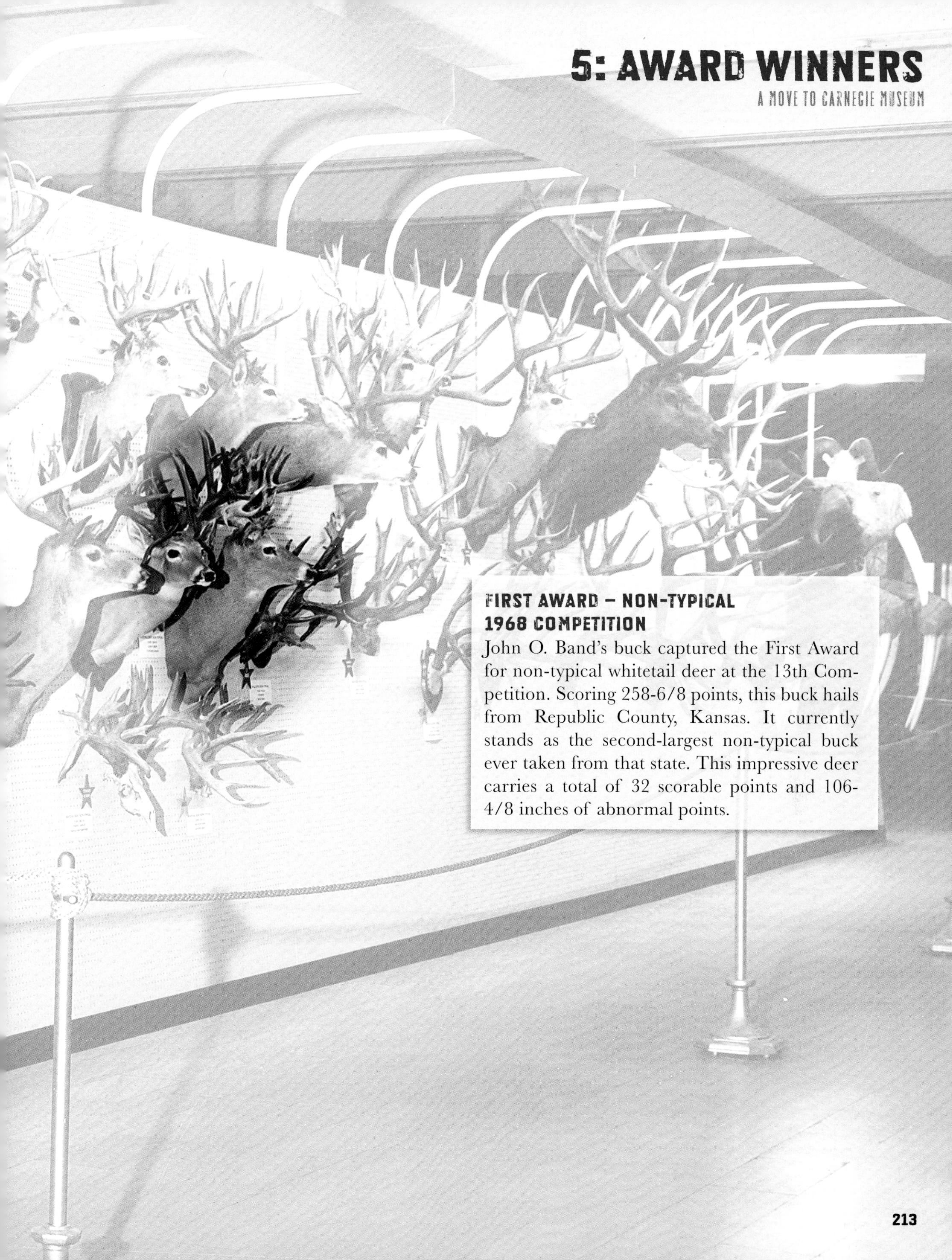

**FIRST AWARD – NON-TYPICAL
1968 COMPETITION**

John O. Band's buck captured the First Award for non-typical whitetail deer at the 13th Competition. Scoring 258-6/8 points, this buck hails from Republic County, Kansas. It currently stands as the second-largest non-typical buck ever taken from that state. This impressive deer carries a total of 32 scorable points and 106-4/8 inches of abnormal points.

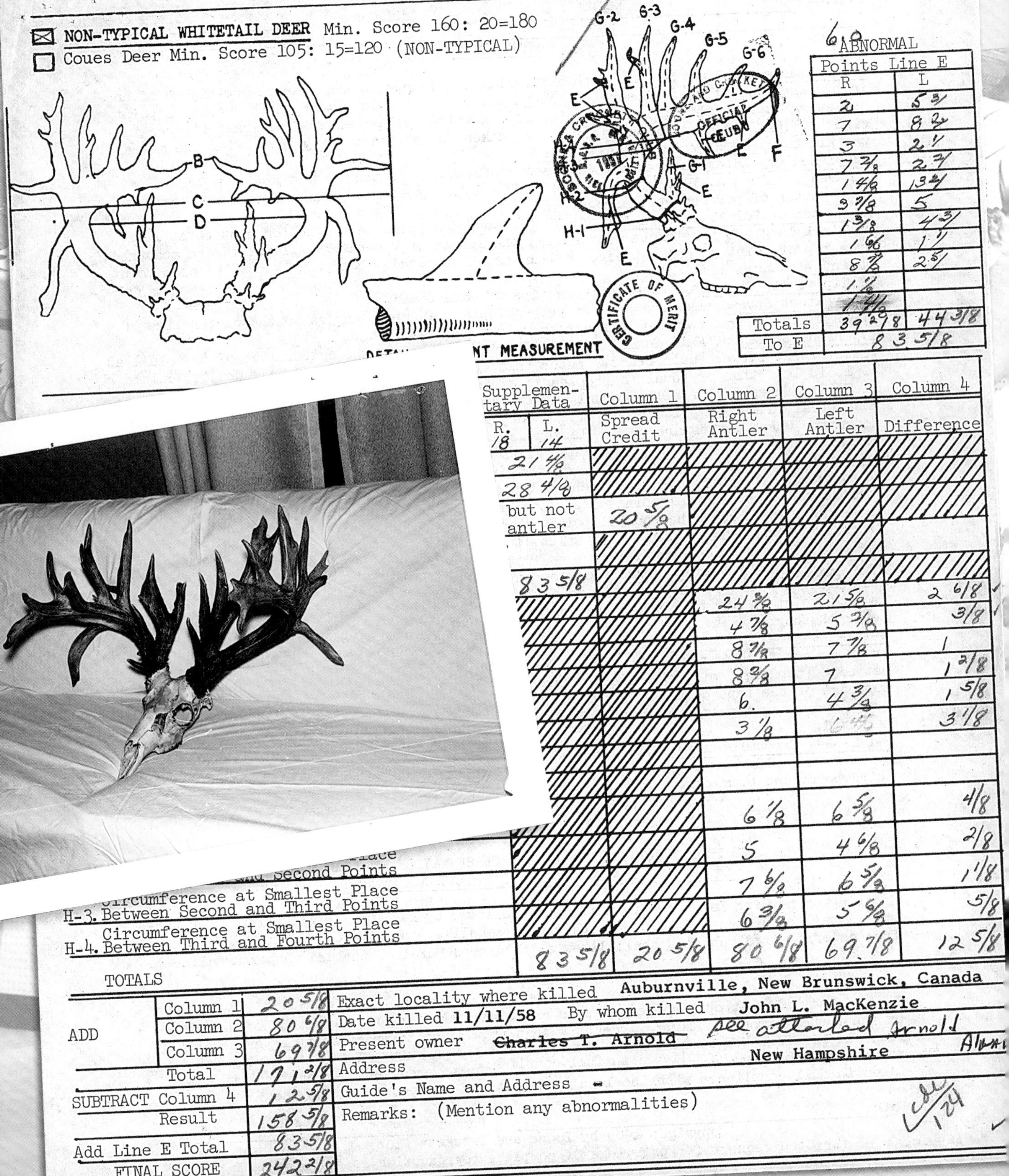

RECORDS OF NORTH AMERICAN BIG GAME COMMITTEE

BOONE AND CROCKETT CLUB

Records of North American Big Game Committee
c/o Carnegie Museum
4400 Forbes Ave. Pittsburgh, Pa. 15213

☒ NON-TYPICAL WHITETAIL DEER Min. Score 160: 20=180
☐ Coues Deer Min. Score 105: 15=120 (NON-TYPICAL)

60

ABNORMAL Points Line E	
R	L
2	5 3/
7	8 2/
3	2 1/
7 2/8	2 7/
1 4/8	13 4/
3 7/8	5
1 3/8	4 3/
1 6/8	1 1/
8 7/8	2 5/
1 1/8	
1 4/8	
Totals 39 2/8	44 3/8
To E 83 5/8	

DETAIL... ...NT MEASUREMENT

	Supplementary Data R. 18	L. 14	Column 1 Spread Credit	Column 2 Right Antler	Column 3 Left Antler	Column 4 Difference
	21 4/8					
	28 4/8					
...but not ...antler			20 5/8			
	83 5/8					
				24 3/8	21 5/8	2 6/8
				4 7/8	5 2/8	3/8
				8 7/8	7 7/8	1
				8 2/8	7	1 2/8
				6	4 3/8	1 5/8
				3 1/8	6 4/8	3 1/8
				6 1/8	6 5/8	4/8
				5	4 6/8	2/8
...Place ...and Second Points				7 6/8	6 5/8	1 1/8
Circumference at Smallest Place H-3. Between Second and Third Points				6 3/8	5 6/8	5/8
Circumference at Smallest Place H-4. Between Third and Fourth Points						
TOTALS	83 5/8		20 5/8	80 6/8	69 7/8	12 5/8

ADD	Column 1	20 5/8	Exact locality where killed **Auburnville, New Brunswick, Canada**
	Column 2	80 6/8	Date killed **11/11/58** By whom killed **John L. MacKenzie**
	Column 3	69 7/8	Present owner ~~Charles T. Arnold~~ see attached Arnold
	Total	171 2/8	Address **New Hampshire**
SUBTRACT	Column 4	12 5/8	Guide's Name and Address -
	Result	158 5/8	Remarks: (Mention any abnormalities)
Add Line E Total		83 5/8	
FINAL SCORE		242 2/8	

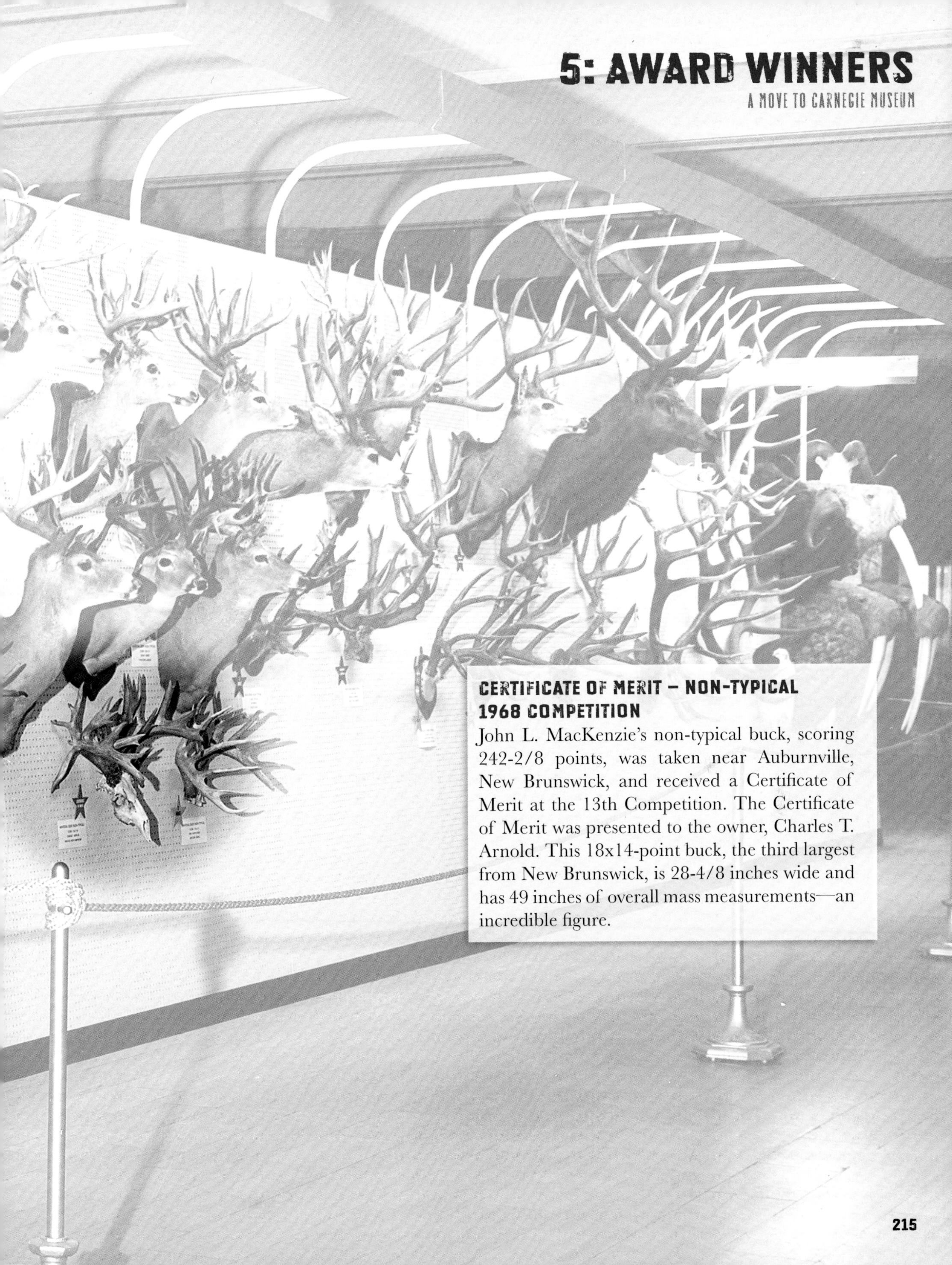

CERTIFICATE OF MERIT – NON-TYPICAL 1968 COMPETITION

John L. MacKenzie's non-typical buck, scoring 242-2/8 points, was taken near Auburnville, New Brunswick, and received a Certificate of Merit at the 13th Competition. The Certificate of Merit was presented to the owner, Charles T. Arnold. This 18x14-point buck, the third largest from New Brunswick, is 28-4/8 inches wide and has 49 inches of overall mass measurements—an incredible figure.

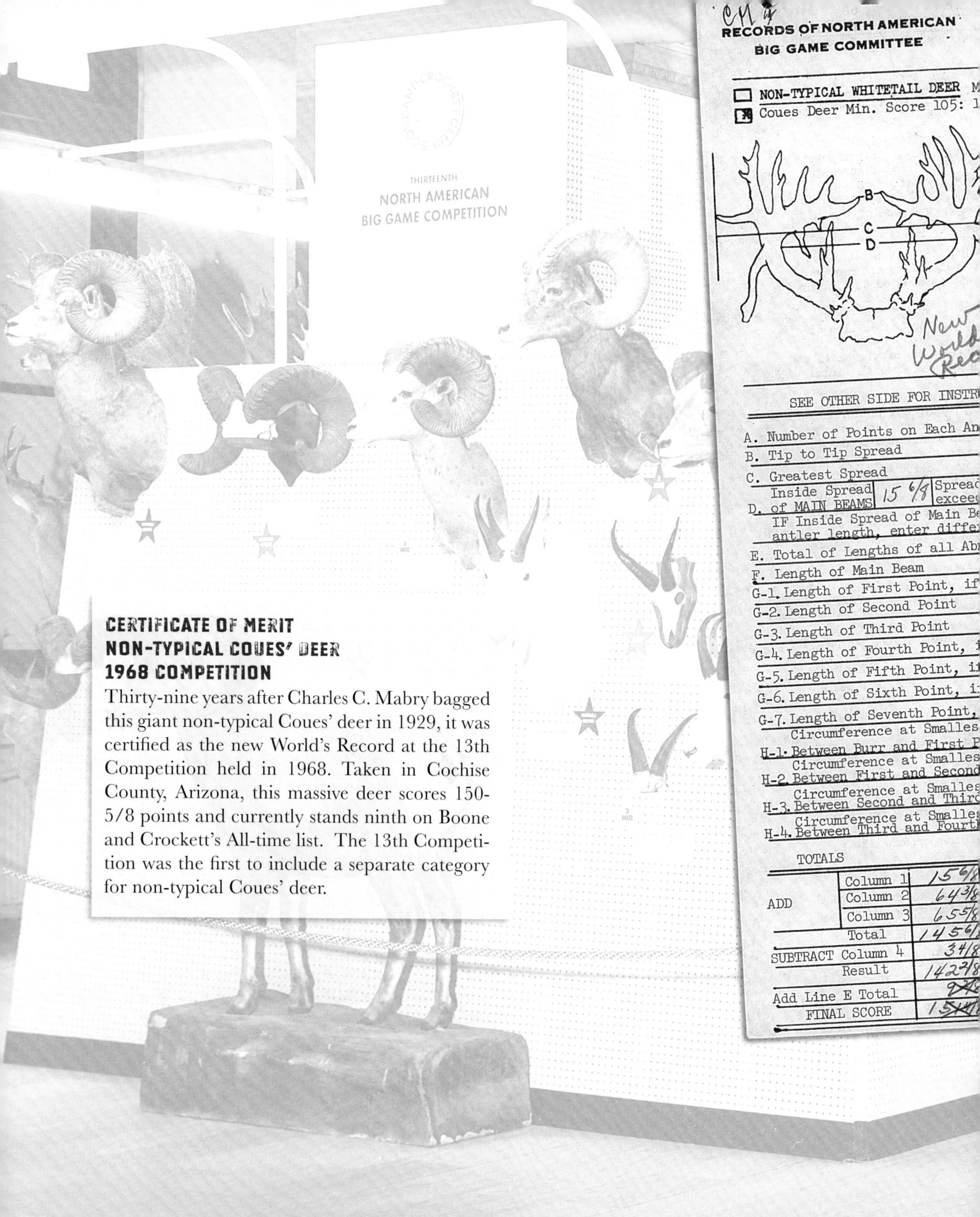

RECORDS OF NORTH AMERICAN
BIG GAME COMMITTEE

☐ NON-TYPICAL WHITETAIL DEER M
☒ Coues Deer Min. Score 105: 1

New World Rec

SEE OTHER SIDE FOR INSTR

A. Number of Points on Each An
B. Tip to Tip Spread
C. Greatest Spread
D. Inside Spread of MAIN BEAMS | 15 6/8 | Spread excee
IF Inside Spread of Main Be antler length, enter diffe
E. Total of Lengths of all Ab
F. Length of Main Beam
G-1. Length of First Point, if
G-2. Length of Second Point
G-3. Length of Third Point
G-4. Length of Fourth Point, i
G-5. Length of Fifth Point, i
G-6. Length of Sixth Point, i
G-7. Length of Seventh Point,
H-1. Circumference at Smalles Between Burr and First P
H-2. Circumference at Smalles Between First and Second
H-3. Circumference at Smalles Between Second and Third
H-4. Circumference at Smalles Between Third and Fourth

TOTALS

ADD	Column 1	15 6/8
	Column 2	64 3/8
	Column 3	65 5/8
	Total	145 6/
SUBTRACT Column 4		3 4/8
	Result	142 2/8
Add Line E Total		9
FINAL SCORE		15

CERTIFICATE OF MERIT
NON-TYPICAL COUES' DEER
1968 COMPETITION

Thirty-nine years after Charles C. Mabry bagged this giant non-typical Coues' deer in 1929, it was certified as the new World's Record at the 13th Competition held in 1968. Taken in Cochise County, Arizona, this massive deer scores 150-5/8 points and currently stands ninth on Boone and Crockett's All-time list. The 13th Competition was the first to include a separate category for non-typical Coues' deer.

ND CROCKETT CLUB

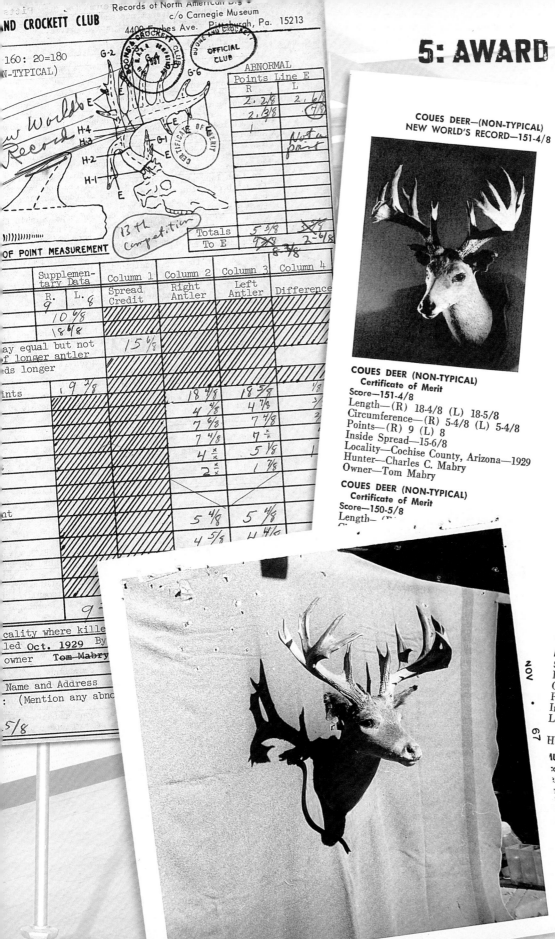

Records of North American B... c/o Carnegie Museum 4400 Forbes Ave. Pittsburgh, Pa. 15213

160: 20=180

N-TYPICAL)

BOONE AND CROCKETT CLUB OFFICIAL CLUB

New World's Record

CERTIFICATE OF MERIT

13th Competition

OF POINT MEASUREMENT

ABNORMAL Points Line E	
R	L
2 2/8	2 6/8
2 3/8	7/8
1	Not a point
Totals 5 5/8	3 5/8
To E 9 3/8 8 3/8	2 6/8

	Supplementary Data R.	L.	Column 1 Spread Credit	Column 2 Right Antler	Column 3 Left Antler	Column 4 Difference
	9	8				
	10 6/8					
	18 6/8					
ay equal but not f longer antler ds longer			15 6/8			
ints	19 2/8			18 4/8	18 5/8	1/8
				4 4/8	4 7/8	3/
				7 6/8	7 7/8	2/
				7 4/8	7 x/x	
				4 x/x	5 1/8	1
				2 x/x	1 7/8	
nt				5 4/8	5 4/8	
				4 5/8	4 4/8	
	9					

cality where kille... led Oct. 1929 By... owner Tom Mabry

Name and Address

: (Mention any abno...

5/8

COUES DEER—(NON-TYPICAL)
NEW WORLD'S RECORD—151-4/8

COUES DEER (NON-TYPICAL)
Certificate of Merit
Score—151-4/8
Length—(R) 18-4/8 (L) 18-5/8
Circumference—(R) 5-4/8 (L) 5-4/8
Points—(R) 9 (L) 8
Inside Spread—15-6/8
Locality—Cochise County, Arizona—1929
Hunter—Charles C. Mabry
Owner—Tom Mabry

COUES DEER (NON-TYPICAL)
Certificate of Merit
Score—150-5/8
Length—(R...

MULE DEER (...
Record—...

MULE DEER (TYPICAL)—1st Aw...
Score—211-2/8
Length—(R) 29-7/8 (L) 29-...
Circumference—(R) 4-5/8 (L...
Points—(R) 7 (L) 8
Inside Spread—30-3/8
Locality—Teton County, Wyom...
Hunter—Dr. Robert V. Parke...
Guide—Lule Beard

MULE DEER (TYPICAL)—2nd Awa...
Score—207-1/8
Length—(R) 26-6/8 (L) 26-2/...
Circumference—(R) 5-6/8 (L)...
Points—(R) 6 (L) 5
Inside Spread—24-1/8
Locality—Golden, Colorado—19...
Hunter—Harold B. Moser

MULE DEER (TYPICAL)—3rd Award
Score—203-4/8
Length—(R) 27 (L) 28-1/8
Circumference—(R) 5-4/8 (L) 5...
Points—(R) 5 (L) 6
Inside Spread—24-4/8
Locality—Rio Arriba County, New... 1965
Hunter—Arnold Wendt
Owner—John Wm. Hughes

MULE DEER (TYPICAL)—Honorable M...
Score—203-7/8
Length—(R) 29-3/8 (L) 29-4/8
Circumference—(R) 5-6/8 (L) 5-5...
Points—(R) 5 (L) 5
Inside Spread—25-5/8
Locality—Jicarilla Reservation, New... —1966
Hunter—Dick Wright

...ULE DEER (TYPICAL)—Honorable Men...
...core—203-2/8
...ength—(R) 25-6/8 (L) 26-6/8
...rcumference—(R) 4-6/8 (L) 4-7/8
...nts—(R) 6 (L) 5
...de Spread—23-3/8
...ality—Garfield County, Utah—1965
...ter—James D. Perkins
...er—Mrs. James D. Perkins

NOV • 67

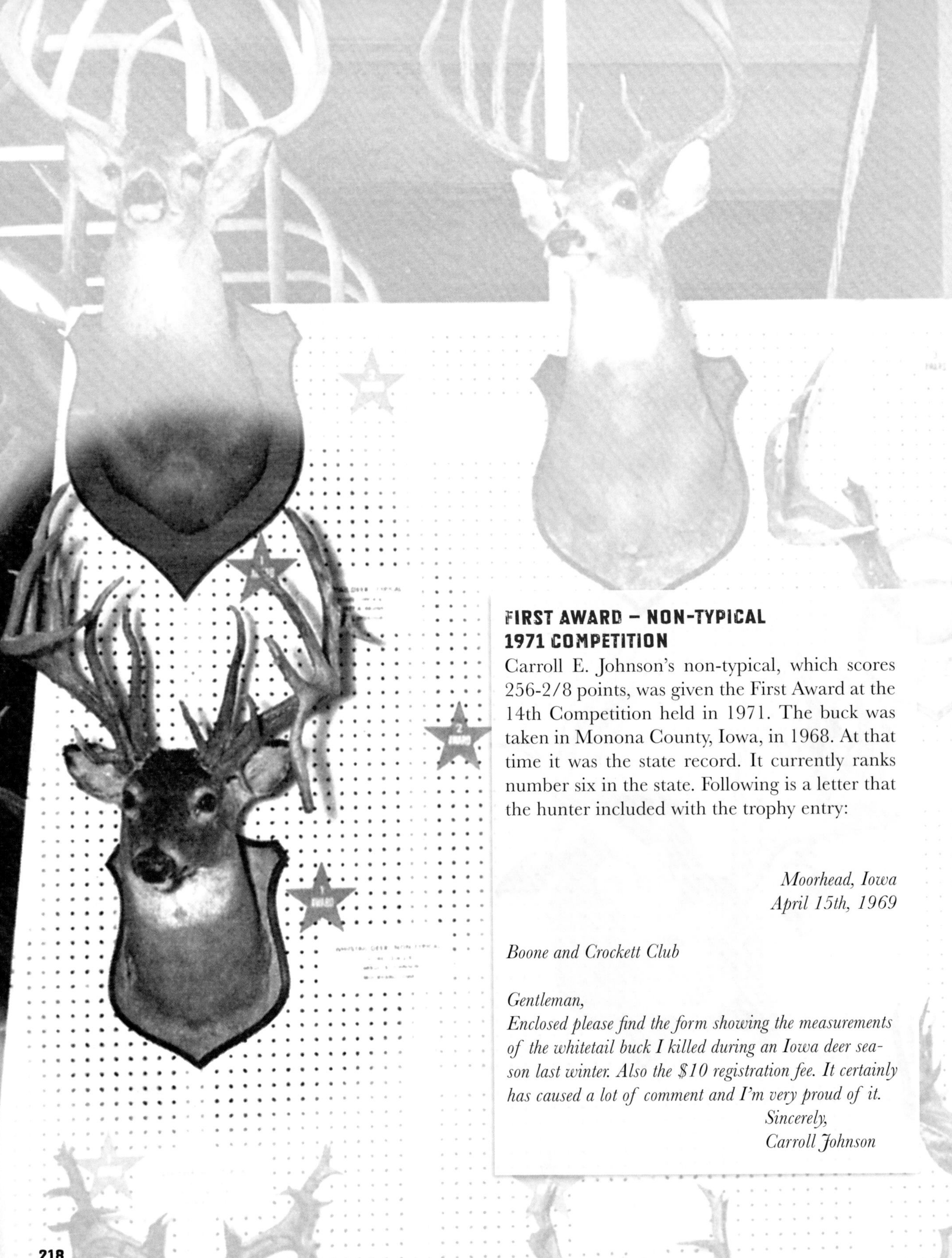

FIRST AWARD – NON-TYPICAL
1971 COMPETITION

Carroll E. Johnson's non-typical, which scores 256-2/8 points, was given the First Award at the 14th Competition held in 1971. The buck was taken in Monona County, Iowa, in 1968. At that time it was the state record. It currently ranks number six in the state. Following is a letter that the hunter included with the trophy entry:

Moorhead, Iowa
April 15th, 1969

Boone and Crockett Club

Gentleman,
Enclosed please find the form showing the measurements of the whitetail buck I killed during an Iowa deer season last winter. Also the $10 registration fee. It certainly has caused a lot of comment and I'm very proud of it.

Sincerely,
Carroll Johnson

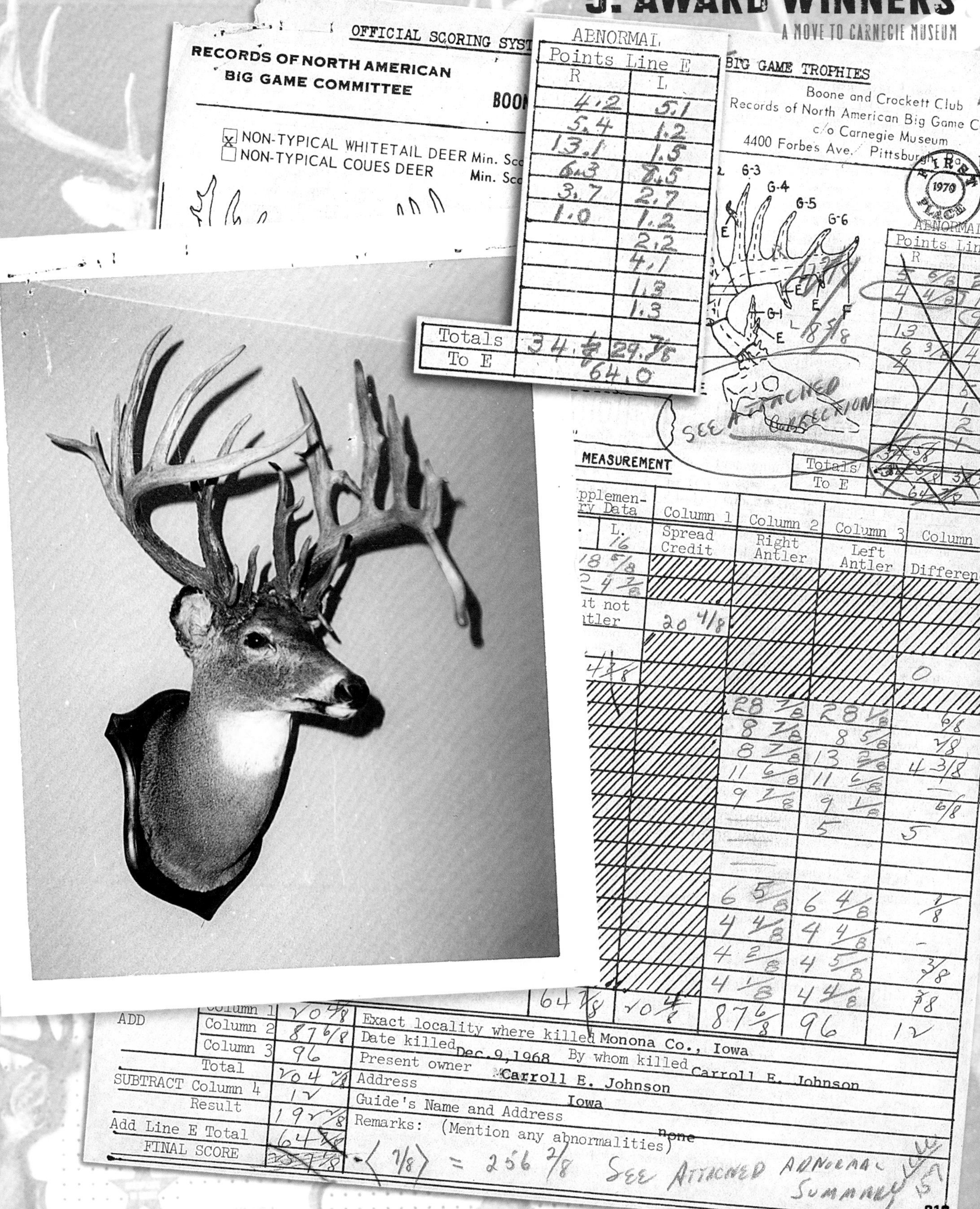

OFFICIAL SCORING SYSTEM FOR NORTH AMERICAN BIG GAME TROPHIES

RECORDS OF NORTH AMERICAN BIG GAME COMMITTEE

Boone and Crockett Club
Records of North American Big Game Committee
c/o Carnegie Museum
4400 Forbes Ave. Pittsburgh

☒ NON-TYPICAL WHITETAIL DEER Min. Score
☐ NON-TYPICAL COUES DEER Min. Score

FIRST PLACE 1970

ABNORMAL Points Line E

R	L
4.2	5.1
5.4	1.2
13.1	1.5
6.3	8.5
3.7	2.7
1.0	1.2
	2.2
	4.1
	1.2
	1.3
Totals 34 1/8	29 7/8
To E 64.0	

SEE ATTACHED CORRECTION

MEASUREMENT

Supplementary Data	Column 1 Spread Credit	Column 2 Right Antler	Column 3 Left Antler	Column 4 Difference
18 5/8				
24 7/8				
	20 4/8			
4 3/8				0
		28 7/8	28 1/8	6/8
		8 7/8	8 5/8	2/8
		8 7/8	13 2/8	4 3/8
		11 6/8	11 6/8	—
		9 7/8	9 1/8	6/8
			5	5
		6 5/8	6 4/8	1/8
		4 4/8	4 4/8	—
		4 2/8	4 5/8	3/8
		4 1/8	4 4/8	7/8
64 7/8	204 4/8	87 6/8	96	12

ADD	Column 1	204 4/8
	Column 2	87 6/8
	Column 3	96
	Total	204 7/8
SUBTRACT Column 4		12
	Result	192 7/8
Add Line E Total		64
FINAL SCORE		257 7/8

Exact locality where killed Monona Co., Iowa
Date killed Dec. 9, 1968 By whom killed Carroll E. Johnson
Present owner Carroll E. Johnson
Address Iowa
Guide's Name and Address
Remarks: (Mention any abnormalities) none

-⟨7/8⟩ = 256 7/8 SEE ATTACHED ABNORMAL SUMMARY

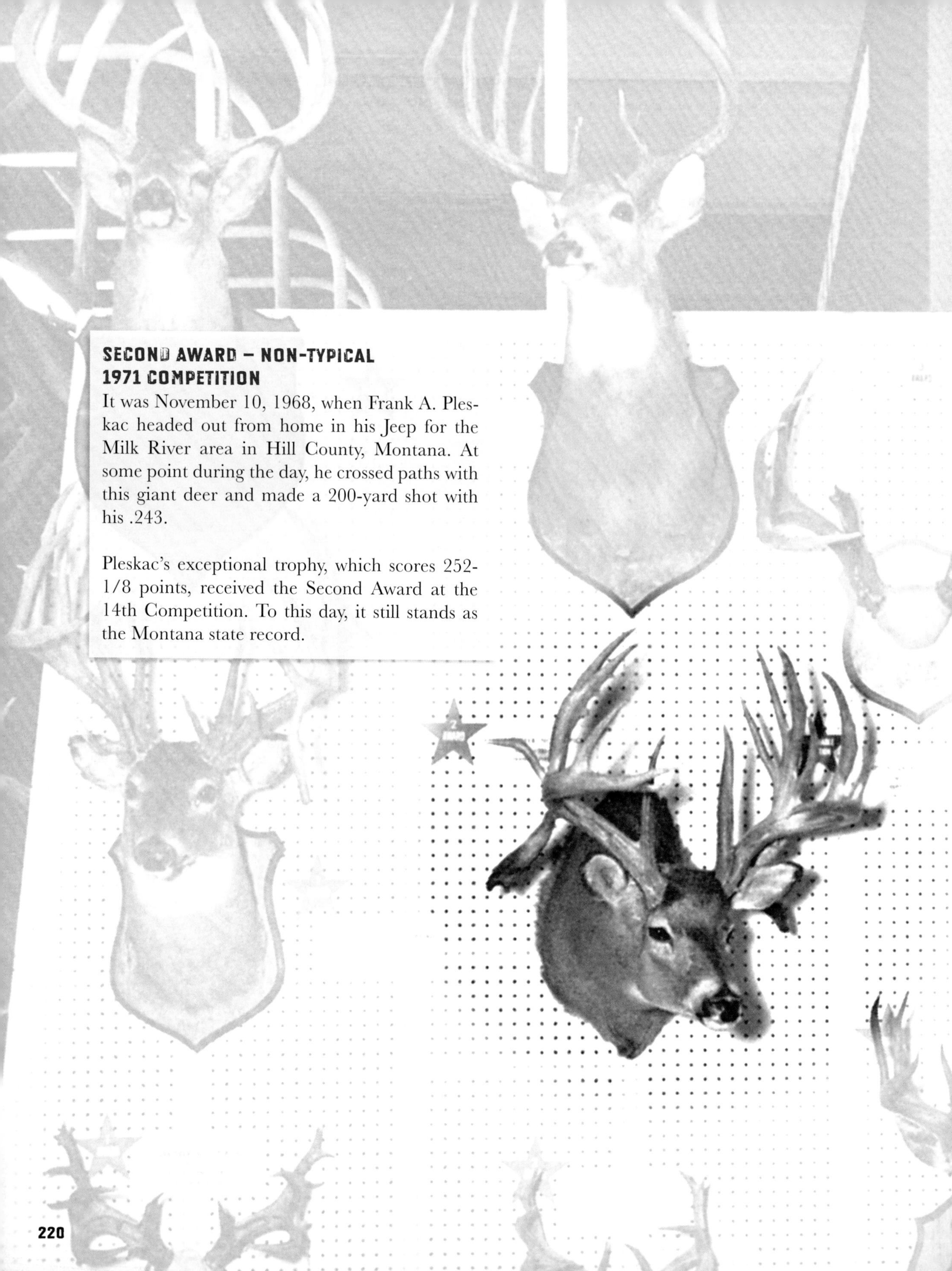

SECOND AWARD – NON-TYPICAL
1971 COMPETITION

It was November 10, 1968, when Frank A. Pleskac headed out from home in his Jeep for the Milk River area in Hill County, Montana. At some point during the day, he crossed paths with this giant deer and made a 200-yard shot with his .243.

Pleskac's exceptional trophy, which scores 252-1/8 points, received the Second Award at the 14th Competition. To this day, it still stands as the Montana state record.

AND BIG GAME TROPHIES 29

Boone and Crockett Club
Records of North American Big Game Committ
c/o Carnegie Museum
4400 Forbes Ave. Pittsburgh, Pa. 15213

SECOND 1970 PLACE

G-2 G-3 G-4 G-5 G-6 E E E E F H-4 H-3 H-2 H-1 G-1 E E

Points	Line
R	L
10.5	10.
7.6	6.
6.0	7.
2.2	9.
Totals	26 5/8
To E	100 6/8

UREMENT

	Column 1 Spread Credit	Column 2 Right Antler	Column 3 Left Antler	Colu Diffe
not tler	19.5			
60 6/8				
E. Total of ...		25.6	28.3	
F. Length of Main Beam		8.2	9.5	
G-1. Length of First Point, if present		14.2	15.1	
G-2. Length of Second Point		12.1	11.5	
G-3. Length of Third Point		6.4	5.7/8	
G-4. Length of Fourth Point, if present				
G-5. Length of Fifth Point, if present				
G-6. Length of Sixth Point, if present				
G-7. Length of Seventh Point, if present		5 3/8	5 6/8	
Circumference at Smallest Place H-1. Between Burr and First Point		4 7/8	4 4/8	
Circumference at Smallest Place H-2. Between First and Second Points		6.0	5 3/8	
Circumference at Smallest Place H-3. Between Second and Third Points		5.0	5.0	
Circumference at Smallest Place H-4. Between Third and Fourth Points				
TOTALS	60 6/8	19 5/8	88 1/8	91 1/8

ADD	
Column 1	19 5/8
Column 2	88 1/8
Column 3	91 1/8
Total	198 7/8
SUBTRACT Column 4	7 4/8
Result	191 3/8

Exact locality where killed West Fork Milk River-NorthHill
Date killed 11/10/68 By whom killed Frank A. Pleskac
Present owner ~~Frank A. Pleskac~~ Dick Idol-see
Montana
Address
Guide's Name and Address none
Remarks: (Mention any abnormalities)
Abnormal point from main beam below first point

HONORABLE MENTION – NON-TYPICAL 1971 COMPETITION

Clifford G. Pickell's 248-7/8 non-typical from Greenwood County, Kansas, received an Honorable Mention at the 14th Competition. He had the following to say about his trials and tribulations while pursuing this great deer:

I hunted an area of Greenwood County every weekend during the 1968 Archery Deer season. Driving from my home in Wichita, Kansas in a 1965 El Camino pick-up to the hunting area.

The trophy deer was first sighted October 13, at about 35 yards. I took five shots at the deer but missed the first four. (Over-excitement I guess.) The fifth arrow hit high in his right shoulder. I followed the blood trail for about one mile before it stopped. The buck apparently did not have a fatal wound.

On Sunday, November 17, I sighted the deer again, but could not get a shot since he was standing in some brush. I was happy to see he had survived our first encounter.

December 1, at 7:00 a.m. the same deer came down the game trail and high in his shoulder was a completely healed over scar. This time it took only one arrow at 20 yards to bring him down. The hit was in the lung area and he traveled only about 200 yards.

When the trophy deer was field dressed, I found the still sharp broadhead of the first encounter by cutting my finger on it. It was completely embedded in the healed scar area.

Members of the 14th Competition Panel of Judges are pictured at right: Peter Haupt, B.A. Fashingbauer, George T. Church, Jr., Philip L. Wright, Ova Uggen, Frank Cook (chairman), Arnold O. Haugen, and Donald S. Hopkins.

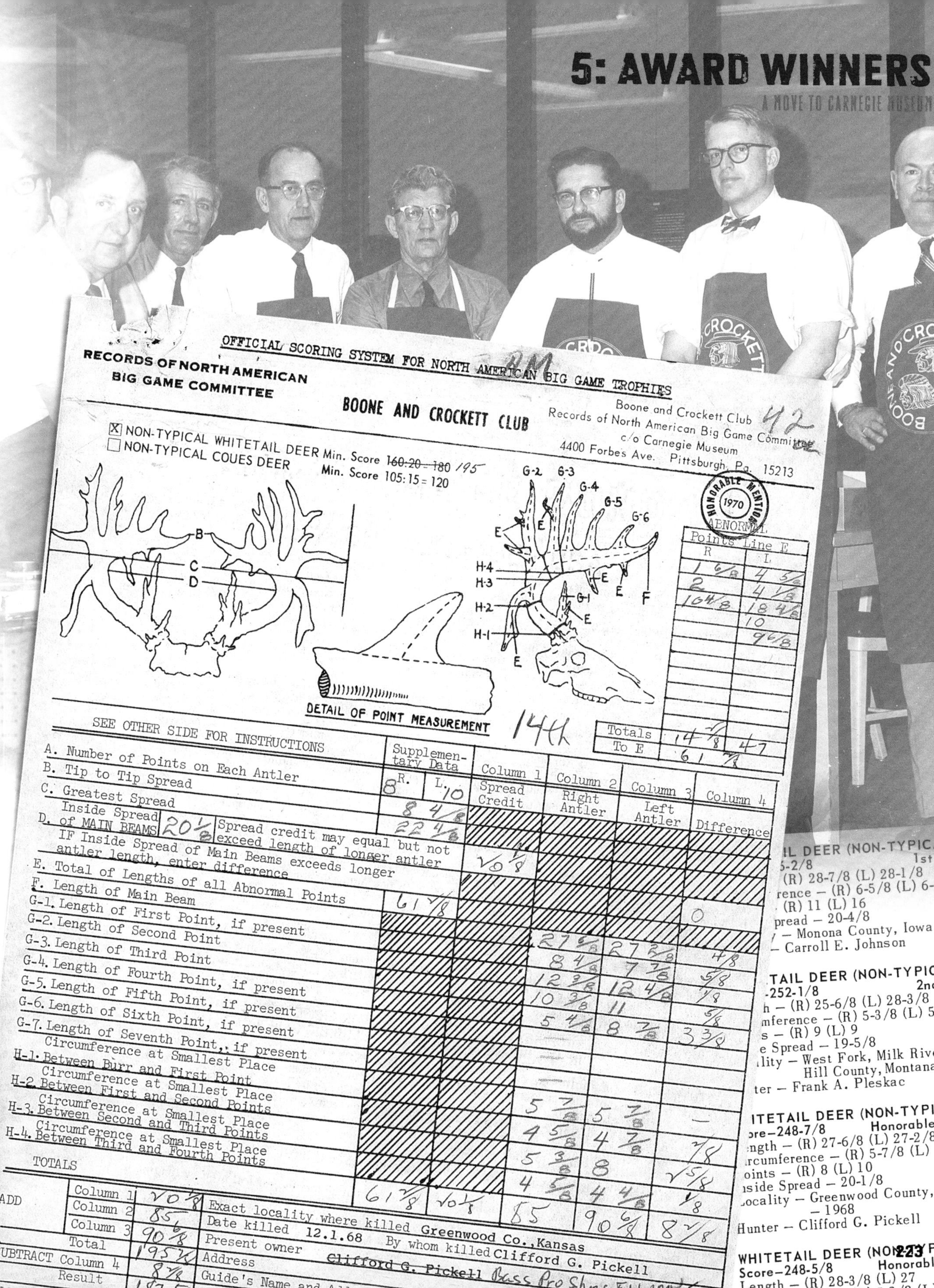

OFFICIAL SCORING SYSTEM FOR NORTH AMERICAN BIG GAME TROPHIES

RECORDS OF NORTH AMERICAN BIG GAME COMMITTEE

BOONE AND CROCKETT CLUB

Boone and Crockett Club
Records of North American Big Game Committee
c/o Carnegie Museum
4400 Forbes Ave. Pittsburgh, Pa. 15213

AM 42

[X] NON-TYPICAL WHITETAIL DEER Min. Score ~~160:20=180~~ 195
[ ] NON-TYPICAL COUES DEER Min. Score 105:15=120

HONORABLE MENTION 1970

DETAIL OF POINT MEASUREMENT

14th

Abnormal Points Line E	R	L
	1 6/8	4 5/8
	2	4 1/8
	10 4/8	18 4/8
		10
		9 6/8
Totals	14 1/8	47
To E	61 7/8	

SEE OTHER SIDE FOR INSTRUCTIONS

	Supplementary Data R.	Supplementary Data L.	Column 1 Spread Credit	Column 2 Right Antler	Column 3 Left Antler	Column 4 Difference
A. Number of Points on Each Antler	8	10				
B. Tip to Tip Spread	8 4/8					
C. Greatest Spread	22 4/8					
D. Inside Spread of MAIN BEAMS 20 1/8 — Spread credit may equal but not exceed length of longer antler			20 1/8			
IF Inside Spread of Main Beams exceeds longer antler length, enter difference						
E. Total of Lengths of all Abnormal Points	61 7/8					0
F. Length of Main Beam				27 6/8	27 2/8	4/8
G-1. Length of First Point, if present				8 4/8	7 7/8	5/8
G-2. Length of Second Point				12 3/8	12 4/8	1/8
G-3. Length of Third Point				10 3/8	11	5/8
G-4. Length of Fourth Point, if present				5 4/8	8 7/8	3 3/8
G-5. Length of Fifth Point, if present				—	—	
G-6. Length of Sixth Point, if present						
G-7. Length of Seventh Point, if present						
Circumference at Smallest Place H-1. Between Burr and First Point				5 7/8	5 7/8	—
Circumference at Smallest Place H-2. Between First and Second Points				4 5/8	4 7/8	2/8
Circumference at Smallest Place H-3. Between Second and Third Points				5 3/8	8	2 5/8
Circumference at Smallest Place H-4. Between Third and Fourth Points				4 5/8	4 4/8	1/8
TOTALS	61 7/8		20 1/8	85	90 6/8	8 2/8

ADD	Column 1	20 1/8
	Column 2	85
	Column 3	90 6/8
	Total	195 7/8
SUBTRACT	Column 4	8 2/8
	Result	187 5/8

Exact locality where killed Greenwood Co., Kansas
Date killed 12.1.68 By whom killed Clifford G. Pickell
Present owner ~~Clifford G. Pickell~~ Bass Pro Shops
Address
Guide's Name and Add...

...IL DEER (NON-TYPICAL)- 1st Aw...
...5-2/8
... (R) 28-7/8 (L) 28-1/8
...rence – (R) 6-5/8 (L) 6-4/8
... (R) 11 (L) 16
...pread – 20-4/8
... – Monona County, Iowa – 1...
... – Carroll E. Johnson

...TAIL DEER (NON-TYPICAL)... 2nd Aw...
...-252-1/8
...h – (R) 25-6/8 (L) 28-3/8
...mference – (R) 5-3/8 (L) 5-6/8
...s – (R) 9 (L) 9
...e Spread – 19-5/8
...lity – West Fork, Milk River, N...
Hill County, Montana – 1...
...ter – Frank A. Pleskac

...ITETAIL DEER (NON-TYPICAL... Honorable Me...
...ore–248-7/8
...ength – (R) 27-6/8 (L) 27-2/8
...rcumference – (R) 5-7/8 (L) 5-7/...
...oints – (R) 8 (L) 10
...side Spread – 20-1/8
...ocality – Greenwood County, Ka...
– 1968
Hunter – Clifford G. Pickell

WHITETAIL DEER (NON-TYPICA... Honorable Me...
Score–248-5/8
Length – (R) 28-3/8 (L) 27

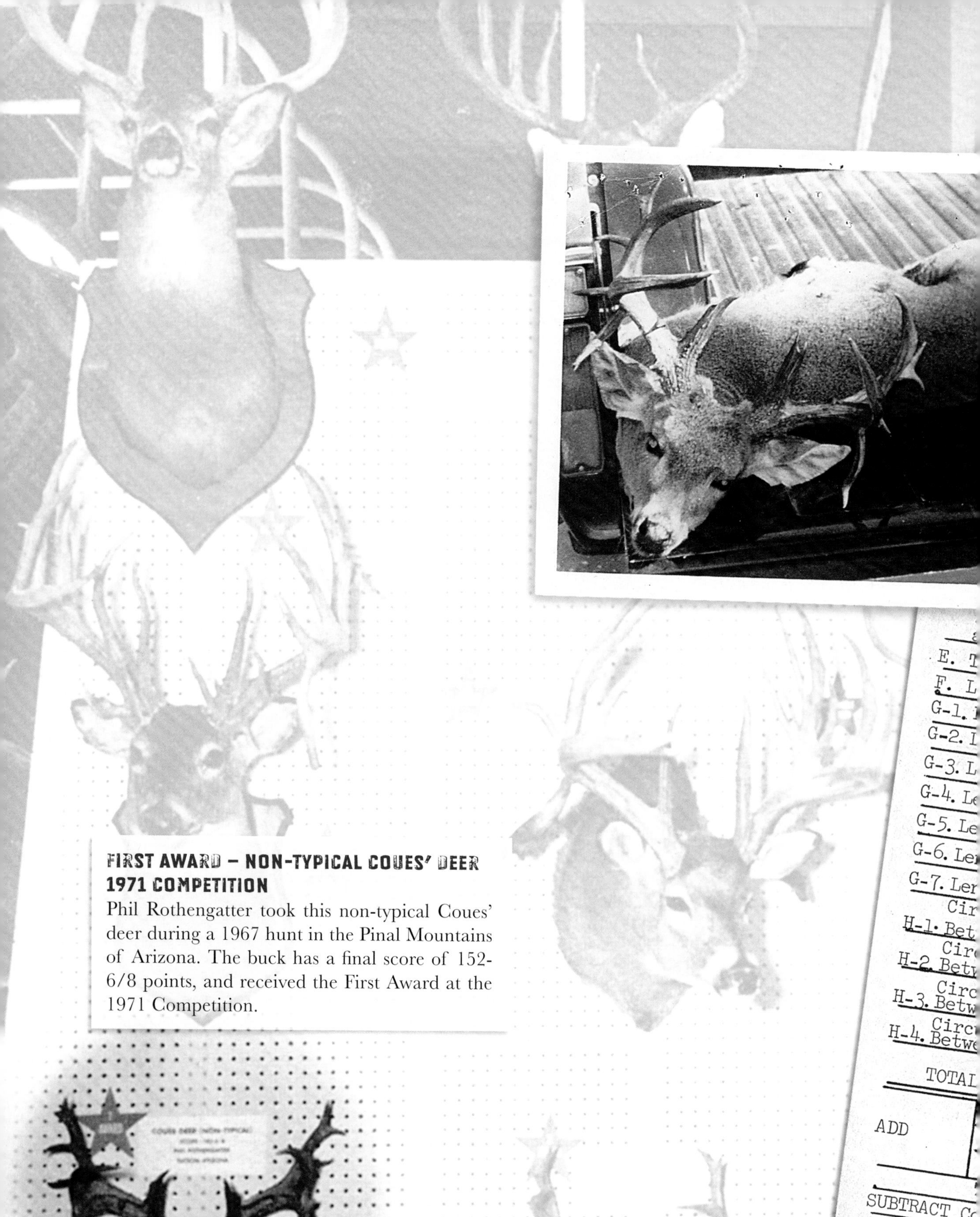

FIRST AWARD – NON-TYPICAL COUES' DEER 1971 COMPETITION

Phil Rothengatter took this non-typical Coues' deer during a 1967 hunt in the Pinal Mountains of Arizona. The buck has a final score of 152-6/8 points, and received the First Award at the 1971 Competition.

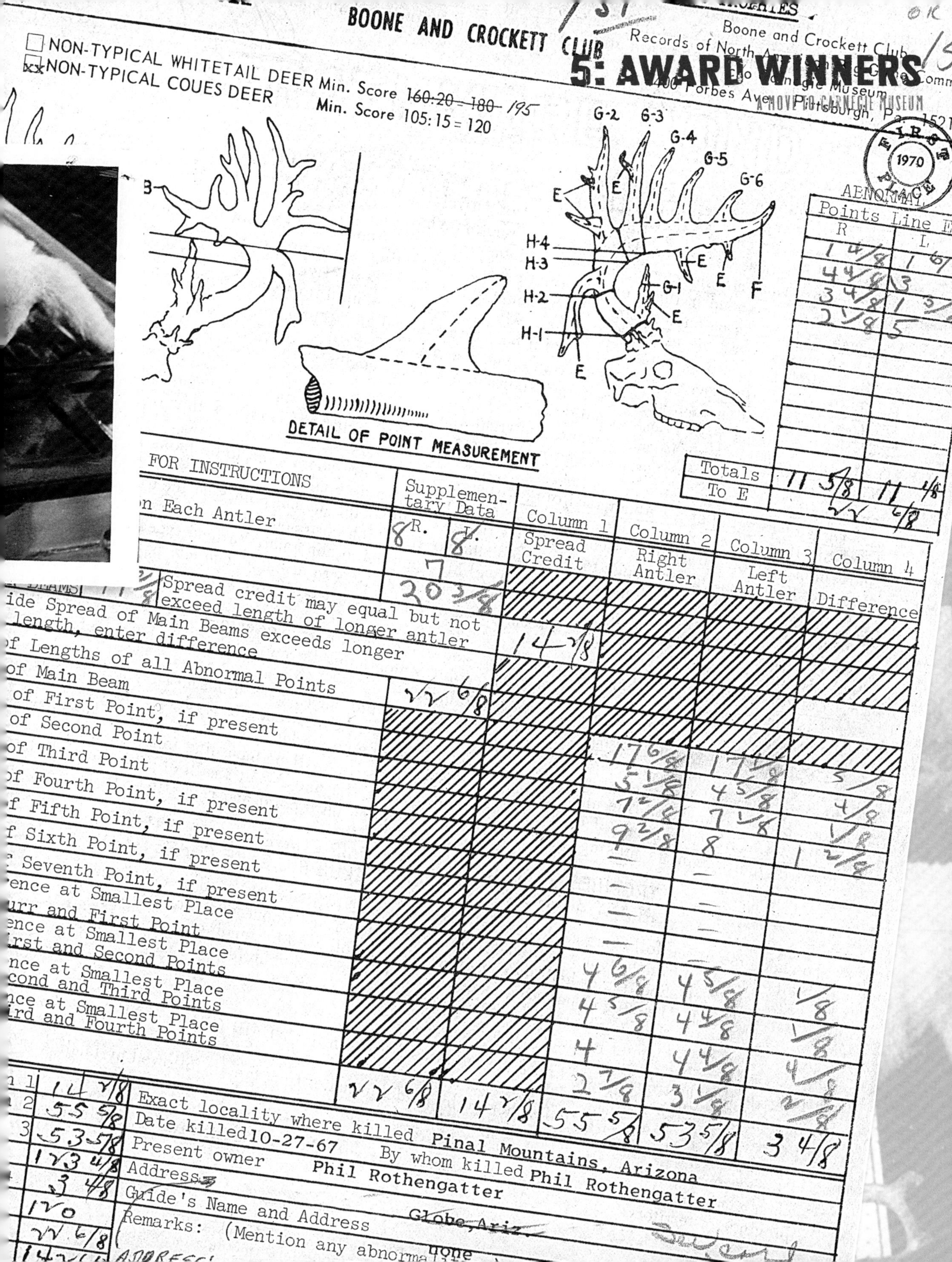

5: AWARD WINNERS

A NOVA TO CARNEGIE MUSEUM

BOONE AND CROCKETT CLUB

Boone and Crockett Club
Records of North A... Game Comm...
...Carnegie Museum
4400 Forbes Ave. Pittsburgh, Pa. 15213

FIRST PLACE 1970

OK 15

☐ NON-TYPICAL WHITETAIL DEER Min. Score ~~160:20 = 180~~ 195
xx NON-TYPICAL COUES DEER Min. Score 105:15 = 120

ABNORMAL Points Line E	
R	L
1 4/8	1 6/8
4 4/8	3
3 4/8	1 5/8
2 1/8	5
Totals To E: 11 5/8	11 1/8
	22 6/8

...FOR INSTRUCTIONS

	Supplementary Data R.	Supplementary Data L.	Column 1 Spread Credit	Column 2 Right Antler	Column 3 Left Antler	Column 4 Difference
...n Each Antler	8	8				
	7					
...Beams 17 ... Spread credit may equal but not exceed length of longer antler	20 3/8					
...ide Spread of Main Beams exceeds longer ...length, enter difference			14 7/8			
...of Lengths of all Abnormal Points	22 6/8					
...of Main Beam				17 6/8	17 1/8	5/8
...of First Point, if present				5 1/8	4 5/8	4/8
...of Second Point				7 2/8	7 1/8	1/8
...of Third Point				9 2/8	8	1 2/8
...of Fourth Point, if present				—	—	
...f Fifth Point, if present				—	—	
...f Sixth Point, if present				—	—	
...Seventh Point, if present				—	—	
...ence at Smallest Place ...urr and First Point				4 6/8	4 5/8	1/8
...ence at Smallest Place ...rst and Second Points				4 5/8	4 4/8	1/8
...nce at Smallest Place ...cond and Third Points				4	4 4/8	4/8
...nce at Smallest Place ...ird and Fourth Points				2 7/8	3 1/8	2/8
		22 6/8	14 7/8	55 5/8	53 5/8	3 4/8

...n 1	14 7/8
... 2	55 5/8
3	53 5/8
	123 4/8
	3 4/8
	120
	22 6/8
	14...

Exact locality where killed **Pinal Mountains, Arizona**
Date killed 10-27-67 By whom killed **Phil Rothengatter**
Present owner **Phil Rothengatter**
Address ~~Globe, Ariz.~~
Guide's Name and Address
Remarks: (Mention any abnormali... none
ADDRESS

P. 39

Pennsylvania

GAME NEWS

JULY, 1964 TEN CENTS

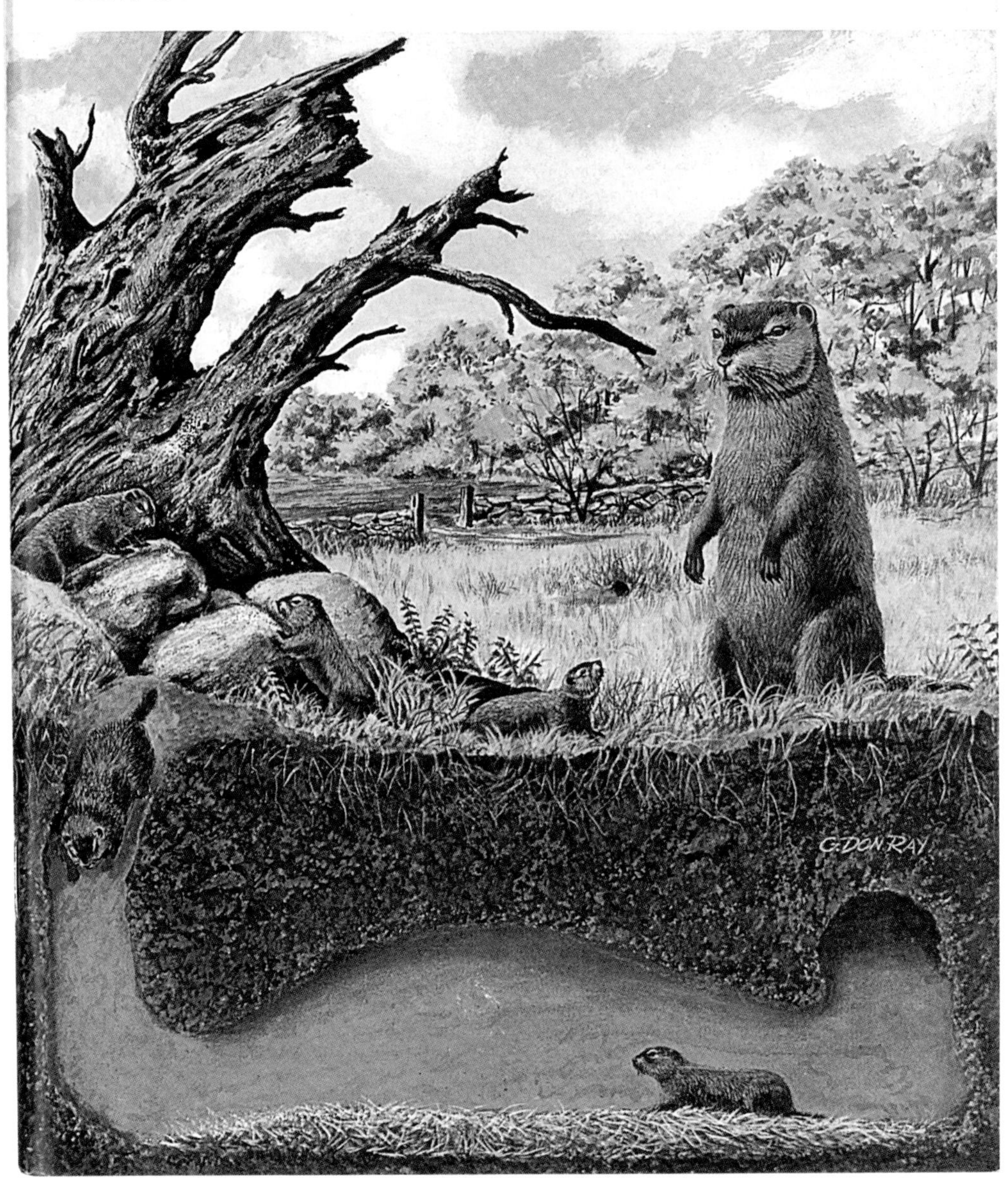

5: PUBLICITY

A MOVE TO CARNEGIE MUSEUM

The next three pages show an article about the Club's first competition held at Pittsburgh's Carnegie Museum in 1963. Prior to that, all of the Competitions had been held at the American Museum of Natural History in New York City.

CONSERVATION NEWS

Boone and Crockett Presents North American Big Game Awards in Pittsburgh

THE Boone and Crockett Club, whose members are leading sportsmen and conservationists of North America, announced the winners of its 1963 North American Big Game Competition. The awards were presented at the Club's Award Ceremony and Dinner at the Carnegie Museum April 30.

Some 330 invited guests assembled in the Museum's Lecture Hall at 5 p.m. on April 30 to witness the awards ceremony. Winners from Mexico, Canada, Alaska and throughout the United States were on hand to receive the coveted medals and certificates.

ADMIRING THE WHITE-TAILED DEER winners are Honorary President of Boone and Crockett Archibald Roosevelt and Pennsylvania Game Commissioner James A. Thompson of Pittsburgh. The exhibit of 131 heads was on display at Carnegie Museum in Pittsburgh throughout the month of May. Roosevelt is the last surviving son of President Theodore Roosevelt, the founder of the Boone and Crockett Club.

PGC Photo by Harrison

Competition was open to all hunters of North American big game. Statistics on all trophies entered in its biennial competitions are maintained by the Records Committee. Robert S. Waters, of Johnstown, Chairman of the Records Committee, pointed out: "This year's entries produced outstanding trophies, and many of the winning trophies will be in the 'first ten' of the all-time record list; this is surprising in view of the reduction in the primitive ranges of our big game animals, caused by increasing population, urbanization, and highway construction in the United States."

Following the awards ceremony, guests moved into the Hall of the Dinosaurs where cocktails were served. Dinner followed in the foyer of the Music Hall.

The viewing of the winning heads and skulls, the highlight of the evening, followed dinner. It was here that guests and winners alike admired North America's finest big game specimens.

The trophies were on exhibition at Carnegie Museum through May 31. The exhibit was free to the public.

Records Committee Chairman Waters remarked:

"The Boone and Crockett Club Competitions help to awaken an interest in outstanding examples of North American big game and arouse sportsmen to the importance of a wise conservation policy. These magnificent mammals," he said, "were an inherited

THE ONLY PENNSYLVANIAN to win a Boone and Crockett award in 1963 competition was Sil first place medal in the Canada Moose Category from Records Committee Chairman Robert S. Wa seated on the stage of the Carnegie Museum Lecture Hall.

natural wildlife asset to which our sportsmen should give zealous protection; otherwise future generations may be deprived of this natural resource."

As outlined in its articles of incorporation, the Club's position as an international repository and clearing house for statistical data on North American big game has been demonstrated in various aspects of its policy for many years.

Individuals and members of the Boone and Crockett Club, all of whom are experts in the field of measuring and scoring, made up the panel of judges.

Trophies killed by accident, pickups, those purchased, or those of unknown methods of capture were not eligible for a Medal but may qualify for a Certificate of Merit. Such trophies will be given their rightful position in the all-time RECORDS OF NORTH AMERICAN BIG GAME. Medal awards were given only to trophies taken since 1958. Those taken at an earlier date were eligible for certificates of merit. Trophies taken in "Unfair Chase" were not eligible for medals or certificates. They are defined as follows: spotting or herding land game from the air, followed by landing in its vicinity for pursuit, and herding or pursuing any game from motor powered vehicles; such are deemed Unfair Chase and unsportsmanlike.

SECOND PLACE WINNER in the white-tailed deer (typical) category is checked here by the hunter who shot it, award winner Arlee McCullough of Newark, Ohio. The 14-point buck was killed in Licking County, Ohio, in 1962. It has a spread of 22⅞ inches.

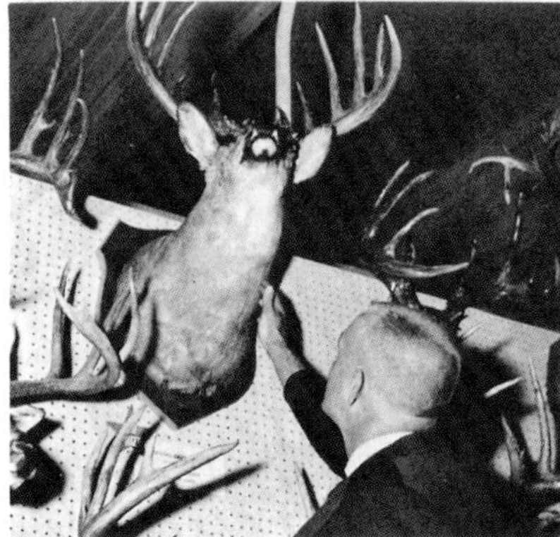

5: PUBLICITY

A MOVE TO THE CARNEGIE MUSEUM

PGC Photos by Harrison

...ene Bracalente of Quakertown. Here he receives his ...ers of Johnstown. The judges for the competition were

NEW WORLD'S RECORD polar bear was taken by Shelby Longoria of Mexico (left). The big bear was killed at Kotezbue, Alaska, in 1963. Here Records Committee Chairman Robert S. Waters (right) presents the medal in Pittsburgh.

In addition to the medals and certificates of award, the Sagamore Hill Medal was presented to Norman Blank, Beverly Hills, Calif., for his outstanding stone sheep killed at Sikanni River, B. C., the finest specimen of this species reported since 1936. This award is in memory of Theodore Roosevelt (first president and founder of the Boone and Crockett Club in 1887), Kermit Roosevelt and Theodore Roosevelt, Jr.

Among this year's award winning entries is a world's record polar bear which was shot by Shelby Longoria, of Matamoros, Tamaulipas, Mexico.

The following trophies will rank in 2nd place in the all-time records: white-tailed deer (nontypical), shot by Del Austin, Hastings, Neb.; mule deer (nontypical), shot by James Austill, Denver, Colo.; cougar, shot by Louis Rebillet, Warren, Idaho, ties for the No. 2 position; stone sheep, shot by Norman Blank, Beverly Hills, Calif.

The Records Committee Chairman said that, "Due to the number of outstanding entries received since the publication of the 1958 Records Book, and as a further encouragement in selective hunting, the minimum qualifying scores for entry in this competition had been raised in most categories and reduced in one." There were 1,930 entries, a reduction of approximately 17 per cent below the number in the previous competition.

TOP BLACK BEAR was killed by Ben Hillicoss of Yorktown Heights, N. Y., in 1963 on Megal Mountain, Newfoundland.

Twenty-six classes were represented at the Exhibition; participating hunters were from 26 states, Canada, Mexico and Switzerland. Most of the trophies including the new world's record polar bear, and 90 of the 130 winners, were taken in the United States. Thirty-seven of the winners were shot in Canada, one in British Honduras, and two in Mexico.

The 131 awards (including the Sagamore Hill Medal) were made as follows: 73 medals and certificates to place winners, 11 honorable mention certificates, 46 certificates of merit (trophies taken prior to 1958, pickups, purchased trophies or those of unknown methods of capture), 1 Sagamore Hill Medal for the outstanding trophy of the exhibit.

Eighty-eight of the 131 award winning and certificates of merit trophies were on exhibition at the Carnegie Museum.

Of the 131 winners, only one is from Pennsylvania. He is Silvene Brocalente, of Quakertown, who won first place in the Canada moose category.

The judges for the 1963 competition were: Dr. Elmer M. Rusten, Chairman, Minneapolis, Minn.; Jack N. Allen, Tacoma, Wash.; John H. Batten, Racine, Wis.; Elgin T. Gates, Newport Beach, Calif.; Edward McGuire, Bergenfield, N. J.; George L. Norris, Game Commission Field Division Supervisor, Ligonier, Pa.; and Arthur C. Popham, Jr., Kansas City, Mo.

Jr. Conservation Camp ...

OFFICIAL SCORING SYSTEM FOR NORTH AMERICAN BIG GAME TROPHIES

RECORDS OF NORTH AMERICAN BIG GAME COMMITTEE

Dwight O. Allen

BOONE AND CROCKETT CLUB

Address Correspondence to:
Mrs. Grancel Fitz, Secretary
5 Tudor City Place, NYC 17. NY.

NON-TYPICAL WHITETAIL DEER #47

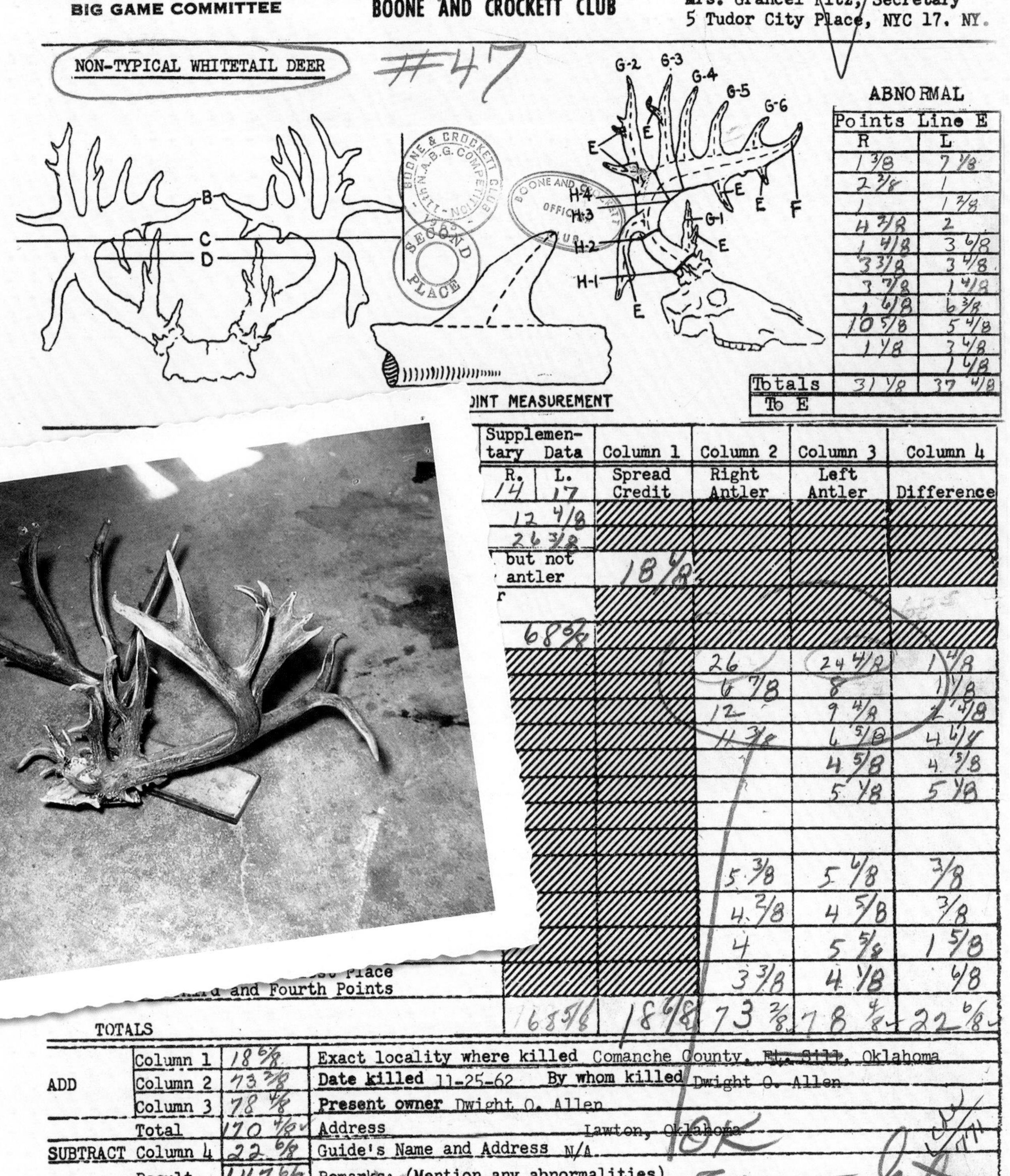

ABNORMAL

Points Line E	
R	L
1 3/8	7 1/8
2 3/8	1
1	1 3/8
4 7/8	2
1 4/8	3 6/8
3 3/8	3 4/8
3 7/8	1 4/8
1 6/8	6 3/8
10 5/8	5 4/8
1 1/8	3 4/8
	1 6/8
Totals 31 1/8	37 4/8
To E	

...OINT MEASUREMENT

	Supplementary Data R. 14	L. 17	Column 1 Spread Credit	Column 2 Right Antler	Column 3 Left Antler	Column 4 Difference
	12 4/8					
	26 3/8					
... but not ... antler			18 6/8			
...r						
	68 5/8					
				26	24 4/8	1 4/8
				6 7/8	8	1 1/8
				12	9 4/8	2 4/8
				11 3/8	6 5/8	4 6/8
					4 5/8	4 5/8
					5 1/8	5 1/8
				5 3/8	5 4/8	3/8
				4 2/8	4 5/8	3/8
				4	5 5/8	1 5/8
...Place ...ird and Fourth Points				3 3/8	4 1/8	6/8
TOTALS	168 5/8		18 6/8	73 2/8	78 4/8	22 6/8

ADD	Column 1	18 6/8	Exact locality where killed Comanche County, ~~Ft. Sill~~, Oklahoma
	Column 2	73 2/8	Date killed 11-25-62 By whom killed Dwight O. Allen
	Column 3	78 4/8	Present owner Dwight O. Allen
	Total	170 4/8	Address Lawton, Oklahoma
SUBTRACT	Column 4	22 6/8	Guide's Name and Address N/A
	Result	147 6/8	Remarks: (Mention any abnormalities)
	Add Line E Total	68 5/8	ok OK Elgin T. Gates
	FINAL SCORE	216 3/8	

A FULL SET. Dwight Allen, 2146 Lincoln, shows his 47-point buck which he killed Sunday in Area 48 of the Military reservation. Allen's kill has one of the largest racks, considering the number of points, ever killed in Oklahoma. (Staff Photo)

Lawton Man Nabs Prize 47-Pointer

DWIGHT Allen of Lawton bagged one of the most impressive of nearly 3,500 deer Sunday as Oklahoma's five-day deer season came to a halt.

Allen, who lives at 2146 Lincoln, dropped an ancient buck in Fort Sill's Military reservation Area 48 which boasted an antler rack of 47 points.

The deer, which was estimated to be 12 years old, was felled by a 12-gauge shotgun about 800 yards north of the spot where Postoak Creek runs off the reservation, Allen said.

Julian Howard, director of the Wildlife Refuge, said he had no information as to a record set of antlers, "but 47 points is a lot of points.

"I haven't seen the deer, but the best explanation I can give is that antlers sometimes become mal-formed after the buck has passed his prime. This rack, I'm told, is mal-formed," he explained.

Allen's kill was one of 3,419 deer slain in Oklahoma during the short season. The total, which includes 425 Sunday, represented totals from all but two of the state's 45 check points.

O. L. Curtis, Oklahoma Wildlife Department big game supervisor, said this year's kill is lower than that of 1961, when a record 3,702 deer were killed. He added that the drop was not surprising, noting that last winter was a hard one and deer were moving quite a bit this year.

Allen's deer weighed 162 pounds, hog-dressed. That is 33 pounds lighter than the biggest kill of the season, a 195-pounder taken the first day.

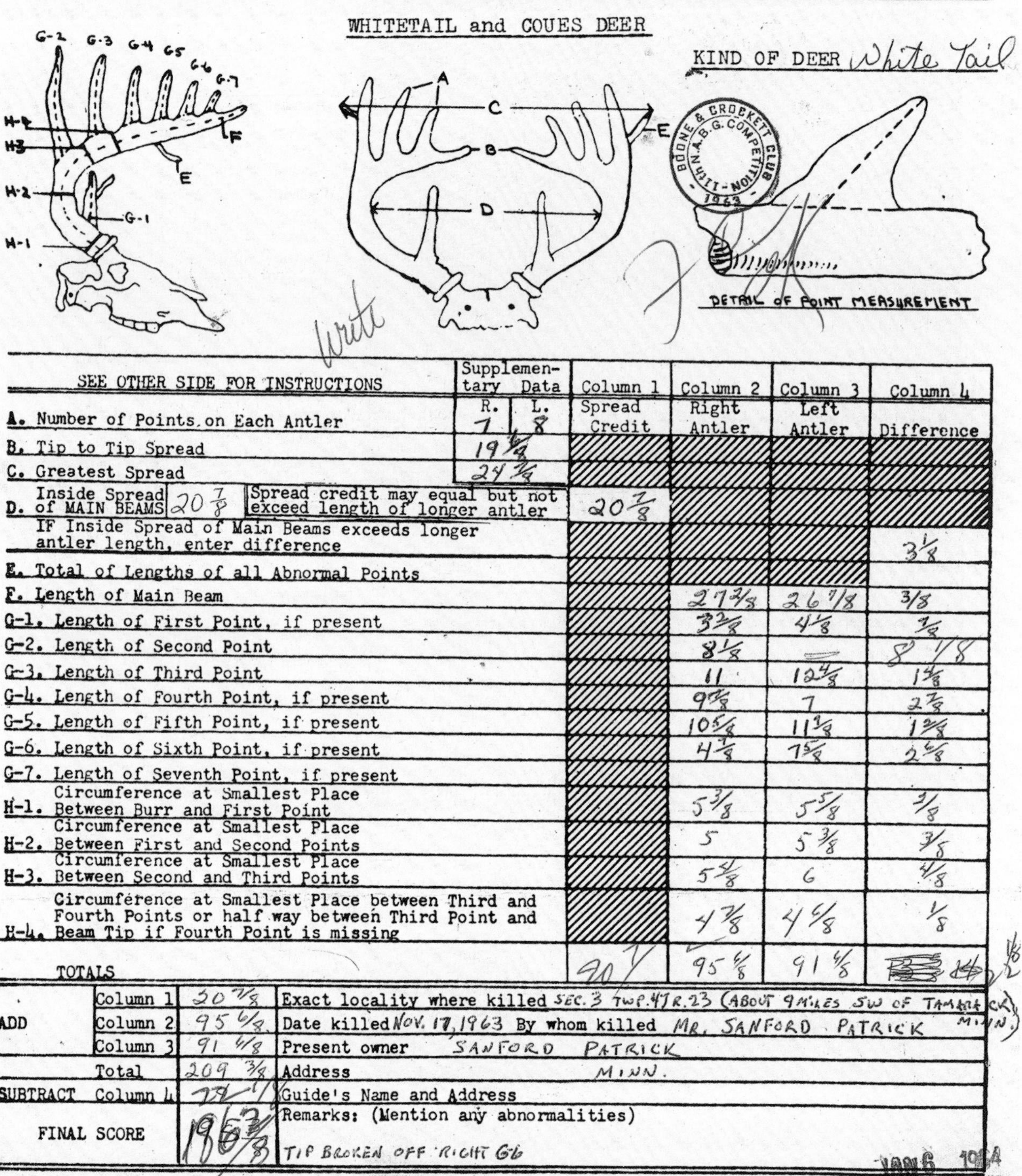

OFFICIAL SCORING SYSTEM FOR NORTH AMERICAN BIG GAME TROPHIES

RECORDS OF NORTH AMERICAN BIG GAME COMMITTEE

BOONE AND CROCKETT CLUB

Address Correspondence to:
Mrs. Grancel Fitz, Secretary
5 Tudor City Place, NYC 17, NY.

WHITETAIL and COUES DEER

KIND OF DEER White Tail

SEE OTHER SIDE FOR INSTRUCTIONS	Supplementary Data R.	Supplementary Data L.	Column 1 Spread Credit	Column 2 Right Antler	Column 3 Left Antler	Column 4 Difference
A. Number of Points on Each Antler	7	8				
B. Tip to Tip Spread	19 4/8					
C. Greatest Spread	24 1/8					
D. Inside Spread of MAIN BEAMS 20 7/8 — Spread credit may equal but not exceed length of longer antler			20 7/8			
IF Inside Spread of Main Beams exceeds longer antler length, enter difference						3 1/8
E. Total of Lengths of all Abnormal Points						
F. Length of Main Beam				27 2/8	26 7/8	3/8
G-1. Length of First Point, if present				3 2/8	4 1/8	7/8
G-2. Length of Second Point				8 1/8	—	8 1/8
G-3. Length of Third Point				11	12 4/8	1 4/8
G-4. Length of Fourth Point, if present				9 7/8	7	2 7/8
G-5. Length of Fifth Point, if present				10 5/8	11 7/8	1 2/8
G-6. Length of Sixth Point, if present				4 7/8	7 5/8	2 6/8
G-7. Length of Seventh Point, if present						
H-1. Circumference at Smallest Place Between Burr and First Point				5 3/8	5 5/8	2/8
H-2. Circumference at Smallest Place Between First and Second Points				5	5 3/8	3/8
H-3. Circumference at Smallest Place Between Second and Third Points				5 4/8	6	4/8
H-4. Circumference at Smallest Place between Third and Fourth Points or half way between Third Point and Beam Tip if Fourth Point is missing				4 7/8	4 6/8	1/8
TOTALS			20 7/8	95 6/8	91 4/8	[illegible]

ADD	Column 1	20 7/8	Exact locality where killed SEC. 3 TWP. 47 R. 23 (ABOUT 9 MILES SW OF TAMARACK, MINN.)
	Column 2	95 6/8	Date killed NOV. 17, 1963 By whom killed MR. SANFORD PATRICK
	Column 3	91 4/8	Present owner SANFORD PATRICK
	Total	209 3/8	Address MINN.
SUBTRACT	Column 4	[illegible] 1/8	Guide's Name and Address
FINAL SCORE		186 3/8	Remarks: (Mention any abnormalities) TIP BROKEN OFF RIGHT G6

JAN 6 1964

5: CORRESPONDENCE FROM THE VAULTS

SANFORD PATRICK

Jan. 10, 1964

Mr. Sanford Patrick
Tamarack
Minn.

Dear Mr. Patrick:

Thank you very much for sending in the chart of your fine Whitetail Deer. We are glad to have this record of your trophy, and if you have scored it correctly, I know that the Judges will want to have your trophy exhibited at the next show. Enclosed is our form letters in re shipment.

If you are not sure that you have scored the rack correctly and would like to have it rechecked before going to the expense of shipping it to Pittsburgh, the following men are official measurers for us:

Dr. Elmer M. Rusten, 1645 Medical Arts Bldg., Minneapolis, Minn.

Mr. B. A. Fashingbauer, Game Biologist, 110 Suzanne Court, St. Paul 10, or Carlos Avery Research Center, Forest Lake, Minn.

Just where is Tamarack? If it is near the border of the state, we might have a man near in one of the other states. Enclosed is a new chart for scoring. From your photograph, it is not possible for me to tell whether all the points, other than the 3 1/8 listed as abnormal, come off the main beam or not. If you will send me a rough sketch of the rack, I could tell better.

We look forward to hearing from you as to whether you will get the trophy officially scored or, if you feel that you have scored the rack correctly, we hope you will be shipping the trophy to Pittsburgh.

Yours sincerely,

bsf

(Mrs. Grancel Fitz)

Copy to Dr. Rusten

Mr. Patrick took the advice in the January 10th letter and had his trophy remeasured by B.A. Fashingbauer. Following is Fashingbauer's conclusion:

CORRESPONDENCE FROM FASHINGBAUER

Dear Dr. R: This trophy has a score of 186-2/8; they had it at 195 3/8, but had not entered a penalty of 8 1/8 for only one 2d point. It's still a fine trophy and I'd take it, wouldn't you? — BF

Sanford Patrick's whitetail was eventually accepted in the 11th Competition as a non-typical with a final score of 199-4/8 points.

Mr. Sanford Patrick
Tamarack
Minn.

Dear Mr. Patrick:

Thank you very much for getting your whitetail deer officially scored. As you know, it is now in the Non-typical class.

Your trophy is eligible for the next record book, but not quite large enough to warrant your shipping to the show. The new book will be out sometime this early fall; we'll let you know in advance of publication.

If you read the magazine, Outdoor Life, the February issue which will be on the newstands soon, has an article by my late husband, Grancel Fitz. Under the Whitetail deer caption he says, "Odds against your whitetail's being a giant are fantastic -- something like 100,000 to 1." When Grancel referred to Giant Whitetails he meant any that make the record lists; therefore, I congratulate you.

Yours sincerely,

bsf

(Mrs. Grancel Fitz)

WALTER BRO
184 6/8
1961

5: CORRESPONDENCE FROM THE VAULTS

WALTER BROCK/LEE PERRY WHITETAIL

REX HANCOCK, D. D. S.
515 SOUTH MAIN STREET
STUTTGART, ARKANSAS 72160

Betty:

I mailed the card to you the other day AIR MAIL indicating that Spears and Neals trophies were on their way.

Be sure both trophies are returned to me via Railway Express, insured for $2,000.00. I will see to it thatt they get to their respective owners.

I would like very much to attend the awards banquet & meet you and the other members of Boone & Crockett Club. When is the date?

The Walter Brock trophy was not a purchased trophy. The man that killed it did not care to have it mounted and gave it to Brock to have mounted.

The real massive bucks are getting a thing of the past in Arkansas, but have seen several real fine trophies that were taken around Stuttgart this past season, but nothing out of the 175 class.

Yours for better sports,

Rex

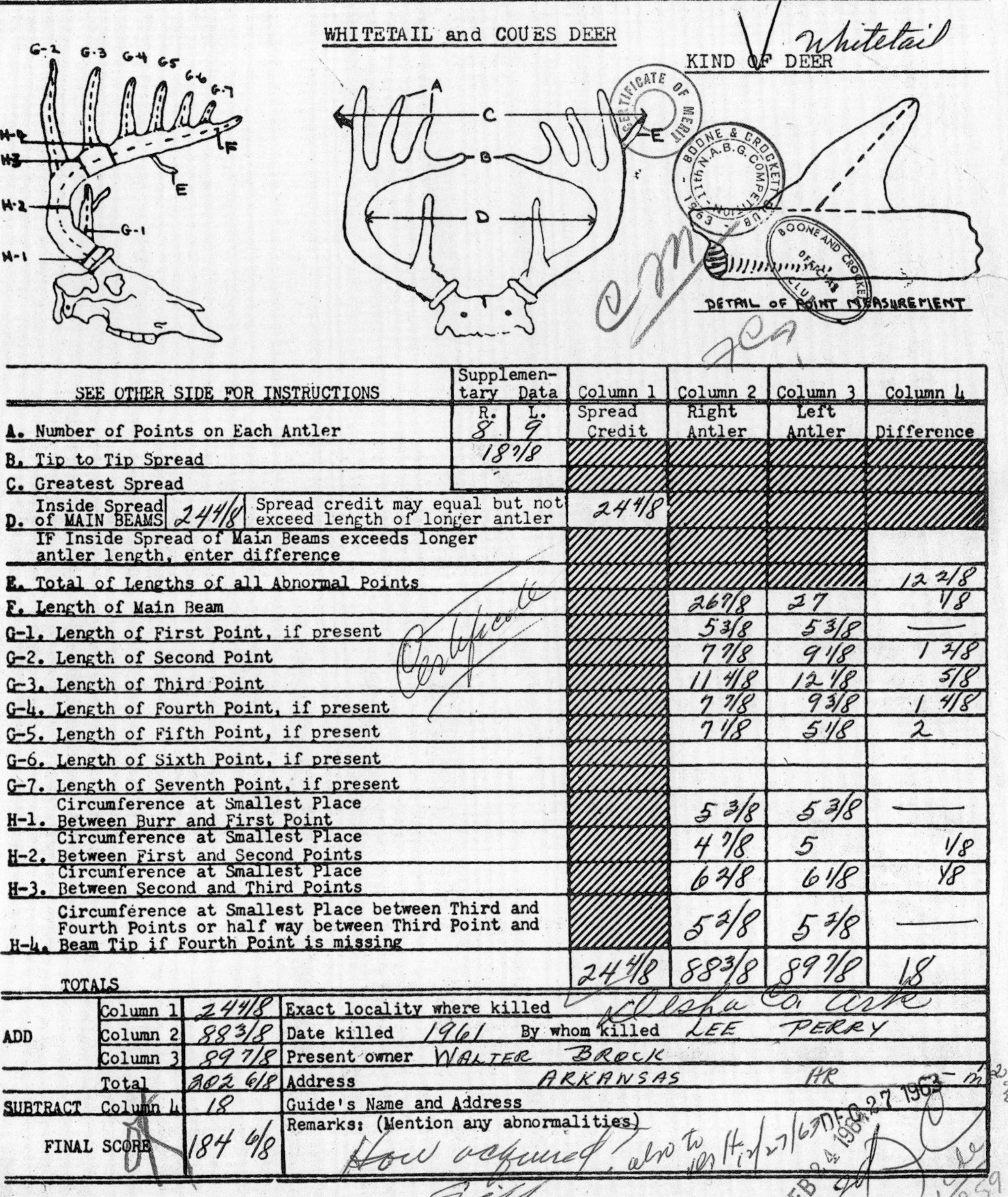
OFFICIAL SCORING SYSTEM FOR NORTH AMERICAN BIG GAME TROPHIES

Records of North American Big Game Committee

BOONE AND CROCKETT CLUB

Address correspondence to:
Dr. Rex Hancock
515 South Main St.
Stuttgart, Arkansas

WHITETAIL and COUES DEER

KIND OF DEER Whitetail

SEE OTHER SIDE FOR INSTRUCTIONS	Supplementary Data R.	Supplementary Data L.	Column 1 Spread Credit	Column 2 Right Antler	Column 3 Left Antler	Column 4 Difference
A. Number of Points on Each Antler	8	9				
B. Tip to Tip Spread	18 7/8					
C. Greatest Spread						
D. Inside Spread of MAIN BEAMS 24 4/8 — Spread credit may equal but not exceed length of longer antler			24 4/8			
IF Inside Spread of Main Beams exceeds longer antler length, enter difference						
E. Total of Lengths of all Abnormal Points						12 2/8
F. Length of Main Beam				26 7/8	27	1/8
G-1. Length of First Point, if present				5 3/8	5 3/8	—
G-2. Length of Second Point				7 7/8	9 1/8	1 2/8
G-3. Length of Third Point				11 4/8	12 1/8	5/8
G-4. Length of Fourth Point, if present				7 7/8	9 3/8	1 4/8
G-5. Length of Fifth Point, if present				7 1/8	5 1/8	2
G-6. Length of Sixth Point, if present						
G-7. Length of Seventh Point, if present						
H-1. Circumference at Smallest Place Between Burr and First Point				5 3/8	5 3/8	—
H-2. Circumference at Smallest Place Between First and Second Points				4 7/8	5	1/8
H-3. Circumference at Smallest Place Between Second and Third Points				6 2/8	6 1/8	1/8
H-4. Circumference at Smallest Place between Third and Fourth Points or half way between Third Point and Beam Tip if Fourth Point is missing				5 2/8	5 2/8	—
TOTALS			24 4/8	88 3/8	89 7/8	18

ADD	Column 1	24 4/8	Exact locality where killed Desha Co. Ark
	Column 2	88 3/8	Date killed 1961 By whom killed LEE PERRY
	Column 3	89 7/8	Present owner WALTER BROCK
	Total	202 6/8	Address ARKANSAS
SUBTRACT	Column 4	18	Guide's Name and Address
FINAL SCORE		184 6/8	Remarks: (Mention any abnormalities) How acquired? Gift

Certificate

DEC 27 1963

FEB 24 1964

REX HANCOCK, D. D. S.
515 SOUTH MAIN STREET
STUTTGART, ARKANSAS 72160

Betty:

I mailed the fair chase cards to both Spears & Brock today.

I was talking to Mr. Brock about the trophy that he has which was killed by Lee Perry. Mr. Perry shot the deer below Elaine in Desha County and did not want to spend the money to have it mounted. Several of his companions wanted it, and he did not know who to give it to. Mr. Brock's store is the checking station for deer and he told Mr. Perry that he would have it mounted and put his name on it and hang it in his store. This is the story of the Brock deer. Mr. Brock does not even know the address of Lee Perry but thought it was somewhere between Marianna & Memphis, Tenn. The buck was taken legally and in fair chase, but it would be an extremely difficult task to locate Lee Perry. He only comes through Elaine during deer season as he hunts with a club below there.

This buck was taken deep in the White River Refuge area where no vehicles can go, so you may take my verification that this trophy was NOT spotted by use of a plane or pursued by vehicle.

Cordially,

Rex

TENNESSEE WILDLIFE RESOURCES AGENCY

1184 HIGHWAY 45 BYPASS
DIRECTOR'S PLAZA
JACKSON, TENNESSEE 38301

Gary T. Myers, Executive Director
Roy H. Anderson, Ass't. Director

February 13, 1980

Mr. Jack Reneau
NABGAP
c/o Hunting Activities Department
1600 Rhode Island Avenue, N.W.
Washington, D. C. 20036

Dear Jack:

It's ironic but our first official act as NABGAP measurers is to request that one of Tennessee's record whitetail entries by deleted from the records.

Tommy Grimsley and I were in Memphis recently and talked with Mr. John J. Heirigs who has two record W.T. entries from Shelby County, Tennessee. Mr. Heirigs advises us that the two deer are one and the same. It's not conspicuous since one entry was in 1962 and one in 1963 with scores of 173 4/8 and 173 1/8 respectively. Mr. Heirigs advises that the entries were submitted by two different measurers and it would please him to set the record straight. That's how we would like to see it.

Please advise us as to what we should do to get the records in order. Meanwhile, we should be sending you a new state record anytime.

Sincerely,

Jim Johnson/g.m.

Jim W. Johnson
Assistant Regional Manager

JWJ:gm

5: CORRESPONDENCE FROM THE VAULTS

TWO FOR THE PRICE OF ONE

North American Big Game Awards Program

27 February 1980

Mr. Jim Johnson
Assis. Regional Manager
Tennessee Wildlife Resources
Agency
1184 Highway 45 Bypass
Director's Plaza
Jackson, Tennessee 38301

Dear Mr. Johnson:

I am responding to your recent letter to Jack Reneau, as Jack Reneau left our staff last July to join the U.S. Forest Service in California.

The situation of Mr. Heirigs' "two" deer entries is indeed an interesting one. We would agree with you that we would like to set the record straight. We would like to begin by finding out the correct kill date for the single deer and we would also like some explanation of why the same deer trophy was measured twice by Jim Gay who is a long-time Official Measurer from Wyoming. Specifically, Mr. Gay is listed on the two score charts as having scored this trophy on January 24, 1963 and again on September 1, 1963.

If you do have any information from Mr. Heirigs regarding the correct date of kill, I would appreciate your forwarding it at your earliest convenience; if not, if you will furnish a recent address for Mr. Heirigs, we will contact him directly regarding this matter.

Thank you in advance for your cooperation in this matter.

Sincerely,

Wm. H. Nesbitt
Coordinator

WHN:iet

OFFICIAL SCORING SYSTEM FOR NORTH AMERICAN BIG GAME TROPHIES

Records of North American Big Game and North American Big Game Competition

BOONE AND CROCKETT CLUB

% Am. Museum of Natural History
Central Park West at 79th Street
New York 24, New York

#182 of 1962

WHITETAIL and COUES DEER

KIND OF DEER Whitetail

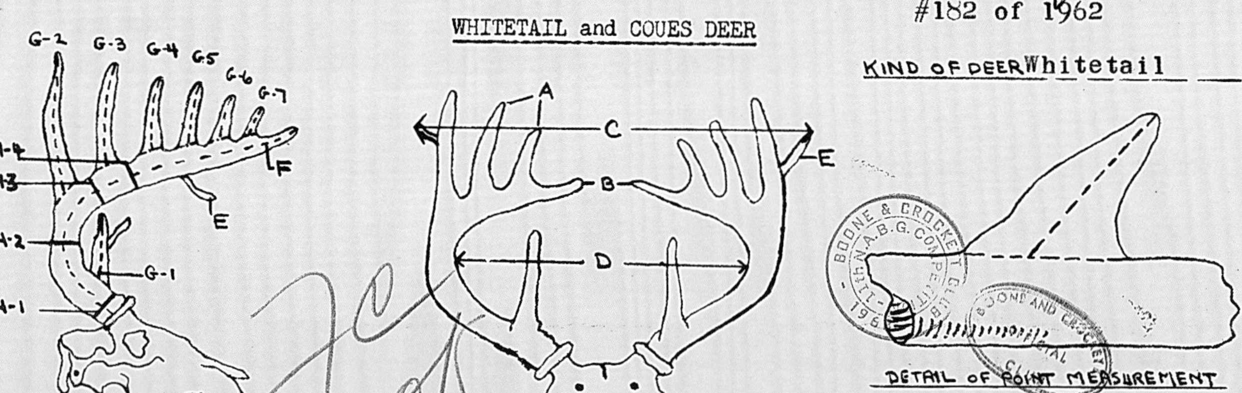

SEE OTHER SIDE FOR INSTRUCTIONS	Supplementary Data R.	Supplementary Data L.	Column 1 Spread Credit	Column 2 Right Antler	Column 3 Left Antler	Column 4 Difference
A. Number of Points on Each Antler	6	6				
B. Tip to Tip Spread	12					
C. Greatest Spread	21-4/8					
D. Inside Spread of MAIN BEAMS 18-7/8 — Spread credit may equal but not exceed length of longer antler			18-7/8			
IF Inside Spread of Main Beams exceeds longer antler length, enter difference						---
E. Total of Lengths of all Abnormal Points						---
F. Length of Main Beam				23-4/8	23-6/8	2/8
G-1. Length of First Point, if present				4-3/8	3-7/8	4/8
G-2. Length of Second Point				8-5/8	10-1/8	1-4/8
G-3. Length of Third Point				9-5/8	10-6/8	1-1/8
G-4. Length of Fourth Point, if present				9	9	---
G-5. Length of Fifth Point, if present				5-6/8	4-4/8	1-2/8
G-6. Length of Sixth Point, if present				---	---	---
G-7. Length of Seventh Point, if present				---	----	---
H-1. Circumference at Smallest Place Between Burr and First Point				5	5	---
H-2. Circumference at Smallest Place Between First and Second Points				4-3/8	4-4/8	1/8
H-3. Circumference at Smallest Place Between Second and Third Points				4-3/8	4-4/8	1/8
H-4. Circumference at Smallest Place between Third and Fourth Points or half way between Third Point and Beam Tip if Fourth Point is missing				4-3/8	4-2/8	1/8
TOTALS			18-7/8	79	80-2/8	5

IF YOU WISH YOUR TROPHY LISTED IN THE 1964 RECORD BOOK, WE MUST HAVE A FAIR CHASE CERTIFICATION BY APRIL 15, 1964.

APR 7 1964

ADD	Column 1	18-7/8	Exact locality where killed	So.west Shelby County, Tennessee in Mississippi River bottoms
	Column 2	79	Date killed Nov.3.1963	By whom killed John J. Heirigs
	Column 3	80-2/8	Present owner	John J. Heirigs
	Total	178-1/8	Address	Memphis, Tennessee
SUBTRACT	Column 4	5	Guide's Name and Address	None
FINAL SCORE		173-1/8	Remarks: (Mention any abnormalities)	

MAR -7 1963

OFFICIAL SCORING SYSTEM FOR NORTH AMERICAN BIG GAME TROPHIES

Records of North American
Big Game Committee

BOONE AND CROCKETT CLUB

Address correspondence to:
Mrs. Grancel Fitz, Secretary
5 Tudor City Place
New York 17, N. Y.

WHITETAIL and COUES DEER

#182 of 1962

KIND OF DEER Whitetail

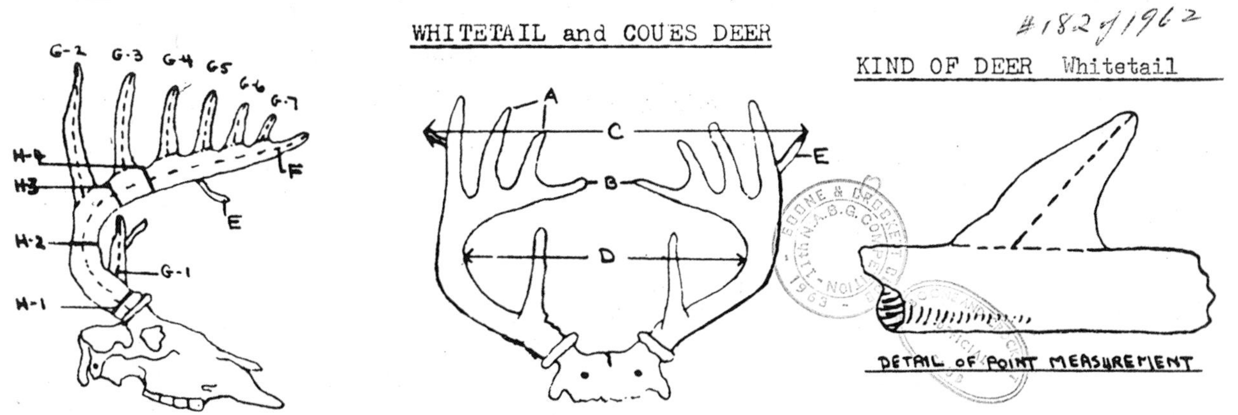

SEE OTHER SIDE FOR INSTRUCTIONS	Supplementary Data R.	Supplementary Data L.	Column 1 Spread Credit	Column 2 Right Antler	Column 3 Left Antler	Column 4 Difference
A. Number of Points on Each Antler	6	6				
B. Tip to Tip Spread	11 - 4/8					
C. Greatest Spread	21 - 4/8					
D. Inside Spread of MAIN BEAMS	Spread credit may equal but not exceed length of longer antler		18 - 6/8			
IF Inside Spread of Main Beams exceeds longer antler length, enter difference						
E. Total of Lengths of all Abnormal Points						
F. Length of Main Beam				23 - 6/8	23 - 7/8	1/8
G-1. Length of First Point, if present				4 - 5/8	4 - 1/8	4/8
G-2. Length of Second Point				8 - 5/8	10 - 2/8	1 - 5/8
G-3. Length of Third Point				9 - 6/8	10 - 5/8	7/8
G-4. Length of Fourth Point, if present				9	9	
G-5. Length of Fifth Point, if present				4 - 6/8	4 - 4/8	2/8
G-6. Length of Sixth Point, if present						
G-7. Length of Seventh Point, if present						
H-1. Circumference at Smallest Place Between Burr and First Point				4 - 6/8	4 - 6/8	
H-2. Circumference at Smallest Place Between First and Second Points				4 - 3/8	4 - 3/8	
H-3. Circumference at Smallest Place Between Second and Third Points				4 - 3/8	4 - 3/8	
H-4. Circumference at Smallest Place between Third and Fourth Points or half way between Third Point and Beam Tip if Fourth Point is missing				4 - 2/8	4 - 1/8	1/8
TOTALS			18 - 6/8	78 - 2/8	80	3 - 4/8

ADD	Column 1	18 - 6/8	Exact locality where killed Shelby County, Tennessee
	Column 2	78 - 2/8	Date killed Nov. 3, 1962 By whom killed John J. Heirigs
	Column 3	80	Present owner John J. Heirigs
	Total	177	Address Memphis, Tennessee
SUBTRACT	Column 4	3 - 4/8	Guide's Name and Address
FINAL SCORE		173 - 4/8	Remarks: (Mention any abnormalities)

DEC 4 1963

TENNESSEE WILDLIFE RESOURCES AGENCY

1184 HIGHWAY 45 BYPASS
DIRECTOR'S PLAZA
JACKSON, TENNESSEE 38301

Gary T. Myers, Executive Director
Roy H. Anderson, Ass't. Director

April 28, 1980

Mr. William H. Nesbitt, Coordinator
NABGAP
c/o Hunting Activities Department
1600 Rhodes Island Ave., N.W.
Washington, D. C. 20036

Dear Mr. Nesbitt:

I talked to Mr. John Heirigs regarding the conflict of records where his deer killed in Shelby County, Tennessee, November 3, 1962 was entered twice in the NABGAP records.

Mr. Heirigs said he has no idea why Mr. Gay of Wyoming measured his animal twice on different dates. He does say that the scoring dates of January 24, 1963 correlates with the month he sent the trophy to Mr. Gay for mounting and September 1, 1963 the month the mounted trophy was returned to Mr. Heirigs. It would seem that Mr. Gay simply forgot that he had measured the trophy when he first received it.

Mr. Heirigs has newspaper clippings of his deer kill from the local Commercial Appeal that documents date and time the animal was taken. Mr. Heirigs address is 1521 Maurine Street, Memphis, Tn. 38116. Please advise if I can assist further.

Sincerely,

Jim W. Johnson/g.m.

Jim W. Johnson
Assistant Regional Manager

RECEIVED
MAY 01 1980
HUNTER SERVICES

JWJ:gm

cc: Tom Grimsley

CLOSURE

On July 8, 1980, Mr. Heirigs received the following correspondence from William H. Nesbitt:

Many thanks for the copy of the local newspaper article (shown at right) concerning your whitetail deer that is shown as two separate entries in the last edition of the records book, North American Big Game. *We will note this kill date in the file for this trophy, and we are returning the newspaper article to you for your files.*

Concerning the two score charts on file, and the corresponding dual listings for this single trophy, we will delete the second (later) scoring for this trophy so that it will be shown in the next edition of the records book at 173-4/8, the score arrived at on 3 November 1962. This would seem to be most fair to the trophy, in all respects.

Thank you very much for your help in unraveling this matter.

'PEAL, MEMPHIS, TUESDAY MORNING, NOVEMBER 6, 1962

Bulldogs Practice Without End Gibbs

Flu May Keep Gene Out Of Auburn Game

STARKVILLE, Miss., Nov. 5 — (UPI) — Mississippi State's first two teams worked out in sweat clothes Monday while the third team scrimmaged with the "B" squad.

The Bulldogs are preparing for Saturday's Southeastern Conference game against Auburn at Auburn, Ala.

Coach Paul Davis took his team indoors after the practice session where they heard a scouting report on the Tigers.

End Gene Gibbs, a first team member, missed Monday's drill and may be out for Saturday's game. He is hospitalized with intestinal flu. Another first stringer, guard Tommy Ranager, played against Alabama last week with a bad shoulder and is not expected to be at full strength for the Auburn tilt.

Auburn Concentrates On Weak Running Game

AUBURN, Ala., Nov. 5 — (UPI) -Auburn viewed films of upcoming foe, Mississippi State, Monday ... workout in sweat clothes.

... perfect season record was shattered in an upset loss to Florida last week, begin a three game home ...

ENSLEY BOTTOMS BUCK—Johnny Heirigs, Whitehaven contractor, shows off the head of a 12-point buck he killed (Saturday morning) in Ensley Bottoms near the steam plant. He plans to have the trophy mounted for the den of his home. —Staff Photo

SATURDAY WOULD BE JUNE 3, 1962

Mid-South Outdoors—

Daring Buck Gives Hunter Second Chance In Bottoms

By HENRY REYNOLDS

Deer hunting entails a lot of luck. There have been more deer killed which walked up on hunters than have been knocked down at 200 yards by a skilled rifleman.

Sometimes deer become inquisitive and show themselves in an effort to learn what's going on in their baliwick. Others race wildly past a stand in an attempt to escape dogs or hunters.

Take the case of Johnny Heirigs of 3546 McCorkle Road, a Whitehaven contractor. Johnny opened the Tennessee season Saturday morning in Ensley Bottoms near the steam plant.

He and Johnny Gallina of 9795 Poplar hit the bottoms before daylight and took their stands. They stayed there until an agreed time of 9:30 when they returned to the truck for a bite to eat.

While nibbling on a sandwich, the Whitehaven sportsman spotted the biggest rack he had ever seen on a deer. It stuck up over a small rise in the ground that hid all the deer but the head and horns.

Lothridge Ret... SEC Offense

Namath Paces Pa... Canale Is Top Pu...

BIRMINGHAM, Nov... (UPI) -- Georgia Tec... threat quarterback Bi... ridge picked up 17... against Duke to contin... Southeastern Conferen... offense leader this we...

Lothridge, who guid... to a 20-9 win over D... week end, leads in... fense with 1,153 yards a... to statistics released by SEC Commissioner Moore's office.

Lothridge has 382 y... the ground to lead in... and 771 yards by pass... ond only to Alabama... back Joe Namath who... yards through the air.

Namath is second in... fense with 941 yards t... 195 yards picked up... bama's 20-0 win over... sippi State. Larry Ra... Georgia signal caller, v... in total offense with 91...

Larry Dupree of Flor... picked up 186 yards... against Auburn, was s... rushing with 367 yar... bama fullback Eddie V... was third with 310 yar...

PAUL FANNIN
Governor

Commissioners

C. J. MANTLE TUCSON
M. N. FORMAN YUMA
HARRY FUNK PRESCOTT
LEE HOVER PHOENIX
O. M. SIZER CLIFTON

ARIZONA GAME & FISH DEPARTMENT
105 State Office Building • Phoenix 7, Arizona • 271-4295

• ROBERT J. SMITH Director WENDELL SWANK Assistant Director

February 2,1962

The Boone and Crockett Club
Mrs Grancel Fitz,
Secretary
5 Tudor City Place
New York 17,New York

Dear Mrs Fitz:

There is quite some misunderstanding in this area as to rulings concerning the legality of Coues deer taken locally. Last year a very fine trophy was taken near here and I understand it was refused recognition although another trophy taken in the same general area was given recognition several years ago. There are a number of trophys unrecorded in this area because of these misunderstandings.

Would you be so kind as to give me the facts concerning these rulings so that these local trophys may receive thier just accreditation.

Sincerely,

William R. Hernbrode

William R. Hernbrode
District Wildlife Manager
Box 131 Payson, Arizona

5: CORRESPONDENCE FROM THE VAULTS

PURE OR HYBRID COUES' WHITETAIL DEER

March 7, 1962

Mr. William R. Hernbrode
District Wildlife Manager
Box 131
Payson, Ariz.

Dear Mr. Hernbrode:

Please excuse the delay in replying to your letter, which came in the rush of closing the 1961 Exhibition.

I know of no ruling concerning the legality of Coues deer taken in Arizona. Neither do I know who refused the recognition of the trophy last year. We would be happy to have charts on any Coues deer taken in Arizona or Mexico.

If you have more data on the ruling, we would be glad to have it for our files. I am most confident that the ruling last year was not one made by the Boone and Crockett Club.

Yours sincerely,

bs f

(Mrs. Grancel Fitz)

P. S. If you'd like an assortment of charts, our prices are:

$3.50 per hundred or 5¢ each in lots less than 100. We pay postage on all orders when check is enclosed.

P. S. Sometime ago some hunter sent in a photograph of a whitetail deer and claimed it was a Coues Deer. Whether this trophy was from Arizona, I do not remember, but I doubt it.

ARIZONA GAME & FISH DEPARTMENT

105 State Office Building · Phoenix 7, Arizona · 271-4295

June 24, 1962

Mrs Grancel Fitz, Secretary
5 Tudor City Place
New York 17, New York

Dear Mrs Fitz:

Enclosed please find chart and photographs concerning Coues Deer referred to in my previous correspondence.

In checking with the hunter and the taxidermist who made the mounting I find that the refusal of the trophy last year was made by Mr Bob Householder. Those of us who have seen this animal and inspected it can see no reason for such refusal. I have personally seen not only color photos of the animal but portions of the hide, the tail, and the head before mounting. It is my feeling that this is a Coues Deer.

The owner of the mount is willing to ship it to you for official measuring and entering.

Sincerely,

William R. Hernbrode
District Wildlife Manager
Box 131 Payson, Arizona

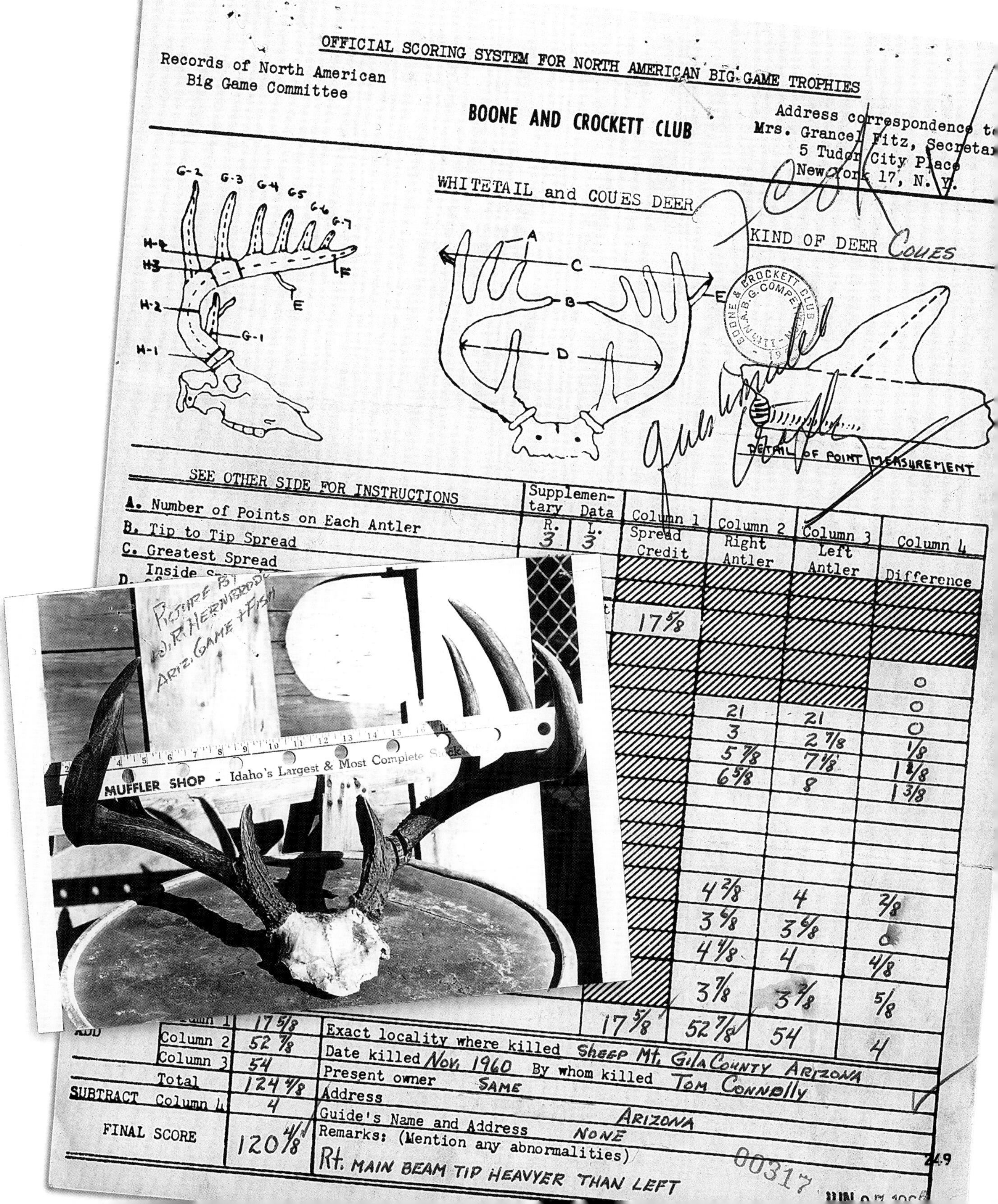

OFFICIAL SCORING SYSTEM FOR NORTH AMERICAN BIG GAME TROPHIES

Records of North American
Big Game Committee

BOONE AND CROCKETT CLUB

Address correspondence to
Mrs. Grancel Fitz, Secretary
5 Tudor City Place
New York 17, N. Y.

WHITETAIL and COUES DEER

KIND OF DEER Coues

SEE OTHER SIDE FOR INSTRUCTIONS

	Supplementary Data R.	Supplementary Data L.	Column 1 Spread Credit	Column 2 Right Antler	Column 3 Left Antler	Column 4 Difference
A. Number of Points on Each Antler	3	3				
B. Tip to Tip Spread						
C. Greatest Spread						
Inside Sp...			17 5/8			
						0
				21	21	0
				3	2 7/8	0
				5 7/8	7 1/8	1/8
				6 5/8	8	1 2/8
						1 3/8
				4 2/8	4	2/8
				3 6/8	3 6/8	0
				4 4/8	4	4/8
				3 7/8	3 2/8	5/8
			17 5/8	52 7/8	54	4

ADD	Column 1	17 5/8	Exact locality where killed Sheep Mt. Gila County Arizona
	Column 2	52 7/8	Date killed Nov. 1960 By whom killed Tom Connolly
	Column 3	54	Present owner Same
	Total	124 4/8	Address Arizona
SUBTRACT	Column 4	4	Guide's Name and Address None
FINAL SCORE		120 4/8	Remarks: (Mention any abnormalities) Rt. main beam tip heavyer than left

00317

THE CORRESPONDENCE INTENSIFIES

Upon receipt of the materials from Mr. Hernbrode, Mrs. Grancel Fitz sent the following letter to Bob Housholder:

We have recently received a Coues Deer chart on a trophy shot in 1960 by Tom Connolly, Payson, Ariz., in Gila County, Ariz. The score on the chart is 120 4/8.

We have been informed by one of the game officials that you had ruled out this trophy as being a Coues' Deer. Will you please let me have any information you have on this deer. Are Whitetail Deer found in Gila County?

Shortly thereafter, Mrs. Fitz received this interesting letter from Householder shown on the opposite page.

In July of 1962, the Records Program requested that Mr. Connolly send the trophy to the 1964 Judges Panel for final determination. You will find the remaining correspondence, as well as the official score chart on the following pages. Mr. Connelly's entry was ultimately determined to be a Coues' whitetail and received a Second Place Award at the 1964 Competition with a final score of 119-7/8 points.

June 30, 1962

Dear Betty

Thanks for the letter. We've got a big splash on the '61 Competition in the July issue, will send you a copy.

Yes, I have seen the "Coues" head, many times, that you spoke of. Betty, that head is questionable. Both Dr. Clare and myself studied the head at length, and both decided it was not and could not be, a true Coues. Further, I went back in my files and found a letter dated Jan. 4, 1954 written by Webb to me--I quote--"undoubtedly mule and whitetail will cross occasionally when their ranges overlap. Our policy is and must be to include all deer taken in these areas in the larger specie category. You will agree with our stand in regard to such cases, otherwise, sooner or later, the records would be topped by questionable heads, rather than by typical fine examples."

Betty, I have been measuring heads in the southwest for 12 years now. I believe that I should know something about the deer in this state. I have known the "Game Dept. official" you spoke of for about 30 years, and he has "crowed" all over Phoenix that he really showed Housholder a thing or two about measuring heads. I have not said a word to this man about the head-he measured it on his own. The owner of the head, Betty, told Mr Sievers and myself that the animal weighed 150 pounds--now that alone would cause me to hesitate to measure it as a true Coues, since any idiot knows that Coues seldom weigh more than 100 pounds ON THE HOOF.

I most strongly urge you not to accept the head as a Coues. Do you know Hoffmeister of Illinois, Curator of the Museum? He has written a book on the "whitetail" of this country. He saw this head and said,"it looks like a white tail, but it's certainly no Coues....."

Another thing. Our"Game Dept. official" didn't even measure it right. Sievers and I gave it a rough tape one day, and came up with, as I remember, about 135 points. Its weight, the "size" of the antlers, and the location of the kill, were enough for Dr. Clare and myself (remembering Webb's remarks) to avoid the head, and to put it in the questionable class.

Yes, there are deer with white tails in Gila County. I remember the deer that brought the comment from Webb. It was taken by Pringle of Phoenix up on the Mogollon Rim. The score was around 145 points and it weighed 155 pounds DRESSED. Lets face it, Betty, that was no true Coues, and it caused the comments from Webb and also Grancel. It's just not logical that a true Coues could weigh 180 plus on the hoof---and this is the main reason Dr. Clare and I agreed not to accept it as a true Coues.

Yes, I (we) ruled out the head as a true Coues, and I (we) will again. This head "looks" like a white tail, but I will never put my name to a Coues chart on this head, neither will Sievers or Clare. What Mr Hernbrode thinks is 100% doubted by the three of us. As a questionable head, I will not enter this head to the Club as a true Coues.

Enough of unpleasantness--the 1963 Shikar*Safari meeting will be held in Phoenix, and I have been asked to help Charley Vorm and General Scott in arranging it. Weatherby is coming out with two new rifles this year. He sent me a .460 to try out-man, that one has a kick-96 pounds. I am leaving Aug. 12 for the Yukon for the stone-my last ram. Have added three names to the slam list-now have 47 names. Will send you a revised list.

Best personal regards

Bob

Grancel gave me this information He thought it was a Coues no 1

July 14, 1962

Dear Bob:

In re the questionable deer entered by Tom Connolly, the report I get, on the evidence of the picture and measurements submitted to us, is that this may really be a legitimate head. It shows no sign of being one of the extremely rare crosses with desert mule deer. The characteristic curvature of the main beams follows a very common Coues deer pattern. We know of absolutely no instance of Coues deer intergrating with larger whitetail races, nor can we find evidence that any of these larger whitetails are found in Arizona. The reported weight, of course, is far out of line, but this may have been a grossly exaggerated estimate, and there is no way to check it. Finally, although the score is high, it is far below the Coues deer record, and therefore not out of line. Under these conditions, the best solution is to call it in to the next show for examination by the judges.

Where

Grancel suggested that I let you know one thing about Mr. Bird's jaguar skull which he recently scored. As noted on his chart, the length measurement was taken to the front edge of the teeth at the outer ends of the front row of incisors, where it is very unusual for them to project farther forward than the center ones. He could find no sign that they had fallen out in the cleaning of the skull and had been cemented back in wrong alignment, but he thinks the judges should consider this abnormality before the score goes into the next book.

Best of luck on your hunt for a Stone ram. We hope you bring back a winner.

Yours sincerely,

(Mrs. Grancel Fitz)

Mr. Bob Housholder
P. O. Drawer 6428
Phoenix, Ariz.

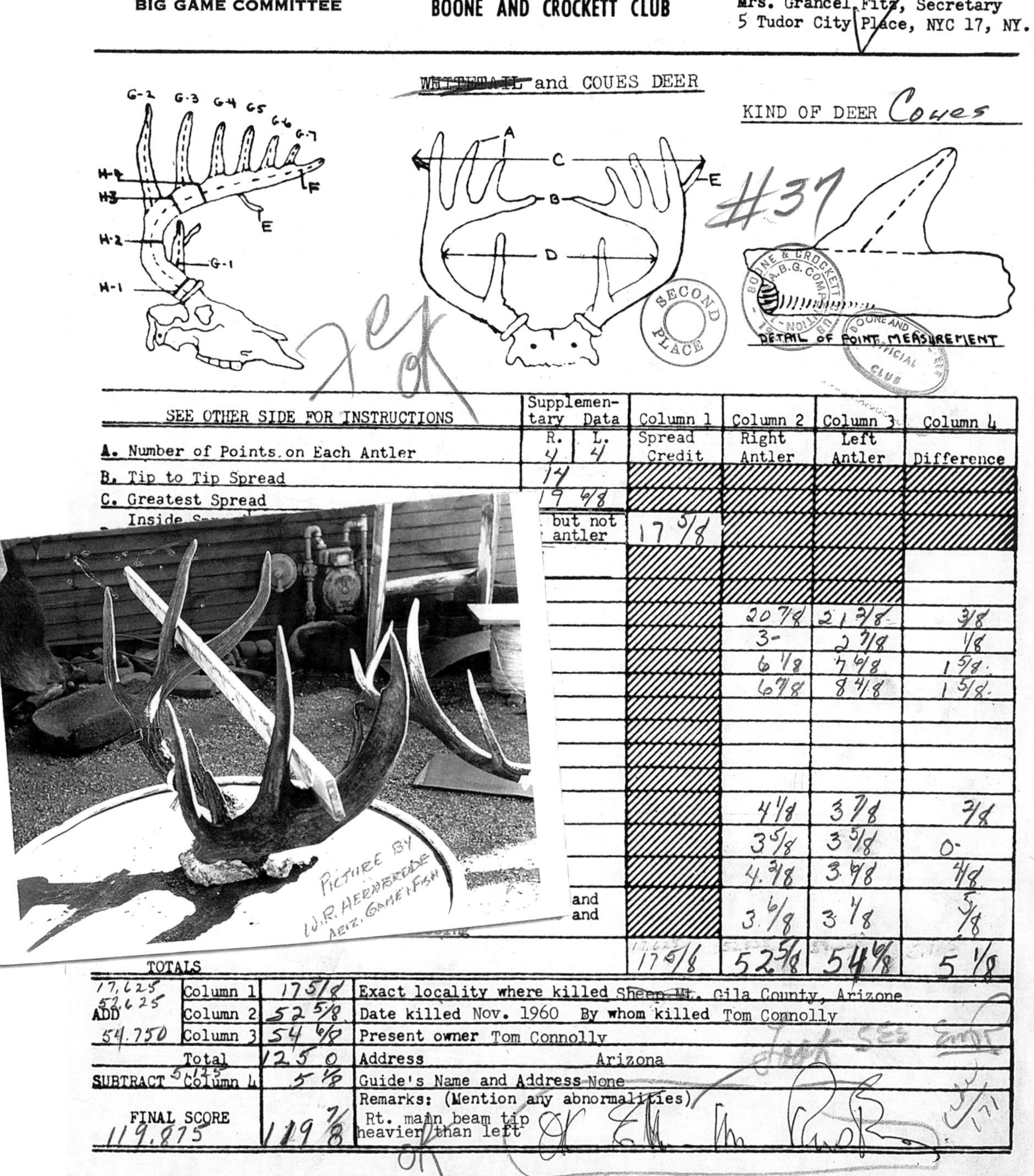

OFFICIAL SCORING SYSTEM FOR NORTH AMERICAN BIG GAME TROPHIES

RECORDS OF NORTH AMERICAN BIG GAME COMMITTEE

BOONE AND CROCKETT CLUB

Address Correspondence to:
Mrs. Grancel Fitz, Secretary
5 Tudor City Place, NYC 17, NY.

~~WHITETAIL~~ and COUES DEER

KIND OF DEER Cowes

#37

SECOND PLACE

DETAIL OF POINT MEASUREMENT

SEE OTHER SIDE FOR INSTRUCTIONS	Supplementary Data R.	Supplementary Data L.	Column 1 Spread Credit	Column 2 Right Antler	Column 3 Left Antler	Column 4 Difference
A. Number of Points on Each Antler	4	4				
B. Tip to Tip Spread	14					
C. Greatest Spread	19 6/8					
Inside Sp[read] … but not … antler			17 5/8			
				20 7/8	21 2/8	3/8
				3-	2 7/8	1/8
				6 1/8	7 6/8	1 5/8
				6 7/8	8 4/8	1 5/8
				4 1/8	3 7/8	3/8
				3 5/8	3 5/8	0-
				4 2/8	3 6/8	4/8
… and … and				3 6/8	3 1/8	5/8
TOTALS			17 5/8	52 5/8	54 6/8	5 1/8

ADD	Column 1	17 5/8	Exact locality where killed ~~Sheep Mt.~~ Gila County, Arizona
	Column 2	52 5/8	Date killed Nov. 1960 By whom killed Tom Connolly
	Column 3	54 6/8	Present owner Tom Connolly
	Total	125 0	Address Arizona
SUBTRACT	Column 4	5 1/8	Guide's Name and Address None
FINAL SCORE		119 7/8	Remarks: (Mention any abnormalities) Rt. main beam tip heavier than left

FIRST FEDERAL SAVINGS AND LOAN ASSOCIATION
OF SAN MARCOS
SAN MARCOS, TEXAS

Nov. 24, 1967

Boone and Crockett Club
Mrs. Grancel Fitz, Secretary
5 Tudor City Place
New York City, New York 17

Dear Mrs. Fitz,

I am submitting to you the measurements of a most significant discovery of antlers of a whitetail deer from this State. It is most possible that these antlers could score the highest number of points in the typical category for the State of Texas and that could be saying an awful lot, so I will leave the final determination to official measurements.

Recently, in our weekly newspaper, there was a picture of the inside of an old grocery store in an advertisement. On the wall were a number of deer heads and horns. One mounted head stood out in particular. My son lives for the hunting season and has a set of antlers officially scoring 168-2/8. Several contacts found the owner, who is Mr. David M. Dailey, 411 W. San Antonio St., ofthis City. The deer had been killed by his grandfather on December 11, 1903. Although the head had been mounted, today it leaves a lot to be desired but the horns are in perfect condition. I asked him to let me borrow the head and turned same over to my son to make an estimation of the points. His estimation is submitted on your form at 198-3/8 with several rather poor polaroid pictures, but I am sure that they will reveal that the head is remarkable.

Mr. David M. Dailey, the grandson of Mr. Basil Dailey, who killed the deer near Pearsall, Texas on the Blackaller Ranch has always thought that same was exceptional but never had any way of knowing really how fine a head same might be. He told me that several times over the years and this is a hunting first area, some exceptional heads were put against this one for comparison and the bets ranged all the way from a shave to 25¢, but none could compare with Mr. Dailey's.

Mr. Dailey recalls that when his grandfather and hunting party returned from that successful trip and passed through San Antonio, that Mr. Albert, the owner of the famous Buckhorn Saloon then, and which outstanding collection was sold to the Lone Star Brewing Company and is on display from their plant there, offered him $100.00 for the head cut from the body, and that was 1903. Mr. Albert knew something about deer heads as the non-typical antlers of a whitetailed deer, now owned by the Lone Star Brewing Company ranks Number 1.

I have nothing to gain in this matter, whatsoever, except the satisfaction to see that this set of horns takes it's rightful place in the records of your distinguished club. So, upon receipt of your further instructions will turn them over to Mr. Dailey for his attention and will assist him any way I can. I am sending a copy of this letter to the Texas Parks and Wildlife publication of our State and would love to see an article in same following the completion of the official measurements and results.

Very truly yours,

Ted MacIntyre

Ted MacIntyre, P O Box 707, San Marcos, Texas

c/c Mr Wayne K. Tiller, Editor
Texas Parks & Wildlife
David M. Dailey

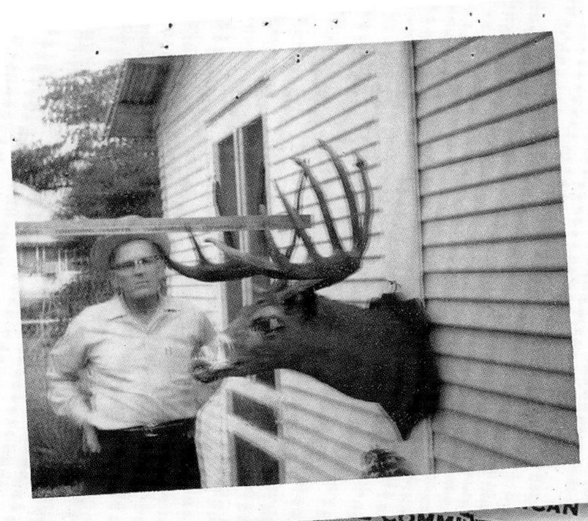

CORRESPONDENCE FROM THE VAULTS

DAILEY'S 1903 WHITETAIL

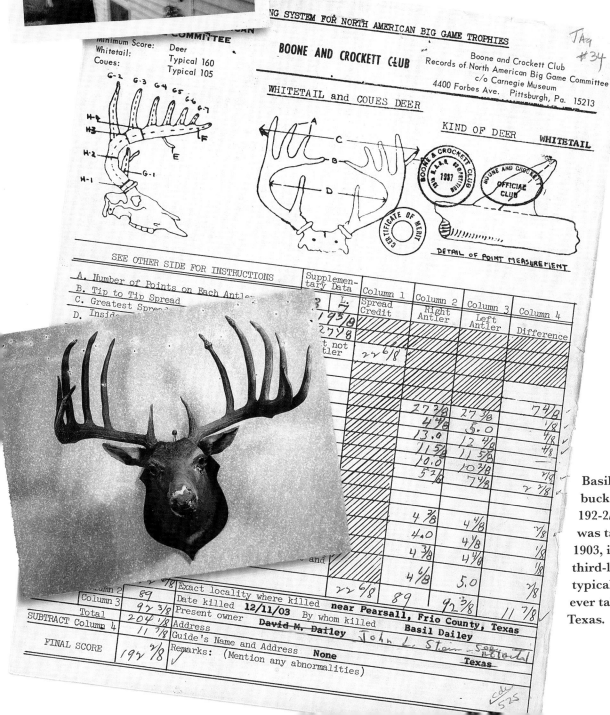

...NG SYSTEM FOR NORTH AMERICAN BIG GAME TROPHIES

JAg #34

...COMMITTEE

Minimum Score: Deer
Whitetail: Typical 160
Coues: Typical 105

BOONE AND CROCKETT CLUB

Boone and Crockett Club
Records of North American Big Game Committee
c/o Carnegie Museum
4400 Forbes Ave. Pittsburgh, Pa. 15213

WHITETAIL and COUES DEER

KIND OF DEER WHITETAIL

SEE OTHER SIDE FOR INSTRUCTIONS

	Supplementary Data		Column 1	Column 2	Column 3	Column 4
	R.	L.	Spread Credit	Right Antler	Left Antler	Difference
A. Number of Points on Each Antler	8	7				
B. Tip to Tip Spread	19 5/8					
C. Greatest Spread	27 1/8					
D. Inside ... not ... tler			22 6/8			
				27 3/8	27 3/8	7 4/8
				4 4/8	5.0	1/8
				13.0	12 4/8	4/8
				11 5/8	11 5/8	4/8
				10.0	10 2/8	—
				5 2/8	7 4/8	2/8
						2 2/8
				4 7/8	4 4/8	3/8
				4.0	4 1/8	1/8
				4 3/8	4 4/8	1/8
... and				4 6/8	5.0	2/8
TOTALS			22 6/8	89	92 3/8	11 7/8

Column 1	22 6/8
Column 2	89
Column 3	92 3/8
Total	204 1/8
SUBTRACT Column 4	11 7/8
FINAL SCORE	192 2/8

Exact locality where killed near Pearsall, Frio County, Texas
Date killed 12/11/03 By whom killed Basil Dailey
Present owner ~~David M. Dailey~~ John L. Stein
Address
Guide's Name and Address None Texas
Remarks: (Mention any abnormalities)

cde 525

Basil Dailey's buck scoring 192-2/8, which was taken in 1903, is the third-largest typical whitetail ever taken in Texas.

OFFICIAL SCORING SYSTEM FOR NORTH AMERICAN BIG GAME TROPHIES #43. Done ✓ (11)

RECORDS OF NORTH AMERICAN BIG GAME COMMITTEE

BOONE AND CROCKETT CLUB

DP17000899

Address Correspondence to:
Mrs. Grancel Fitz, Secretary
5 Tudor City Place, NYC 17. NY.

NON-TYPICAL WHITETAIL DEER

Work Sheet

1st

11th Comp 1962-63

2.7	
3.1	1.6
ABNORMAL	
Points	Line E
R 3.7	L 1.1
10.	2.4
1.2	8.
2.2	3.4
2.0	3.
1.2	2.3
1.4	1.4
3.5	1.6
4.5	4.
2.	1.6
1.4	4.6
9.2	4.3
Totals 51 1/8	40 3/8
To E ~~91 4/8~~	

SEE OTHER SIDE FOR INSTRUCTIONS	Supplementary Data		Column 1	Column 2	Column 3	Column 4 (89-4/8)
A. Number of Points on Each Antler	R. 19	L. 18	Spread Credit	Right Antler	Left Antler	Difference
B. Tip to Tip Spread	13.5					
C. Greatest Spread	29.5					
D. Inside Spread of MAIN BEAMS 21.1 — Spread credit may equal but not exceed length of longer antler			21.1			
IF Inside Spread of Main Beams exceeds longer antler length, enter difference						
E. Total of Lengths of all Abnormal Points	91 4/8					
F. Length of Main Beam				28.1	28.3	.2
G-1. Length of First Point, if present				8.1	6.5	1.4
G-2. Length of Second Point				11.	11.6	.6
G-3. Length of Third Point				6.7	(9.6)	2.7
G-4. Length of Fourth Point, if present				7.5	8.1	.4
G-5. Length of Fifth Point, if present						
G-6. Length of Sixth Point, if present						
G-7. Length of Seventh Point, if present						
Circumference at Smallest Place H-1. Between B[...]				6.5	6.7	.2
Circumfer[...] H-2. Between F[...]				5.3	(5.2)	.1
Circumfer[...] H-3. Between S[...]				5.	(5.1)	.1
Circumfer[...] H-4. Between Thi[...]				6.1	(5.2)	.7
TOTALS ~~Legendary Whitetails~~	91 4/8		21 1/8	84.7	87 1/8	7 2/8

Owner: **Bass Pro Shops**
2500 E. Kearney
Springfield, MO 65898
417/873-5237

ADD	Column 1	21.1	Exact locality where killed ~~Shelton, Nebr.~~ Hall Co
	Column 2	84.7	Date killed 11/1/62 By whom killed Del Austin
	Column 3	87.1	Present owner ~~[illegible]~~ · John D. Morgan NA Whitetail
	Total	193.1	Address Hastings, Nebr. [illegible]
SUBTRACT	Column 4	7.2	Guide's Name and Address Al Dawson
	Result	185.7	Remarks: (Mention any abnormalities)
Add Line E Total		91 4/8	~~[illegible]~~ 50
FINAL SCORE		277 3/8	

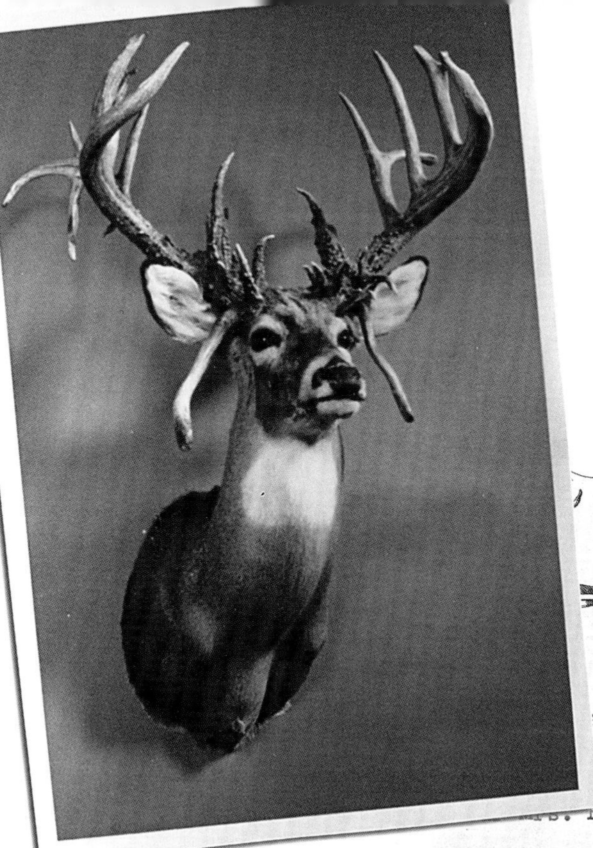

5: SPECIAL TROPHY

DEL AUSTIN'S AWARD-WINNING WHITETAIL

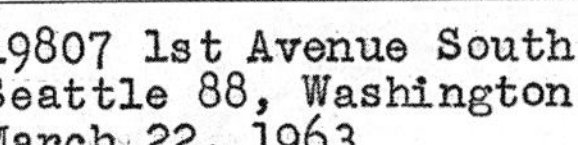

19807 1st Avenue South
Seattle 88, Washington
March 22, 1963

el Fitz
y Place
, New York

s. Fitz:

Enclosed find forms for a non-typical whitetail and a Rocky Mountain goat.

According to your last published book, the non-typical whitetail score would place it about third in the World Records. You will note by the picture that this rack has many long points on the burrs. The measurements were taken with a quarter inch steel tape. Although it took us 3½ hours, we realize there could be some discrepancies while taking into consideration all aspects of these odd points. It will, without question, be the new World Record for the Pope and Young Club. It was sent into this office for official measurement and for registering with the Boone and Crockett Club.

This deer lived on an island in the Platte River where these fellows had been stalking it for the past two or three years. There is quite a story behind the hunt and I am told that it will be published very soon in one of the outdoor magazines.

If there is any further question regarding this fine non-typical trophy, please write to me or directly to the owner as indicated on the form. I will have the rack in my possession for a few more days before returning it to Hastings, Nebraska.

Sincerely yours,

Glenn St. Charles

Glenn St. Charles

GS:rm
Enclosure

When Del Austin arrowed one of the most recognizable whitetails in history on November 1, 1962, it turned the whitetail world on its ear. It quickly became the largest known hunter-taken trophy in history (number two all-time next to the unknown 284-3/8 deer from the Buckhorn Saloon). Not only that, but he had taken it with a bow! Add to that fact that the photo of Austin with his deer is one of the more historic in B&C's files, and it's evident why this great whitetail is a special trophy. Austin's buck received a First Award at the 11th Competition, and was also recognized as a World's Record for the Pope and Young Club, where it currently maintains its number one rank.

THE BEEF STATE

BOONE AND CROCKETT CLUB
1963 North American
Big Game Competition
sponsored by
BOONE AND CROCKETT CLUB
WHITETAIL DEER (Non-Typical)—1st Award
Score—185-7/8+91-4/8=277-3/8
Length—(R) 28-1/8 (L) 28-3/8
Circumference—(R) 6-5/8 (L) 6-7/8
Points—(R) 19 (L) 18
Inside Spread—21-1/8
Locality—Hall County, Nebr.—1962
Hunter—Del Austin
Guide—Al Dawson
SAGAMORE HILL AWARD
STONE SHEEP—1st Award
Score—190
Length—(R) 46-6/8 (L) 46-6/8
Basal Circumference—(R) 15-2/8
(L) 15-1/8
Locality—Sikanni River, B. C.—1962
Hunter—Norman Blank
Guide—R. Lynn Ross
4th PRIZE

OFFICIAL SCORING SYSTEM FOR NORTH AMERICAN BIG GAME TROPHIES

ecords of North American
Big Game Committee

BOONE AND CROCKETT CLUB

Address correspondence to:
Mrs. Grancel Fitz, Secretary
5 Tudor City Place
New York 17, N. Y.

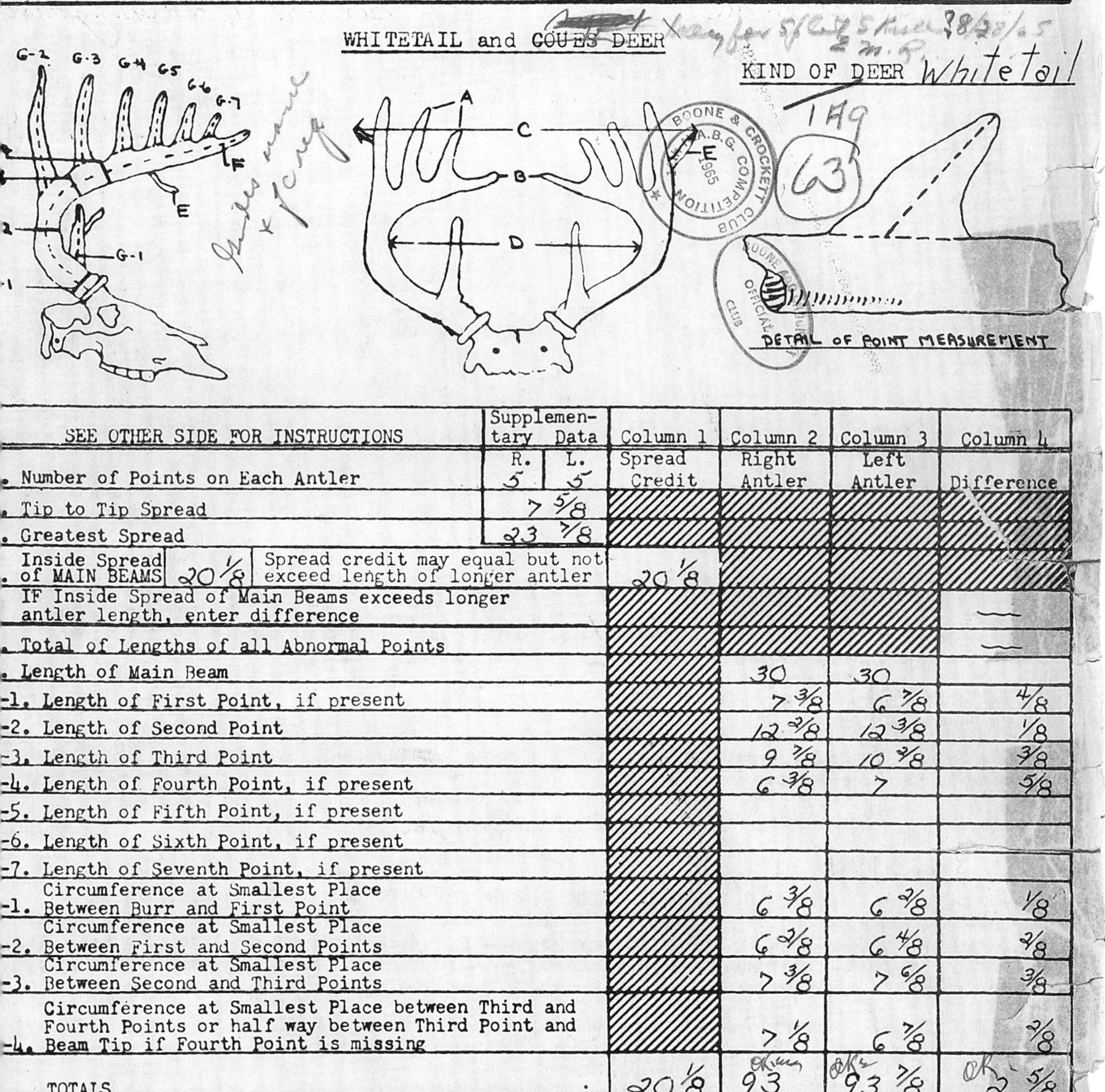

SEE OTHER SIDE FOR INSTRUCTIONS	Supplementary Data R.	Supplementary Data L.	Column 1 Spread Credit	Column 2 Right Antler	Column 3 Left Antler	Column 4 Difference
. Number of Points on Each Antler	5	5				
. Tip to Tip Spread	7 5/8					
. Greatest Spread	23 7/8					
Inside Spread . of MAIN BEAMS 20 1/8 — Spread credit may equal but not exceed length of longer antler			20 1/8			
IF Inside Spread of Main Beams exceeds longer antler length, enter difference						—
. Total of Lengths of all Abnormal Points						—
. Length of Main Beam				30	30	
-1. Length of First Point, if present				7 3/8	6 7/8	4/8
-2. Length of Second Point				12 2/8	12 3/8	1/8
-3. Length of Third Point				9 7/8	10 2/8	3/8
-4. Length of Fourth Point, if present				6 3/8	7	5/8
-5. Length of Fifth Point, if present						
-6. Length of Sixth Point, if present						
-7. Length of Seventh Point, if present						
Circumference at Smallest Place -1. Between Burr and First Point				6 3/8	6 2/8	1/8
Circumference at Smallest Place -2. Between First and Second Points				6 2/8	6 4/8	2/8
Circumference at Smallest Place -3. Between Second and Third Points				7 3/8	7 6/8	3/8
Circumference at Smallest Place between Third and Fourth Points or half way between Third Point and -4. Beam Tip if Fourth Point is missing				7 1/8	6 7/8	2/8
TOTALS			20 1/8	93	93 7/8	2 5/8

	Column 1	20 1/8	Exact locality where killed Probably vicinity Sandstone, Minn.
D	Column 2	93	Date killed ? By whom killed ?
	Column 3	93 7/8	Present owner Robert Ludwig
207	Total	206 8/8	Address Sandstone, Minnesota
BTRACT	Column 4	2 5/8	Guide's Name and Address
FINAL SCORE		204 3/8	Remarks: (Mention any abnormalities) Fourth point on right is deformed - blunt tip. Third point on left is sharply ridged along outer edge.

Beams massive - tending toward palmation.

OCT 13 1964

5: SPECIAL TROPHY

JAMES JORDAN WORLD'S RECORD WHITETAIL

STATE OF MINNESOTA
DEPARTMENT OF CONSERVATION
SAINT PAUL 1

Carlos Avery Research Center
Forest Lake, Minnesota

August 13, 1964

Mrs. Grancel Fitz, Secretary,
5 Tudor City Place,
New York 17, N. Y.

Dear Mrs. Fitz:

Here it is - possibly a new world's record whitetail trophy. I had written to you about this trophy at an earlier date but I was not able to measure it until only a few days ago.

There were one or two instances in which minor abnormalities necessitated a decision regarding alternatives in making the measurements. The most pronounced of these abnormalities pertained to a sharp ridge along the outer curve of the third point - left antler. If measured along the peak of the undulating ridge the greater measurement obtained would not be representative of the actual length of the point. Also, a slight difference in measurement could occur in considering the location of the abnormally blunted "tip" on the fourth point - right antler. However, I do not believe the questioned measurements would total more than an inch or so and the total score would not change more than a full point. Regardless of how it is measured it is quite likely that the score will exceed the present record of 202.

I was not able to obtain photographs of this trophy but intend to do so within the next few weeks.

The history of this trophy remains unknown. It was purchased by the present owner, Mr. Ludwig, at some sort of farm sale in Sandstone, Minnesota in 1959. A few old timers in the vicinity believe it was shot in that vicinity many years back. The mounted head appears to be at least 35 or more years old. No taxidermist marks are evident.

I'll continue to work on the trophy's past history. These antlers are very impressive and I'd welcome any suggestions you may have. Too bad this trophy could not have been included in the forthcoming record book.

Sincerely,

BA Fashingbauer

B. A. Fashingbauer
Research Biologist

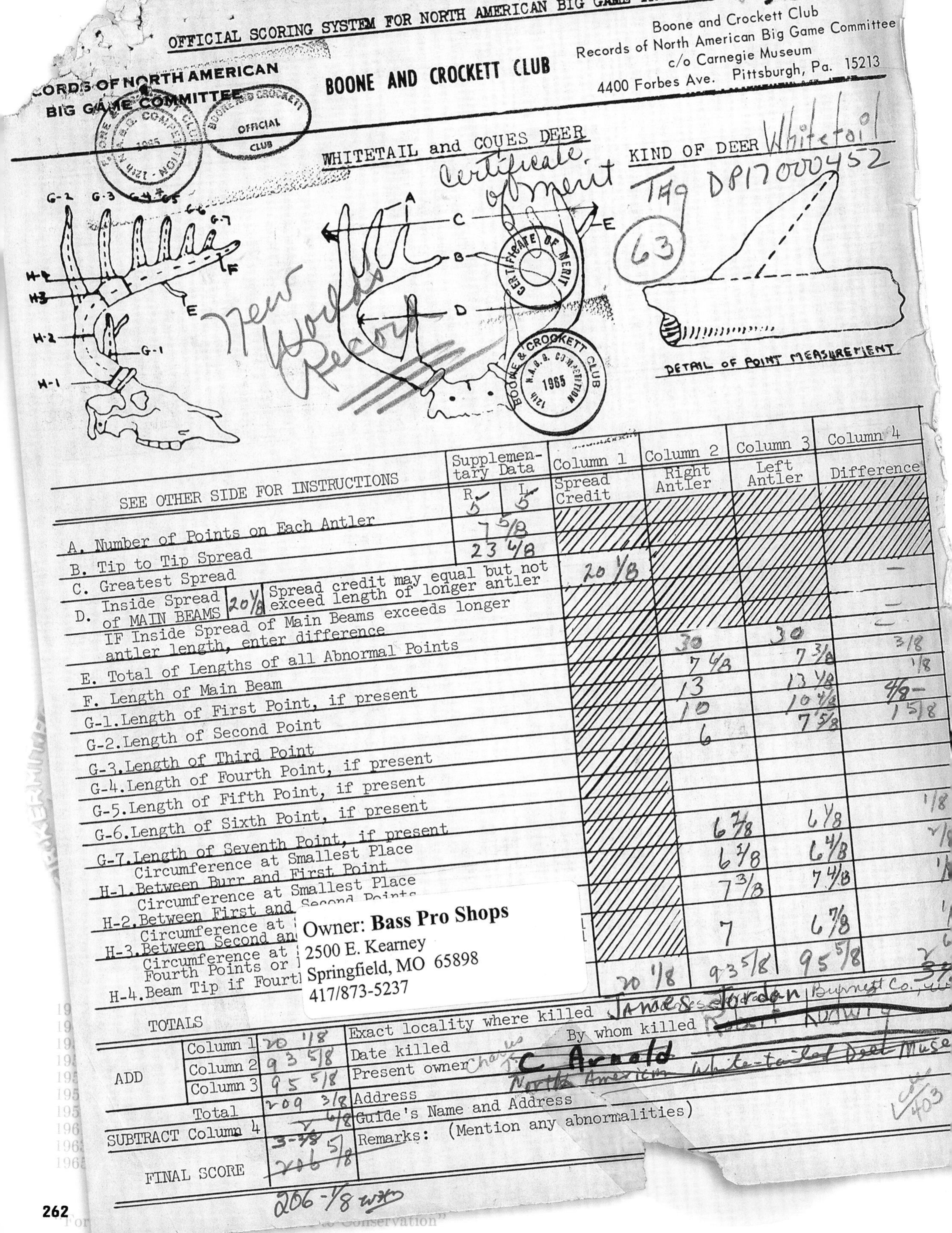

OFFICIAL SCORING SYSTEM FOR NORTH AMERICAN BIG GAME TROPHIES

RECORDS OF NORTH AMERICAN BIG GAME COMMITTEE

BOONE AND CROCKETT CLUB

Boone and Crockett Club
Records of North American Big Game Committee
c/o Carnegie Museum
4400 Forbes Ave. Pittsburgh, Pa. 15213

WHITETAIL and COUES DEER

KIND OF DEER Whitetail

Certificate of merit

TAG DP17000452

63

New World Record

DETAIL OF POINT MEASUREMENT

SEE OTHER SIDE FOR INSTRUCTIONS	Supplementary Data R.	Supplementary Data L.	Column 1 Spread Credit	Column 2 Right Antler	Column 3 Left Antler	Column 4 Difference
	5	5				
A. Number of Points on Each Antler	7 5/8					
B. Tip to Tip Spread	23 4/8					
C. Greatest Spread						—
D. Inside Spread of MAIN BEAMS 20 1/8 — Spread credit may equal but not exceed length of longer antler			20 1/8			—
IF Inside Spread of Main Beams exceeds longer antler length, enter difference						—
E. Total of Lengths of all Abnormal Points						
F. Length of Main Beam				30	30	3/8
G-1. Length of First Point, if present				7 4/8	7 3/8	1/8
G-2. Length of Second Point				13	13 4/8	4/8
G-3. Length of Third Point				10	10 4/8	1 5/8
G-4. Length of Fourth Point, if present				6	7 5/8	
G-5. Length of Fifth Point, if present						
G-6. Length of Sixth Point, if present						
G-7. Length of Seventh Point, if present						1/8
Circumference at Smallest Place H-1. Between Burr and First Point				6 7/8	6 1/8	
Circumference at Smallest Place H-2. Between First and Second Points				6 3/8	6 4/8	
Circumference at ... H-3. Between Second and ...				7 3/8	7 4/8	
Circumference at ... Fourth Points or ... H-4. Beam Tip if Fourth ...				7	6 7/8	
TOTALS			20 1/8	93 5/8	95 5/8	2 6/8

Owner: **Bass Pro Shops**
2500 E. Kearney
Springfield, MO 65898
417/873-5237

ADD			
ADD	Column 1	20 1/8	Exact locality where killed: Burnett Co., Wis. — By whom killed: James Jordan
	Column 2	93 5/8	Date killed
	Column 3	95 5/8	Present owner: Charles T. C. Arnold
	Total	209 3/8	Address
SUBTRACT Column 4		2 6/8	Guide's Name and Address
			Remarks: (Mention any abnormalities)
FINAL SCORE		206 5/8	

206-1/8 WHN

WHITETAIL DEER

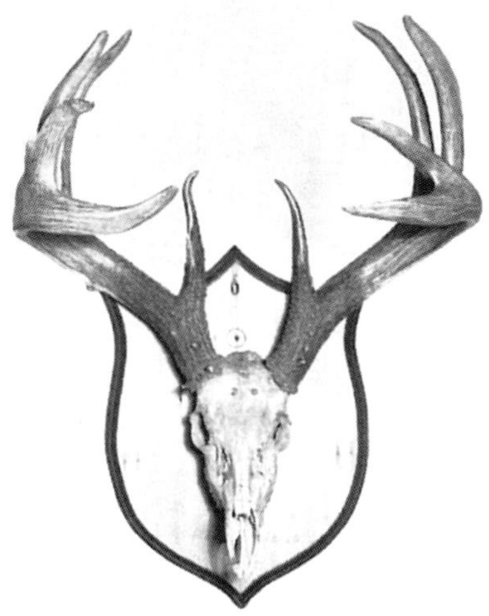

NEW WORLD'S RECORD

WHITETAIL DEER (Typical)
Certificate of Merit
Score — 206-5/8
Length—(R) 30 (L) 30
Circumference—(R) 6-2/8 (L) 6-1/8
Points—(R) 5 (L) 5
Inside Spread—20-1/8
Locality—Probably vicinity Sandstone, Minn. — Date killed unknown
Owner—Robert Ludwig

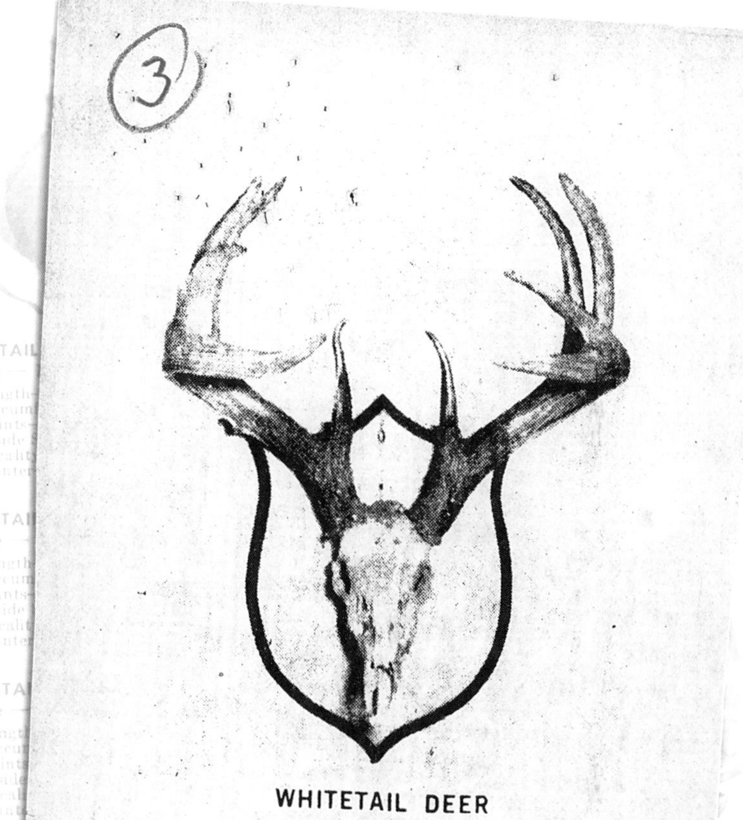

WHITETAIL DEER
(Score: 206⅝)

I purchased the horns at a rummage-type sale in Sandstone, Minn., in the summer of 1959. Realizing their size and uniformity, I wanted them for my collection. Not knowing that they were a record at that time, I didn't inquire as to who had brought them in. From their appearance (they were very dirty) and old style of mounting (plaster of Paris), they probably had been in someone's attic for years. I attempted to trace their origin, with no success.

ROBERT LUDWIG, Sandstone, Minn.

Unfortunately, there are inaccuracies on the photo brochure that proclaimed this whitetail as the new World's Record: The hunter was still listed as unknown; it would later be discovered that the antlers were from Wisconsin, and a 4/8-inch adding error was discovered nearly two decades later, which ultimately (and correctly) put the final score at 206-1/8. It wasn't until the 1981 All-time book that the final score was correctly published.

Copy of James Jordan's letter of Jan. 23, 1971 regarding Danbury deer:
Typed from original letter submitted in long hand by Mr. Jordan

Dear Mr. B. A. Fashingbauer:

I have your letter in hand, and glad to hear from you. I know Grant Peterson. And Grant heard Mrs. Bob Ludwig say "We know, Uncle Jim, that you killed the deer". Mrs. Bob Ludwig is my sister's daughter. Bob Ludwig is related to me. He told untrue stories about me and the deer. He knows I killed the deer but he is afraid I might take the horns. But I won't. All I want to do is (have) the name of killing the deer. His father-in-law told my wife and I (that) he saw the board it was on and the writing on the board said "Killed in 1914". That is the year I killed it. And I have plenty of witnesses that will swear to that.

I showed the picture of the horns to one guy and he said that is off the deer I helped you pull out of the river in 1914. He was 14 years (old) at the time. And I have two more guys that knew the guy that took the head to mount. I never mentioned the name of the guy who mounted the head in the story I am sending you, but I had known the guy. He meant to steal the head when he took it to mount. One guy told me that not long ago. I have lots of proof that I killed the deer.

About 18 months 1½ years ago my wife and I stoked in to see Bob Ludwig and had coffee. And he brought out the horns and showed them to my wife and I. When I saw the (horns), blood rushed to my head. I knew that was the horns off of that long lost deer head that was stolen from me. I could not say much but "we better go home" to my wife. I never slept that night. The next morning I called him and told him to stop in if he went this way. Well, him and his wife come over that night and I told him the story. He acted like he believed it. And all the time he knew it was killed in 1914. Now he has sold the horns. I heard he was afraid I was getting too close.

We knew the guy that stole the horns or head. He lived in Hinckley, Minn. and when Webster, Wisconsin first started, he lived there. Him and his wife both died. My wife and I are getting up in years, married 57 years. Live right by the St. Croix Bark (Park?) in Minnesota, 18 miles east of Hinckley, Minn. Get our mail route out of Danbury, Wisconsin.

I have a large story written about that big buck and other things. I have lived out here way since 1900. When we moved out here our neighbors were Indians. I shot my first deer when I was 11 years old. And trapped lots of wolves and mink and fox. I have lots of deer horns. I am too old to tell a lie about some horns I did not get myself.

Well thank you and do what you can about the horns. I can get some proof of what I said.

And good luck

James Jordan

R 1, Box 71
Danbury, Wis. 54830

JAMES JORDAN TELLS HIS STORY

This letter from James Jordan, himself, is very intriguing and open. It is also a very important piece of hunting history. B&C was actively involved in getting to the bottom of this mystery, and Jordan was ultimately credited as being the hunter. Sadly, that happened two months after his death.

Pictured at left are James and his wife, Lena, when he was 21 — one year before he shot the buck.

North American Big Game Awards Program

News Release

WORLD'S RECORD WHITETAILED DEER TROPHY FROM WISCONSIN

FOR IMMEDIATE RELEASE
15 FEBRUARY 1979

Some 65 years have now passed since James Jordan shot a whitetail buck with an exceptionally large rack near Danbury, Wisconsin, along the Yellow River, in 1914. Although no one viewing this rack could remember a larger one, no one suspected this trophy of being a world record The date was long before the formal records—keeping for native, North American big game was begun by the Boone and Crockett Club in 1932. Through a peculiar series of events, Jordan would not again see his trophy for more than a half—century.

Shortly after killing his deer, Jordan accepted the offer of a part-time taxidermist, George Van Castle of Webster, Wisconsin to mount his trophy for 5 dollars. Van Castle took the rack and hide to his home to work on it, but soon moved to Hinckley, Minnesota after the death of his wife. Jordan later heard that Van Castle had moved to Florida, making a trip to Hinckley to recover his trophy useless, although Jordan himself moved to Hinckley in his later life.

When Van Castle moved to Florida, he left Jordan's mounted deer head behind in the home he had occupied. Apparently, it then gathered dust in an attic corner until it was purchased in 1964 at a rummage sale for 3 dollars by Robert Ludwig.

Passing through Sandstone, Minnesota, Ludwig decided that the exceptional antlers were worth the price although the cracked and peeling mount would have to be thrown away. Ludwig retained the antlers in his home in Sandstone until he sold them to Dr. Charles T. Arnold of New Hampshire, whose hobby is collecting exceptional deer antler racks.

In 1964, Bernard A. Fashingbauer of St. Paul, Minnesota, measured this rack in his capacity as an Official Measurer for the Boone and Crockett Club big game records and found it to surpass the score of the then world record. Later, a select panel of judges, chosen from the ranks of the Official Measurers, certified this trophy as the world record at 206—5/8 points. At that time, the trophy was still the property of Robert Ludwig. By the time it was first published in the records book (1971 edition: North American Big Game) it was the property of Dr. Arnold so that it was shown with hunter "unknown".

In 1964, when James Jordan first viewed the huge deer rack owned by Robert Ludwig (a distant relative) he knew it was the same deer he had shot so many years ago. For more than a decade, Jordan would be frustrated in his quest to be recognized as the hunter for this deer in the records book.

Jordan's claim to this trophy was convincing to many of those who talked to him about the matter. Ron Schara, Outdoor Writer for the Minneapolis Tribune, featured Jordan's story on several occasions. The current trophy owner (Dr. Arnold) wrote to the North American Big Game Awards Program (NABGAP) in late 1977, suggesting that Jordan's story be fully explored and that he be designated as the hunter, if the records office were convinced. *Continued on next page...*

— Continued from the press release on the previous page —

The NABGAP office asked Bernard Fashingbauer to gather all evidence that he could find on this trophy, in order that Jordan's claim could be fully considered by the Boone and Crockett Club's Records of North American Big Game Committee. Under the terms of the 1973 records keeping agreement, the club renders the final decision in cases such as this, while NRA staff perform the everyday program administration.

Information gathered by Fashingbauer, and from other sources, was considered by the Records Committee at their December 1978 meeting. After review, the committee decided to list James Jordan as the hunter for the world record whitetail deer (typical antlers), with a kill date and location of 1914 on the Yellow River, near Danbury, Wisconsin.

The next edition of the records book, North American Big Game, will be corrected with this information; expected publication is in 1983. (The current edition was published in 1977; usual publication cycle is six years.)

Unfortunately, James Jordan died in October 1978, at age 86, before he could be informed of the decision. His heirs have been informed of the decision, and they are pleased that his hunting achievement of more than a half century ago has finally been properly recognized.

Picture at top: Fashingbauer took this photo of Lena and Jim Jordan when he met with them in April of 1978 to discuss the whitetail buck.

Pictured at right: Jordan with his buck that he took over 60 years earlier.

5: SPECIAL TROPHY

MELVIN J. JOHNSON'S SAGAMORE HILL AWARD-WINNING WHITETAIL

OPPOSITE: Melvin J. Johnson harvested one of North America's finest trophies. Johnson's buck is currently the number four typical of All-time, but remains the Pope and Young Club's World's Record

WHITETAIL DEER (Typical) — 1st Award
Score — 204-4/8

Length—(R) 27-5/8 (L) 26-6/8
Circumference—(R) 6-1/8 (L) 6-2/8
Points—(R) 7 (L) 6

Inside Spread—23-5/8
Locality—Peoria Co., Ill. — 1965
Hunter—M. J. Johnson

The Sagamore Hill Medal is given by the Roosevelt family in memory of Theodore Roosevelt, Founder and first President of Boone and Crockett Club, Theodore Roosevelt, Jr., and Kermit Roosevelt. It was created in 1948. It **may** be awarded by the Competition Judges, if in their opinion there is an outstanding trophy worthy of great distinction. It may also be awarded by the Executive Committee of Boone and Crockett Club for distinguished devotion to the objectives of the Club. The Sagamore Hill Medal is the highest award given by Boone and Crockett Club. Only one may be given in any Big Game Competition and only eleven have been awarded altogether.

SAGAMORE HILL AWARDS

1948—Robert C. Reeve	Alaskan Brown Bear
1949—E. C. Haase	Mountain Goat
1950—Dr. R. C. Bentzen	Wapiti
1951—George H. Lesser	Woodland Caribou
1953—Edison A. Pillmore	Mule Deer
1957—Frank Cook	White Sheep
1959—Fred C. Mercer	Wapiti
1961—Harry L. Swank, Jr.	White Sheep
1963—Norman Blank	Stone Sheep
1965—Melvin J. Johnson	Whitetail Deer (Typical)

SPECIAL AWARD
1952—DeForest Grant
"For long and distinguished service to Conservation"

Medal & Certificate

OFFICIAL SCORING SYST

RECORDS OF NORTH AMERICAN
BIG GAME COMMITTEE

BOONE

WHITET

G-2 G-3 G-4 G-5 G-6 G-7
H-4 H-3 H-2 G-1 H-1

SAGAMORE HILL AWARD

BOONE AND CROCKETT CLUB 12th N.A.B.G. COMPETITION 1965

OFFICIAL CLUB

SAGAMORE HILL AWARD

FIRST PLACE

DETAIL OF POINT MEASUREMENT

DP17000454

BOONE AND CROCKETT CLUB
Records of North American Big Game
Committee
c/o Carnegie Museum RECD JAN 24 1
4400 Forbes Avenue
Pittsburgh, Pennsylvania 15213

BOONE AND CROCKETT CLUB · BIG GAME COMPETITION

T49 (2)

Please check one of these sections and return at once.

(X) I will send my trophy prepaid to the Carnegie Museum to arrive February 15th. When you return my trophy, please insure it f

$ 1500.00

( ) I will not send my trophy to the Carnegie Museum

Kind of trophy Whitetail Deer (Typical)

Date January 21, 1966 Signature Melvin J. Johns

SEE OTHER SIDE FOR INSTRUCTIONS	Supplementary Data R.	Supplementary Data L.	Column 1 Spread Credit	Column 2 Right Antler	Column 3 Left Antler	Column 4 Difference
A. Number of Points on Each Antler	7	6				
B. Tip to Tip Spread	22 5/8					
C. Greatest Spread	26 1/8					
D. Inside Spread of MAIN BEAMS 23 5/8 — Spread credit may equal but not exceed length of longer antler			23 5/8			
IF Inside Spread of Main Beams exceeds longer antler length, enter difference						—
E. Total of Lengths of all Abnormal Points						1 1/8
F. Length of Main Beam				27 5/8	26 6/8	7/8
G-1. Length of First Point, if present				5 4/8	7 2/8	1 6/8
G-2. Length of Second Point				11 3/8	12	5/8
G-3. Length of Third Point				12 6/8	12	6/8
G-4. Length of Fourth Point, if present				10 1/8	9 7/8	2/8
G-5. Length of Fifth Point, if present				5 7/8	4 4/8	1 3/8
G-6. Length of Sixth Point, if present						
G-7. Length of Seventh Point, if present						
Circumference at Smallest Place H-1. Between Burr and First Point				6 1/8	6 2/8	
Circumference a… H-2. Between First a…				5	5	
Circumference a… H-3. Between Second a… and				5 1/8	5 1/8	
Circumference a… Fourth Points… H-4. Beam Tip if Fou… and				4 6/8	5 1/8	
TOTALS			23 5/8	94 2/8	93 7/8	7

Owner: **Bass Pro Shops**
2500 E. Kearney
Springfield, MO 65898
417/873-5237

ADD	Column 1	23 5/8	Exact locality where killed Peo County Ill.
	Column 2	94 2/8	Date killed 29 Oct 65 By whom killed M. J. Johnson
	Column 3	93 7/8	Present owner ~~M. J. Johnson~~ ~~Legendary Whitetails~~ ~~Ill.~~
	Total	211 6/8	Address ~~Peoria, Ill~~
SUBTRACT Column 4		7 2/8	Guide's Name and Address None
FINAL SCORE		204 4/8	Remarks: (Mention any abnormalities) ~~North American Whitetail Deer Museum~~

PLEASE SIG
P
vic
or
Chas
defin
spott
I fur
vehic
provin
Date J

chart being Xroxed - 6/9/66

Dear Sirs.

I would like at this time to thank you all at Boone and Crockett for giving me the biggest thrill of my life. I was really to stunned at the time to show my appreciation.

I was wondering if you would send me a copy of the official scoring form with the final measurments. Would you also send me a copy or tell me where I could get one of the picture of the antlers as shown in the booklet.

Thanks Again
Mel Johnson
3513 N. Monroe St.
Peoria, Ill. 6160

RECD JUN 3 1966

RN TO PITTSBURGH TO COMPLETE YOUR FILE FOR COMPETITION FOR 1965
M.J. JOHNSON WHITETAIL DEER 197-4/8

and return to: Boone and Crockett Club
Records of North American Big Game Committee
c/o Carnegie Museum
4400 Forbes Avenue
Pittsburgh, Pa. 15213

NO TROPHY OBTAINED BY UNFAIR CHASE MAY BE ENTERED
IN ANY BOONE & CROCKETT BIG GAME COMPETITION

or herding land game from the air, followed by landing in its
ursuit, shall be deemed UNFAIR CHASE and unsportsmanlike. Herding
Y game from motor powered vehicles shall likewise be deemed Unfair
ortsmanlike.

* * * * * *

hat the trophy scored on this chart was taken in Fair Chase as
the Boone & Crockett Club. I certify that it was not taken by
ing from the air followed by landing in its vicinity for pursuit.
y that it was not taken by herding or pursuing from motor powered
it was taken in full compliance with the local game laws of the
.

3, 1966 Hunter Melvin J. Johnson

PHOTOGRAPH

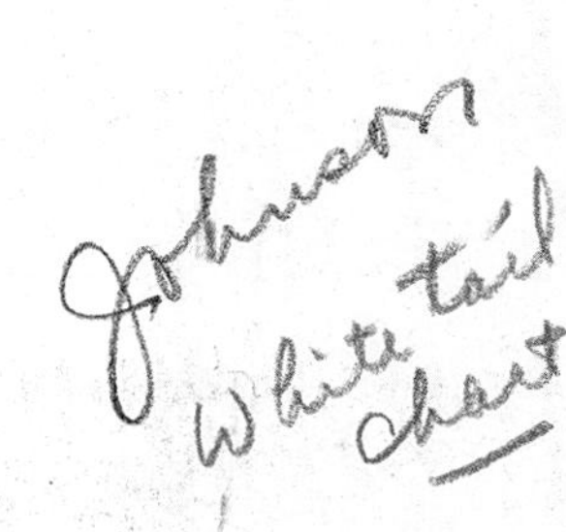

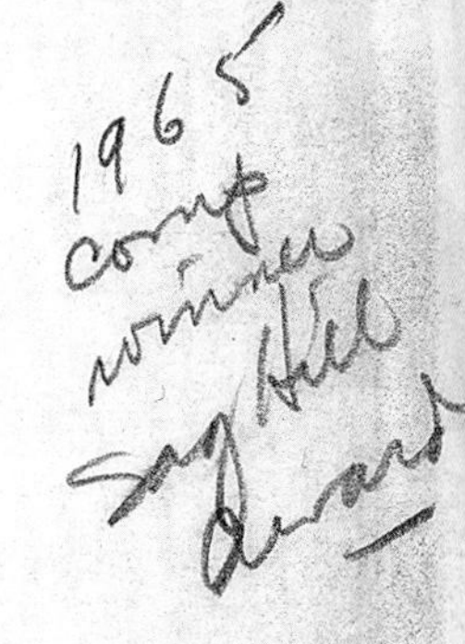

June 14, 1966

Mr. Melvin J. Johnson

Peoria, Illinois 61603

Dear Mr. Johnson:

We wish to acknowledge receipt of your letter of May 31. No wonder you were thrilled at getting one of the highest awards that can be given to a hunter, the Sagamore Hill Award! It is understandable that you would be too stunned to have much to show how pleased you were. All we had to do was to look at you to know how happy you were.

Enclosed is a copy of the final measurements submitted by the judges of the 12th Competition. We cannot send you a picture of the antlers at the present time but will do so in the near future when they will be available.

You found in your "back yard" what many hunters have traveled and spent a great deal of money trying to achieve. Congratulations!

Sincerely,

Elmer M. Rusten, M.D.
Chairman

ET:caw

Enclosure

cc: E. M. Rusten
File ✓

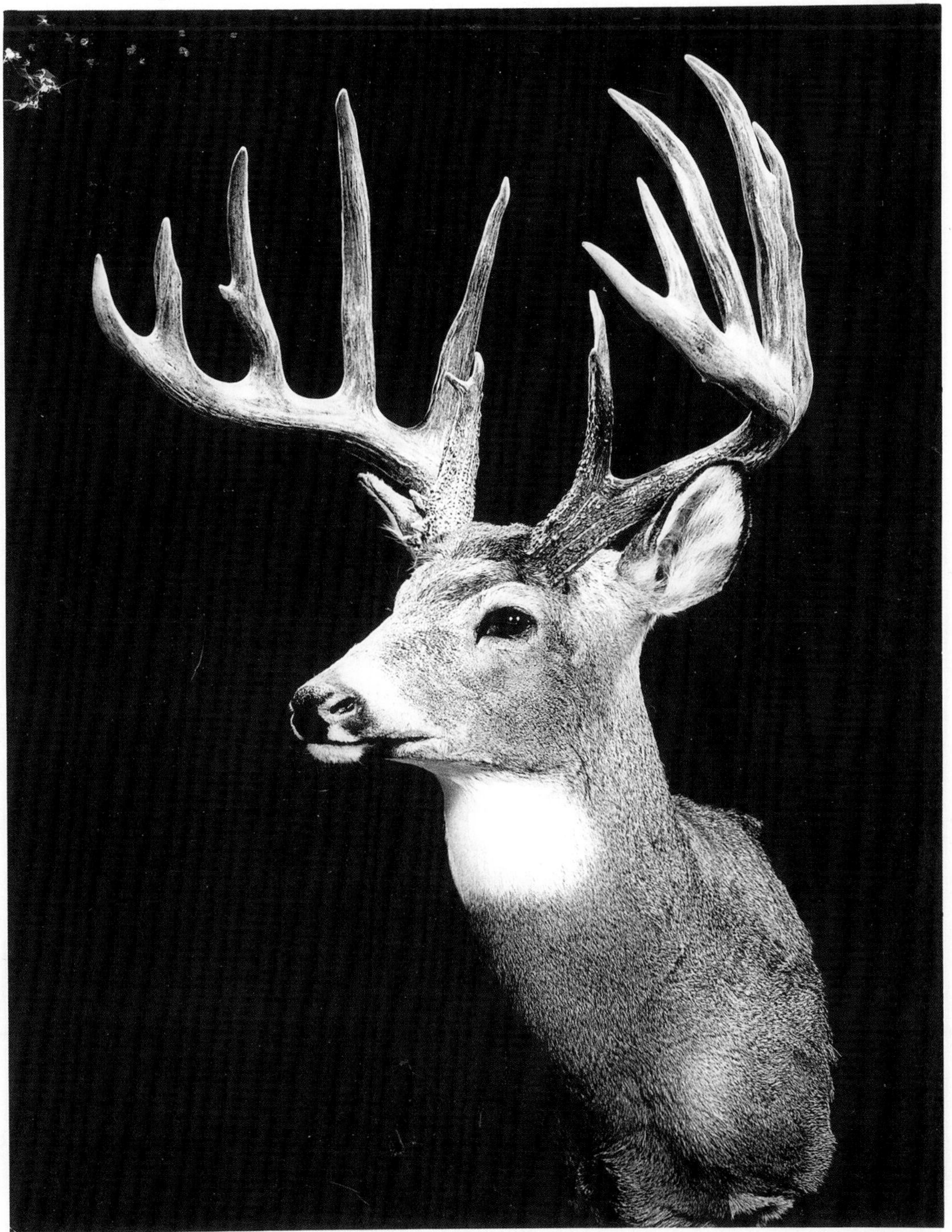

Johnson's 204-4/8 typical whitetail was certified at the 12th Competition Judges Panel. At that time, it was the Number Two in the world. Only the Jordan buck was bigger, and was certified by the same Judges Panel. Jordan's trophy is currently second on the All-time list, and Johnson's (pictured above) is fourth.

The National Rifle Association of America

and The

Boone and Crockett Club

In consideration of common goals

To conserve North American wildlife resources;

To establish high ethical standards for all participants in the sport of hunting;

To foster the rules and principles of fair chase;

To recognize outstanding achievements by sportsmen in taking select trophy game animals; and

To promote public understanding and appreciation of the ancient and noble sport of hunting in relation to the wise use of our natural resources, the

National Rifle Association of America and the Boone and Crockett Club agree to join together in support and sponsorship of

North American Big Game Trophy Programs

For the Boone and Crockett Club

For the National Rifle Association

June 30, 1973

6: NABGAP BEGINS

BY TOMMY CARUTHERS

The North American Big Game Awards Program (NABGAP) got its start in June of 1973 when the National Rifle Association (NRA) and the Boone and Crockett Club (B&C) signed an agreement to co-sponsor the Boone and Crockett Records Program. A records committee was soon formed with NRA and B&C representation to steer the effort.

This historic agreement had a profound effect on the future of the B&C Records Program. First, it was an agreement between two established organizations, both dating to the late 1800s (B&C from 1887 and NRA from 1871). Both clubs had viable hunting programs, ethical hunting definitions, and hunter-achievement awards programs.

Traditionally, B&C club members had performed big-game awards data entry in their homes, but the dramatic increase in volume made this process cumbersome, at best. The NRA offered the benefit of a huge membership and national exposure.

B&C was a small club in numbers (100 regular members), but had unbelievable political clout and extremely well-to-do members. The NRA had the ability to staff data entry and depended on B&C to govern the records program in the same manner as had been done since publishing the 1932 Records Book. The effort was a perfect fit for NRA and B&C, wildlife managers and sportsmen.

LEFT: The agreement between the Boone and Crockett Club and the National Rifle Association to create the North American Big Game Awards Program (NABGAP) ushered in a new era for big-game records-keeping. Milestones during this time period included the establishment of a training manual for all measurers and a standard for all materials submitted for entry into the program.

This was an exciting period for several reasons. Both organizations wanted the Awards Program to reward fine trophies taken under fair-chase conditions; both wanted to avoid quarrelsome and debilitating competition between hunters for trophy animals.

The Awards Program also had a conservation element; both clubs were interested in rewarding the trophy, the game management and the habitat management programs required to produce such impressive specimens, again under fair-chase conditions.

The record books provided the ancillary value of providing critical data for wildlife managers, enabling them to gauge their programs, both in terms of quantity and trophy quality (size). As an added feature, hunters could use the record books to conduct research before selecting areas to hunt or areas for which they might apply for permits.

The second great advantage of the B&C/NRA merger was the creation of a records-measuring manual to universally train measurers. Previously, non-standardized scoring measures had been applied. A new, uniform measurement system was required.

Harold Nesbitt set about creating a manual that contained explicit instructions for trophy measurement. This manual was used as the text-

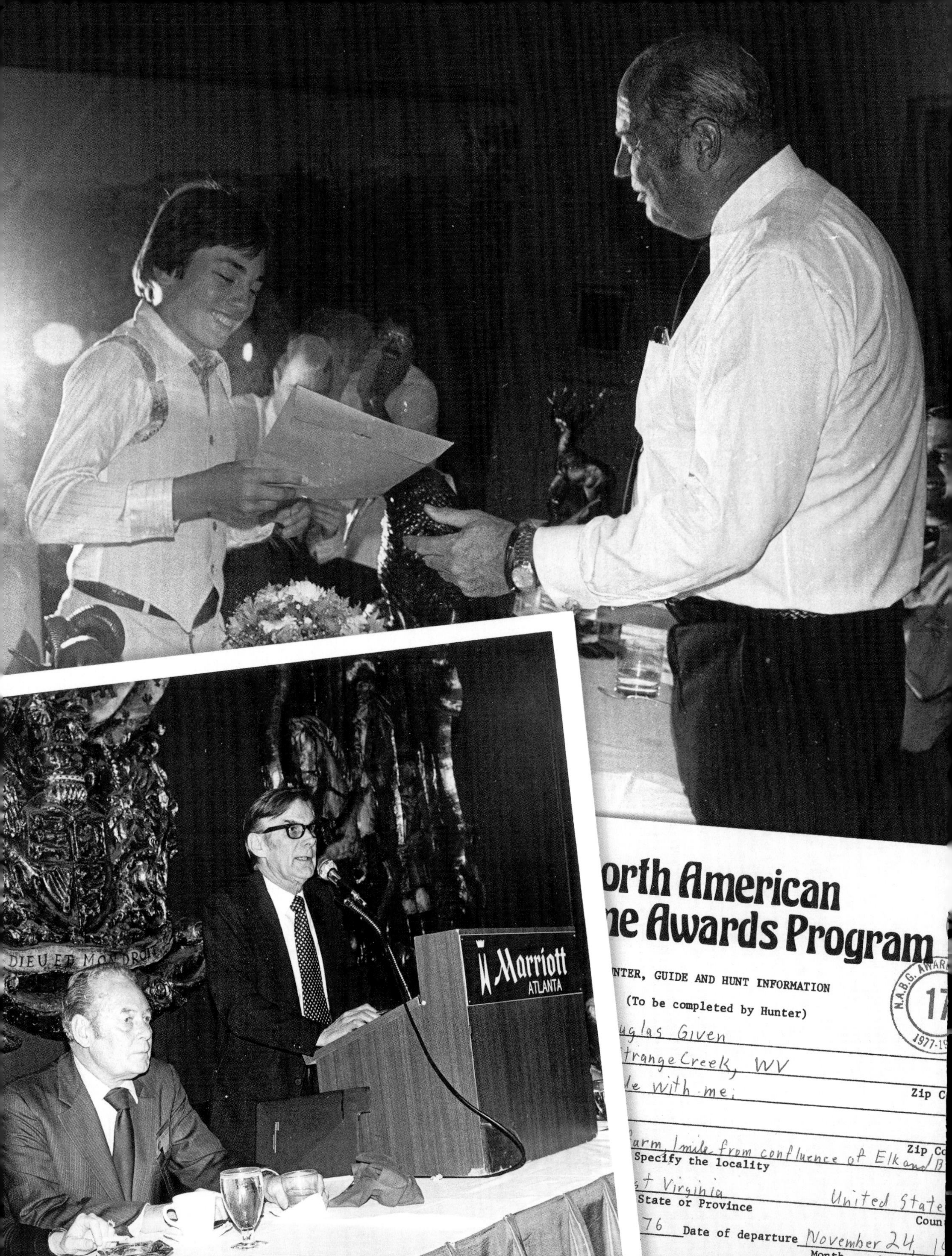

Marriott
ATLANTA
orth American
ne Awards Program
NTER, GUIDE AND HUNT INFORMATION
(To be completed by Hunter)
uglas Given
Strange Creek, WV
le with me.
Zip C
Farm, 1 mile from confluence of Elk and B
Zip Co
Specify the locality
st Virginia
United State
State or Province
Coun
76
Date of departure November 24, 1
Month

book for scoring schools that were held to train all future measurers since 1976; this program was also administered by NRA.

A standard of entry requirements was created that required photographs of both sides and the front of each trophy (aside from skulls, which also requires a top view).

The fair-chase statement now required notarization (later, the fair chase statement could also be witnessed by the official measurer or by a notary). A copy of the hunting license was also required. Previously, all that had been required was an original score chart, the $10.00 entry fee, and a completed Hunter, Guide and Hunt Information Form.

Such changes provided the records committee a much greater ability to detect unscrupulous or erroneous entries as well as enforce the accurate and consistent measuring of trophies.

The agreement between the NRA and the B&C remained in place until 1980. During that seven-year period, three awards programs and one all-time awards program were co-sponsored. The demise of the joint effort came about when NRA deemed the records-program data entry too time consuming for its staff.

Again, this effort fell to the B&C staff and club members. During the collaborative years, Harold Nesbitt had been employed by NRA to run the Awards Program. After the agreement was dissolved, Harold went to work for B&C to continue the Program.

Over the years, entry requirements have changed only slightly, minimums raised occasionally, and the Fair Chase Statement altered somewhat to encompass the technological changes that have occurred in hunting methods and equipment.

The current system of measuring North American big-game trophies was adopted prior to the 1952 edition of the records book and has served the records program well. This is a reflection of the fine work and careful evaluation exemplified by committee members tasked with developing a single, standardized system of trophy evaluation.

TOP: Jack S. Parker, Chairman of the Boone and Crockett Club's Records of North American Big Game Committee, presents one of the trophy owners a Boone and Crockett medal and award. The 17th Awards Entry Period from 1977-1979 was the last Awards Program cosponsored by B&C and the NRA. BOTTOM LEFT: The Boone and Crockett Club held its first cosponsored Awards Banquet with the NRA in Atlanta, Georgia, on March 24, 1974. General Max Rich, Executive Director of the NRA, was in attendance to speak the attendees. Seated to his left is Boone and Crockett Club member John E. Rhea, who was also the Chairman of the NRA Coordinating Committee for the 15th Awards.

6: VINTAGE PHOTOS*

NABCAP BEGINS

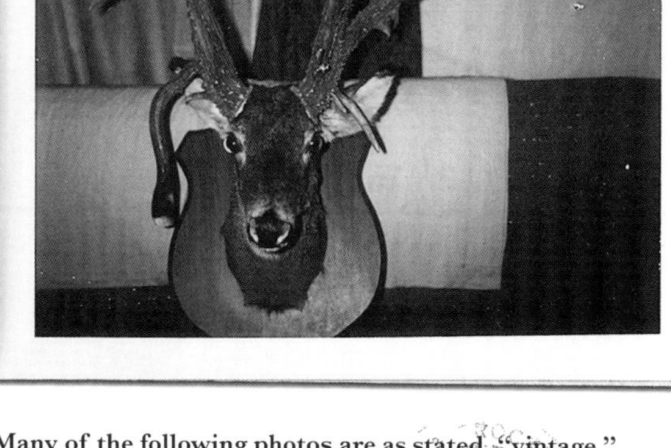

ABOVE: This massive Coues' deer was taken by Arcenio G. Valdez in Pima County, Arizona, in 1971. This rack, with characteristic massiveness and compact look, is very typical for Coues' deer. Smooth bases and relatively short G1s also fit the mold.

RIGHT: This non-typical, which scores 203-5/8 points, is a unique trophy. Wesley Gilkey was hunting in Meigs County, Ohio, on November 30, 1970, when he had a fateful encounter with this buck.

LEFT: In the remarks section of this deer's score chart, it notes, "Palmate antler development." That would be an apt statement for this one-of-a-kind whitetail. Scoring 227 points, this Miami County, Kansas, non-typical has H3 measurements over 10 inches. Gary A. Smith was the lucky hunter.

***Many of the following photos are as stated, "vintage." The Boone and Crockett Club has carefully ushered in a new era with the advancement and availability of photographic equipment. Today, our expectations consist of presenting a blood-free trophy and hunter in an uncluttered, natural environment. These guidelines were born out of respect for the animal and its habitat.**

N.A.B.G. AWARDS PROGRAM
17

ABOVE: Chester T. Veach was carrying his 20-gauge slug shotgun in Pike County, Ohio, on this fateful day in 1971. He was able to drop this All-time non-typical giant at 83 yards. The buck scores 267 points and is the second-largest Ohio buck ever recorded in the Boone and Crockett Club records. Only the Hole-in-the-Horn buck scoring 328-2/8 points ranks higher.

RIGHT: Morris Sather's compact non-typical, which scores 211-2/8 points, was taken near Hughenden, Alberta, in 1966. The rack shows tremendous mass throughout. Sather used a .30-06 on his successful hunt.

LEFT: Joe A. Rose, Jr., was hunting in Osago County, Kansas, on a cold and foggy December morning in 1977 when he made good on a 250-yard shot on this non-typical, scoring 198 points.

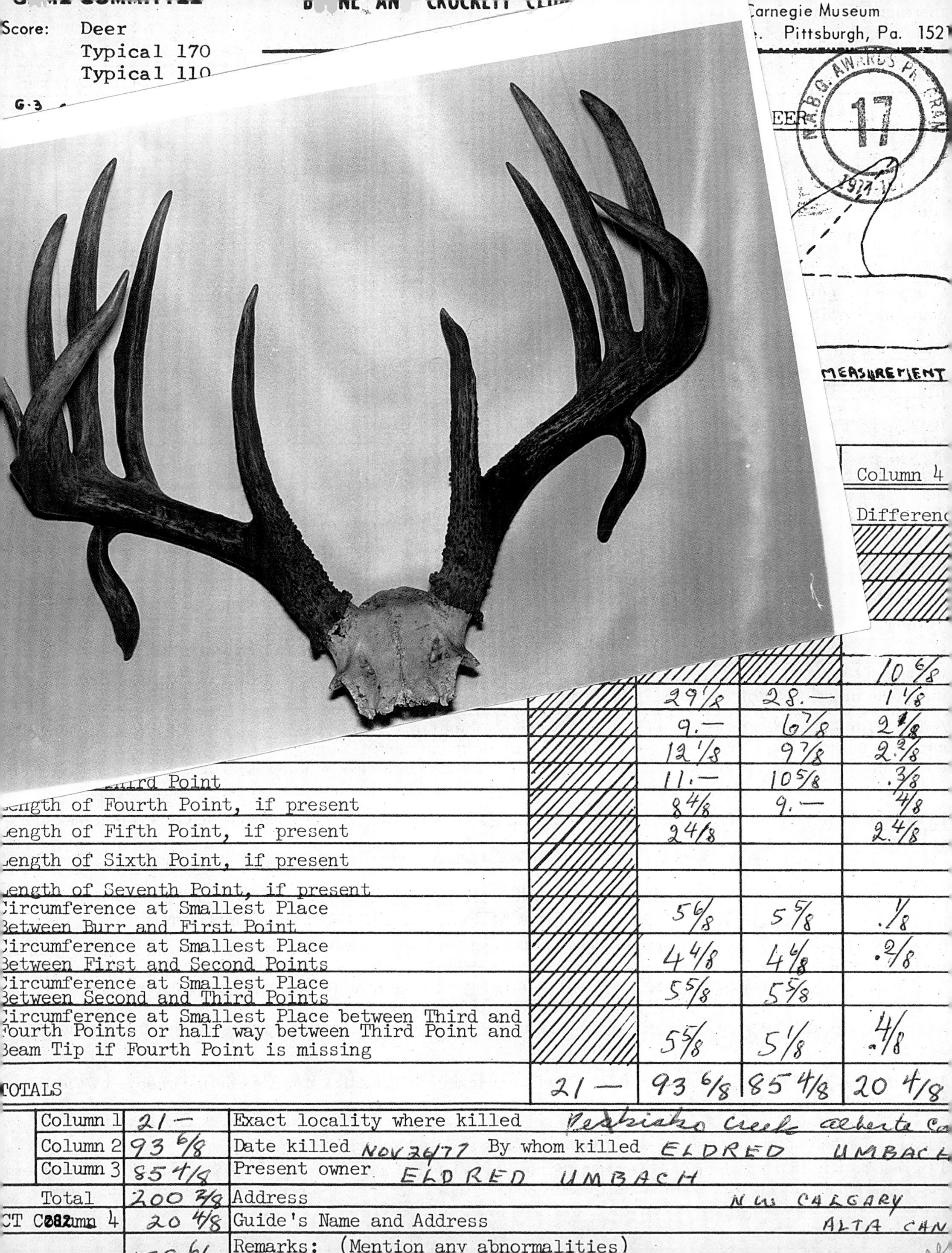

Score: Deer
Typical 170
Typical 110

Carnegie Museum
Pittsburgh, Pa. 152

MEASUREMENT

				Column 4
				Difference
				10 6/8
		29 1/8	28.—	1 1/8
		9.—	6 7/8	2 1/8
		12 1/8	9 7/8	2 2/8
…ird Point		11.—	10 5/8	3/8
Length of Fourth Point, if present		8 4/8	9.—	4/8
Length of Fifth Point, if present		2 4/8		2 4/8
Length of Sixth Point, if present				
Length of Seventh Point, if present				
Circumference at Smallest Place Between Burr and First Point		5 6/8	5 5/8	1/8
Circumference at Smallest Place Between First and Second Points		4 4/8	4 6/8	2/8
Circumference at Smallest Place Between Second and Third Points		5 5/8	5 5/8	
Circumference at Smallest Place between Third and Fourth Points or half way between Third Point and Beam Tip if Fourth Point is missing		5 5/8	5 1/8	4/8
TOTALS	21 —	93 6/8	85 4/8	20 4/8

Column 1	21 —	Exact locality where killed Pekisko Creek Alberta Ca…
Column 2	93 6/8	Date killed NOV 24/77 By whom killed ELDRED UMBACH
Column 3	85 4/8	Present owner ELDRED UMBACH
Total	200 2/8	Address NW CALGARY ALTA CAN
…CT Column 4	20 4/8	Guide's Name and Address
	…6…	Remarks: (Mention any abnormalities)

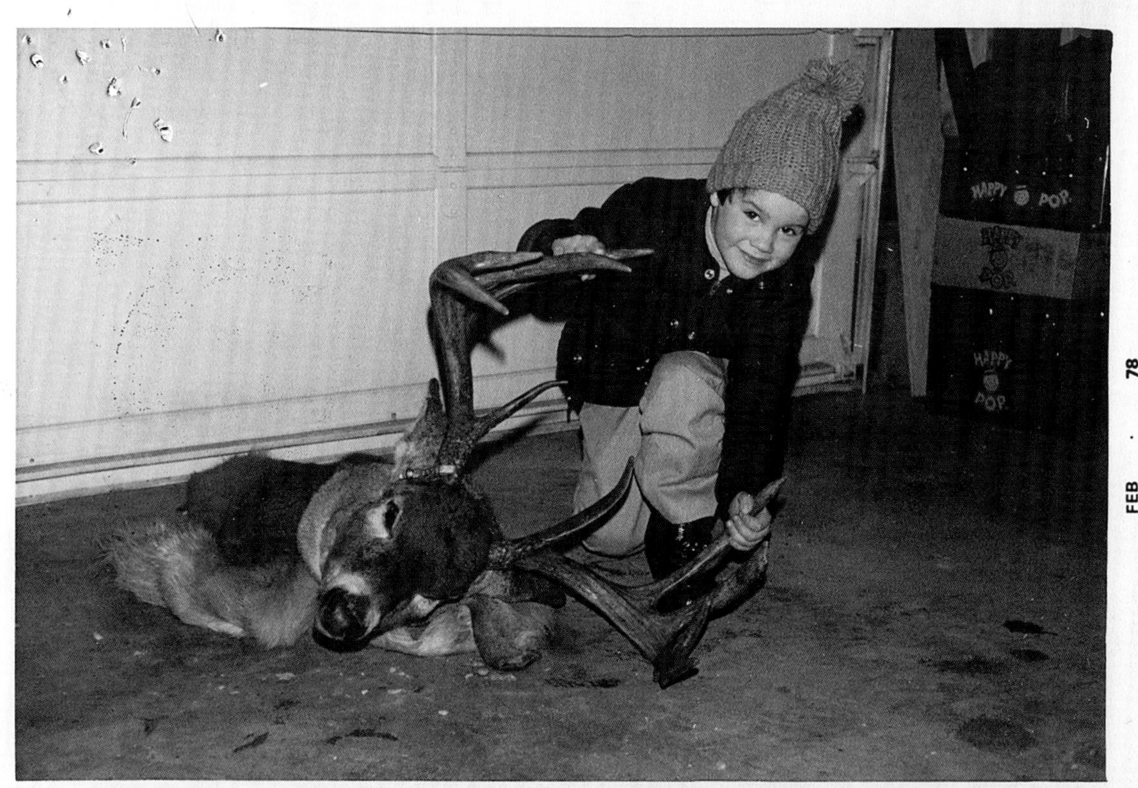

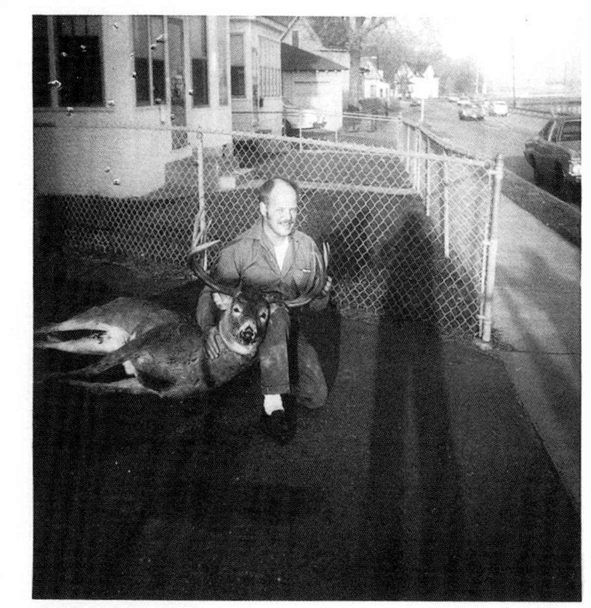

ABOVE: A 1977 hunt on the Athabasca River in Alberta yielded this great buck for Ron J. Holm. At 171-3/8 points, this typical buck just makes the All-time records book.

RIGHT: Harland A. Kern holds his typical whitetail, which scores 179-6/8 points, following a successful hunt in Aitkin County, Minnesota, in 1973.

LEFT: Scoring 179-6/8 points, this great typical was taken by Eldred Umbach in 1977 near Longview, Alberta.

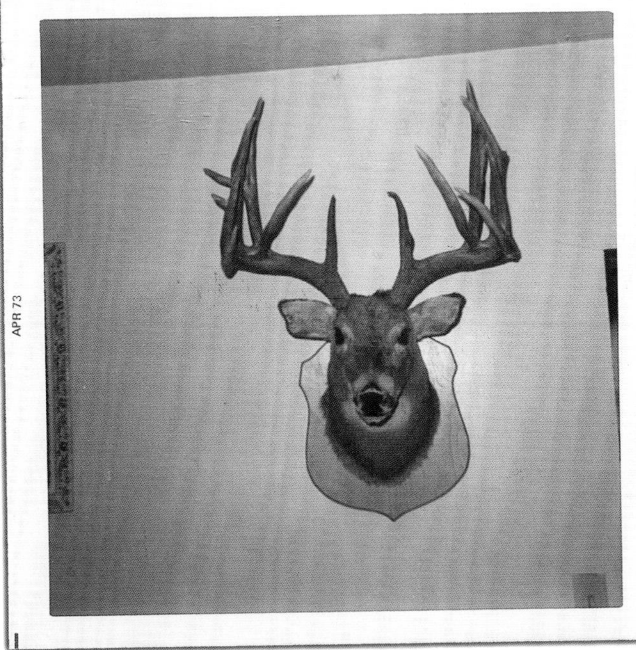

ABOVE: This eye-catching non-typical was taken by Richard O. Rivera in Webb County, Texas, in 1972. The matching G2s both have trident-like forking. The final score on this buck is 219-3/8 points.

RIGHT: Mike Unzen used a 16-gauge shotgun slug to down this 224-3/8 non-typical. Taken in Lac qui Parle County, Minnesota, in 1969, this buck has a 192-6/8 typical frame and 31-5/8 inches of abnormal points.

LEFT: This breath-taking non-typical has some of the longest tines ever measured on a white-tail, including a 16-4/8-inch right G2. The hunter is unknown, but the records indicate this giant scoring 234-1/8 points was from Glacier County, Montana.

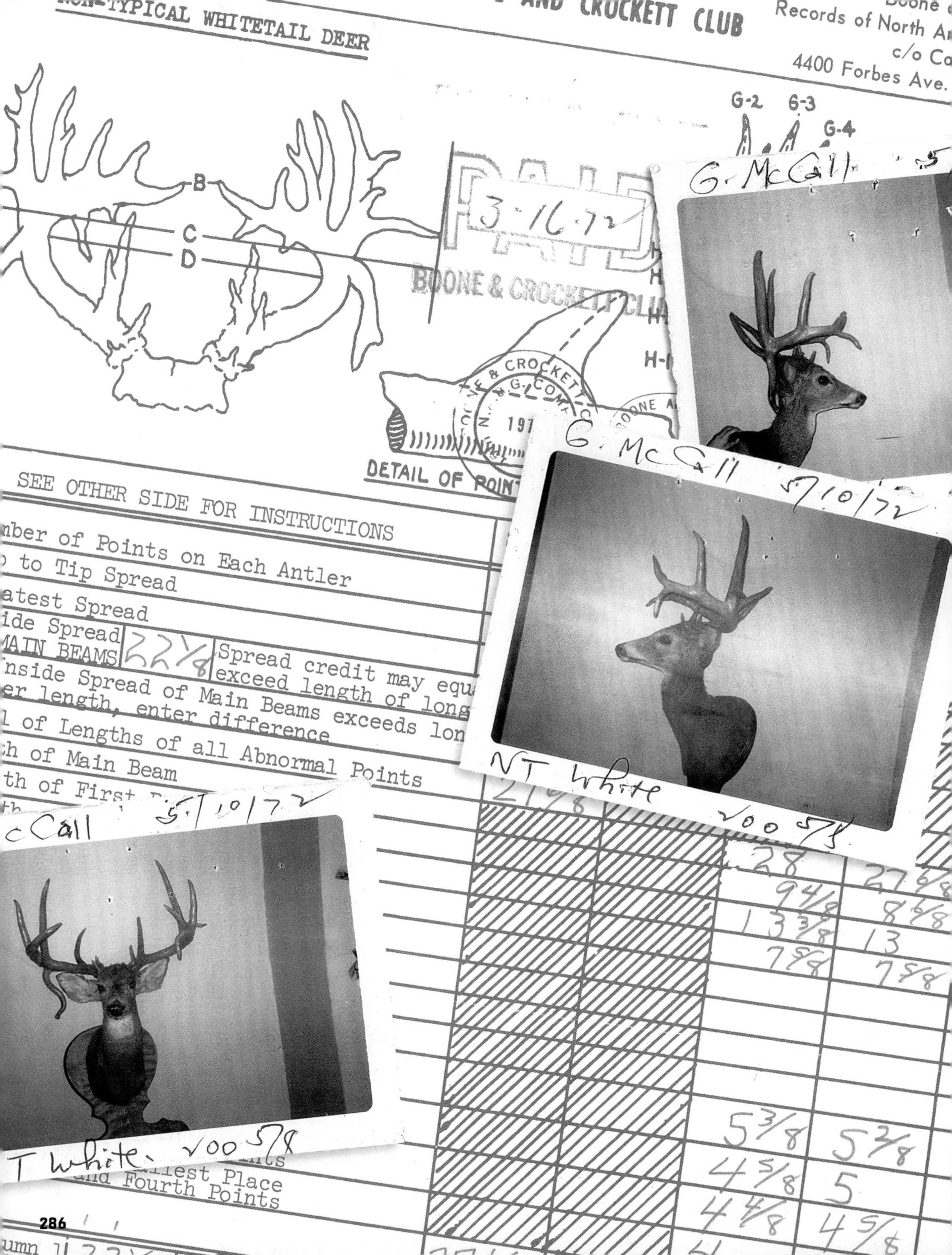
NON-TYPICAL WHITETAIL DEER
CROCKETT CLUB
Records of North A
4400 Forbes Ave.
G-2
G-3
G-4
B
C
D
3-16-72
BOONE & CROCKETT CLU
DETAIL OF POINT
SEE OTHER SIDE FOR INSTRUCTIONS
Number of Points on Each Antler
Tip to Tip Spread
Greatest Spread
Inside Spread of MAIN BEAMS
22 1/8
Spread credit may equa
exceed length of long
Inside Spread of Main Beams exceeds lon
er length, enter difference
l of Lengths of all Abnormal Points
h of Main Beam
th of First
Smallest Place
and Fourth Points
G. McCall
G. McCall 7/10/72
NT White 20057
5/10/72
T White 20057
28
27 6/8
9 4/8
8 6/8
13 3/8
13
7 6/8
7 5/8
5 3/8
5 2/8
4 5/8
5
4 4/8
4 5/8

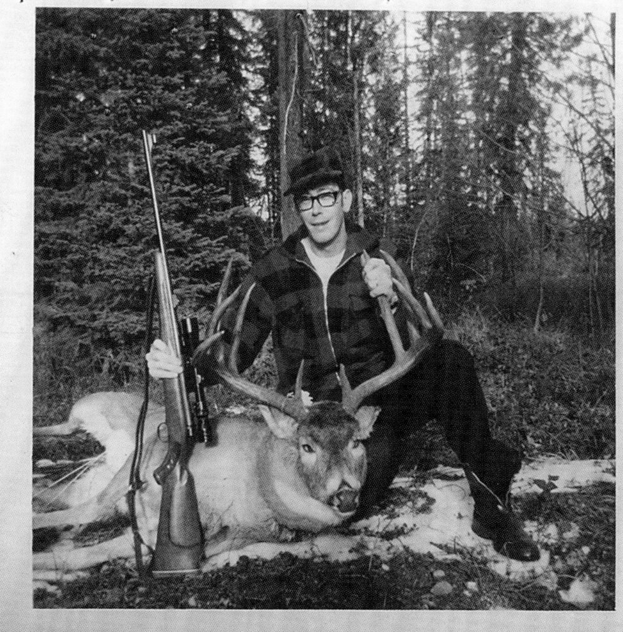

ABOVE: Logan County, Ohio, was the hunting location for this 1975 typical taken by David Sutherly. With a score of 176-7/8 points, this trophy was entered into the 16th Awards Program, 1974-1976.

RIGHT: Darrell Brist used a .338 Winchester Mag. to bag this fine trophy. He was hunting in Lake County, Montana, in November of 1977 when he met this buck at 120 yards. The final score is 173-1/8 points.

LEFT: Glenn McCall harvested this big-framed non-typical, which scores 200-5/8 points, with one slug from a 12-gauge shotgun at 70 yards. This successful hunt took place in Jackson County, Ohio.

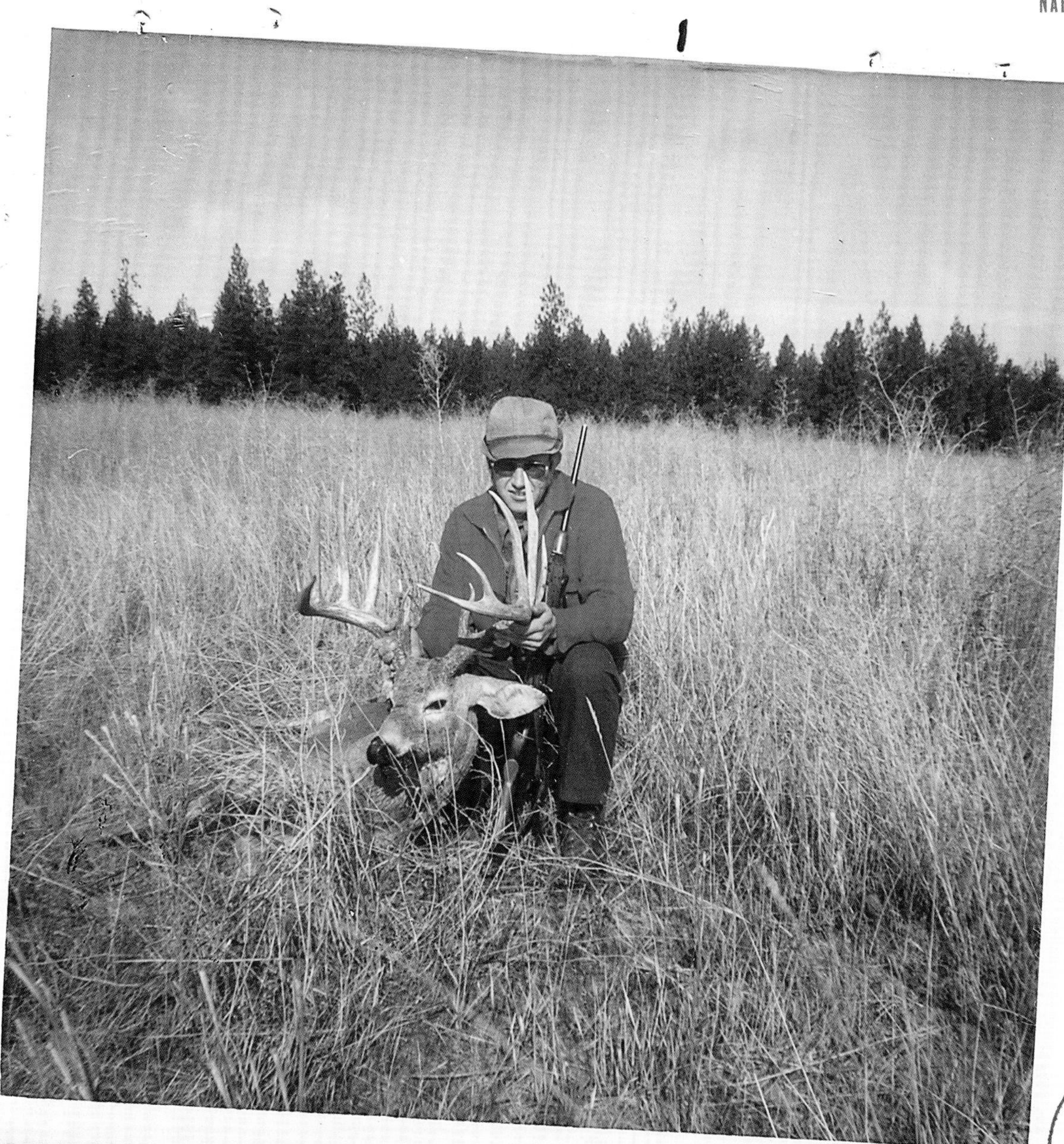

LEFT: This magnificent non-typical, which scores 240-3/8 points, was taken by John L. Hatton, Jr. and is the Georgia State Record. He was hunting in Monroe County on November 17, 1973, when he downed this buck with a .44 Magnum. This fantastic buck sports 38 scorable points and has base circumferences of 7-2/8 inches each. Note the plaque with upturned hooves, which was popular for this era.

ABOVE: A Spokane County, Washington, hunt in 1972 produced this typical whitetail scoring 179-4/8 points for Bert E. Smith. This typical is the third-largest ever recorded from Washington.

North American Big Game Awards Program

N.A.B.G. AWARDS PROGRAM 17 1977-1979

HUNTER, GUIDE AND HUNT INFORMATION

(To be completed by Hunter)

Hunter's Name William Douglas Given

Mailing Address Strange Creek, WV

Zip Code

Guide's Name none. No guide with me.

Mailing Address

Zip Code

Location of hunt Our family farm, 1 mile from confluence of Elk and Birch Riv

Specify the locality

Braxt... West Virginia United States

State or Province Country

1976 Date of departure November 24, 1976

Year Month Day Year

foot

Out

no if so, specify type and purpose

:00 AM PM at distance of 50 (fifty) (yards)

ullet type/weight 150 grain PSP Sierra

(or broadhead type/arrow weight)

at time of kill:

y Raining Lightly snowing

y Raining Heavily snowing

mph 1/2 inches snow on ground

RECEIVED JUL 18 1977 N.A.B.G. AWARDS

ther (specify) The snow was so thick before I shot, I had to use binoculars to identify it as a deer. When I got ready to fire, the snow almost stopped

NABGAP:77

~~June~~ July 16, 1977 — date

William Douglas Given — signature of hunter

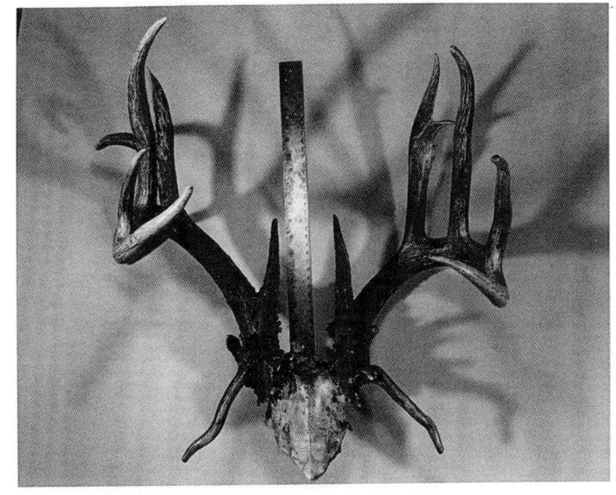

ABOVE: The Pajarito Mountains of Santa Cruz County, Arizona, provided the backdrop for W.C. Grant's successful 1973 hunt. At 112-3/8 points, Grant's typical Coues' deer is a great trophy.

RIGHT: This unique 215-7/8 non-typical was taken by Thomas H. Cooper in Putnam County, Georgia, in 1974. The matched drop points look as though they could have given this buck a permanently-obstructed view.

LEFT: The photo of William D. Given's typical scoring 182-3/8 points and accompanying Hunter, Guide and Hunting Information form help tell his story. Given's 6x6 trophy was taken in Braxton County, West Virginia, in 1976.

224 16th

ABOVE: Charlton County, Missouri, was where Vernon Sower harvested this big 203-5/8 point non-typical. This buck's turned-down main beams measure 26-6/8 and 28 inches in length.

RIGHT: Terry L. Halgrimson poses with his typical whitetail deer scoring 177-5/8 points. The deer was taken near Endeavor, Saskatchewan, in 1971.

LEFT: This magnificent deer, scoring 224 points, is listed as being from Hancock County, Maine. The hunter is unknown. At 34-4/8 inches, this is the sixth-widest whitetail in the records books. It also has main beams measuring 29-2/8 inches each.

ABOVE: William E. Schaefer harvested this 216-3/8 non-typical in Powhatan County, Virginia, in 1970. The most outstanding features on this buck are his eye guards, which measure 13-5/8 and 13-4/8 inches – easily some of the largest ever recorded.

RIGHT: Scoring 258-2/8 points, this fantastic whitetail is the second largest ever recorded in Minnesota. J.J. Matter was the successful hunter, taking the deer in Becker County, in 1973. Matter used a .308 at 250 yards to bring this great buck down.

LEFT: Joseph P. Culbertson takes a moment to preserve history in 1972. His non-typical scoring 216-2/8 points taken in Richland County is one of Montana's largest bucks.

RECEIVED

AUG29 1979

ABOVE: It was a rainy day in November of 1946 when Donald Torgerson encountered this giant 220-6/8 non-typical. Torgerson was hunting in Anoka County, Minnesota.

RIGHT: A 45-yard shot with a 65-pound bow netted this big 182-7/8 typical for Gary E. Landry. The deer was taken in Wayne County, Ohio, on December 30, 1975.

LEFT: This buck was submitted as a Coues' whitetail, with an entry score of 152-1/8 points. After further examination of the pictures and the location of kill, it was determined that it was not a Coues' deer and therefore not eligible for entry. The buck was taken in 1942 in Hidalgo County, New Mexico, by George Turner.

Decembe
Month

apon 357 MAG

let 158 GR.

f bow and arrow

istance from tr

May, 1975,

1977

, 1600 Rhode Island

erican
ds Program

76

RECEIVED
JUN 16 1975
N.A.B.G. AWARDS

T INFORMATION

y Hunter

RRY

GRAYSVILLE, PA. 15337

ALEPPO Twp.

ify Locality

A. U.S.A.

vince Country

Day Year

Day Year

WALK

Out

O if so, specify type

11 1974

Day Year

458 Win. MAG.

510 GR.

NONE

11 YDS. pistol 250 YDS. RIFLE

an Parry

Signature of hunter

,Wash., D.C. 20036 Telephone (202) 783-6505

ABOVE: This non-typical, which scores 251-1/8 points, is the sixth largest buck in Kansas history. It was taken by Theron E. Wilson in Mitchell County in 1974. Wilson made a 250-yard shot with a .300 Winchester Magnum. Interestingly, both bucks on these two pages were taken on the same day – December 11, 1974.

LEFT: This huge typical, scoring 184-6/8 points, is the Pennsylvania State Record. Ivan Parry was hunting in Greene County on December 11, 1974, when he encountered this buck. Parry used both a .357 pistol and a .458 Winchester Magnum to down this historic trophy. The deer was entered into the 16th Big Game Awards Program, 1974-1976.

ABOVE: A total of seven drop tines make this non-typical, which scores 211 points, a fascinating trophy. D.V. Day was hunting in Dimmitt County, Texas, when the area yielded this fine trophy in 1948.

RIGHT: As bowhunting became more popular and practical, field photos like this one were more common. Myles T. Keller took this typical whitetail, scoring 174-7/8 points, on a cold day in late December of 1977. Keller was hunting in Burnett County, Wisconsin.

LEFT: Barry L. Wensel was hunting in Flathead County, Montana, in 1976 when he was able to arrow this 201-4/8 point non-typical. The shot was from 12 yards using a 77-pound Widow recurve bow. This extremely heavy buck has base circumferences of 6-7/8 inches each.

Records of North American
Big Game Committee

c/o Carnegie Museum
4400 Forbes Avenue
Pittsburgh, Pa. 15213

Hunter's name *William B. Heller*

Address *Dallas, Texas*
City State Province Zip

Guide's name *NA*

Address
City State Province Zip

Location of hunt *Love Valley (Love Co., Okla)*

Date of arrival *11* *14* *70*
Month Day Year

Date of departure *70*
Year

walk
Out

? *yes* If so, specify type

carry it out

15 *70*
Day Year

shotgun

used *NA*

Approximate distance from trophy *60-75 yds*

William B. Heller
Signature of Hunter

ABOVE: This big non-typical, which scores 202-3/8 points, is the 13th largest ever taken in Wyoming. Marshall Miller bagged this buck in November of 1968 while hunting in Crook County. Interestingly, all 19 inches of this buck's abnormal points are on the right antler.

RIGHT: Alfred C. Pieper proudly poses with his trophy deer from 1977. This 212-6/8 non-typical was taken in Houston County, Minnesota, on a cold November day, with a 12-gauge shotgun slug at 20 yards.

LEFT: This 10x11 non-typical, scoring 204-4/8 points, was harvested by William B. Heller in Love County, Oklahoma, during the 1970 season.

FIRST AWARD – TYPICAL
15TH BIG GAME AWARDS

Larry W. Gibson harvested an award-winning typical whitetail with a shot from his .308 at only 28 feet. Originally scored at 201-5/8 points, the 15th Awards Judges Panel in Atlanta arrived at a final score of a staggering 205 points – good enough to become the second-best whitetail in the world in 1974.

This tremendous whitetail, with great balance throughout the rack, was taken in Randolph County, Missouri, in November of 1971. A broken and healed right G2 likely kept this deer from becoming the new World's Record at that time.

6: AWARD WINNERS

NABCAP BEGINS

25

OFFICIAL SCORING SYSTEM FOR NORTH AMERICAN BIG GAME TROPHIES

RECORDS OF NORTH AMERICAN BIG GAME COMMITTEE

BOONE AND CROCKETT CLUB

RETURN TO:
N. A. B. G. Awards P
1600 Rhode Island Av
Washington, D. C. 2

Minimum Score: Deer
Whitetail

WHITETAIL and COUES DEER

KIND OF DEER

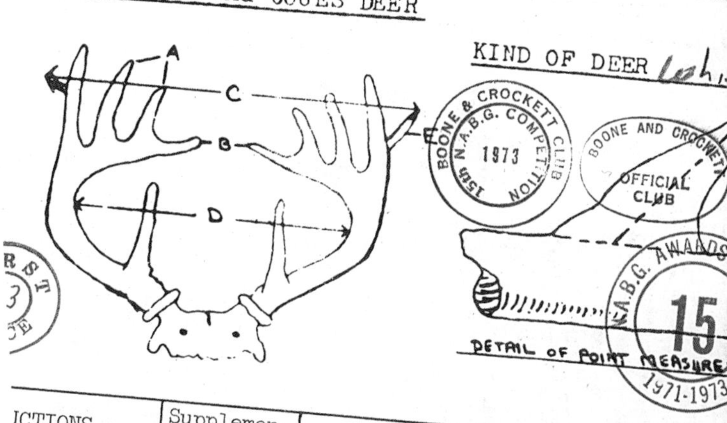

…CTIONS	Supplementary Data R.	Supplementary Data L.	Column 1	Column 2	Column 3	Colum…
…ler	6	6	Spread Credit	Right Antler	Left Antler	Diffe…
	22 4/8					
	25 4/8					
…dit may equal but not …th of longer antler			24 3/8			
…s exceeds longer …e						
…al Points						
…ent				26 6/8	25 4/8	1
				5 6/8	8 3/8	
				11 7/8	14 4/8	
…ent				12 6/8	13 2/8	
…nt				10 5/8	10 6/8	1/8
…nt				6 2/8	5	1
…oint, if present				–	–	
H-1. Circumference at Smallest Place Between Burr and First Point				–	–	
H-2. Circumference at Smallest Place Between First and Second Points				4 6/8	4 6/8	–
H-3. Circumference at Smallest Place Between Second and Third Points				4 1/8	4 1/8	
H-4. Circumference at Smallest Place between Third and Fourth Points or half way between Third Point and Beam Tip if Fourth Point is missing				4 7/8	5	1/8
TOTALS				5 1/8	5 1/8	–
			24 7/8	97 7/8	96 3/8	8 4/8

ADD	Column 1	24 7/8	Exact locality where killed Randolph Co., Mo. 8 mi E Moberly
	Column 2	97 7/8	Date killed 11-21-71 By whom killed LARRY W. GIBSON
	Column 3	96 3/8	Present owner Same
	Total	218 4/8	Address
SUBTRACT Column 4		8 4/8	Guide's Name and Address
FINAL SCORE			Remarks: (Ment…

FIRST AWARD – NON-TYPICAL
15TH BIG GAME AWARDS

Taken in Johnston County, Oklahoma, in 1970, this extraordinary non-typical scoring 247-2/8 points remains the State Record to this day. Bill M. Foster was the hunter fortunate enough to harvest this magnificent buck. Foster used a 12-gauge shotgun from "70 steps" to take the trophy.

Foster's buck received a First Award at the 15th Big Game Awards Program held in Atlanta, Georgia in 1974.

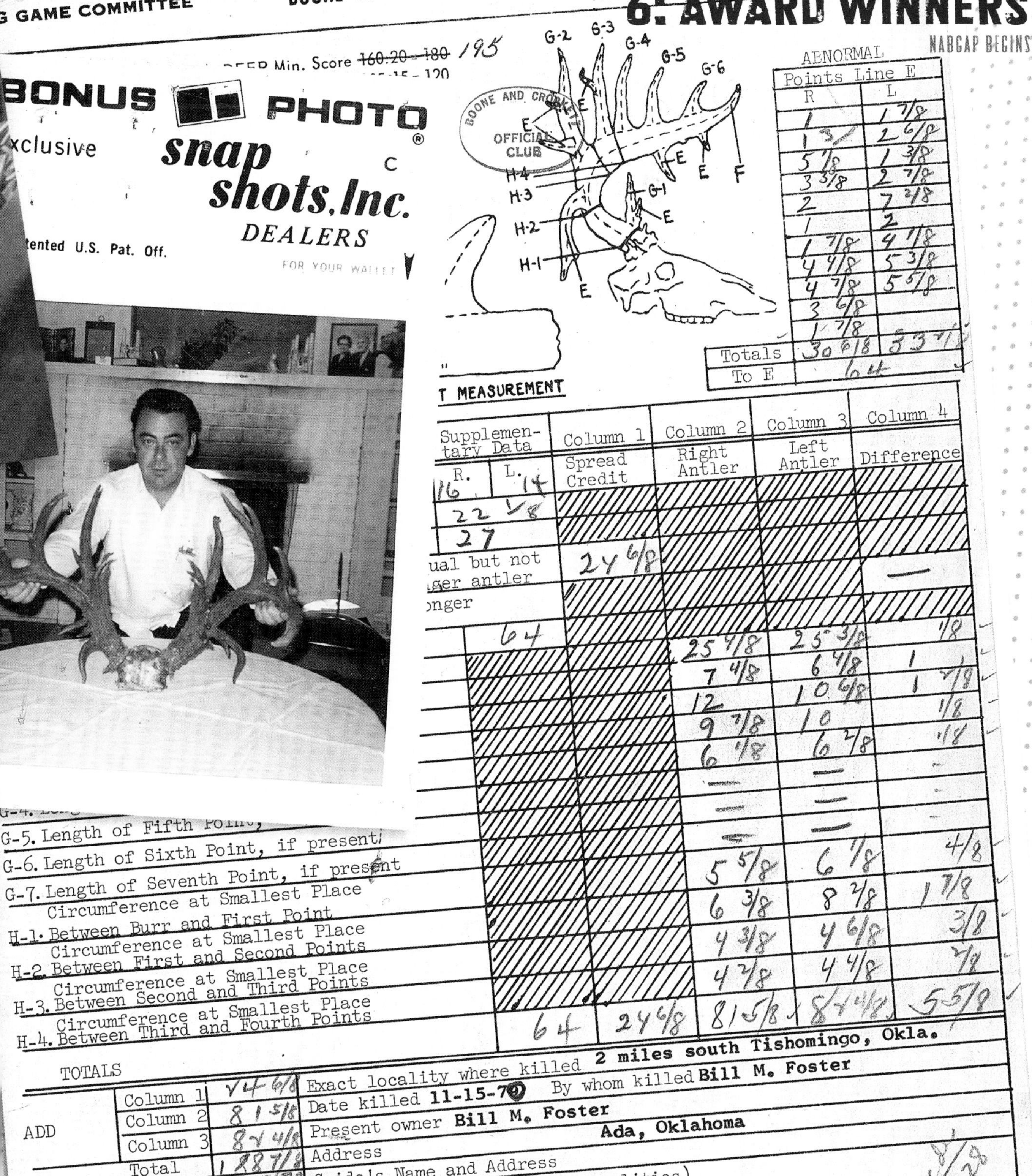
OFFICIAL SCORING
RECORDS OF NORTH AMERICAN
BIG GAME COMMITTEE
BOONE AND CROCKETT CLUB
Records of North American Big Game
c/o Carnegie Museum
4400 Forbes Ave. Pittsburgh, Pa. 15213
DEER Min. Score 160-20-180 195
BONUS PHOTO
Exclusive
snap shots, Inc.
DEALERS
Patented U.S. Pat. Off.
FOR YOUR WALLET
BOONE AND CROCKETT OFFICIAL CLUB
G-2 G-3 G-4 G-5 G-6
E F G-1 H-4 H-3 H-2 H-1
ABNORMAL
Points Line E
R L
1 1 7/8
1 3/8 2 6/8
5 1/8 1 3/8
3 3/8 2 7/8
2 7 2/8
1 2
1 7/8 4 1/8
4 4/8 5 3/8
4 7/8 5 5/8
3 6/8
1 7/8
Totals 30 6/8 33 2/8
To E 64
MEASUREMENT
Supplementary Data
R. L.
16 14
22 1/8
27
Column 1 Spread Credit
Column 2 Right Antler
Column 3 Left Antler
Column 4 Difference
24 6/8
64
25 4/8 25 3/8 1/8
7 4/8 6 4/8 1
12 10 6/8 1 2/8
9 7/8 10 1/8
6 1/8 6 2/8 1/8
G-5. Length of Fifth Point, if present
G-6. Length of Sixth Point, if present
G-7. Length of Seventh Point, if present
Circumference at Smallest Place
H-1. Between Burr and First Point 5 5/8 6 1/8 4/8
Circumference at Smallest Place
H-2. Between First and Second Points 6 3/8 8 2/8 1 7/8
Circumference at Smallest Place
H-3. Between Second and Third Points 4 3/8 4 6/8 3/8
Circumference at Smallest Place
H-4. Between Third and Fourth Points 4 2/8 4 4/8 2/8
TOTALS 64 24 6/8 81 5/8 84 4/8 5 5/8
Exact locality where killed 2 miles south Tishomingo, Okla.
ADD Column 1 24 6/8
Column 2 81 5/8
Column 3 84 4/8
Total 188 7/8
SUBTRACT Column 4 5 5/8
Result 183 2/8
Add Line E Total 64
FINAL SCORE 247 2/8
Date killed 11-15-79 By whom killed Bill M. Foster
Present owner Bill M. Foster
Address Ada, Oklahoma
Guide's Name and Address
Remarks: (Mention any abnormalities)

FIRST AWARD
NON-TYPICAL COUES' DEER
15TH BIG GAME AWARDS

Carlos G. Touche was hunting in the San Cayetano Mountains of Santa Cruz County, Arizona, when he came across this amazing trophy. In 1968, a shot from his 7mm at nearly 200 yards gave him this fine non-typical trophy scoring 128 points.

21

RECORDS OF NORTH AMERICAN BIG GAME COMMITTEE

OFFICIAL SCORING SYSTEM FOR NORTH AMERICAN BIG GAME TROPHIES

BOONE AND CROCKETT CLUB

Boone and Crockett Club
Records of North American Big Game C
c/o Carnegie Museum
4400 Forbes Ave. Pittsburgh, Pa.

☐ NON-TYPICAL WHITE

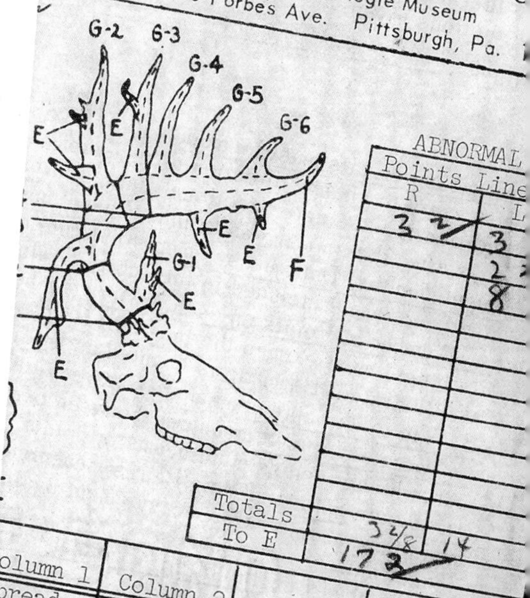

	Column 1 Spread Credit	Column 2 Right Antler	Column 3 Left Antler	Column 4 Difference
E. Total of Lengths of all Abnormal Points	16 2/8			
F. Length of Main Beam	17 3/8	18 6/	19 2/	
G-1. Length of First Point, if present		4 2/	3	3/8
G-2. Length of Second Point		7 1/8	6	1 2/8
G-3. Length of Third Point		8 5/8	5	1 7/8
G-4. Length of Fourth Point, if present			1 5/8	3 5/8
G-5. Length of Fifth Point, if present				1 5/8
G-6. Length of Sixth Point, if present				
G-7. Length of Seventh Point, if present				
Circumference at Smallest Place H-1. Between Burr and First Point		5 2/8	4 3/8	7/8
Circumference at Smallest Place H-2. Between First and Second Points		3 7/8	3 6/8	1/8
Circumference at Smallest Place H-3. Between Second and Third Points		4 1/8	3 4/8	5/8
Circumference at Smallest Place H-4. Between Third and Fourth Points		2 3/8	2 7/8	
TOTALS	17 2/8 / 16 2/8	54 7/8	49 2/8	9 5/8

Column 1	16 2/8
Column 2	54 7/
Column 3	49 2/8
Total	120 3/
SUBTRACT Column 4	9 5/
Result	110 6/8
Line E Total	17 2/
FINAL SCORE	[illegible]

Exact locality where killed **San Cayetano Mts., Santa Cruz, Ariz.**

Date killed **11-3-68** By whom killed **Carlos G. Touche**

Present owner **Carlos G. Touche**

Address **Tucson, Ariz.**

Guide's Name and Address **None**

Remarks: (Mention any

FIRST AWARD – TYPICAL
16TH BIG GAME AWARDS

On November 23, 1974, Thomas H. Dellwo had the good fortune of finding himself 75 yards away from the biggest buck of his life. A well-placed shot from his .30-06 landed him a 199-3/8 typical that would become the Montana State Record. Taken in Missoula County, Dellwo's giant typical was verified at the 16th Awards Judges Panel at the Denver Museum of Natural History in 1977.

1st place 16th

OFFICIAL SCORING SYSTEM FOR NORTH AMERICAN BIG GAME TROPHIES

RECORDS OF NORTH AMERICAN BIG GAME COMMITTEE

BOONE AND CROCKETT CLUB

RETURN TO:
N.A.B.G. Awards Program
1600 Rhode Island Ave.,
Washington, D.C. 20036

Minimum Score: Deer
Whitetail: Typical 170
Coues: Typical 110

WHITETAIL and COUES DEER

N.A.B.G. AWARDS PROGRAM 16 1974-1976

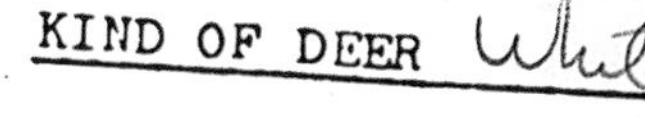
KIND OF DEER Whit[...]

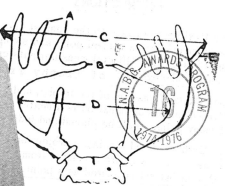

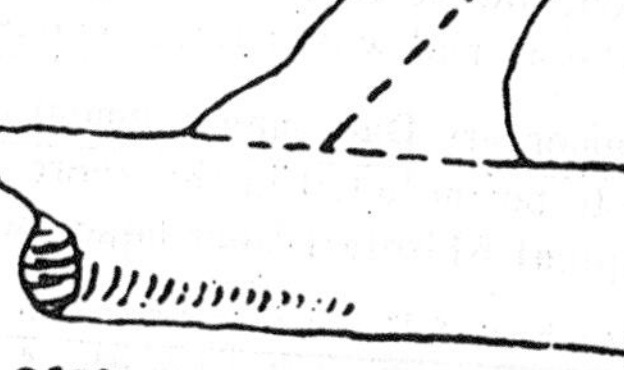
DETAIL OF POINT MEASUREMENT

	Supplementary Data R.	Supplementary Data L.	Column 1 Spread Credit	Column 2 Right Antler	Column 3 Left Antler	Column 4 Difference
	6	7				
	13 4/8					
	24 3/8					
equal but not longer antler			22 3/8			
ds longer						
ts						
						1 1/8
				27 3/8	27 4/8	1/8
				5 7/8	6 3/8	4/8
				11 1/8	9 5/8	1 4/8
				12 1/8	12 1/8	—
				10 1/8	10 1/8	—
				6 4/8	6	4/8
				—	—	—
				—	—	—
				4 4/8	4 6/8	2/8
				4	4	—
				4 7/8	5	1/8
ird and oint and ssing				4 4/8	4 4/8	—
			22 3/8	91	90	4

ADD	Column 1	22 3/8	Exact locality where killed Missoula Co., Mont.
	Column 2	91	Date killed Nov 23, 1974 By whom killed Tom Dellwo
	Column 3	90	Present owner Bass Pro Shops
	Total	203 3/8	Address
SUBTRACT Column 4		4	Guide's Name and Address
FINAL SCORE		199 3/8	Remarks: (Mention any abnormalities)

SECOND AWARD – TYPICAL
16TH BIG GAME AWARDS

At 198-2/8 points, Dennis P. Finger's 1974 typical from Nemaha County stands as the largest hunter-taken typical whitetail in Kansas history, and second overall to a picked-up head. It received the Second Award at the 16th Awards Program held at the Denver Museum of Natural History. Dennis used a .25-06 to bring this buck down at 130 yards. Perhaps the most outstanding feature on this deer are his eye guards, which measure 12-5/8 and 12-4/8 inches.

2nd place 16th PLW

GAME TROPHIES

RETURN TO:
A.B.G. Awards Program
600 Rhode Island Ave., N.W.
ashington, D.C. 20036

KIND OF DEER Whitetail
ATYPICAL

E

DETAIL OF POINT MEASUREMENT

…US PROGRAM 16 1974-1976

	lumn 1	Column 2	Column 3	Column 4
	read edit	Right Antler	Left Antler	Difference
	20 2/8			
				4 6/8
		27 7/8	26 7/8	0 6/8
		12 5/8	12 4/8	0 1/8
G-2. Length of Second …		13 6/8	14 4/8	0 6/8
G-3. Length of Third Point		11 7/8	11 6/8	0 1/8
G-4. Length of Fourth Point, if present		6 6/8	8 2/8	1 4/8
G-5. Length of Fifth Point, if present		1 6/8	4 5/8	2 7/8
G-6. Length of Sixth Point, if present				
G-7. Length of Seventh Point, if present				
Circumference at Smallest Place H-1. Between Burr and First Point		5 0/8	5 0/8	—
Circumference at Smallest Place H-2. Between First and Second Points		4 3/8	4 3/8	—
Circumference at Smallest Place H-3. Between Second and Third Points		4 3/8	4 5/8	0 2/8
Circumference at Smallest Place between Third and Fourth Points or half way between Third Point and H-4. Beam Tip if Fourth Point is missing		4 2/8	4 3/8	0 1/8
TOTALS	20 2/8	92 3/8	96 7/8	11 2/8

ADD	Column 1	20 2/8	Exact locality where killed Nemaha Co., Kan
	Column 2	92 3/8	Date killed 12/10/74 By whom killed Dennis P. Finger
	Column 3	96 7/8	Present owner DENNIS P FINGER
	Total	209 4/8	Address
SUBTRACT Column 4		11 2/8	Guide's Name and Address
			Remarks: (Mention any abnormalities)

2nd place 16th comp.

OFFICIAL SCORING SYSTEM FOR NORTH AMERICAN BIG GAME TROPHIES

OF NORTH AMERICAN
GAME COMMITTEE

BOONE AND CROCKETT CLUB

Boone and Crockett Club
Records of North American Big Game Committee
c/o Carnegie Museum
4400 Forbes Ave. Pittsburgh, Pa. 15213

TYPICAL WHITETAIL DEER

Taken with a T-square

ABNORMAL Points Line E		
R	L	
4 0	2 1	3 0
1 5	2 7	3 6
11 6	1 2	1 0
8 2	6 4	
7 4	1 0	
3 6	2 4	
1 3	6 1	
3 4	6 4	
3 5	5 2	
2 7	1 4	
2 0	1 1	
Totals 73 5/	44 6/8	
To E 118 3/8		

16
1974-1976

Column 1 Spread Credit	Column 2 Right Antler	Column 3 Left Antler	Column 4 Difference
19 2/8			
	20 6/8	24 6	4 0
	8 3	4 1	4 2
	9 1	10 4	1 3
	6 4	7 3	0 7/8
	5 3	6 3	1 0
		5 7	5 7
	—	3 5	3 5
	—	—	
	6 4	5 3	1 1
	4 7	5 2	0 3
	6 3	6 6	0 3
	5 4	9 6	4 2
118 3	14 2	73 3	89 6	27 1/8

ADD	Column 1	14 2/
	Column 2	73 3/
	Column 3	89 6/
	Total	177 3/8
SUBTRACT Column 4		27 1/8
	Result	150 2/8
Add Line E Total		118 3/
FINAL SCORE		268 5/8

Exact locality where killed
Date killed 11-9-74 By whom killed Mitchell A. Vakoch
Present owner Bass Pro Shops F&W Mus.
Address
Guide's Name and Address
Remarks: (Mention any abnormalities)

SECOND AWARD – NON-TYPICAL
16TH BIG GAME AWARDS

This unique non-typical received the Second Award at the 16th Awards in Denver. Scoring 268-5/8 points, this buck was taken by Mitchell A. Vakoch, in Norman County, Minnesota, in 1974. A 12-gauge shotgun slug from 50 feet yielded this great trophy for Vakoch. Currently the Minnesota State Record, this historical deer has 41 scorable points and a staggering 50-3/8 inches of mass measurements.

3rd place 16th ov pub

...ME TROPHIES

RETURN TO:
...B.G. Awards Program
... Rhode Island Ave., N.W.
...ington, D.C. 20036

5 7/8
1

ABNORMAL Points Line E	
R	L
2	1 7/8
1 1/8	5
1 1/8	2 3/8
3 3/8	5 3/8
4 5/8	2
7	2 3/8
1 2/8	1 7/8
2 7/8	1 7/8
4	2 6/8
3 6/8	2
1 7/8	2 2/8
Totals 2 7/8	
To E 1 3/8	(29 6/8)

(37 2/8) 67

	...lumn 2	Column 3	Column 4
	...ight ...ntler	Left Antler	Difference
			—
	...5/8	23 5/8	2 0/
	8	7 4/8	4/8
			—
	12 2/8	12 2/8	1/8
	11 2/8	11 3/8	3/8
...gth of Third Point	7 6/8	7 3/8	4/8
...gth of Fourth Point, if present	2	2 4/8	
...gth of Fifth Point, if present	—	—	
...gth of Sixth Point, if present	—	—	
...gth of Seventh Point, if present	4 6/8	4 4/8	2/8
...rcumference at Smallest Place ...tween Burr and First Point	4 4/8	4 6/8	2/8
...rcumference at Smallest Place ...tween First and Second Points	5 5/8	6	3/8
...rcumference at Smallest Place ...tween Second and Third Points	5	5 5/8	5/8
...rcumference at Smallest Place ...tween Third and Fourth Points	86 6/8	85 4/8	5
...OTALS 73 7/8	16 2/8		

		Exact locality where killed *Elkhorn, Man.*
Column 1	16 2/8	Date killed *11-22-73* By whom killed *Harvey Olsen*
Column 2	86 6/8	Present owner *Harvey Olsen*
Column 3	85 4/8	Address
Total	188 4/8	Guide's Name and Address
...RACT Column 4	5	Remarks: (Mention any abnormalities)
Result	183 4/8	

THIRD AWARD – NON-TYPICAL
16TH BIG GAME AWARDS

Harvey Olsen used a 6mm to harvest Manitoba's third-largest, non-typical whitetail. Olsen was hunting near Elkhorn, Manitoba, on November 22, 1973, when he and his 257-3/8-point buck met at 60 yards. The deer has a total of 38 scorable points and 73-7/8 inches worth of abnormal point lengths. Olsen's buck received the Third Award for non-typical whitetail deer at the 16th Awards Program.

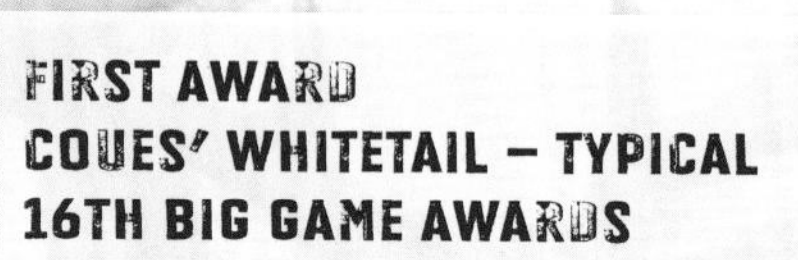

FIRST AWARD
COUES' WHITETAIL – TYPICAL
16TH BIG GAME AWARDS

T. Reed Scott's typical Coues' deer, which scores 121-1/8 points, won the First Award at the 16th Big Game Awards Program held in 1977. Scott was hunting in the Catalina Mountains of Pima County, Arizona, on November 27, 1975, when he harvested this buck from 200 yards with his .30-06.

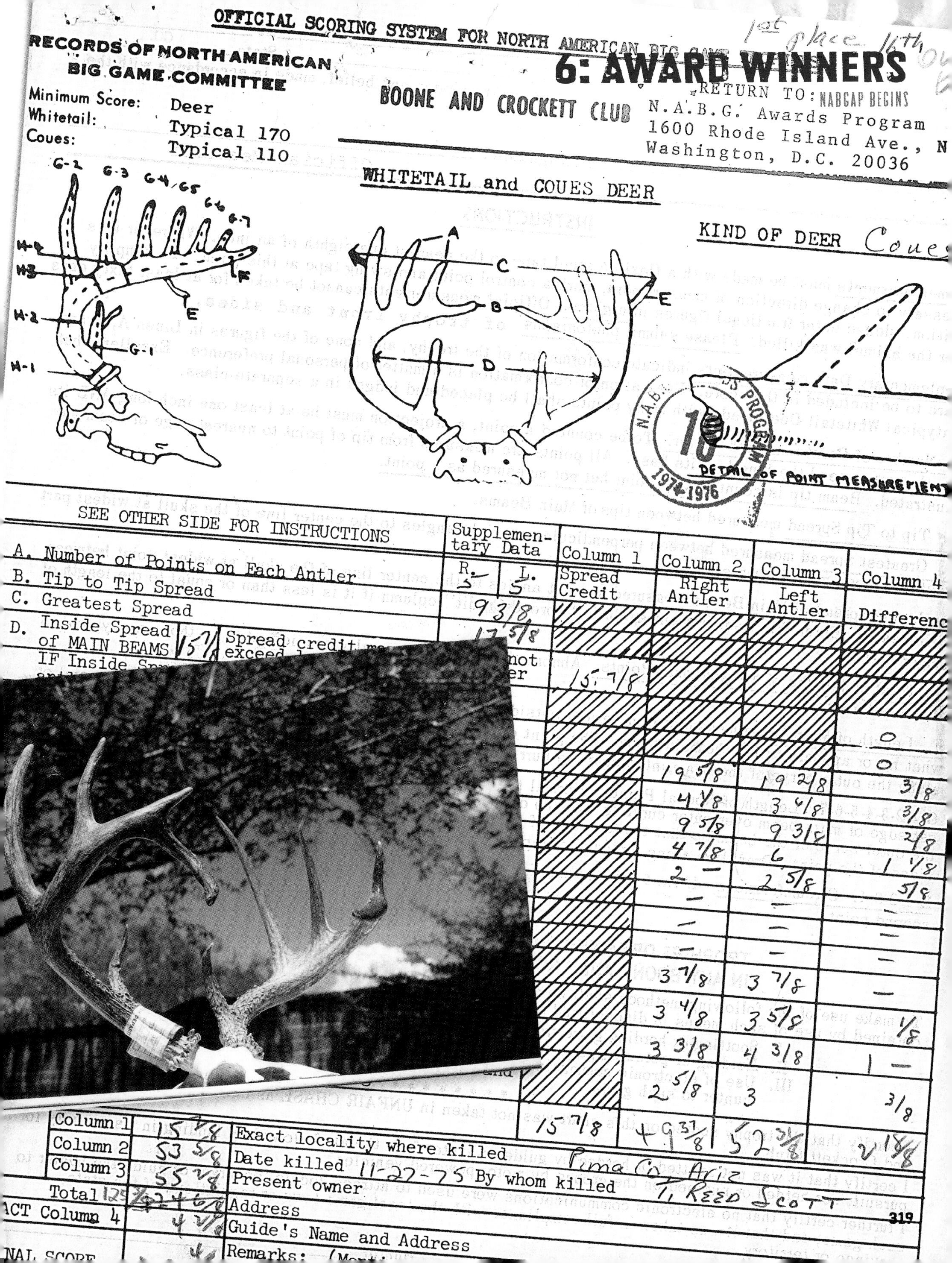

OFFICIAL SCORING SYSTEM FOR NORTH AMERICAN BIG GAME TROPHIES

1st place 11th

RECORDS OF NORTH AMERICAN BIG GAME COMMITTEE

BOONE AND CROCKETT CLUB

RETURN TO: N.A.B.G. Awards Program
1600 Rhode Island Ave., N
Washington, D.C. 20036

NABCAP BEGINS

Minimum Score:	Deer
Whitetail:	Typical 170
Coues:	Typical 110

WHITETAIL and COUES DEER

KIND OF DEER Coues

SEE OTHER SIDE FOR INSTRUCTIONS

	Supplementary Data R.	Supplementary Data L.	Column 1 Spread Credit	Column 2 Right Antler	Column 3 Left Antler	Column 4 Difference
A. Number of Points on Each Antler	5	5				
B. Tip to Tip Spread	9 3/8					
C. Greatest Spread	17 5/8					
D. Inside Spread of MAIN BEAMS 15 7/8 — Spread credit may ... exceed ...			15 7/8			
IF Inside Spr... ... not ... er						
						0
						0
				19 5/8	19 2/8	3/8
				4 1/8	3 4/8	3/8
				9 5/8	9 3/8	2/8
				4 7/8	6	1 1/8
				2 —	2 5/8	5/8
				—	—	—
				—	—	—
				—	—	—
				3 7/8	3 7/8	—
				3 4/8	3 5/8	1/8
				3 3/8	4 3/8	1 —
				2 5/8	3	3/8
			15 7/8	+ 9 37/8	52 31/8	2 1/8

Column 1	15 7/8	Exact locality where killed	Pima Co. Ariz
Column 2	53 5/8	Date killed 11-27-75	By whom killed T. Reed Scott
Column 3	55 7/8	Present owner	
Total	125 3/8 ~~124 6/8~~	Address	
SUBTRACT Column 4	4 2/8	Guide's Name and Address	
FINAL SCORE		Remarks: (Ment...	

WHITETAIL DEER — NON-TYPICAL ANTLERS — 1st Award
Score — 238-2/8
Length — (R) 27-1/8 (L) 26-2/8
Circumference — (R) 5-5/8 (L) 5-7/8
Points — (R) 12 (L) 17
Inside Spread — 21-4/8
Locality — Bay County, Michigan — 1976
Hunter — Paul Mickey

WHITETAIL DEER — NON-TYPICAL ANTLERS — 2nd Award
Score — 216-3/8
Length — (R) 27-3/8 (L) 24-6/8
Circumference — (R) 4-6/8 (L) 5-3/8
Points — (R) 14 (L) 14
Inside Spread — 23
Locality — Carroll County, Mississippi — 1978
Hunter — Mark Hathcock

FIRST AWARD – NON-TYPICAL
17TH AWARDS PROGRAM
Not only did Paul Mickey's 238-2/8 non-typical receive the First Award at the 17th Awards Program in Columbia, Missouri, it also became the Michigan State Record. Taken in Bay County in 1976, Mickey used a .30-06 at 200 yards to bag the state's biggest buck.

Hunter — Olaf P. Anderson
Owner — Burton L. Anderson

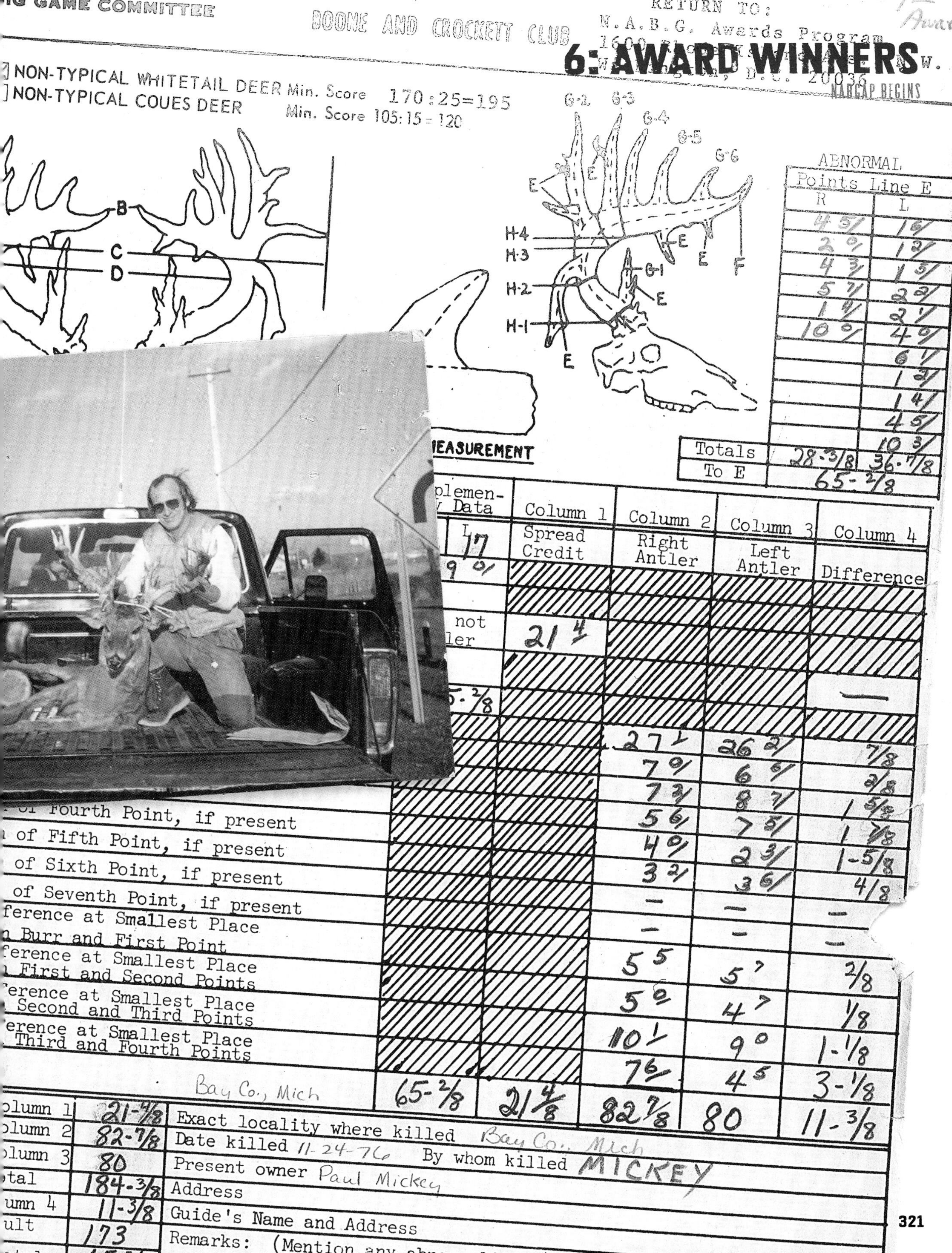

IG GAME COMMITTEE — BOONE AND CROCKETT CLUB

RETURN TO:
N.A.B.G. Awards Program
1600 ...
W..., D.C. 20036 ... N.W.

NABCAP BEGINS

[ ] NON-TYPICAL WHITETAIL DEER Min. Score 170:25=195
[ ] NON-TYPICAL COUES DEER Min. Score 105:15=120

ABNORMAL Points Line E	
R	L
4 5/	1 6/
2 0/	1 2/
4 3/	1 5/
5 7/	2 2/
1 4/	2 1/
10 0/	4 0/
	6 1/
	1 2/
	1 4/
	4 5/
	10 3/
Totals 28-3/8	36-7/8
To E 65-2/8	

...EASUREMENT

	...plemen-...y Data	Column 1 Spread Credit	Column 2 Right Antler	Column 3 Left Antler	Column 4 Difference
	L 17				
	9 0/				
...not ...ler		21 4			
	5-2/8				—
			27 1/	26 2/	7/8
			7 0/	6 0/	2/8
			7 2/	8 7/	1 5/8
... of Fourth Point, if present			5 6/	7 5/	1 7/8
... of Fifth Point, if present			4 0/	2 3/	1-5/8
... of Sixth Point, if present			3 2/	3 6/	4/8
... of Seventh Point, if present			—	—	—
...ference at Smallest Place ...n Burr and First Point			—	—	—
...ference at Smallest Place ...n First and Second Points			5 5	5 7	2/8
...erence at Smallest Place ... Second and Third Points			5 6	4 7	1/8
...erence at Smallest Place ... Third and Fourth Points			10 1	9 0	1-1/8
			7 6	4 5	3-1/8
Bay Co., Mich	65-2/8	21 4/8	82 7/8	80	11-3/8

...olumn 1	21-4/8	Exact locality where killed Bay Co., Mich
...olumn 2	82-7/8	Date killed 11-24-76 By whom killed MICKEY
...olumn 3	80	Present owner Paul Mickey
...tal	184-3/8	Address
...umn 4	11-3/8	Guide's Name and Address
...ult	173	Remarks: (Mention any abnormalities)
...otal	65-2/8	

SECOND AWARD — NON-TYPICAL 17TH BIG GAME AWARDS

With 14 points per side, this non-typical, scoring 217-5/8 points, is Mississippi's sixth-largest buck. Mark T. Hathcock was the successful hunter, taking the buck in Carroll County in January of 1978. Hathcock's buck received the Second Award for non-typical whitetail deer at the 17th Awards Banquet.

The 17th Awards Judges Panel is pictured in background. Standing from left to right: Wm. Harold Nesbitt – Coordinator, Scott Showalter, Philip L. Wright, Dean A. Murphy, Frank Cook, Bernard A. Fashingbauer, William I. Crump, and kneeling are Glen C. Sanderson, left, and Glenn St. Charles – Chairman.

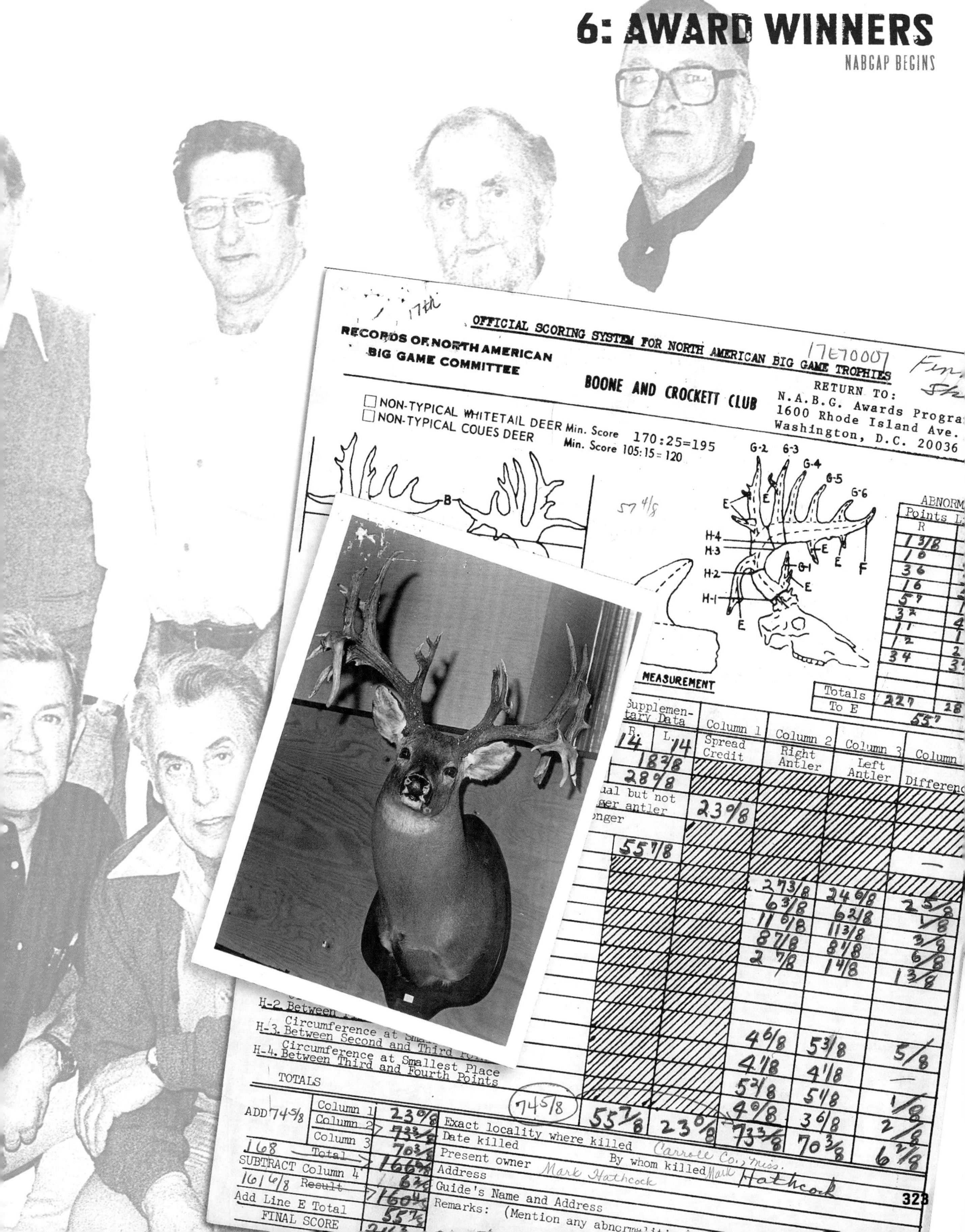

17th

OFFICIAL SCORING SYSTEM FOR NORTH AMERICAN BIG GAME TROPHIES

17E70007

RECORDS OF NORTH AMERICAN BIG GAME COMMITTEE

BOONE AND CROCKETT CLUB

RETURN TO:
N.A.B.G. Awards Progra
1600 Rhode Island Ave.
Washington, D.C. 20036

☐ NON-TYPICAL WHITETAIL DEER Min. Score 170:25=195
☐ NON-TYPICAL COUES DEER Min. Score 105:15=120

57 4/8

ABNORM Points R
1 3/8
10
36
16
57
32
11
12
34
Totals 227
To E 557

MEASUREMENT

Supplementary Data R.	L.	Column 1 Spread Credit	Column 2 Right Antler	Column 3 Left Antler	Column 4 Difference
14	14				
18 2/8					
28 4/8					
...ual but not ...ger antler ...onger		23 4/8			
55 7/8					
					—
			27 3/8	24 6/8	2 5/8
			6 3/8	6 2/8	1/8
			11 6/8	11 3/8	3/8
			8 7/8	8 1/8	6/8
			2 7/8	1 4/8	1 3/8
H-2. Between ...					
Circumference at Sma... H-3. Between Second and Third Poi...			4 6/8	5 3/8	5/8
Circumference at Smallest Place H-4. Between Third and Fourth Points			4 1/8	4 1/8	—
			5 2/8	5 1/8	1/8
			4 0/8	3 6/8	2/8
TOTALS		55 7/8	23 0/8	73 3/8	70 3/8	6 2/8

74 5/8

ADD 74 5/8	Column 1	23 4/8
	Column 2	73 3/8
	Column 3	70 3/8
168	Total	166 [illegible]
SUBTRACT Column 4		6 2/8
161 6/8	Result	160 [illegible]
Add Line E Total		55 7/8
FINAL SCORE		2[illegible]

Exact locality where killed Carroll Co., Miss.
Date killed By whom killed Mark Hathcock
Present owner Mark Hathcock
Address
Guide's Name and Address
Remarks: (Mention any abnormali...

OFFICIAL SCORING SYSTEM FOR NORTH AMERICAN BIG GAME TROPHIES

RECORDS OF NORTH AMERICAN BIG GAME COMMITTEE

BOONE AND CROCKETT CLUB

RETURN TO:
N.A.B.G. Awards Program
1600 Rhode Island Ave., N.W.
Washington, D.C. 20036

DP17000943

☐ NON-TYPICAL WHITETAIL DEER Min. Score 170:25=195
☐ NON-TYPICAL COUES DEER Min. Score 105:15=120

DETAIL OF POINT MEASUREMENT

ABNORMAL Points Line E R	L
1¼	1¼
5	3 5/8
7¼	7¼
6–	1 2/8
5¼	3 2/8
Totals 24 6/8	17 1/8
To E 41 7/8	

CERTIFICATE OF MERIT –NON-TYPICAL
17TH BIG GAME AWARDS

Harvested in 1886, this non-typical, scoring 232-1/8 points, is one of the oldest trophies listed in the Boone and Crockett Club's records books. Olaf P. Anderson was hunting in McLean County, North Dakota, after arriving by train and horseback, when he encountered this huge deer.

His grandson Burton L. Anderson entered the trophy, which received a Certificate of Merit at the 17th Big Game Awards Banquet.

	Supplementary Data R	L	Column 1 Spread Credit	Column 2 Right Antler	Column 3 Left Antler	Column 4 Difference
A. Number of Points on Each Antler		11				
B. Tip to Tip Spread	6 3/8					
C. Greatest Spread	24 5/8					
D. Inside Spread of MAIN BEAMS — Spread credit may equal but not exceed length of longer antler			16 4/8			
IF Inside Spread of Main Beams exceeds longer antler length, enter difference						–
E. Total of Lengths of all Abnormal Points	41 7/8					
F. Length of Main Beam				24 5/8	24 5/8	–
G-1. Length of First Point, if present				6 6/8	5 2/8	1 4/8
G-2. Length of Second Point				12 1/8	11 2/8	7/8
G-3. Length of Third Point				9 7/8	11 5/8	1 6/8
G-4. Length of Fourth Point, if present				9 –	10 –	1
G-5. Length of Fifth Point, if present				5 4/8	6 7/8	1 3/8
G-6. Length of Sixth Point, if present						
G-7. Length of Seventh Point, if present						
Circumference at Smallest Place H-1. Between Burr and First Point				4 7/8	4 6/8	1/8
Circumference at Smallest Place H-2. Bet…				4 6/8	4 7/8	1/8
Cir… H-3. Bet…				5 4/8	5 5/8	1/8
Cir… H-4. Bet…				6 4/8	6 3/8	1/8
TOT…	41 7/8		16 4/8	89 4/8	91 2/8	7 6/8

Owner: **Bass Pro Shops**
2500 E. Kearney
Springfield, MO 65898
417/873-5237

ADD	Column 1	16 4/8	Exact locality where killed Ft. Stevenson, N.D.
	Column 2	89 4/8	Date killed 1886 By whom killed Olaf P. Anderson
	Column 3	91 2/8	Present owner ~~Burton L. Anderson~~ Head
	Total	197 2/8	Address ~~Wat Miller~~ see attached
SUBTRACT	Column 4	7 6/8	Guide's Name and Address
	Result	190 2/8	Remarks: (Mention any abnormalities)
Add Line E Total		41 7/8	
FINAL SCORE		232 1/8	

OFFICIAL SCORING SYSTEM FOR NORTH AMERICAN BIG GAME TROPHIES

RECORDS OF NORTH AMERICAN BIG GAME COMMITTEE

BOONE AND CROCKETT CLUB

Boone and Crockett Club
Records of North American Big Game Committee
c/o Carnegie Museum
4400 Forbes Ave. Pittsburgh, Pa. 15213

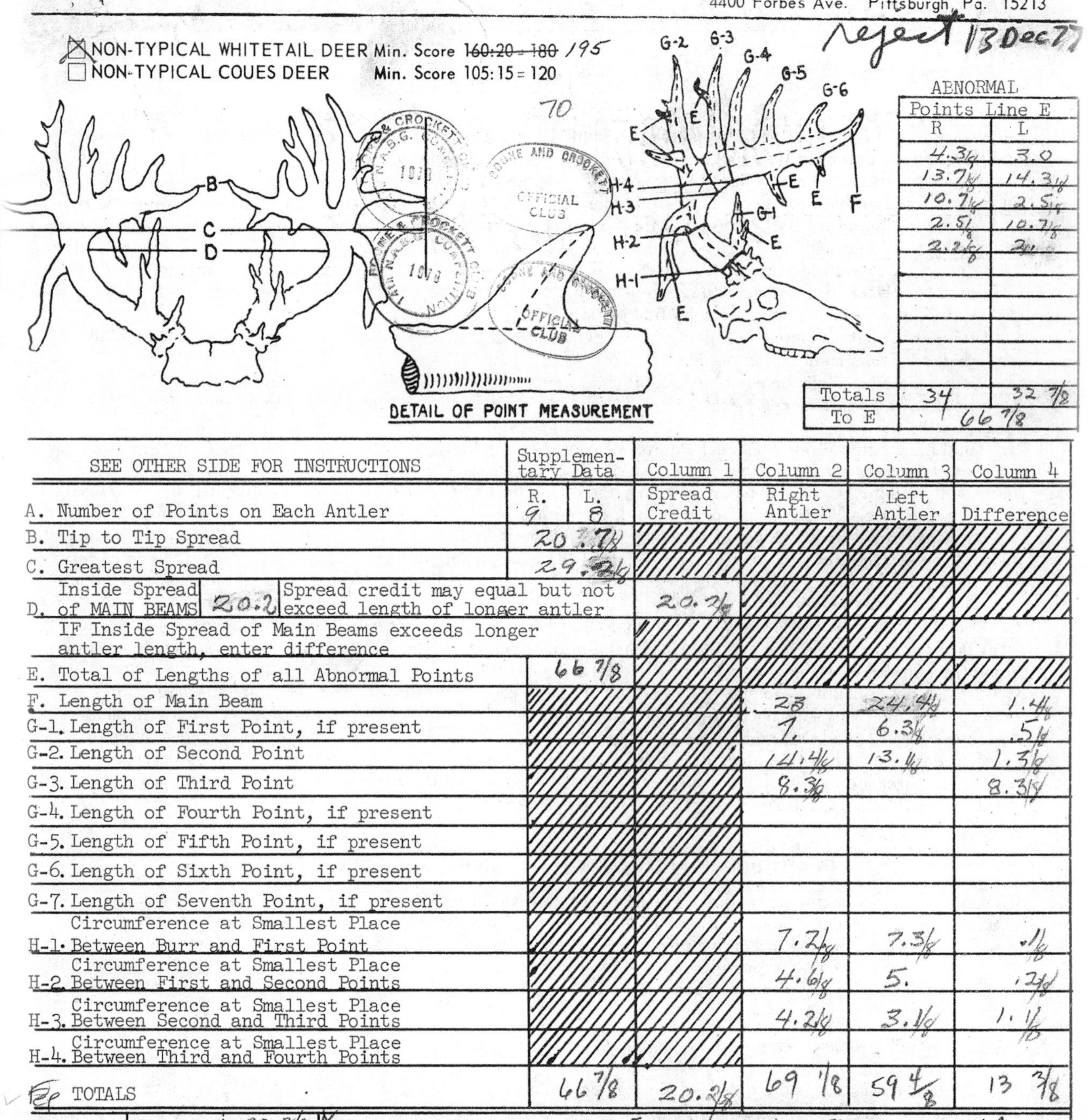

Reject 13 DEC 77

[X] NON-TYPICAL WHITETAIL DEER Min. Score ~~160:20 = 180~~ 195
[ ] NON-TYPICAL COUES DEER Min. Score 105:15 = 120

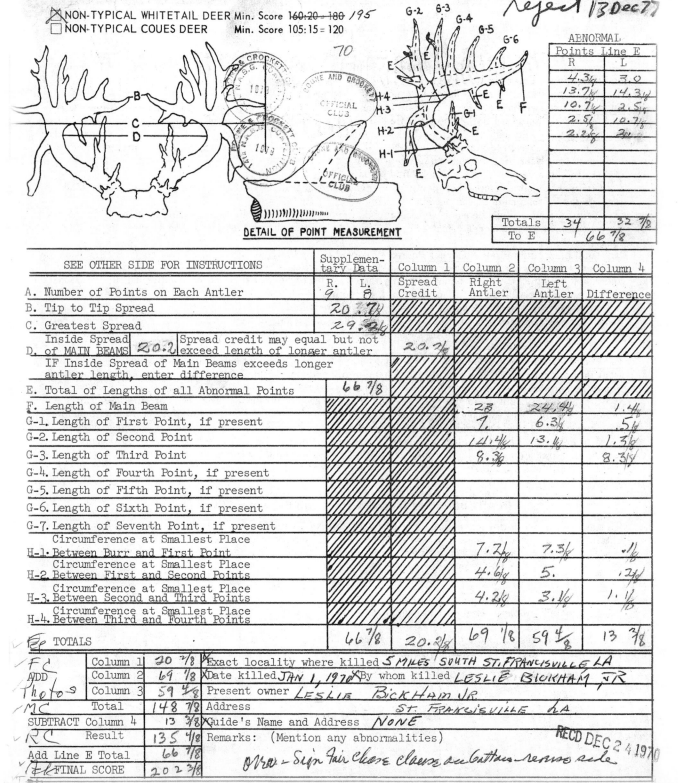

70

ABNORMAL Points Line E	
R	L
4.3/8	3.0
13.7/8	14.3/8
10.7/8	2.5/8
2.5/8	10.7/8
2.2/8	2.0
Totals 34	32 7/8
To E	66 7/8

SEE OTHER SIDE FOR INSTRUCTIONS	Supplementary Data R.	Supplementary Data L.	Column 1 Spread Credit	Column 2 Right Antler	Column 3 Left Antler	Column 4 Difference
A. Number of Points on Each Antler	9	8				
B. Tip to Tip Spread	20.7/8					
C. Greatest Spread	29.2/8					
D. Inside Spread of MAIN BEAMS 20.2 — Spread credit may equal but not exceed length of longer antler			20.2/8			
IF Inside Spread of Main Beams exceeds longer antler length, enter difference						
E. Total of Lengths of all Abnormal Points	66 7/8					
F. Length of Main Beam				23	24.4/8	1.4/8
G-1. Length of First Point, if present				7.	6.3/8	.5/8
G-2. Length of Second Point				14.4/8	13.1/8	1.3/8
G-3. Length of Third Point				8.3/8		8.3/8
G-4. Length of Fourth Point, if present						
G-5. Length of Fifth Point, if present						
G-6. Length of Sixth Point, if present						
G-7. Length of Seventh Point, if present						
H-1. Circumference at Smallest Place Between Burr and First Point				7.2/8	7.3/8	.1/8
H-2. Circumference at Smallest Place Between First and Second Points				4.6/8	5.	.2/8
H-3. Circumference at Smallest Place Between Second and Third Points				4.2/8	3.1/8	1.1/8
H-4. Circumference at Smallest Place Between Third and Fourth Points						
TOTALS	66 7/8		20.2/8	69 1/8	59 4/8	13 3/8

ADD Column 1	20 2/8	Exact locality where killed 5 MILES SOUTH ST. FRANCISVILLE LA
Column 2	69 1/8	Date killed JAN 1, 1970 By whom killed LESLIE BICKHAM, JR
Column 3	59 4/8	Present owner LESLIE BICKHAM JR.
Total	148 7/8	Address ST. FRANCISVILLE LA
SUBTRACT Column 4	13 3/8	Guide's Name and Address NONE
Result	135 4/8	Remarks: (Mention any abnormalities)
Add Line E Total	66 7/8	
FINAL SCORE	202 3/8	Over - Sign fair chase clause on bottom reverse side

FC Photos MC RC

RECD DEC 24 1970

6: CORRESPONDENCE FROM THE VAULTS

BICKMAN'S THREE-ANTLERED DEER

In December of 1970, B&C received the following letter and score chart initiating the entry process for a big non-typical taken in Louisiana. For several years this buck was officially listed in B&C's records books.

LESLIE BICKHAM, JR.
ROUTE 5-B BOX 930
PHONE 635-3942
ST. FRANCISVILLE, LOUISIANA 70775

December 16, 1970

Elmer M. Rusten, M.D.
c/o Doctors Building Pharmacy
82 South 9th Street
Minneapolis, Minnesota 55402

Doctor Rusten,

We certainly do appreciate your taking the time and trouble to measure Leslie's deer head for the Boone and Crockett Club records. As of this evening it has not returned but we anticipate no difficulties with the trip home.

Leslie signed the form which you sent him, but just for a more complete record, I shall give you a few additional facts.

Deer was killed January 1, 1970 about 30 minutes before dark while still hunting. The location was approximately 5 miles south of St. Francisville, La., 25 miles north of Baton Rouge, and 2 miles east of the Mississippi River in West Feliciana Parish. It was killed with a model 742 Remington 30-06 automatic with a Weaver model K4 scope. The weight of the deer was 265 pounds when field dressed.

Enclosed you will find the ten dollars requested by your last letter. Also, we are wondering if there is some sort of magazine or publication of the Club which Leslie may subscribe to or some sort of guidebook which explains the purpose of the Club with a list of the records set in each class?

My husband has an uncle who lives in Pittsburg whom we have never been able to visit. Needless to say we are all keeping our fingers crossed hoping that Leslie's trophy will merit the award for his class and he will be entitled to go to Pennsylvania.

Many thanks again for your patience and help.

Sincerely,
Nancy Bickham
Mrs. Leslie Bickham, Jr.

Outdoor Writers

A non-profit pro

307-9 Outdoors Bldg., Colu

Don G. Cullimo

May 4, 19

Boone & Crockett Cl
c/o Carnegie Museum
4400 Forbes Avenue,
Pittsburg, Pa. 1521

Sirs;

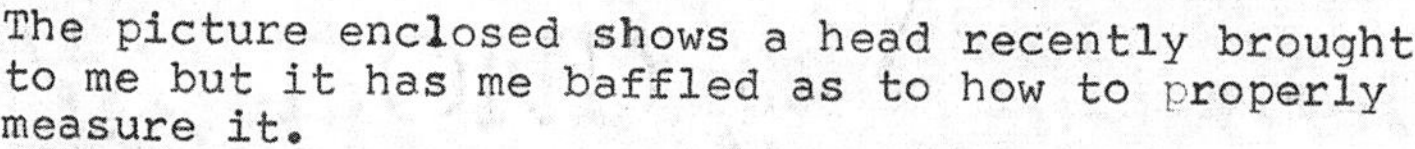

The picture enclosed shows a head recently brought to me but it has me baffled as to how to properly measure it.

As I taped it the head went 122 6/8:92 6/8 for a total of 215 4/8. BUT I know I made one error in not measuring the circumference of each horn between the only typical point and the tip of the main beam - this would add points to the typical score. Also, I'm not certain as to whether or not the circumference of the third horn between the point and the tip should be measured and added to the non-typical score.

If you can help me I'd certainly appreciate it. If you think the head would score high enough to make it feasible for the owner to ship it to you for certification he is willing to do it.

The black lines I have marked on the horns show the portion measured as typical - all the other was marked as non-typical. The "X'S" are the circumferences I did not measure but now believe should be included.

I'd appreciate hearing from you.

Sincerely,

Hurley Campbell

Hurley Campbell

To Dr. Ruster
5/7/70

RECD MAY 6 1970

16 September 1976

LZ S

Dr. Philip Wright
Department of Zoology
University of Montana
Missoula, Montana 59801

Dear Phil:

I'm enclosing copies of two score charts and photos for what appears clearly to be a three-antlered whitetail. Perhaps you are familiar with this one, since the scoring that appears in the current records book was done by Rusty.

My question is simple. Is it really correct to include this trophy in the archives and records book? I personally dont't think so since there is an obvious lack of overall symmetry caused by the third antler. The distinct patch of hide and hair between the right and middle antlers weakens the possible interpretation that the middle antler is an offshoot of the right antler. It does appear from the score chart that Rusty treated it this way.

My feeling is that this trophy is one of those freaks that the scoring system was not designed to recognize. What do you think? By the way, the black lines on the photo were apparently put there by Rusty to show his interpretation of this trophy.

Sincerely,

Wm. H. Nesbitt
Coordinator

DISCUSSION ABOUT THREE-ANTLERED DEER

During an audit of the records files in 1976, the deer came up for discussion due to the third antler projecting out from the deer's forehead. Wm. Harold Nesbitt wrote, "My feeling is that this is one of those freaks that the scoring system was not designed to recognize." Members of the Records Committee agreed, feeling that to allow those rare deer in would give them an unfair advantage over the vast majority of animals that only grow two normal antlers. The trophy was removed from the records. Nonetheless, this great buck remains an incredible trophy any hunter would be excited to take.

OFFICIAL THREE-ANTLERED DEER POLICY

Deer with three (or more) antlers are not eligible for entry in the Club's records archives or for listing in the records books. The Club's scoring system was designed to recognize massiveness and symmetry. Numerous measurements are taken to account for massiveness of a trophy. Symmetry is taken care of by comparing the measurements of one antler with the same measurements on the opposite antler and deducting the differences. The system was not designed to record measurements of a third antler.

This policy applies to a third antler that is completely separated from either of the other antlers with flesh and hide and has its own pedicle and is shed separately from the other two antlers each winter. In some cases the third antler may actually arise from one of the two normal pedicles, but it is shed separately from the other two normal antlers. This policy does not apply to normal points that branch off one of the antlers near the burr. Several of these trophies have been entered in the non-typical categories.

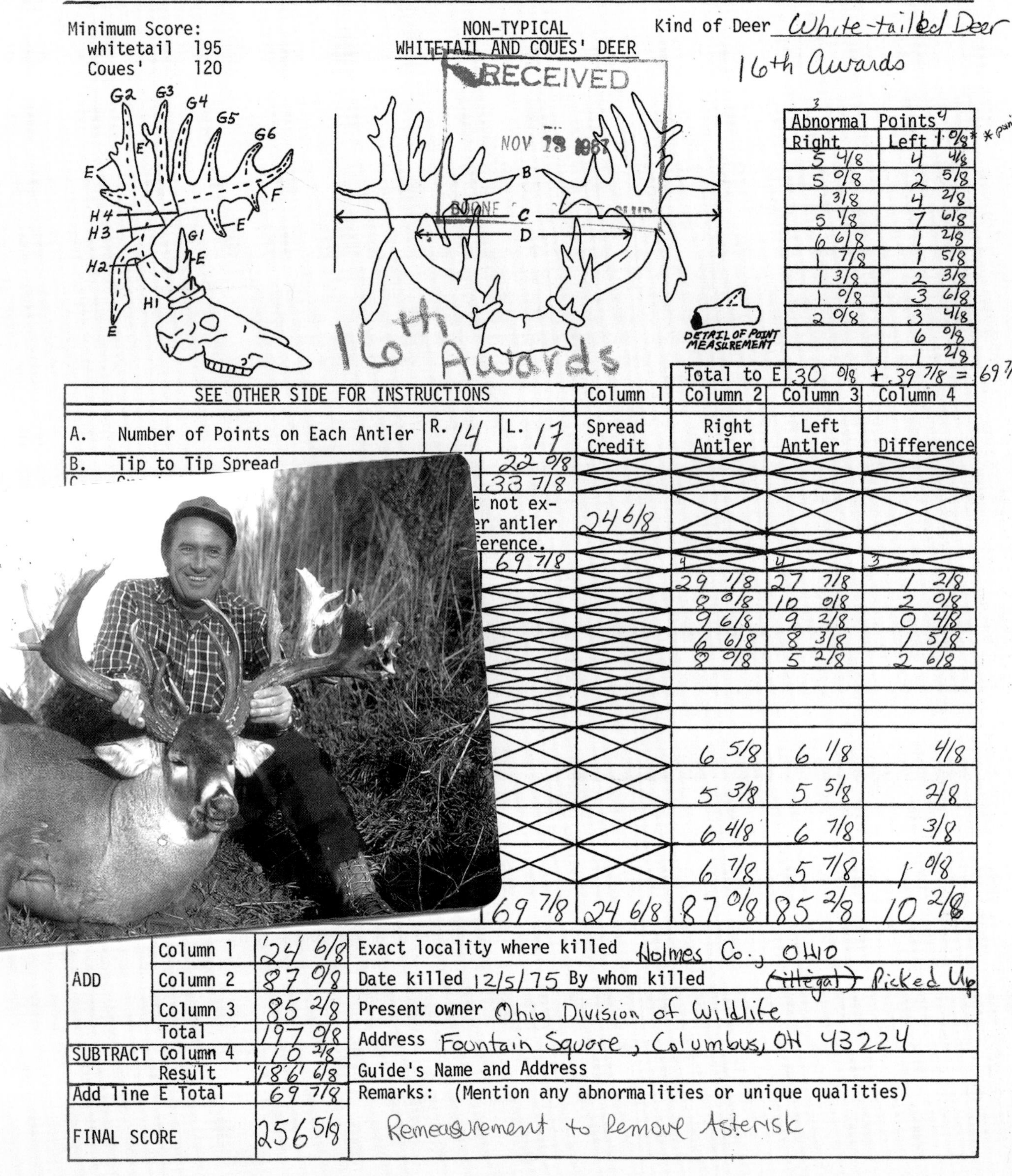

OFFICIAL SCORING SYSTEM FOR NORTH AMERICAN BIG GAME TROPHIES

Records of North American Big Game

BOONE AND CROCKETT CLUB

241 South Fraley Boulevard
Dumfries, Virginia 22026

Minimum Score:
whitetail 195
Coues' 120

NON-TYPICAL
WHITETAIL AND COUES' DEER

Kind of Deer White-tailed Deer

16th Awards

RECEIVED
NOV 13 1987
BOONE AND CROCKETT CLUB

Abnormal Points Right	Abnormal Points Left
5 4/8	4 4/8
5 0/8	2 5/8
1 3/8	4 2/8
5 1/8	7 6/8
6 6/8	1 2/8
1 7/8	1 5/8
1 3/8	2 3/8
1 0/8	3 6/8
2 0/8	3 4/8
	6 0/8
	1 2/8
Total to E 30 0/8	+ 39 7/8 = 69 7/8

SEE OTHER SIDE FOR INSTRUCTIONS			Column 1	Column 2	Column 3	Column 4
A. Number of Points on Each Antler	R. 14	L. 17	Spread Credit	Right Antler	Left Antler	Difference
B. Tip to Tip Spread		22 0/8				
C.		33 7/8				
...t not ex- ...r antler ...erence.			24 6/8			
		69 7/8				
				29 1/8	27 7/8	1 2/8
				8 0/8	10 0/8	2 0/8
				9 6/8	9 2/8	0 4/8
				6 6/8	8 3/8	1 5/8
				8 0/8	5 2/8	2 6/8
				6 5/8	6 1/8	4/8
				5 3/8	5 5/8	2/8
				6 4/8	6 7/8	3/8
				6 7/8	5 7/8	1 0/8
		69 7/8	24 6/8	87 0/8	85 2/8	10 2/8

ADD	Column 1	24 6/8	Exact locality where killed Holmes Co., OHIO
	Column 2	87 0/8	Date killed 12/5/75 By whom killed ~~(illegal)~~ Picked Up
	Column 3	85 2/8	Present owner Ohio Division of Wildlife
	Total	197 0/8	Address Fountain Square, Columbus, OH 43224
SUBTRACT	Column 4	10 2/8	
	Result	186 6/8	Guide's Name and Address
Add line E Total		69 7/8	Remarks: (Mention any abnormalities or unique qualities)
FINAL SCORE		256 5/8	Remeasurement to Remove Asterisk

6: CORRESPONDENCE FROM THE VAULTS

NOT ALL STORIES HAVE A HAPPY ENDING

Record deer hunter tried, stripped of hunting honors

BY DENNIS LUCAS

"The worst punishment for you is being stripped of the record," Judge Francis Smith told Eli Hochstetler, 47, after finding the Berlin man guilty of shooting a deer out of season. The action came Monday in Holmes County Court in a trial presented to the court by the state and defense attorneys for Hochstetler. A jury trial originally requested was dropped.

The deer in question was shot Dec. 5, 1975 and is the largest non-typical deer shot in Ohio and the fourth largest ever taken in the country of its type. Hochstetler was fined $250 and costs.

Hochstetler was also charged with shooting from a public highway but the charge was dismissed on a motion by the defense for a directed verdict. Smith ruled that the state had not presented enough evidence for a conviction on the charge because the testimony of an accomplice, if not corroborated, is not enough for conviction.

Received Honors

Hochstetler has received awards such as the Buckeye Big Bucks Club award for most outstanding deer which was presented to him last March at a banquet in Marietta. The Boone and Crockett Club also honored Hochstetler in July at its North American Big Game Awards program held in Denver, Colo. Boone and Crochett Club standards are used to measure antlers for the competition.

According to Holmes County Game Protector John Latecki who brought the charges against Hochstetler, the Berlin man will also lose his hunting license for three years as a result of the conviction.

Holmes County Prosecutor Robert Beck, who presented the state's case, reported Monday after the trial that the state will take custody of the antlers from the deer after a taxidermist removes them. The antlers are currently on another mounted deer and on display at Eastern Sports, Inc., a sporting goods store in Berlin. The record setting deer was originally mounted life-size but shrank and so the antlers were mounted on another animal.

The rack is 35 inches on the outside spread and has 31 points. Non-typical antlers are asymmetrical and are believed by biologists to be caused by high calcium levels in the animal's diet.

The state called three witnesses Monday morning, the first of which was Marion Weaver, who testified that he was with Hochstetler the day the deer was killed.

Partner Testifies

Weaver, a mail carrier from the Berlin area, told the court that Hochstetler shot the deer from his car before dawn on Ohio 39 just east of the Village of Nashville.

He said that he helped load the animal into the trunk of his car which had been pulled over to the side for Hochstetler to shoot the animal which was stopped about 20 feet from the road, according to Weaver.

Weaver, after being informed by the court at the suggestion of Hochstetler's defense attorney Dave Noble, of his fifth amendment rights concerning self-incrimination and the possibility that he too could be prosecuted for any illegal acts, waived his rights and proceeded to testify against Hochstetler. He told the court that he and Hochstetler had disagreements and ill feelings existed between them.

Weaver also told the court that he felt all of the men in the car (Clyde Gerber in addition to Hochstetler) were aware that the animal was shot illegally and that they stopped and covered up the antlers with Hochstetler's jacket so no one could see them on the return trip to Hochstetler's house.

Prosecutor Beck asked Weaver why he waited so long to report the illegal shooting and Weaver replied, "The pressure became so great that I didn't feel like lying anymore and I decided to tell the truth."

On cross examination, Noble asked Weaver whether he shot a deer the same week, to which Weaver replied that he had. He also told the court on questioning that he used illegal ammo in the kill. He denied carrying a gun when the men went hunting on Friday when Hochstetler shot the big buck.

Weaver also told the court during questioning by Noble that the deer was first seen in the headlights of the car and that he went to the next farmhouse and turned around and came back to where the deer was standing before it was shot.

Shot Too Early

The key witness for the state was Henry B. Yoder of Millersburg RD 4 who told the court that he was working in the shop next to Eli's house on Dec. 5, 1975 when he saw Eli showing the deer to his wife in the back of his pickup truck. Yoder told the court that he checked his watch because he thought it was early for them to be back with a deer and noticed that it was 7:30 a.m. Deer season opens each day at 7:30 a.m., and Yoder, who testified that he arrived at work at 7 a.m., said he was certain of the time on the shop clock. Yoder also said he went into the Hochstetler basement and viewed the deer with some other workers from the shop after Hochstetler and the other men had left to go hunting again.

Following Yoder's testimony, Noble moved for a directed verdict and asked the court to dismiss the charge of shooting from the road against his client which Smith proceeded to do on the basis of lack of corroboration between Yoder's and Weaver's testimony.

Hochstetler was called to the stand by Noble as the first defense witness.

Testimony Differs

Hochstetler told the court that he shot the deer on the Conrad Stitzlein farm near Glenmont and about 100 yards from the road and that he returned to his house at 8:30 a.m.

Hochstetler also testified concerning the bad feelings between he and Weaver and alleged that Weaver vowed to get even.

Hochstetler also told the court that he did not field dress the deer on the spot where it was shot. Weaver allegedly talked him into hunting some more the same day and not tagging the deer.

Judge Smith asked Hochstetler when the Berlin man set the blame on Weaver, "How old are you?" to which Hochstetler gave his age of 47 and replied, "I shouldn't have let myself be talked into it."

Hochstetler's wife, Betty, was the next to testify and told the court that she recalled the deer being brought home around 8:30 a.m. as her sons were getting off to school.

Following Mrs. Hochstetler's testimony, Smith receased the court until 1 p.m. when final arguments began.

Express Concern

At that time, Beck told the court the big question was not if the deer was shot but when, before or after 7:30 a.m. when deer season opens. "I know Eli and he's not a bad person and it was not a malicious act but other hunters are very concerned about the outcome of this case."

Noble claimed that the state failed to prove its burden beyond a reasonable doubt because of a question when the picture was taken after the deer was field dressed at Hochstetler's warehouse and because Noble said, "I find it hard to believe that you could shoot a deer in the dark."

Smith then made his guilty finding on the shooting out of season charge on the basis of Yoder's testimony who told the judge that he testified at great reluctance and because of Hochstetler's own testimony.

Smith told Hochstetler, "There are rules by which we play the game in life. Guilty as charged. I don't think Mr. Hochstetler has much regard for game laws, and because Hochstetler chose not to field dress the deer at the spot where he shot the animal as is customary and that he went out to hunt again after taking the animal home."

Appeal Considered

Hochstetler's attorney Dave Noble said after court adjourned that he and his client would consider appeal and would not give up the deer without a fight. Later in the afternoon, however, the defense attorney and the state agreed to turn over the antlers to the state.

The story of Hochstetler's record deer appeared in national sporting publications and several Ohio newspapers.

In a letter to Dale Haney (Chief of the Ohio Division of Wildlife) dated November 17, 1977, Wm. Harold Nesbitt wrote:

I'm enclosing a newspaper clipping (left) you may have already seen concerning Eli Hochstetler's non-typical whitetail taken in Ohio during 1975. To clarify an inaccuracy in this article, Hochstetler was not honored at the 16th N.A.B.G. Awards in Denver this past July. Hochstetler was indeed invited to send his trophy to Denver for the Final Awards Judging, but he did not accept the invitation.

Mr. Hochstetler's trophy is shown in the 1977 edition of the records book, North American Big Game, as no. 6 for the category... Mr. Hochstetler's conviction of violation of Ohio hunting regulations in taking this trophy means that it will be removed future editions of the records books and disqualified as an entry into the program.

Unfortunately, not all stories have happy endings. This magnificent non-typical, scoring 256-5/8 points, making it the fourth-largest in Ohio history, was entered as a legal, hunter-taken trophy, complete with a signed Fair Chase statement. An ensuing investigation revealed that the buck was taken illegally, and the deer was confiscated. Now owned by the Ohio Department of Natural Resources, this trophy remains in B&C's listings as a "picked up" head, giving the poacher no credit for his actions.

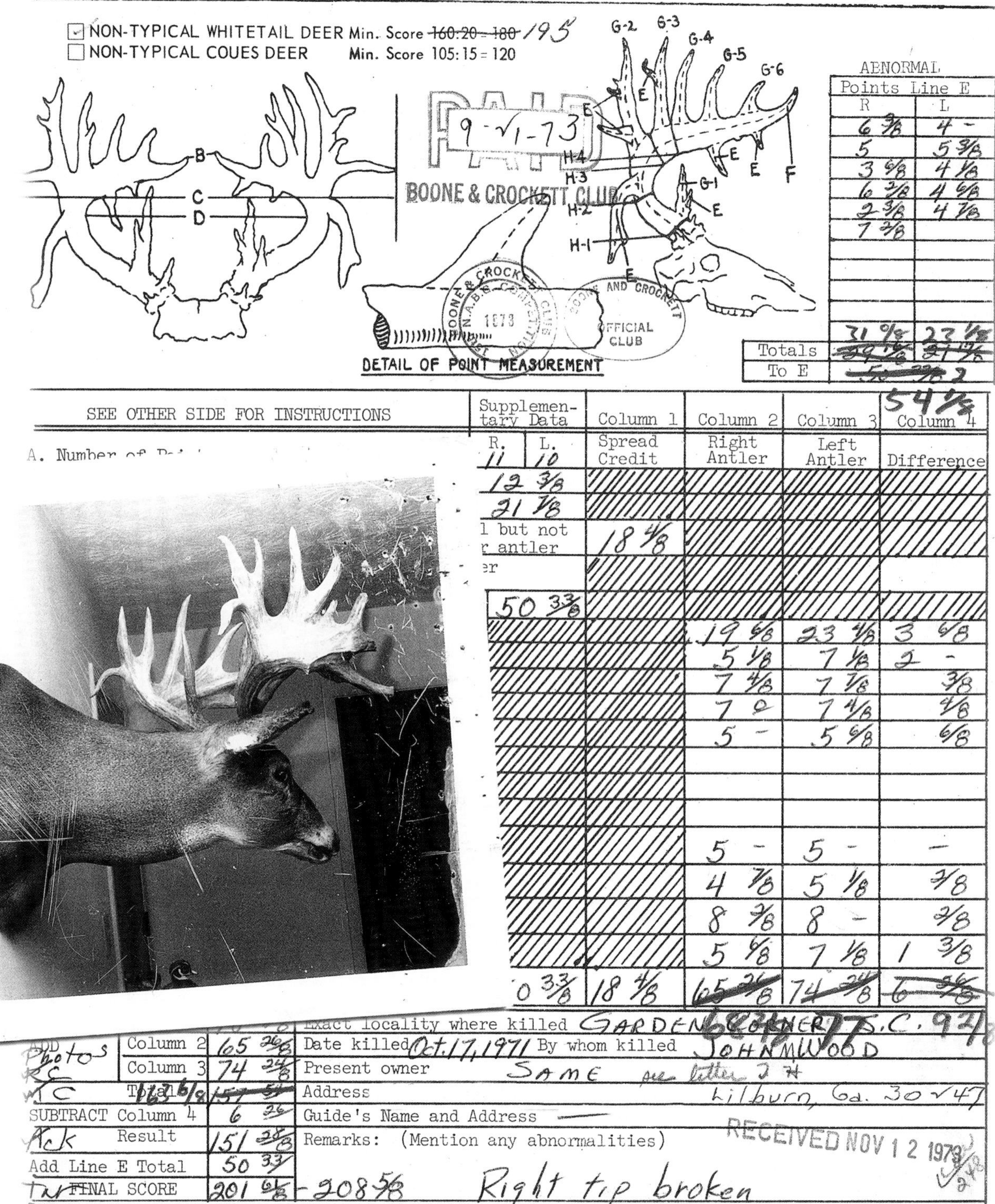

OFFICIAL SCORING SYSTEM FOR NORTH AMERICAN BIG GAME TROPHIES

RECORDS OF NORTH AMERICAN BIG GAME COMMITTEE

BOONE AND CROCKETT CLUB

Boone and Crockett Club
Records of North American Big Game Committee
c/o Carnegie Museum
4400 Forbes Ave. Pittsburgh, Pa. 15213

☑ NON-TYPICAL WHITETAIL DEER Min. Score ~~160:20=180~~ 195
☐ NON-TYPICAL COUES DEER Min. Score 105:15=120

ABNORMAL Points Line E	R	L
	6 3/8	4 -
	5	5 3/8
	3 6/8	4 1/8
	6 2/8	4 6/8
	2 3/8	4 7/8
	7 2/8	
Totals	31 6/8	23 1/8
To E	54 7/8	

SEE OTHER SIDE FOR INSTRUCTIONS	Supplementary Data R.	L.	Column 1 Spread Credit	Column 2 Right Antler	Column 3 Left Antler	Column 4 Difference
A. Number of Points	11	10				
	12 3/8					
	21 1/8					
…l but not …r antler			18 4/8			
…er						
	50 33/8					
				19 6/8	23 4/8	3 6/8
				5 1/8	7 1/8	2 -
				7 4/8	7 7/8	3/8
				7 2	7 4/8	4/8
				5 -	5 6/8	6/8
				5 -	5 -	-
				4 7/8	5 1/8	2/8
				8 2/8	8 -	2/8
				5 6/8	7 1/8	1 3/8
TOTALS	…0 33/8		18 4/8	65 26/8	74 24/8	6 26/8

ADD Column 2	65 26/8	Exact locality where killed GARDEN CORNER, S.C.
Column 3	74 24/8	Date killed Oct. 17, 1971 By whom killed JOHN M. WOOD
Total	163 6/8	Present owner SAME see letter
SUBTRACT Column 4	6 26/8	Address Lilburn, Ga. 30247
Result	151 28/8	Guide's Name and Address —
Add Line E Total	50 33/8	Remarks: (Mention any abnormalities)
FINAL SCORE	201 61/8	208 5/8 Right tip broken

RECEIVED NOV 12 1973

6: CORRESPONDENCE FROM THE VAULTS

SOUTH CAROLINA STATE RECORD

Boone and Crockett Club
c/o Carnegie Museum
4400 Forbes Avenue
Pittsburgh, Pa. 15213

RECEIVED SEP 21 1973

To Whom it may concern,

In October of 1971 I killed what I hope is the South Carolina State Record (non-typical) white-tailed deer. At the time, I was told by the State Game officals that it would have to be measured by an offical measurer of your Club. They told me to contact Mr. Jack Crockford here in Atlanta, which I did, and he scored the rack at 208 3/8. Now they tell me it will be the State Record and possibly the Southern or Southeaster Record. But the game officals now say that it can't be re-conized offically until it is accepted by the Boone and Crockett Club as the largest re-

An excited John M. Wood wrote this letter to B&C about his non-typical whitetail, which he hoped might be the South Carolina State Record. He was right on track. At 208-5/8 points, it is not only the state record, but also one of only three non-typicals ever entered from South Carolina. The mass and palmation on this deer are considerable.

OFFICIAL SCORING SYSTEM FOR NORTH AMERICAN BIG GAME TROPHIES

RECORDS OF NORTH AMERICAN BIG GAME COMMITTEE

Minimum Score: Deer
Whitetail: Typical 160
Coues: Typical 105

BOONE AND CROCKETT CLUB

Boone and Crockett Club
Records of North American Big Game Committee
c/o Carnegie Museum
4400 Forbes Ave. Pittsburgh, Pa. 15213

WHITETAIL and COUES DEER

KIND OF DEER Whitetail

G-2 G-3 G-4 G5 G6

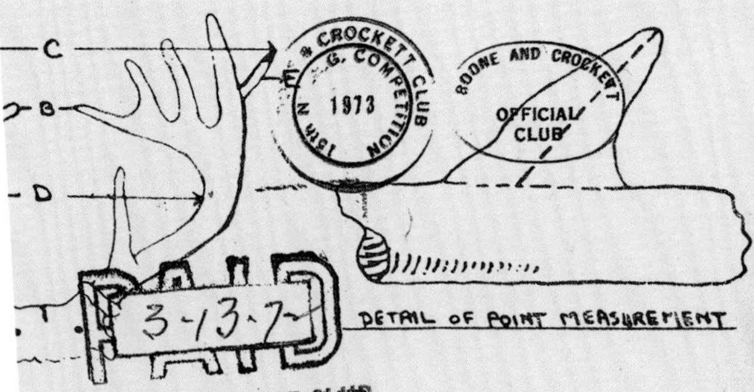

CROCKETT CLUB

Supplementary Data R. 10	L. 14	Column 1 Spread Credit	Column 2 Right Antler	Column 3 Left Antler	Column 4 Difference
13 5/8					
21 7/8					
but not antler		16 1/8			
ger					
					1 7/8
			22 2/8	22 1/8	1/8
			8 1/8	9	7/8
			9	7 2/8	1-6/8
			6 2/8	6 7/8	5/8
			5 5/8	6 7/8	1-2/8
			4	3 4/8	4/8
			6	6	
			5 2/8	5 1/8	1/8
			7 2/8	6/6/8	4/8
...rd and ...Third Point and ...Tip if Fourth Point is missing			4 1/8	4 5/8	4/8
Fee TOTALS		16 1/8	77 7/8	78 1/8	8-1/8 ~~1 7/8~~

ADD	Column 1	16 1/8	Exact locality where killed Pickerel River, Parry Sound area
	Column 2	77 7/8	Date killed Nov. 12/70 By whom killed Jack Baker
Photos	Column 3	78 1/8	Present owner Jack Baker
	Total	171 9/8	Address Aylmer West, Ontario
SUBTRACT Column 4		8-1/8 ~~1 7/8~~	Guide's Name and Address ---
			Remarks: (Mention any abnormalities)
FINAL SCORE		~~170 1/4~~ 164	

Tab. ✓Perm

MAR 13 1972

6: CORRESPONDENCE FROM THE VAULTS

ERRORS IN MEASUREMENT

October 5, 1972

Mr. Jack Baker
Talbot
Aylmer,West, Ontario, Canada

Dear Mr. Baker:

When we sent you an acknowledgment form on July 11, 1972 for your Whitetail Deer score chart it signified our acceptance, guided by the minimum score of 160 which is printed at the top of the sheet. This was an inadvertant oversight, however; the chart is an outdated one since the minimum score was raised to 170 as of January 1, 1968.

The final score of 164 which we show on your chart is correct. You will see that we had to carry figures over to Column 4 on Lines F through H-4, because they had not been written in at the time the chart was mailed to us.

We cannot understand the high figure of 217-1/4 which you arrived at originally. We are enclosing a score chart so that you will be able to follow the measuring instructions on the reverse side. If there is still a great' variance we can appreciate your desire for a remeasurement, and enclose a list of our Official Measurers in Ontario and New York.

Thank you for writing, and we hope this question can be settled satisfactorily. Please let us hear from you at your early convenience so that, if necessary, your chart, fee, etc. may be returned without undue delay.

Very truly yours,

(Mrs.) Dorothy G. Petrovsky
Administrative Assistant

In a letter dated September 16, 1972, Jack Baker wrote the following letter to the Club:

Enclosed is the "Certificate" of fair chase requested. I would like to have this head measured again. When we measured, we arrived at 217-1/4 points, and when measured in Toronto it was 170-1/4 and now it is 164.

It seems this deer has shrunken right out of the record book. I would appreciate having it measured again by you or someone you suggest.

Confusion on this nice deer seems to have come from mistakes on multiple levels. First, it appears that most of the abnormal points were never recorded on the chart. Second, the typical frame interpretation was incorrect. Third, an adding error further complicated matters. This deer should have been scored as a non-typical. Its current status is "unresolved." Since the score fell below the minimum, paperwork was never completed.

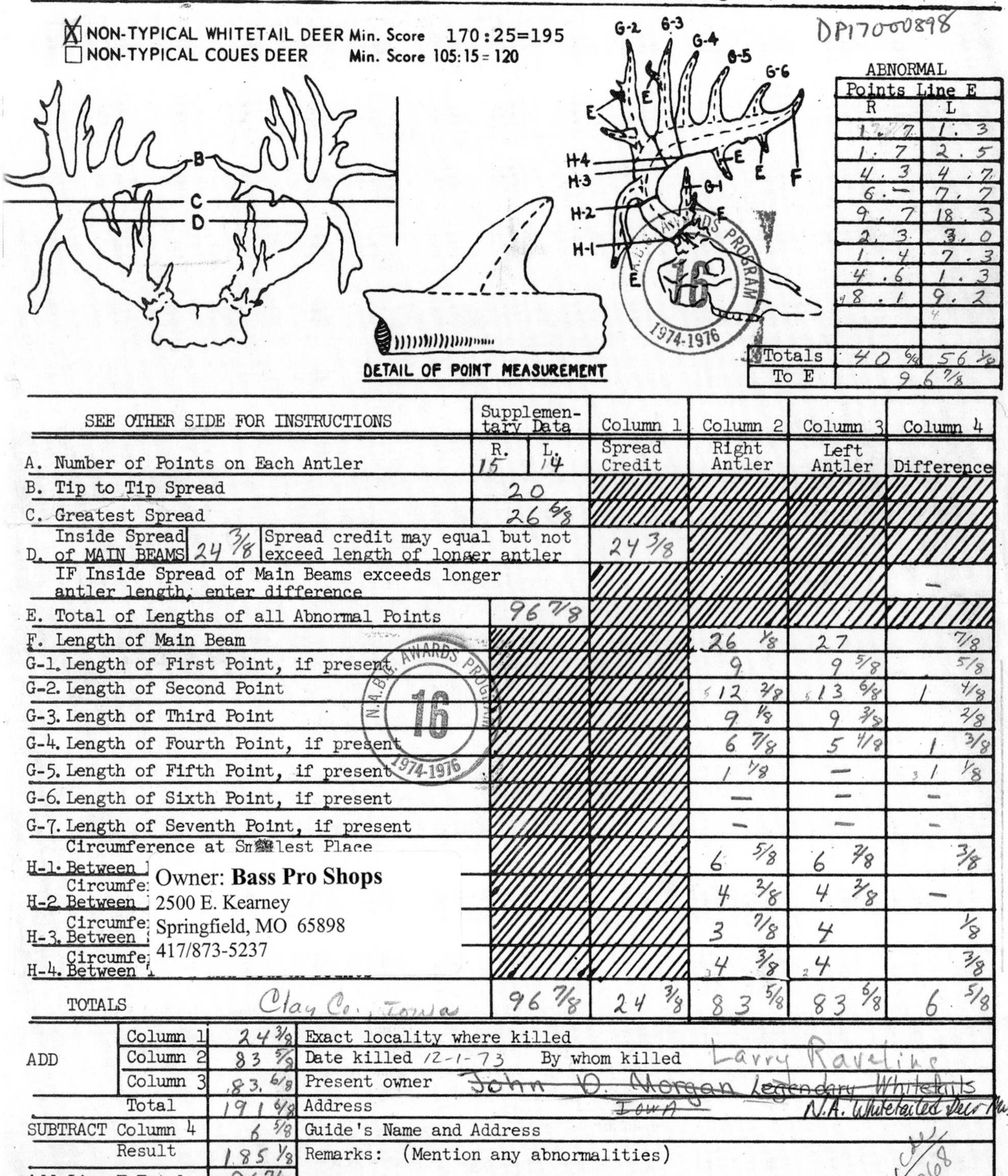

1st place 16th OY PLW

OFFICIAL SCORING SYSTEM FOR NORTH AMERICAN BIG GAME TROPHIES

RECORDS OF NORTH AMERICAN BIG GAME COMMITTEE

BOONE AND CROCKETT CLUB

RETURN TO:
N.A.B.G. Awards Program
1600 Rhode Island Ave., N.W.
Washington, D.C. 20036

DP17000898

[X] NON-TYPICAL WHITETAIL DEER Min. Score 170:25=195
[ ] NON-TYPICAL COUES DEER Min. Score 105:15=120

ABNORMAL Points Line E R	L
12.7	1.3
1.7	2.5
4.3	4.7
6.–	7.7
9.7	18.3
2.3	3.0
1.4	7.3
4.6	1.3
8.1	9.2
Totals 40 6/8	56 1/8
To E 96 7/8	

SEE OTHER SIDE FOR INSTRUCTIONS	Supplementary Data R.	Supplementary Data L.	Column 1 Spread Credit	Column 2 Right Antler	Column 3 Left Antler	Column 4 Difference
A. Number of Points on Each Antler	15	14				
B. Tip to Tip Spread	20					
C. Greatest Spread	26 6/8					
D. Inside Spread of MAIN BEAMS 24 3/8 — Spread credit may equal but not exceed length of longer antler			24 3/8			
IF Inside Spread of Main Beams exceeds longer antler length, enter difference						–
E. Total of Lengths of all Abnormal Points	96 7/8					
F. Length of Main Beam				26 1/8	27	7/8
G-1. Length of First Point, if present				9	9 5/8	5/8
G-2. Length of Second Point				12 2/8	13 6/8	1 4/8
G-3. Length of Third Point				9 1/8	9 3/8	2/8
G-4. Length of Fourth Point, if present				6 7/8	5 4/8	1 3/8
G-5. Length of Fifth Point, if present				1 1/8	–	1 1/8
G-6. Length of Sixth Point, if present				–	–	–
G-7. Length of Seventh Point, if present				–	–	–
H-1. Circumference at Smallest Place Between ...				6 5/8	6 7/8	3/8
H-2. Circumfe... Between ...				4 3/8	4 3/8	–
H-3. Circumfe... Between ...				3 7/8	4	1/8
H-4. Circumfe... Between ...				4 3/8	4	3/8
TOTALS	96 7/8		24 3/8	83 5/8	83 6/8	6 5/8

Owner: **Bass Pro Shops**
2500 E. Kearney
Springfield, MO 65898
417/873-5237

ADD	Column 1	24 3/8	Exact locality where killed Clay Co., Iowa
	Column 2	83 5/8	Date killed 12-1-73 By whom killed Larry Raveling
	Column 3	83 6/8	Present owner ~~John D. Morgan~~ ~~Legendary Whitetails~~
	Total	191 6/8	Address ~~Iowa~~ N.A. Whitetailed Deer Mus
SUBTRACT Column 4		6 5/8	Guide's Name and Address
	Result	185 1/8	Remarks: (Mention any abnormalities)
Add Line E Total		96 7/8	
FINAL SCORE		282	(3)

268

6: SPECIAL TROPHY

LARRY RAVELING'S AWARD-WINNING WHITETAIL

1973 IOWA STATE CONSERVATION COMMISSION
RESIDENT DEER HUNTING LICENSE

5421

The licensee described below is hereby licensed to hunt deer according to the laws of the State of Iowa and the Departmental Rules of the State Conservation Commission.

AGE	HEIGHT	WGT	EYES	HAIR	S	C
20	5 11	160	BR	BR	M	2

RESTRICTIONS
KIND OF LICENSE

RAVELING, LARRY
R R 1
LINN GROVE, IA 51033

SHOTGUN
SEASON DATES
DEC 1 - DEC 5, 1973

LICENSE 14107

SEX OF DEER
ANTLERED ONLY
ZONE

[signature], DIRECTOR, STATE CONSERVATION COMMISSION

When Larry Raveling's non-typical, scoring 282 points, received the First Award at the 16th Awards Banquet in Denver, it was ranked second in the world. Only the Texas buck from the famous Buckhorn Museum and Saloon ranked higher. From the time it was killed in 1973 up until 2003 (an incredible 30 years) this historic whitetail reigned as the Iowa State Record. It stands today as the seventh-largest non-typical ever recorded by B&C. Overall, Raveling's fine trophy, with 29 scorable points, also has 96-7/8 inches of abnormal point lengths.

On the following pages, you will see a candid and interesting account written by Raveling of the day he encountered one of the world's biggest whitetails.

I started the 1973 deer season on Dec. 1st with high hopes of getting a buck, the same as nine other guys hunting with me who also had buck only licenses. We would be hunting in a timber area near Peterson, Iowa about a mile and a half west of town.

My job was the stand while some of the other men were driving. After a little while on the stand I heard a shot, and thought somebody had gotten his buck. Pretty soon I heard him yell that he had hit a buck but only wounding it in the back leg. A friend of ours was sitting in his pickup on the road just watching, when he saw a big buck run across the road and into another piece of timber.

We went across the road and into a piece of timber that bordered a game reserve. Being Careful not to go into the game reserve, I walked towards the west when I came to a pretty good sized ravine. I started to walk down into it and saw a buck standing on the other side - part way down the side of the bank. I didn't know if it was the wounded buck or not. I shot, hitting the deer in the front leg at the knee. That downed him and it turned out to be the wounded deer. It was a generally agreed upon rule in our group that if you shot a deer but didn't down it, it belonged to whoever did down it.

I was not only glad to get such a nice big buck, but also to have gotten the wounded one which otherwise would have gotten away, suffered and died later.

The buck field dressed out at 160 lbs. I had the rack mounted by Jim Hartman of Estherville, Iowa in which I was extremely pleased with the job he did.

N.A.B.G. AWARDS PROGRAM 16 1974-1976

This story may not sound as interesting as a long stalk and a fine long running shot, but that is not the way we can hunt here in Iowa. We have to use shotguns and we hunt in timber so thick with underbrush, you have to use a group of guys and drive the deer or they can slip right by you.

ACKNOWLEDGEMENTS

A WHITETAIL RETROSPECTIVE

First, we would like to extend a special thank you to all of the past chairmen of the Boone and Crockett Club's Records Committee for their hard work and dedication:

Alfred Ely, Jr. *(deceased)*
Harold E. Anthony *(deceased)*
Samuel B. Webb *(deceased)*
Robert S. Waters *(deceased)*
Elmer M. Rusten *(deceased)*
Jack S. Parker
Philip L. Wright *(deceased)*
Walter H. White *(deceased)*
C. Randall Byers *(deceased)*
Eldon L. "Buck" Buckner – Current

Images and Memorabilia selected from the Boone and Crockett Club's Archives in Missoula, Montana, by:

Mark B. Steffen – Publications Chairman
Ryan Hatfield
Julie T. Houk
Jack Reneau

Editorial Contributors:

Gilbert T. Adams
Eldon L. "Buck" Buckner
Ryan Hatfield
Joel W. Helmer
Frederick J. King
John Poston
Jack Reneau
Tommy Caruthers, Sr.

Proofreading by: Todd Woodard

Scanning Assistance: Dariusz Janczewski

OCR Specialist: Sandy Poston

A Whitetail Retrospective was designed by Julie T. Houk, Director of Publications, for the Boone and Crockett Club using Baskerville and Roadkill typefaces

Printed and bound in Canada by Friesens

11TH COMPETITION — 1964
CARNEGIE MUSEUM